MW00445673

# *INSIDE HONORS 2018-2019:*

## Ratings and Reviews of 50 Public University Honors Programs

©Copyright 2018 John Willingham

# CONTENTS

PREFACE                                                                                    4

RATINGS, RANKINGS, AND EVALUATIONS                                                         6

ALL ABOUT HONORS CLASSES—PLEASE READ THIS!                                                 8

HONORS COMPLETION RATES: 'A Dirty Little Secret' or a (Very) Complicated Issue?           11

HONORS COLLEGES VERSUS HONORS PROGRAMS: What Are The Differences?                         17

CHOOSING AN HONORS PROGRAM: 20 QUESTIONS TO ASK                                           21

PRESTIGIOUS AWARDS                                                                       24

STATISTICAL SUMMARY                                                                      26

METHODOLOGY                                                                              28

RATED HONORS COLLEGES AND PROGRAMS:

Arizona Honors College                                                                   30
Arizona State, Barrett Honors College                                                    38
Arkansas Honors College                                                                  45
Auburn Honors College                                                                    53
Clemson, Calhoun Honors College                                                          60
Colorado State Honors Program                                                             67
CUNY, Macaulay Honors College                                                            74
Delaware Honors Program                                                                   82
Florida Atlantic Wilkes Honors College                                                   89
Georgia Honors Program                                                                    97
Georgia State Honors College                                                            105
Houston Honors College                                                                  113
Illinois, Campus Honors Program (CHP)                                                   121
Indiana, Hutton Honors College                                                          128
Iowa Honors Program                                                                     134
Kansas Honors Program                                                                   141
LSU Honors, Ogden Honors College                                                        148
Massachusetts, Commonwealth Honors College                                             155
Minnesota Honors Program                                                                163
Mississippi, Sally McDonnell Barksdale Honors College                                  171
Missouri Honors College                                                                177
Nevada Reno Honors Program                                                              185
New Jersey Inst of Technology, Albert Dorman Honors College                            191
New Mexico Honors College                                                               198
Oklahoma, OU Honors College                                                            204

# CONTENTS

Oklahoma State Honors College                           212
Oregon, Clark Honors College                            219
Oregon State Honors College                             226
Penn State, Schreyer Honors College                     233
Purdue Honors College                                   240
Rutgers Honors College                                  248
South Carolina Honors College                           256
Texas Tech Honors College                               264
UAB Honors College                                      272
UCF, Burnett Honors College                             280
USF Honors College                                      287
UT Austin, Plan II Honors Program                       295
Vermont Honors College                                  303
Virginia Commonwealth Honors College                    310
Washington State Honors College                         316
West Virginia Honors College                            323

## SUMMARY REVIEWS, WITHOUT RATINGS

Alabama Honors College                                  331
Florida International Honors College                    336
Kentucky, Lewis Honors College                          340
Mississippi State, Shackouls Honors College             344
North Carolina-Chapel Hill, Honors Carolina             349
Portland State Honors College                           355
Rowan University Bantivoglio Honors                     360
Texas A&M Honors Program                                365
UC Irvine, Campuswide Honors Program                    369

AFTERWORD: Elitism and Public University Honors Programs 373

**Glossary of Honors Terminology**                      377
About Us                                                380

All college reviews, rankings, and ratings are subjective. I believe that ratings are the least subjective because they are data-driven but do not rank ordinally based on miniscule differences in numerical scores.

Rating honors colleges and programs requires close analysis of extensive data. (From now on I will use the generic term "honors programs.") Honors programs are in fact complicated and vary greatly. Often the variations seem impossible to quantify, much less to describe.

However, in the case of honors programs it is not the devil who resides in the details but, instead, the most significant indicators of excellence. For excellence is what honors programs augment in our public universities. Yet excellence can be elusive to define. You might think you know it when you see it, or when you feel it, but such is not always the case.

Some critics of honors programs say that they are elitist with their sometimes fancy dorms and other perks, and with the generous scholarships that they often provide. Others say that they exist mainly to raise the selectivity rankings of the universities to which they belong, meanwhile providing little of real value to the talented students they are supposed to serve. They talk a good game, but when all is done, they do not deliver. And it is sometimes the case that the universities in which honors programs are but a part do not support honors education as they should. Only a very few public universities have endowments that match those of the elite private institutions, and even if the public endowments are at a high level, the funds still must be spread among far more students than at an elite private university.

On the whole, however, many public universities *are* increasingly committed to honors education. In just the seven years I have spent gathering and analyzing data about public university honors programs, I have observed dramatic growth in honors enrollment and in the private and institutional support for their mission. That mission, by the way, gains the most traction because of necessity, and not only financial necessity. Yes, highly talented students *might* find a place in a relatively small number of very selective institutions. The fact is, however, that many of the most selective schools reject 85% to 95% of applicants for reasons that no one fully understands.

If you have a son or daughter with an ACT of 29 or higher and a (new) SAT of 1360 or higher, the number of colleges and universities with student bodies that, on average, meet that profile is approximately 100. In an analysis two years ago using test scores in place at that time, I found strong evidence that the number of first-year places in all these schools is also less than the number of students with the credentials listed above. Only when public and private honors programs and colleges with similar admissions requirements are included does the number of places approximate the number of highly qualified students. Public honors programs provide the great majority of these additional places. (These views appear in detailed form on our website, in a post titled "Is It True that 80% of Elite Students Are Accepted by Elite Colleges?")

Granting this need for honors colleges and programs, how does one have any idea about the true quality of an honors program, assuming that the students enrolled have met high admission standards? Well-known college rankings generally focus on university-wide "inputs" and "outcomes" while often conflating the two. This book covers some of the same ground: class sizes and graduation rates, for example. These do not tell the full story, however.

Understanding what makes a program substantial must begin with an analysis of the "ground game," the time spent in honors classes, the thesis and research requirements, the specific mix of classes by discipline, the total number of honors sections—and, yes, the availability of special housing and perks.

It is not enough, for example, to know that University A has an excellent physics or political science department, and that one's son or daughter wants to major in one of those disciplines. If a family is trying to decide between one or more elite private universities and one or more public honors programs, it may be decisive to know that the public honors program has *honors level* courses in those subjects.

Or if a family is drawn to an excellent private liberal arts college that will require the student to open up, to present and defend arguments, and to learn to accept criticism, the option of a public honors program might depend on how many small honors classes are available in both discussion-based seminars and courses in the disciplines. Is the honors program really a combination of a "liberal arts college in the midst of a prominent research university, with all the advantages of both"? This typical description of public honors programs is sometimes true, sometimes misleading, and fairly often offset by equivalent values that are not mentioned in the hype.

And of course the choice almost always involves money. Is that private college that your National Merit Scholar has always dreamed of attending really worth an extra $30,000 a year, since all merit aid at the private college is need-based, and your income, even with a family of four, leaves such a big balance. In short, who can say exactly what fact or feature will help a family to decide?

It might be those eight honors math sections, or those interdisciplinary seminars at every class level, or that study-abroad stipend to attend Oxford in the summer, or that (mostly) quiet honors dorm with on-site dining, mentors, and study lounges on every floor, or the combination of writing, rhetoric, and honors business classes that will make your student a well-rounded success in life. And, often, it might be that merit award worth $10,000 a year, to go with a waiver of out-of-state tuition.

Yes, honors programs are complicated, but so are your college choice decisions. To understand *exactly* what those programs offer in order to make your decision, a parent, a prospective student, needs to look inside honors.

That is what this book tries to do, however many statistics it takes to do the job.

John Willingham, Editor

Ever since the *U.S. News Best Colleges* rankings commenced about three decades ago, the American public has been, if not obsessed with, then keenly interested in the numerical rankings of hundreds of colleges and universities.

Rankings are more interesting than ratings, and ratings are more interesting, to the general public at least, than "evaluations" or "assessments."

All have their uses, and their shortcomings.

Rankings presume a perfection that they cannot meet. If one claims that Princeton is better than Harvard based on a difference of one point out of a possible 100, then one is mighty certain that the methodology being used must inexorably lead to a real distinction arising from such a piddling difference. In the real world, inexorable truths are elusive, but the September ranking operettas featuring Harvard and Princeton—Stanford, Yale?—have taken on the aura of natural recurrences, like the stages of the moon or the orbital course of the planet.

Now, if the colleges were *rated* instead of *ranked*, who could have much doubt that both Harvard and Princeton—and Yale, Stanford, Chicago, Columbia, MIT, Penn, Duke—would all be in the highest group. For ratings are relatively humble, as against the hubris of rankings. It might seem un-American not to be Number One, or anyway not to assume that there *is* a Number One, but ratings are satisfied with a Number One *Group*. In the sciences, mathematics, computer science, and engineering, a methodology well applied to observable phenomena or established patterns can lead to precision, and sometimes to what abides as certainty. Yes, a university's football team might win the national title, but the whole university is a sprawling complex of traditions, cultural conflict, cutthroat politics, inspired or ill-fated leaders, competing ideologies, and students and professors of all stripes. No methodology can be precise enough to place a college on the sharp and narrow point of Number One. But, as Hemingway wrote, it is pretty to think so. And, by the way, a lot of fun. So hats off to *U.S. News* for being entertaining and for providing excellent data about class sizes, grad rates, test scores and so on.

We opted for rankings in the first edition, and it was a big mistake. If anything, honors colleges and programs are more heterogeneous than universities, being in some ways schools within schools. And speaking of heterogeneous, Malcolm Gladwell, writing in *The New Yorker* a few years back, argued that one can compare many things using a few criteria, but not many things using many criteria. Our own hubris, offset to some extent by the use of ratings instead of rankings, is that we are comparing 41 "things"—honors programs—using 13 criteria (and defying superstition). Whether or not that is too many criteria for Mr. Gladwell, one consolation is that *U.S. News* compares hundreds of colleges using even more criteria. What is significant is that we do recognize fully the variety and complexity of honors programs. People sometimes ask, "Why don't you include a hundred programs—500 programs?" Well, it has taken almost a thousand spreadsheets and documents to rate 40-50 programs, each with 7-8 pages of narrative, so that is the best answer we have.

Finally, a word about evaluations and assessments. In the academic world, these terms are used to describe internal and external studies of academic components—individual departments, schools and colleges within the university, special programs, teaching effectiveness, faculty productivity, student learning, and so on. We actually considered producing a "study" that presented all of our data and resulting calculations in a more or less anonymous fashion, that is, without attaching any results to individual programs. It is possible that much of our data might have been more or less suitable for an academic paper or for assessment purposes, but that approach would not have given parents and prospective students any of the comparative information that they need in order to make the best decision possible about which college is best for them. (But this edition, however, does include the results of a detailed statistical study—presented without some of the wonkishness in the following section titled "Honors Completion Rates: A 'Dirty Little Secret' or a Very Complicated Issue?")

In the end this book is a hybrid: one part study replete with statistics, and the other part perhaps a distant relative of the *Fiske Guide to Colleges,* which has also used ratings instead of rankings. There is no number one, but we do identify (below) the top two groups, which include the honors colleges and programs in the top half of the overall ratings. But even these groups are only representative of the rated programs *in this edition.* It is all but certain that hiding out there in the growing universe of honors programs are several that could receive the highest rating.

We assign "mortarboards" instead of stars, asterisks, or other symbols that may represent a range of estimated quality. The highest rating overall or in a particular category is 5.

In this edition, the honors colleges and programs with an overall rating of 5 mortarboards would rank in the top 7 out of 41 rated programs. Here they are, in ***alphabetical*** order:

Arizona State, Barrett Honors College
CUNY, Macaulay Honors College
Florida Atlantic Wilkes Honors College
Kansas Honors Program
Penn State, Schreyer Honors College
South Carolina Honors College
UT Austin Plan II Honors Program

Florida Atlantic Wilkes Honors College was not rated previously. In previous editions, the following programs also received five mortarboards: Clemson Calhoun Honors College, Georgia Honors Program, Houston Honors College, New Jersey Inst of Technology Dorman Honors College, Michigan LSA Honors Program, Oregon Clark Honors College, and the Virginia Echols Scholars Program. When our methodology changed after 2014, the data available (or not) from Michigan and UVA was insufficient for rating purposes. And the fact is that both universities are elite overall by any realistic measure. *The other programs formerly rated 5.0 are all now rated 4.5 (below) illustrating that each data set is different—and that those programs remain excellent.* Another factor is that this edition only rates 41 programs versus 50 in 2016, causing the 5.0 category to shrink.

Honors colleges and programs in this edition with an overall rating of 4.5 mortarboards would rank in the 8-20 range, including ties. Here they are, again in ***alphabetical order:***

Clemson Calhoun Honors College; Delaware Honors Program; Georgia Honors Program; Houston Honors College; Illinois CHP Program; LSU Ogden Honors College; Mississippi, Sally McDonnell Barksdale Honors College; Nevada Reno Honors Program; NJIT Dorman Honors College; Oregon, Clark Honors College; Rutgers Honors College; Texas Tech Honors College; UCF, Burnett Honors College; and the Virginia Commonwealth University Honors College.

*ALL ABOUT HONORS CLASSES—PLEASE READ THIS!*

Much of the information in this edition is based on course and section data. Very few people know about or understand the different types of honors classes. To make an informed decision about choosing an honors college or program over a liberal arts college or an elite private university, parents and prospective students really need to consider the types of classes and how those offered by a given honors program will match the preferences and needs of the student.

First, there are four major types of honors classes are honors-only classes, mixed sections, contract (option, conversion) sections, and "experiential" sections.

In most selective private colleges and universities, a class is a class. By this we mean that within each class section, there is not a mix of especially talented students with "regular" students. At the most elite level, this means that all classes at the college are presumably equal in their elite-*ness*.

Yes, elite private universities do have some large classes, especially in the sciences and in extremely popular lecture sections. But most classes are relatively small, with the amount of discussion being limited more by the subject matter than by the number of students involved. Debate in a linear algebra section of 15 students is unlikely to be extensive; but in a seminar in history, philosophy, literature, or political science the same number of students might bring the roof down.

In public university honors programs, about 25%-30% of an honors student's *total* coursework will be in honors classes, although in a few programs that can be as much as 40%. Some of these honors classes will be large, typically in the introductory science courses, but also perhaps in marketing, management, economics, and political science courses. The **honors-only classes**, especially in the first two years, are likely to be small—averaging 17.5 students across the 41 rated programs in this edition. So, in these classes, the comparability to liberal arts and private elite classes is greatest, especially in honors seminars and interdisciplinary sections in which class discussion is a prominent feature. These classes, along with an honors thesis requirement if there is one, are, in the public university setting, most likely to differentiate the honors and non-honors experience.

Unlike liberal arts colleges and elite private universities, some honors classes in the academic disciplines (e.g., biology, chemistry, computer science) are mixed honors sections or, especially in the last two years, honors contract sections, in any discipline. The offering of some mixed and contract sections is still the norm, even though most of the honors sections offered by the rated honors programs in this edition are honors-only classes.

The percentage of honors enrollment, by section type, for all rated programs rated in this edition is 75.8% in honors-only sections; 15.4 % in mixed honors sections; and 8.8% in contract sections. Compared to the 2016 programs we reviewed, the percentage of mixed and contract sections in 2018 has increased, but not dramatically. Honors colleges and programs are growing rapidly; sometimes the only way they can keep up with additional enrollment is to add honors students to already existing sections.

So…**what is a mixed section?** In honors programs, a mixed section for honors credit usually takes one of two forms. The majority of mixed sections are larger than honors-only sections, averaging 68.6 students, including honors *and* non-honors students (this is what makes them "mixed"). This average has gone up since 2016. Some of these sections have no honors-only labs or discussion (breakout) sections in addition to the main mixed section. For these classes, the honors students may do extra work for honors credit, but often the sections are advanced and include students majoring in the discipline or pursuing departmental honors, as well as students in the honors program. Other mixed sections include "regular" students along with honors students, but the honors students meet in their own labs or in 1-2 credit discussion sections outside of the main section. In either of these instances, the mixed section is very likely an improvement over a regular class in the subject.

**A contract section** (also called an honors option, honors conversion, honors enhancement) is a regular section in which one or a few honors students enter into a written agreement with the instructor to do extra work for honors credit and, preferably, also to meet with the instructor one on one at regular intervals. Generally, honors staff must approve these agreements, but the amount of administrative oversight and quality of the extra work can vary considerably. In the best case, there is consistent oversight and evaluation of the contracts; in the worst case, which does exist, honors staff have little or no involvement in the process and might not even have a record of what the extra work was supposed to be.

This is not to say that honors contracts are necessarily inferior to honors-only courses or mixed honors sections. Even though the quality can be uneven, the contract courses can lead to extremely valuable mentoring relationships between instructors and students. Another positive factor is that students often take upper-division honors contract courses, sometimes including courses needed for majors, minors, or for graduating on schedule. The contract courses are also a way for motivated students to continue to be challenged while working on an honors thesis outside of class. Contract courses do tend to be larger, averaging 56.6 students per section. (This class average is better than in 2016.) Proponents of honors contracts contend that the larger class sizes are more than offset by the one-on-one contact that should occur between the student and instructor outside of class. Out of 41 rated programs, 26 allow credit for contract courses, and 15 do not. Arizona State, Penn State, LSU, and Oklahoma State all have 20% or more of their honors enrollment in contract sections.

**Experiential sections** are the honors response to a fairly recent revival of "learning by doing" in higher education. The idea is that students should combine classroom learning with (usually) related experience outside the classroom. In principle, and probably for the most part in practice, experiences directly tied to a specific course do enhance student learning and promote enthusiasm for the subject. The implementation of more of these courses is not limited to public universities. Liberal arts colleges, especially in the wake of the 2008 Great Recession, have also responded to the sense of vocational urgency that most parents and prospective students now feel. Like their public honors counterparts, liberal arts colleges offer internships, leadership training, and group projects, at least in part to boost the resumes of their students. Service learning, which aligns students with community needs, is often the altruistic side of the experiential coin. So from one direction colleges are pushed to respond to material self-interest, while from the other they are tasked with the rejuvenation of community involvement.

A certain amount of experiential learning is all to the good, so to speak. Students in engineering classes surely benefit from group projects; history majors—if they still exist—should by all means take that internship at the state capital (and enroll in an econ class); finance majors will love the idea of an internship at a major brokerage firm; and just about any student will delight in three honors credits for studying Spanish during a Maymester in Seville. Community gardens, fundraisers, tutoring disadvantaged children, all of these are good things. One question, however, is whether experiential learning untethered to classroom work or language study should count for as much as a third of honors completion requirements, as is now the case in some programs. Another development is that even non-credit experiences can count toward honors completion.

Honors programs seek to combine the best of the liberal arts/private elite education model with the advantages of large research universities. But an admittedly non-scientific search for experiential learning programs at the nation's leading private colleges found many examples of such learning connected to coursework or simply offered for students to do on their own time, but nothing to indicate that non-course, non-credit work could be counted toward graduation.

A final question: Should public honors colleges and programs take the risk of carving out a unique place in higher education where activities unrelated to actual classes or earned credits expand to the potential detriment of rigorous academic coursework? Experiential learning can be valuable, and experiential programs might cost less to implement than academic course sections; but the identity, the "brand" of honors programs, will not be the same.

Much less typical than any of the four class types discussed above is the **honors tutorial**. In a tutorial, made famous by the British universities of Oxford and Cambridge, the whole course is a series of one-on-one meetings between the student and instructor. The only honors program to make extensive use of this method is the Honors Tutorial College at Ohio University in Athens, Ohio, but most honors students have at least one tutorial experience, especially if they are doing an honors thesis. Tutorials can be the most demanding, rewarding, and anxiety-producing experiences in undergraduate education (and graduate school, for that matter!), depending on the personalities and expectations of the participants.

So what is the main takeaway for prospective students? Try to understand who you are, who you want to be, what you need in the way of change and development, which fears you want to overcome, and which subjects you want to study. Then decide if an honors program offers the right combination of honors classes and course types for *your* purposes. If you are comfortable with being assertive and participating in small classes, then look for those small classes and a sizable number of honors seminars. If you are uneasy about asserting yourself in class, then you can choose to confront that issue or select a program that emphasizes honors classes in the academic disciplines, especially courses in your proposed major. And if you want as much individual attention as possible, then look for a program with a good mix of class types and activities, including small seminars, undergraduate research opportunities, an honors thesis requirement—and maybe a couple of those contract courses too.

*HONORS COMPLETION RATES: 'A DIRTY LITTLE SECRET' OR A (VERY) COMPLICATED ISSUE?*

First of all, what is an honors completion rate?

It is the percentage of honors program entrants who complete the required honors curriculum by the time of graduation. Many programs have more than one honors curriculum completion option; for example, entering freshmen may be required to finish 30 honors credits and write a thesis for the main option, or they might need to complete only 18 credits without a thesis for a lower option. Honors completion rates are not the same as graduation rates. Entering honors students, because of their strong credentials, will have very high graduation rates regardless of honors completion.

Completing the requirements of an honors program is typically not directly related to graduating with Latin honors (*cum laude, magna cum laude, summa cum laude*) even though some universities do make the connection. Latin honors are most often tied to a student's university grade point average or class standing. In many colleges and universities a student can graduate with Latin honors without taking any honors courses or writing a thesis. Many, if not most, honors program completers do also earn Latin honors.

At least two researchers have written that honors completion rates can be extremely low (in the 30 percent range) and that, because publicizing completion rates can be embarrassing to some programs and their parent institutions, the rates are a "Dirty little secret." Academic studies leave the impression that having 50 percent or more of honors students complete one or more options could be, if not desirable, then acceptable. Using any set percentage as a standard is, however, questionable. (Please see below.)

The data we have received does provide evidence that some program completion rates are as low as 30 percent. On the other hand, the mean six-year honors curriculum completion rate in our own study of 31 honors programs, enrolling more than 64,000 honors students, was 58 percent. The years covered were 2010-2011—2015-2016.

Some honors educators believe that offering the lower, "mid-career" options increases the likelihood of at least some level of completion. The researchers cited above found evidence that mid-career completers are also inclined to add higher levels of honors completion before graduation.

Academic studies of honors retention, completion, and university graduation rates have focused on individual programs rather than on a significant range of programs. These studies have evaluated the impact that program curriculum requirements, entrance test scores, high school GPAs, housing, co-curricular activities, first-year seminars, and other factors have had on honors retention, completion, and graduation.

Our own work began with an analysis of 14 factors: program size; mean test scores of admitted students; number of honors credits required for completion; six-year graduation rate of honors entrants; six-year university graduation rates; university freshman retention rates; number of honors sections offered; average size of honors classes; number of honors sections in key academic disciplines; percentage of honors program members occupying classroom seats; comparison of main option and multiple option program completion rates; impact of a thesis requirement; the percentage of honors residence hall places available for the first two years; and the impact of requiring a separate honors application or credentials.

## IT'S COMPLICATED

Honors educators and university administrators have a keen interest in achieving high honors completion rates. Honors students bring higher test score profiles to the university as a whole, and one would anticipate that being in an honors program would make it even more likely that these students would go on to graduate and, in the process, improve the university's retention and graduation rates.

While the academic studies make it clear that honors student entrants, whether completers or not, have high retention and graduation rates, it is not altogether clear that they have higher rates than those of non-honors students who entered the university with equivalent credentials.

Evidence does indicate, however, that after one or two years in an honors program, students do have better critical thinking skills than similarly qualified non-honors students, probably due to smaller, interdisciplinary classes in the first year and greater interaction with faculty, mentors, and fellow students. And of course these skills and a greater likelihood of obtaining strong faculty recommendations should help students to gain entrance to prestigious graduate and professional schools or find highly desirable and remunerative employment.

Students who do not actually complete all honors requirements do not perform as well academically as honors completers and also take somewhat longer to complete their undergraduate work. One reason: almost all honors students enjoy some form of priority registration.

The principal goals of honors educators and administrators are to improve the metrics of the host university by enrolling high quality students and to provide those students with an enhanced education that can compare favorably with the education one might receive in an elite private college or university.

Our data and other studies show that honors programs do meet the goal of improving university metrics. Honors entrants (not necessarily program completers) on average graduate at a rate 19.7 percentage points higher than the rate for their parent universities as a whole, according to our data. For programs housed in universities with relatively low university graduation rates, the difference can be more than 35 percentage points. (Of course, honors entrants who graduate make up a part of the graduation rate of the university as a whole.)

The main goal of honors educators, however, is to provide an enhanced education.

Honors completion rates should surely be one measure of meeting this goal. Low completion rates are an especially discouraging result given the cost and effort allocated to honors. "Non-participation or minimal participation of honors students is the honors equivalent of poor overall university retention and graduation rates," according to one paper on the subject.

The quote is probably accurate when it comes to describing the mindset of honors educators. But comparing honors completion rates to, for example, the graduation rates of elite colleges and universities is problematic. Honors programs are a hybrid; this all but universal, structural reality clearly differentiates honors programs from most elite colleges, which generally do not have honors programs. (More on the hybrid issue below.)

Comparing honors completion rates with the graduation rates of the parent university as a whole is more reasonable, provided that there is some baseline ratio of honors completion rates to university graduation and freshman retention rates. Programs in our study with completion rates above the mean of 58 percent do, on the whole, achieve honors curriculum completion rates that match the graduation rates for the parent universities. Programs with completion rates below the mean, on average, fail to match the university graduation rate by about 20 percentage points.

Honors programs seek to combine the best qualities of an elite private college with those of a large research university. In general, this means that the "elite private college" components of this hybrid model are smaller classes, more interdisciplinary sections and class discussion, more faculty mentoring, completion of a substantial honors curriculum and sometimes an undergraduate thesis, and a high level of collegiality in the form of co-curricular activities and access to honors housing.

The advantages of the "large research university" include academic majors in abundance, relationships with a broader range of students, more undergraduate research opportunities, study under nationally recognized scholars, the enjoyment of big college football and other athletics, larger alumni networks, and life in a "college town" that is centered on the large university. Some of these advantages are, however, double-edged (see below).

The hybrid model, if realized, would be for many students an ideal college experience. But one can imagine how daunting it is to meet such expectations–to match private elites at their own game and to optimize the research university experience–all simultaneously. Honors and university administrators would like to see honors completion rates that equal or exceed parent university graduation rates, or even the graduation rates of elite colleges. But in the context of honors completion rates, some of the hybrid components are positive while others can work to lower completion rates.

## THE HYBRID MODEL: WHAT MAKES IT WORK?

Six of the 31 programs in our study had six-year honors curriculum completion rates of 80 percent or higher. (But recall that honors entrants, regardless of honors completion, do graduate from the host university at a much higher rate than the rate for all students, on average about 87 percent.)

These programs are, in alphabetical order, by university: Arizona State Barrett Honors College; CUNY Macaulay Honors College; University of Illinois Campus Honors Program; Penn State Schreyer Honors College; University of South Carolina Honors College; and the UT Austin Plan II Honors Program. Programs with rates of 70 percent or higher, in alphabetical order, are Clemson Calhoun Honors College and the Colorado State Honors Program.

The six programs with completion rates of 80 percent or higher have striking differences. Barrett Honors College at ASU and the Schreyer Honors College at Penn State make very extensive use of honors contracts and mixed sections. Compared with the funding required for separate honors sections, the cost of contract and mixed sections is much less. Honors contracts allow a student to take a non-honors course for honors credit if the student "contracts" with the instructor to do some form of additional work. Mixed sections are those that include honors and non-honors students; they should be more rigorous or have an honors-only discussion or lab section. Schreyer Honors College at Penn State has an extremely large percentage of mixed sections—but honors students make up a high percentage of total students in those sections.

The UIUC Campus Honors Program and the UT Plan II program, both small in size, have a far more structured curriculum that does not include contract or mixed section credit. Plan II students receive most of their honors credit through Plan II-specific courses, even in subjects such as physics. CUNY's Macaulay Honors College students take honors-only classes offered by the honors college or by academic departments. The South Carolina Honors College offers an impressive range of honors-only classes of the same type, and only about 11 percent of sections are mixed. The program does not offer contract options.

Contract and mixed sections give students a lot of flexibility. Many of these courses are upper-division, so students can continue to receive honors credit throughout their time in the program, without having to wait for a specific honors-only course to open. It is difficult for many large honors programs to achieve four-year involvement without utilizing contract and mixed sections. Yet the South Carolina Honors College and the Macaulay Honors College at CUNY both have more than 2,000 honors students and also have strong four-year participation.

One thing is clear: the hybrid structure itself has many variations. Here we should note that one honors college, the *Wilkes Honors College of Florida Atlantic University, is not a hybrid at all because the whole campus is dedicated to honors education.*

But based on statistical analyses of the data from all 31 programs, common predictive factors emerge: high university freshman retention rates; a substantial honors curriculum (30 credits or more); an emphasis on one completion option; and enhanced access to honors housing. Other positive factors include higher test scores, important to freshman retention rates; and smaller class sizes. Both of these factors have their greatest impact in programs with multiple, lower completion requirements.

It is somewhat unusual for honors curriculum completion rates to equal or exceed university graduation rates. Eleven of the 31 programs achieved such rates, according to our data. In alphabetical order, they are Arizona State's Barrett Honors College; Colorado State Honors Program; CUNY Macaulay Honors College; University of Houston Honors College; University of Illinois Campus Honors Program; University of Kansas Honors Program; University of Nevada Reno Honors Program; University of South Carolina Honors College; Texas Tech Honors College; UT Austin Plan II Honors Program; and the Virginia Commonwealth University Honors College.

## CHOICES, AND MORE CHOICES

The part of the hybrid structure that is related to the "large public research university" component is difficult to measure. Of course the resources allocated by the university make possible the scores of academic departments and sub-disciplines available for majors and fund the honors program, or programs, as well. Relatively generous funding allows for more honors sections, smaller classes, undergraduate research, and more housing, all of which are important to participation.

But the one characteristic of honors programs and the public universities in which they reside that receives little attention, in relation to completion rates, is the enormous range of choices that are available. An honors student at a major public university can choose to persevere through a demanding honors curriculum, or not; can choose to attend every home football game and party, or not; can choose among hundreds of degree plans and change to one that is too time-consuming to allow for honors work, or not; join eight or ten of the two hundred groups on campus, or not; and choose to live off-campus or with a non-honors friend, or not.

Their counterparts at elite private colleges do not have a hybrid structure that allows such a range of choices. Of course they can change majors, or, perhaps, change residence halls. They can also choose to spend too much time partying. But they have a smaller range of majors and college organizations from which to choose; and college sports often have limited appeal. And most do not experience large, sprawling campuses where one can feel overwhelmed, although honors programs certainly make big-campus life more collegial.

A larger range of choices, then, is an inherent piece of the "research university" component of the hybrid model, and in our opinion, it can contribute to lower honors completion rates. Some characteristics of a large public university campus (large class sizes, registration issues, social distractions) often cause parents and students to choose smaller, private colleges even at greater cost. Honors programs mitigate but do not eliminate the potential impact of these factors.

The real question is whether greater choice is ultimately negative or positive. All students make good choices and bad choices; college is often the place where they learn the first big lessons about choice. Clearly, however, students who are mature and focused enough to enjoy the large university experience without overindulgence are most likely to take full advantage of their honors opportunities.

Students should also be strongly motivated on their own if they are to undertake honors study and succeed. Their counterparts at elite private colleges must demonstrate their motivation repeatedly, not least during the application process. Our study shows that, for main option programs only, honors admission requirements that require an honors-specific application or credentials beyond those required for regular university admission do have a relation to honors completion rates.

Twelve of 15 main option programs require honors-specific application materials. Eleven of 16 multiple option programs do. (Some programs simply gather data from the admissions office and then issue invitations to top students already admitted to the university.)

## PUBLIC HONORS VS. PRIVATE ELITES

The issue of honors completion is not only linked to the question: Do honors programs actually deliver? Another question often follows: How do honors programs really compare with private elite colleges?

Assuming that a student is in a public honors program with a strong curriculum requirement, including a thesis, and a high completion rate, does that student graduate with an education comparable with that attained by a student at an elite private college?

The hybrid model carries with it the assumption that students at elite private colleges complete a rigorous curriculum that usually includes extensive undergraduate research and an honors thesis, and that the honors model should strive to do the same.

Like the perception that honors completion rates should approximate graduation rates at elite colleges, the perception that most or all students at elite colleges necessarily pursue an especially rigorous path is inaccurate.

Princeton is the only university in the Ivy League that requires an undergraduate thesis for graduation. Likewise, Stanford, MIT, Duke, Swarthmore, Amherst, Williams, and other elite schools do not require a thesis. Reed, Chicago, and Bates do have a high number of students who complete an undergraduate thesis. If a student wants to graduate with Latin honors at many elite colleges, or especially to graduate magna cum laude or summa cum laude, or departmental honors, only then would the student have to write a thesis.

Anecdotal information suggests that only 20-25 percent of students at elite colleges complete a thesis or equivalent project. In addition, grades at elite institutions hover around an A-minus average, bringing into question just how much many of them are actually challenged by the courses they take.

So, yes, given appropriate effort, a student in a public honors program with a strong curriculum requirement and a thesis should receive an equivalent education or, perhaps, even a better education than most students at a private elite college. One can certainly argue, however, that the relatively few students pursuing Latin or departmental honors at elite private schools can receive an even better education.

Finally, another comparison: Does the education of an honors student who is in a program with, say, a 55 percent completion rate, a 24-credit completion requirement, and no requirement for a thesis compare with that of his or her counterpart at an elite private college?

The elite private college will have a graduation rate about 5-10 points higher than the graduation rate of public university's honors students. The student body at the private elite will, on the whole, be "smarter" but less diverse, less "real-life," economically and otherwise. The honors student may well be challenged more by honors work than most students at the private elite are in regular classes. Both students may receive some financial aid, but at the private elite most of the aid is need-based or leaves funding gaps that could leave the student with large student loans. Meanwhile, the honors student and many of his classmates receive a large, renewable merit scholarship.

Not a simple choice.

Undoubtedly, the current trend in higher education is to develop new honors colleges or to integrate existing honors programs into a separate honors college. This can lead to the perception that honors colleges are inherently better, more advanced, or more in tune with the need to create centers of greater excellence in public universities.

But in the case of most of the public universities with an average *U.S. News* ranking of about 60 or higher, the preference is to offer an honors program—or programs—rather than establish a separate honors college within those universities. It is no coincidence that these schools, most notably UCLA, Virginia, Michigan, UNC-Chapel Hill, UC Santa Barbara, UC Irvine, Illinois, UT Austin, UW-Madison, Ohio State, and Washington have very strong overall academic reputations *and* high faculty rankings across all major disciplines. (UC Berkeley and William and Mary do not have any university-wide honors programs at all.)

When greater selectivity is combined with outstanding academic reputation and stellar faculty, students with Ivy-ish ambitions can say, with considerable confidence, that the smaller communities and classes created by the honors programs at these schools are the final steps that make them equivalent to (if different from) elite private universities. The university-wide academic reputation is present, and the faculty and most of the students are of a high caliber even in non-honors courses. For many extremely qualified students who care little about the prestige of an elite private college, these universities are sufficiently appealing as they are, with or without honors. There is no urgent competitive need, then, for these universities to establish a separate, often larger and more expensive honors college (please see "Size" comparisons at the end of this section).

There are exceptions, of course. When highly-ranked public universities receive generous private endowments or donations to establish honors colleges, they have done so. The Schreyer Honors College at Penn State is an outstanding example.

The University of Maryland Honors College is another exception. Though not named for wealthy benefactors, the college was created almost half a century ago, in 1966, making it one of the oldest and best-known honors colleges in the nation. (The Missouri Honors College is the oldest, established in 1958.) The highly regarded Calhoun Honors College at Clemson is now in its sixth decade of operation. The impressive new Rutgers Honors College just opened in 2015.

Private endowments and remarkable institutional support can also fund honors colleges within flagships that are not rated among the top 60 national universities, making those honors colleges so notable that they often compete with public and private elites. Examples include the University of South Carolina Honors College, ASU's Barrett Honors College, Clark Honors College at the University of Oregon, the Sally McDonnell Barksdale Honors College at Ole Miss, and the Shackouls Honors College at Mississippi State. A new, generously endowed Lewis Honors College has recently opened at the University of Kentucky. The presence of these excellent honors colleges no doubt enhances the student profiles of the universities of which they are a part and makes the universities more competitive in keeping the brightest students in state. Often, the best honors colleges attract out-of-state students as well, especially if their resources permit generous merit scholarships.

As for **basic types of honors colleges and programs,** the type is not dependent on whether the university has an honors program or an honors college. Programs and colleges can all be roughly characterized as being **core programs, blended programs, or discipline (department)-based programs.**

*Core Programs* are almost always smaller in size, anywhere from a few hundred to about 800 students, although a few are larger than that. They emphasize interdisciplinary classes and lots of seminars in the first two years, especially, and these courses are offered directly by the honors college or program. Some have relatively few sections in the academic disciplines based in the various departments. The UT Austin Plan II Honors Program and Oregon's Clark Honors College, while they are essentially core programs, also offer their own courses in English, math, and physics.

*Blended Programs* offer a combination of seminars, interdisciplinary classes, and more courses across a broader range of subjects than core programs do. There are many examples, but the South Carolina Honors College is one of the best.

*Department-based (or discipline-based) Programs* look mostly to the academic departments across the university to designate honors courses in a wide range of subjects. In these programs, such as Penn State's Schreyer Honors College, the University of Georgia Honors Program, and the University of Arkansas Honors College, the honors administration devotes even more time to coordinating the best possible relationships with Deans and Department Chairs, not to mention Provosts, in order to have as many honors courses as possible.

Now, here are the specific differences between honors colleges and honors programs.

In the 2016-2017 edition, 62% of our ratings were for honors colleges and 38% were for honors programs. The current edition is 78% honors colleges and 22% honors programs. (The change is not only the result of the trend toward converting programs to colleges; some programs that we have rated previously lack the staff or inclination to provide the data we now require.) Honors colleges have higher ratings in seven of 13 categories, but honors programs have a slightly higher overall ratings edge.

**Here are the categories in which honors colleges have better overall ratings:**

*Honors curriculum requirements*—for honors graduation, honors colleges require only ¼ of a semester credit more than honors programs require for honors completion. Both round to 30 credits on average.

*Honors-only class size*—the average honors-only class size in honors colleges is 17.4 students; the average honors-only class size in honors programs is 18.0 students.

*Overall class size*—this measure includes mixed and contract honors classes, both of which have non-honors students. The overall class size in honors colleges, including honors-only classes as well, is 23.5 students. In honors programs, the overall class size is 30.0 students. (Honors programs, in general, offer more discipline-specific courses; these often feature more mixed and contract sections.)

*Honors perks (priority registration, dorm features, room availability)*—honors colleges all have priority registration in some form; a few honors programs do not have priority registration or only offer it with later dates. Honors colleges have better dorm and, especially, space availability ratings than honors programs. Honors residential living is emphasized more in honors colleges than in honors programs, although honors programs do not ignore this aspect of honors education.

*Number of students per honors staff member*—this is the most significant difference. Honors colleges average 119 students per staff member; honors programs average 165 students per staff member.

**On the other hand, honors programs have the edge in several important categories.**

*Number of honors classes*—honors programs offer an honors class for every 13 students; honors colleges offer an honors class for every 16 students.

*Number of honors classes in key disciplines*—honors programs offer a class in a key discipline for every 20 students; honors colleges offer a class in a key discipline for every 26 students.

*Extent of honors participation*—for each member in good standing in honors programs, 1.4 honors classroom seats are occupied; for each member in good standing in honors programs, 1.3 honors classroom seats are occupied.

*Honors graduation rates adjusted to SAT*—This is the six-year honors entrant graduation rate compared with the honors graduation rates for other honors programs with the same test score range for admission. Adjusted rates for programs are about 2/3 of a point higher for programs.

*Honors grad rate adjusted to university freshman retention*— This rating simply compares the six-year graduation rate for honors entrants with the freshman retention rate for the university as a whole. University freshman retention rates often have a significant relationship to honors graduation rates. Adjusted rates for programs are about 1.2 points higher.

*Prestigious scholarships (Rhodes, Marshall, Truman, Goldwater, etc.)*—the fact that honors programs are often located in higher-ranking universities likely contributes to students' winning a significantly higher total of prestigious awards versus those won by students in universities with honors colleges. Programs are also significantly more selective in admissions (below).

**Selectivity**

Although selectivity is not a rating category, the mean (**new** SAT) admissions score for honors programs is 1446, versus the mean score for honors colleges of 1398. This factor also contributes to the higher graduation rates and a greater success at winning prestigious scholarships on the part of universities with honors programs instead of honors colleges. If we had included the honors programs at the University of Michigan
and the University of Virginia, as in previous editions, the differences in test scores would have been even greater.

**Size**

The average number of members in good standing in the 32 honors colleges rated in this edition is 2,142, slightly down from 2016 but only because we did not rate the Alabama Honors College in the current edition. (There is a summary review, however.) The growth in the size of honors colleges is a definite trend.

- The Alabama Honors College does not list its total membership, but it is probably at least 9,000 students, and in any case is the largest in the nation. (We wish they would remove all doubt.)
- The Barrett Honors College at Arizona State University reported 4,800 members in 2014; in 2016, the member total was 6,247; and in this edition the total is 7,228.
- The approximate number of members in the Hutton Honors College at Indiana University was 4,000; in 2016 it was 5,000; and now it is 5,532.
- At the South Carolina Honors College, the 2014 number was approximately 1,400; in 2016 it was 1,620; and now it is 2,021.
- At Ole Miss, the Sally McDonnell Barksdale Honors College reported 1,123 members in 2014, up to 1,251 in 2016, and now up to 1,521.
- The Purdue Honors College reported 1,555 members in 2014, a number which rose to 1,888 members in 2016 and in 2018 reached 2,060
- Washington State Honors College had 703 members in 2016. Now there are 929.

On the other hand, the Commonwealth Honors College at UMass Amherst and CUNY Macaulay Honors College have about the same enrollment as in 2016, probably because they have chosen not to expand, for now.

We have noticed that many students apply to prominent public universities and then, almost as an afterthought, begin to wonder if the honors program at University A makes that school a better choice than regular admission to the higher-ranked University B.

A far better way to look at honors is to evaluate programs in some depth at the earliest stages of the college application process. Otherwise, students realize too late that the honors application or scholarship deadlines have already passed, or find themselves searching for anecdotal evidence with little time to spare.

Honors colleges and programs differ greatly in size, quality, curricula, housing, overall philosophy, and financial aid opportunities. Working through the maze of differences can be a daunting prospect, especially when time is an issue. When it comes to honors programs, many of the most important questions can be answered only by consideration of those all-important "details." Below are twenty steps that should be very useful in helping you make the best decision regardless of whether you want a public or private university honors program:

1. Match <u>basic</u> admission requirements with your test scores, GPA, and essays.

2. Request <u>actual average</u> admission statistics. These may vary greatly from basic (minimum) requirements. In general, honors students will have average test scores 6-10% higher than the 25th percentile of accepted students for the university as a whole. The 25th percentile scores are available from *U.S. News* and other sources. If there is a wide gap between the basic and average stats, and your stats are much closer to the basic stats, then you can probably find a better option. That said, if the admissions requirements are more holistic and less stats-driven, you may be fine.

3. Determine the size of the honors program (mean size in major public universities is 1,742, but programs may be as small as 140 or as large as 9,000).

4. Ask the fish-to-pond question: Are honors students big fish in a small pond or is the pond full of sizable fish? The more selective the university as a whole, the bigger all the fish. Some parents and prospective students might prefer an honors program that stands apart on campus, while others might like a program that is more expansive. Perhaps if you are not sold on the overall quality of the university, you might choose the former; if you think the university as a whole has a strong student body or you simply prefer a non-elitist atmosphere, then you might like the latter.

5. Assess the quality of the city, surrounding area, and climate.

6. Determine the curriculum requirements as a percentage of graduation requirements. Generally, the number of honors hours should be at least 25% of the total required for graduation.

7. Determine the number of honors sections per semester/quarter.

8. Evaluate the reputation of university in preferred or likely areas of study.

9. Ask whether there are special research opportunities for undergrads **and if an honors thesis is required.** Some students do not want the extra challenge; others realize how important it can be for attending graduate or professional school, or even for employment opportunities.

10. Ask about staff size, the number of advisers, and availability to students, as well as special freshmen orientation programs.

**If the above check out, then:**

1. Ask about the number of honors sections, by subject, per semester or quarter and try to verify; determine the average enrollment in honors seminars and sections. The average class size can vary greatly among honors programs, from fewer than 10 students per class to more than 35. Most seminars and all-honors sections should have around 20-25 students or fewer, although in almost every case you will find that there are a few large classes, notably in first-year sciences, business, economics, and political science. Some honors programs have few or no honors courses in certain disciplines.

2. Ask about the types of honors sections: all-honors seminars; all-honors sections offered by honors or a department; "mixed" sections of honors and non-honors students; and the percentage of honors contract/option/conversion courses per average student at time of graduation. **Mixed sections may** be small or, more often, larger sections that can have more than 100 total students in 3-4 credit hour courses. Of these students, maybe 10-20 could be honors students, who then meet for one hour a week (rarely, two hours a week) in separate "discussion" or "recitation" sections. These sections can be led by tenured professors but are typically led by adjunct faculty or graduate students. Ask how many sections are mixed, and of these, ask how many of the main section classes are large.

**Contract courses** are regular–and often larger–sections with both honors and non-honors students, mostly the latter, in which honors students do extra work and meet occasionally with the instructor one-on-one. While most programs have some contract courses, they are generally more prevalent in large honors colleges and programs. There are advantages and disadvantages associated with contract courses. They can speed up graduation, offer more flexibility, expand the influence of honors in the university as a whole, and foster contacts with mentoring faculty. But their quality and class size may vary greatly.

**Experiential courses** are something of a trend in honors education. Some are service-oriented (think volunteering, community service) and some are related to developing leadership skills or practical knowledge through internships. Experiential courses can be exciting, broadening, and influential. They can also be time-consuming, and some do not offer course credits. *It is wise to check out this aspect of an honors curriculum and take care in judging your commitment.*

3. Ask about tuition discounts, scholarships, continuing financial aid, including special recruitment of National Merit Scholars.

4. Determine if there is priority registration for honors students and, if so, type of priority registration.

5. Research the types of special honors housing for freshmen and upperclassmen, if any, including basic floor plans, on-site laundry, suite or corridor-style rooms, air-conditioning, location of nearest dining hall, proximity of major classroom buildings (especially in preferred subjects), and availability of shuttles and other transportation on campus. If there is no special honors housing, it is often a sign that the honors

program does not want to foster an elitist atmosphere. The absence of priority registration may be an additional sign.

6. Research the study-abroad opportunities; some universities have a separate division for study-abroad programs.

7. Ask about the presence and involvement of advisers for prestigious scholarships, such as Goldwater, Rhodes, Marshall, Truman, etc., and program success in achieving these awards.

8. Ask about additional fees for participation in honors **and ask about the percentage of honors "completers."** These are honors students who actually complete all of the honors requirements and graduate with some form of honors. There are some programs that have completion rates as low as 25% and a few with completion rates higher than 80%. (This is different from the graduation rate, which, for freshmen honors entrants, is anywhere from 75%–99% after six years.)

9. Now, try to assess the quality of the honors program versus quality of university as a whole.

10. VISIT the college if you have not done so and try to question current honors students. Some of the information mentioned above can only come from a personal visit or be learned after a student has been accepted.

In each of our profiles of public honors programs in national universities, there is a section titled "Prestigious Awards" that provides a summary of the awards earned by undergraduates and graduates of the universities as a whole. The awards that we track include the Rhodes Scholarship, Marshall Scholarship, Gates Cambridge Scholarship, Truman Scholarship, Churchill Scholarship, National Science Foundation Graduate Research Fellowships, and Fulbright Student Scholarships, most of which are for college upperclassmen or graduates. Undergraduate awards include the Goldwater Scholarships, Udall Scholarships, Boren Scholarships, and Gilman Scholarships. *Until readers become familiar with these scholarships, it will be useful to refer to this page when reading the "Prestigious Awards" section in each profile*

It is a great honor for an undergraduate or graduate to win a prestigious award, and many of the awards lead to notable success in graduate school and public life. Below are brief descriptions of each award.

**Boren Scholarships** provide $20,000-$30,000 to U.S. undergraduate students, including freshmen, to study abroad in areas of the world that are critical to U.S. interests and underrepresented in study abroad, including Africa, Asia, Central & Eastern Europe, Eurasia, Latin America, and the Middle East. The countries of Western Europe, Canada, Australia, and New Zealand are excluded. The GPA requirement is 3.50, with a relevant background and language ability.

**Churchill Scholarships** are valued at approximately $60,000 for 9-12 months of study at Cambridge University. Eligibility requires at least a bachelor's degree and a 3.70 GPA; however, the average GPA is closer to 3.90. Students in the STEM disciplines and public health are eligible. Only 14 scholars are chosen each year.

**Fulbright Student Scholarships** are for graduating seniors or graduates who are selected to study or teach overseas. The award has a value of at least $25,000 for one year, including room and board. Depending on whether the recipient is teaching English or conducting research, the GPA requirements vary from 3.40 (teaching English) to 3.90.

**Gates Cambridge Scholarships** are the most generous multi-year awards we track, currently providing *full tuition and fees and $23,000 per year* in living costs, for up to three years of graduate study at Cambridge University. Students with dependents receive generous funding in addition to the basic funding. Successful candidates must have at least a 3.80 GPA and be graduating seniors or graduates. Although many Gates Cambridge Scholars are STEM students, the award is not restricted to scholars in the STEM disciplines. About 95 scholars are chosen annually from more than 4,000 candidates.

**Gilman Scholarships** allow students of limited means and students in underrepresented disciplines to study or participate in internships abroad. The average value is $4,000. Required GPA is 3.20 to 3.50.

**Goldwater Scholarships** are perhaps the most prestigious undergraduate awards. They are valued at $7,500 per year, and successful candidates are outstanding students in the STEM fields with a GPA of 3.80 and higher. There have been a few two-time winners. A university may nominate up to four candidates a year. About 300 scholars are chosen each year from among thousands of sophomore and junior candidates. Many Goldwater Scholars go on to win major post-graduate awards.

**Marshall Scholarships** are extremely prestigious awards granted to about 40 American graduating seniors in all majors each year. Scholars currently receive approximately $40,000 per year to study at one of scores of universities in the United Kingdom, usually for two years, but sometimes for three years. A large number of Marshall Scholars study at the universities of Cambridge and Oxford; the University of London (King's College, University College, Imperial College); and the London School of Economics and Political Studies (LSE). The GPA requirement is 3.80 and higher.

**National Science Foundation Graduate Research Fellowships** are awarded to 900-1,000 students annually to fund three years of graduate study in a STEM field or a social or behavioral science discipline. Fellows receive about $10,500 for each of the three years. A minimum GPA of 3.70 and very high GRE scores (99th percentile) are required.

**Rhodes Scholarships** remain the best-known and most prestigious of all awards, in addition to being the oldest. Each year 32 Americans are chosen to study for two (and sometimes three) years at the University of Oxford, in all majors. The dollar value of the award is similar to the value of the Marshall Scholarship but could be as high as $50,000 per year; the minimum GPA requirement is also 3.80.

**Truman Scholarships** are awarded to 55-60 juniors at participating U.S. universities who want to go to graduate school in preparation for a career in public service (government or the nonprofit and advocacy sectors). The minimum GPA requirement is 3.80. Awardees receive $2,000 to complete their undergraduate education and $30,000 total for up to three years of postgraduate study.

**Udall Scholarships** now provide $7,000 toward tuition for undergraduates interested in environmental, sustainability, or planning issues, or for Native Americans focusing on health care or tribal policy. Only 50 awards are granted each year.

Although we are not ranking honors colleges and programs in numerical order, the summary below provides average (mean) overall results for the 50 programs that we rated, and additional data.

**Size of Honors Colleges/Programs:**

Average size of all colleges/programs=2,030
Average size of 32 honors colleges=2,144
Average size of 9 honors programs=1,633
Largest of all 41 colleges/programs=7,228
Smallest of all 41 colleges/programs=411

**Curriculum Requirements:**

Average number of honors credit hours required for program completion=30.0 semester credits
Required honors credit hours as a percentage of total credits required for graduation=25.0%
Highest credit hour completion level of the 50 colleges and programs=50 credits
Lowest credit hour completion level of the 50 colleges and programs=18 credits

**Honors Enrollment, by Type of Honors Class Section:**

Average percentage of honors classroom seats in honors-only sections=75.8%
Average percentage of honors classroom seats in mixed honors sections=15.4%
Average percentage of honors classroom seats in honors contract sections=8.8%

**Number and Percentage of Programs with 90%-100% of Honors Classroom Seats in Honors-Only Sections**= 16 programs, or 39%

**Number of Honors Classes Offered:** One honors section for every 15.0 honors individuals enrolled in the term reported.

**Number of Honors Classes in Key Disciplines:** One honors section in each key discipline for every 24.7 honors individuals enrolled in the term reported.

**Average Ratio of Honors Classroom "Seats" to Total Number of Honors Members in Good Standing:** 1.30 classroom seats per 1.0 member in good standing. Range= 3.59 to .46.

**Average Honors-only Class Size:** 17.5 students.

**Average Honors Overall Class Size, including Mixed and Contract Sections:** 24.9 students. The average mixed section had an average 68.6 students in the main course section. The average honors contract section had an average of 56.6 students.

**Honors Graduation Rate (6-year), Freshman Entrants, not necessarily Honors "Completers":**
Average raw honors grad rate for programs with SAT requirement of:

1471-1510= 94.0%.
1420-1461= 86.1%.

1370-1403= 85.5%.
1286-1365= 85.5%.

**Ratio of Honors Students to Honors Staff:**

Average number of honors students to honors staff person=127.9
Highest average number of honors students to staff=398.0
Lowest average number of honors students to staff=28.3

**Ratio of Honors Dorm Spaces to total of First- and Second-Year Members of Program:**

Average ratio of honors dorm spaces to students=.60 (median .49)
Highest ratio of honors dorm spaces to students=1.39
Lowest ratio of honors dorm spaces to students=.04

**Test Scores:**

Mean new SAT for enrolled students in all rated programs=1409
Lowest average SAT score=1286
Highest average SAT score=1510

**Ranking Data for Academic Departments:** For business and engineering, the rankings are of the undergraduate programs; for all other departments, the rankings are of graduate programs.

**Much of our data is unique and is therefore not available in any other publication or online. Some of these unique data elements include:**

• Comparative statistics on the number of prestigious scholarships won by each national university
• Actual honors class sizes from 100% of the rated 41 public honors programs
• Actual honors graduation rates from 100% of the 50 rated honors programs
• Comparative information about the honors residence halls (or lack thereof) designated by all rated honors programs, including room configurations, amenities, and nearest dining facilities
• Ratios of honors students to administrative staff, 100% of rated programs
• Descriptions of the types of honors courses offered by each program, including the percentage breakdown of honors-only class sections, mixed sections, and contract sections

A list of honors colleges and programs with 5.0 and 4.5 ratings appears at the bottom of page 7.

**Curriculum Requirements (20 pts):** For each program, we (1) determine the highest level of honors completion, or an average level if there are multiple completion options; (2) determine the minimum number of credits required to fulfill the requirements; (3) calculate a small percentage credit for the number of engineering graduates from the university;* (4) take the total raw number derived from the previous steps; and (5) standardize and weight the raw data (the final step for all categories before they are summed to a total rating score).

*Developing an extensive honors curriculum in a university with a high percentage of engineering students puts a strain on honors programs (absent generous endowments) because those universities must allocate so many of their resources to engineering equipment, labs, and instruction. The greater demand on resources can limit the honors courses and requirements in several of these universities. The small proportional adjustment that we make for all programs is an attempt to even the playing field just a bit for those that operate in the context of an engineering-heavy university.

**Number of Honors Classes (10 pts):** Using the detailed data we received from respondents about the number and type of honors class sections, we (1) determine the total number of honors individuals (please see Glossary) enrolled for the term reported, (2) assign a prorated value to each honors credit section, depending on the number of credit hours and the percentage of honors student enrollment in each section, and (3) divide the number of individuals by the number of adjusted honors class sections.

**Number of Honors Classes in Key Disciplines (10 pts):** Using the same data as above, we (1) determine the total number of honors individuals enrolled for the term reported, (2) identify the class sections with a threshold percentage of honors enrollment in each key discipline, (3) prorate the value of each section as above, and (4) divide the number of individuals by the number of adjusted honors class sections in key disciplines. The key disciplines are biological sciences; business (all); chemistry; communications (especially public speaking); computer science; economics; engineering (all); English; history; math (all); philosophy; physics; political science; psychology; and sociology/anthropology/gender studies combined. *Each section has equal value, and there is no penalty for not having sections in one or more key disciplines.*

**Extent of Honors Enrollment (10 pts):** Each program provides the total number of honors students in good standing for the term reported. Not all of these students take an honors course in every term. For this measure, we divide the number honors classroom "seats" by the total number of students in good standing in the term reported. A desirable result is a number greater than 1.0, thus showing a reasonably high degree of honors enrollment and participation. In part, this can indicate whether honors students have honors course opportunities in the last two years of college. Most honors courses are offered in the first two years. *(Please see Glossary for a definition of honors "seats.")*

**Average Class Size, Honors-only Sections (6.25 pts):** For this measure, we add the total number of honors classroom seats in sections that have only honors students enrolled. We then divide this total by the number of honors-only sections.

**Average Class Size, Overall (6.25 pts):** On average, honors programs have six basic types of classes or activities that carry honors credit: (1) honors-only sections; (2) mixed sections, in which a sizable number of honors students shared the main section with non-honors students and, often, have additional honors-only labs or discussion sections; (3) contract (option, conversion, enhancement) sections, in which one or a few honors students in a regular non-honors section enter into a formal agreement with the instructor to do extra work for honors credit; (4) experiential courses or activities for honors credit, including internships, special research projects, leadership education, teaching assistantships, public service, and mentoring; (5) thesis preparation and completion; and (6) study abroad. For this measure, we count the *total* enrollment of students, honors and non-honors, in the *main* sections of classes in the first four categories. Many honors professionals believe that the relevant enrollment figures should only be for honors-only main sections or honors-only labs and discussion (breakout) sections, the latter offered primarily in introductory science courses and some business, economics, and political science courses. Our view is that when most parents think about class sizes, they have main course sections in mind. The overall average class size is *not a raw average of class sizes, however.* We do calculate the raw average class sizes for honors-only main sections, mixed sections, and contract sections—but then we use a proportional formula to arrive at the overall average class size. In other words, we take the percentage of enrollment in each section type (honors-only, mixed, contract) and then multiply the raw average class size for each type by the percentage of enrollment for each type. The products are then summed for the overall class size average.

**Honors Graduation Rate Adjusted to SAT (5.0 pts)**--Using the six-year graduation rate for honors entrants, whether or not they completed the honors program, would essentially tie this metric to selection criteria alone—if you set the bar really high, a lot of the students you admit will graduate regardless. So we took the six-year honors entrant graduation data and then compared it to the honors graduation rates for other honors programs with the same test score range for admission. The result is an adjusted honors graduation rate.

**Graduation Rate Adjusted to Freshman Retention (5.0 pts):** This rating simply compares the six-year graduation rate for honors entrants with the freshman retention rate for the university as a whole. University freshman retention rates often have a significant relationship to honors graduation rates.
**Honors Staff (7.5 pts):** Another simple rating, this one derives from dividing the total number of honors students in good standing by the number of full-time equivalent honors staff.

**Priority Registration (2.5 pts):** The maximum rating is assigned to programs that allow honors students to register for all courses, honors and non-honors, in the first group of students regardless of class year. Lesser points are assigned if honors students register first within their class year, or register with the class ahead.

**Honors Residence Halls, Amenities (7.5 pts):** We evaluated the room configurations, locations, amenities, and dining options of honors residence halls and then assigned values according to room type (suite-style and apartments receive the highest value), location, dining options, air-conditioning, proximity to honors administration and programming, in-house laundry, and options for housing upperclassmen as well as first-year students.

**Honors Residence Halls, Availability (2.5 pts):** For this measure, we (1) take the total number of honors dorm places, (2) count the total number of honors students in good standing, divide that total by two (= an approximation of first- and second-year students in good standing), and then divide the number of honors dorm places by the number of first- and second-year students.

**Prestigious Awards (7.5 pts)**--(1) We used raw totals for the entire history of the following: Rhodes, Marshall, Gates Cambridge, Churchill, Truman, Udall, and Goldwater; (2) we used raw totals for three most recent years of Fulbright Student and Boren, three most recent years of NSF GRG awards, and (3) a percentage of Gilman awards during the same period.

**NAME**: UNIVERSITY OF ARIZONA HONORS COLLEGE

**Date Established:** 1999. (Preceded by Honors Program, 1962.)

**Location**: Tucson, Arizona

**University Full-time Undergraduate Enrollment (2017):** 34,072.

**Honors Members in Good Standing**: 4,667; (mean size of all programs is 2,030).

**Honors Average Admission Test Score(s)**: ACT, 30.14; SAT, 1403. Highest score from single sitting.

**Basic Admission Requirements:** None reported.

**Average High School GPA/Class Rank:** 3.86, unweighted.

**Application Deadline(s):** *Please verify with each program, as some deadlines could change.* Priority deadline is December 2, 2018.

**Honors Programs with SAT scores from 1370—1403:** Arizona, CUNY Macaulay, Georgia State, Houston, Indiana, LSU, Massachusetts, New Mexico, Purdue, Texas Tech, UAB.

**Administrative Staff:** 30.

**RATINGS AT A GLANCE:** For all mortarboard ratings immediately below, a score of 5 is the maximum and represents a comparison with all rated honors colleges and programs. More detailed explanations follow the "mortarboard" ratings.

**PERCEPTION* OF UNIVERSITY AS A WHOLE, NOT OF HONORS:** 🎓🎓🎓🎓

*Perception is based on the university's ranking among public universities in the 2018 U.S. News Best Colleges report. Please bear in mind that the better the U.S. News ranking, the more difficult it is for an honors college or program to have a rating that equals or improves on the magazine ranking.

**OVERALL HONORS RATING:** 🎓🎓🎓🎓

**Curriculum Requirements:** 🎓🎓🎓🎓

**Number of Honors Classes Offered:** 🎓🎓🎓 1/2

**Number of Honors Classes in Key Disciplines:** 🎓🎓🎓 1/2

**Extent of Honors Enrollment:** 🎓🎓🎓 1/2

**Honors-only Class Size:** 🎓🎓🎓 1/2

**Overall Class Size (Honors-only plus mixed, contract):** 🎓🎓🎓

**Honors Grad Rate Adjusted to SAT:** 🎓🎓🎓 1/2

**Grad Rate Adjusted to Freshman Retention Rate:** 🎓🎓🎓🎓 1/2

**Ratio of Staff to Students:** 🎓🎓🎓 1/2

**Priority Registration: Yes,** juniors and seniors (by credit count) register with first group; freshmen and sophomores (also by credit count) register with second group.

**Honors Housing Amenities:** 🎓🎓🎓🎓

**Honors Housing Availability:** 🎓🎓🎓

**Prestigious Awards:** 🎓🎓🎓🎓🎓

## RATING SCORES AND EXPLANATIONS:

**Curriculum Requirements (4.0):** The most important rating category, the curriculum completion requirement (classes required to complete honors) defines not only what honors students should learn but also the extent to which honors students and faculty are connected in the classroom. If there is a thesis or capstone requirement, it reinforces the individual contact and research skills so important to learning.

The average number of honors semester hours required for completion across all programs is 30.0.

The highest completion option at the Arizona Honors College is 30 credits, including 24 course credits and a 6-credit thesis. Up to 12 credits may be earned by honors contract in a regular course section (honors student does extra work). This track is for students entering the Honors College with less than 30 college credits.

Students who have completed between 30 and 59 college credits before entering the Honors College can complete the HONR 24 option, which requires 18 course credits and a 6-credit thesis. Up to 9 credits may be earned in honors contract sections.

Students who have completed between 60 or more college credits before entering the Honors College can complete the HONR 18 option, which requires 12 course credits and a 6-credit thesis. Up to 6 credits may be earned in honors contract sections.

For students completing a degree in Engineering, Honors students will automatically receive seven units of Honors credit for design work in their major. They are required to complete a senior design project which can also double as the thesis. Up to 9 credits may be earned in honors contract sections.

**AP/IB credits AP/IB credits** are **not** counted as replacements for honors courses.

**No. Honors Classes Offered (3.5):** This is a measure of the total **adjusted** honors main sections available in the term reported, not including labs and thesis. An adjusted main section has 3 or more semester credits, or equivalent, and sections with fewer credits receive a lower prorated value.

Arizona honors offered a section for every **15.6** enrolled students. The average for all programs was **15.0**. The lower the number, the better.

In the term reported, **58.2%** of honors enrollment was **in honors-only sections; 33.3% in mixed honors sections (honors and non-honors students); and 8.5% in contract sections (regular sections in which honors students "contract" to do extra work).** This represents an increase in contract sections since 2016. For all programs under review, enrollment by type of honors section was 75.8% honors-only, 15.4 % mixed, and 8.8% contract.

**No. Honors Classes in Key Disciplines (3.5):** The 15 "key" disciplines are biological sciences; business (all); chemistry; communications (especially public speaking); computer science; economics; engineering (all); English; history; math (all); philosophy; physics; political science; psychology; and sociology, anthropology, and gender studies. Interdisciplinary sections, such as those often taken for General Education credit in the first two years, do receive a lesser, prorated discipline "credit" because they introduce students to multiple disciplines in an especially engaging way, often with in-depth discussion.

For this measure, mixed and contract sections are not counted as a section in a key discipline unless students taking the sections for honors credit make up at least 10% of the total section enrollment.

In the term reported, the honors college offered a section in a key discipline for every **25.1 honors students.** The average for all programs is **24.7.** The lower the number, the better.

Out of **99 adjusted sections in key disciplines, 35 were honors-only sections.** The most sections by far were in English, and a very high number of physics sections, a fact noted in the last review. Business was another key discipline represented strongly. There was one adjusted section in computer science, and four or five in philosophy, political science, and psychology. Two sections were in math and four in history.

The college does offer interdisciplinary courses including about 20 in social sciences and humanities. These include were "Experiences in the Humanities" and "Exploring Electronic Presence." The honors college is a **blended** program, with a significant tilt toward a department-based type.

**Extent of Honors Enrollment (3.5):** Not all honors students take an honors class each term, especially after the first two years. Programs that have fewer honors classes and thesis options for upper-division honors students will *generally* have fewer total members in good standing who are actually enrolled in a given term. (Please be aware, however, that honors students not enrolled in a class for a term are still tied to the honors community through residential and extracurricular activities.) Our research shows that this measure is closely related to honors completion rates, i.e., the number of students who complete honors requirements by the time they graduate.

For example, if a program has 1,800 individual students enrolled in a given term, and 3,000 students in good standing, the level of enrollment was .67, an indication that honors class enrollment is somewhat

below average, especially in upper-division classes. **Arizona has a ratio of 1.13**, below the average of 1.30 for all programs.

**Average Class Size, Honors-only Sections (3.5):** Offered mostly in the first two years, honors-only classes tend to be smaller and, as the name implies, have no or very few students other than those in the honors program. These class sections always are much smaller than mixed or contract sections, or regular non-honors class sections in the university.

The average honors-only class size at the honors college is **18.1 students**. The average for all programs is **17.5 students.**

**Average Class Size, Overall (3.0):** The overall class calculation is based on the *proportion* of honors students in each type of class (honors-only, mixed honors, and honors contract sections). Thus it is not a raw average. The overall honors-credit class size is **34.2 students**, versus the average for all programs of **24.9 students**. Nevertheless, UA has significantly improved its overall class size since 2016.

These class size averages also do not correspond to the number of students per honors sections numbers above. The reason is that, in computing average class size metrics, we include enrollment in each 1-2-credit section, not just sections with 3 or more credits.

Along with the honors-only average of 18.1 students, at Arizona the mixed honors sections average **50.6 students,** and the contract sections with honors credit for individual honors students average **90.2 students.** Across all programs, the average mixed honors section has 68.6 students, and the average contract section has 56.6 students.

**Honors Grad Rate Adjusted to SAT (3.5):** The rating is the based on the actual grad rate for students who entered the program six years earlier, whether or not the students remained in honors. The **actual rate of 84.4%** is also compared to the rates of other programs with the same test score entry requirement range, and then adjusted upward if the program is performing above other programs in the same range, or downward if the performance is less than other programs in the same range. The rate here is slightly downward, to **84.0%.**

**Grad Rate Adjusted to Freshman Retention Rate (4.5):** This rate compares the actual grad rate above to a predicted grade rate when freshman retention rates are considered. The actual grad rate is **3.1 points higher** than the predicted rate. For all programs, the actual grad rate is **.33 points lower** than the predicted rate.

**Ratio of Staff to Honors Students (3.5):** There is 1 staff member for every 1**55.6** students. (Mean ratio for all programs is 1 staff member for every **127.9** students.)

**Honors Residence Halls, Amenities (4.0):** Árbol de la Vida is the largest and newest Honors hall comprised of five buildings connected by bridges. The building has solar-heated water, low-flow water fixtures, smart thermostats, 'green' outlets, and passive water harvesting. There are common spaces including study rooms, living rooms, recreation and media center, exercise spaces and gathering places indoors and out. Honors classes and Honors advising are also offered on-site. More than 75% of honors students living on campus live in Árbol de la Vida. The rooms are traditional rooms with hall baths, and, of course, air-conditioned.

Yuma Hall is listed on the National Register of Historic Places and features the classic red brick tradition of UA campus. Its location in the historic north area of campus is close to the Eller College of Management, College of Engineering, College of Fine Arts and Memorial Student Union. Community spaces include a sunken living room, kitchen, multi-media study space, recreation room and large patio. Yuma hall was the first Honors hall and celebrated its 30th anniversary as Honors housing in 2018.

UA honors is determined to make improvements, with a new honors dean and **a big new honors residence hall on the way:**

*"Additionally, opening in Fall 2019 will be an as-yet unnamed Honors Facility that will house 1054 Honors students," according to Kevin Hall, senior director of recruitment and marketing. "It will also include all faculty & staff offices, a dining facility, 7 classrooms (one outdoor), courtyard space, and a new Campus Recreation / Health Center directly across the street."*

**Honors Residence Halls, Availability (3.0):** This rating compares the number of occupants in honors residence halls to the number of honors freshman and sophomore members in good standing. The ratio for the college is **.31** places for each first- and second-year student. The *median* for all programs is .49 places.

**Prestigious Awards (5.0):** The awards that we track and include are listed in the section titled "Prestigious Scholarships." The awards are sometimes won by students who are not in an honors college or program, but increasingly many are enrolled in honors programs. It is also a trend that honors colleges and programs help to prepare their students for the awards competitions.

Arizona students, many of them from the honors college, have won a very impressive 24 Rhodes scholarships 13 Truman awards, four Marshall Scholarships, six Gates Cambridge awards and 4 Churchill awards. Arizona students have earned an impressive 40 Goldwater scholarships for undergrads in STEM fields, and the university is a leader in winning Udall awards. It also has a strong record in winning Boren and Gilman foreign study and travel scholarships.

**UNRATED FEATURES**

**Cumulative GPA: 3.40 (pending).**

**Academic Strengths, National Rankings:** This is based on national rankings of *graduate* programs in all but engineering and business, where undergraduate rankings are used. One of the weaknesses of the *U.S. News* rankings is that they focus on too many wealth-related metrics while ignoring their own assessments of academic departments. The rankings listed below are for all universities, public or private.

The University of Arizona is a prime example. The average national departmental ranking across 15 departments at UA is an impressive 43. Leading departments are earth sciences (8), business (21), sociology (24), physics (37), chemistry (41), economics (42), and computer science (43).

**Internships, Professional Development, Community Engagement:** "The UA Honors College has developed a range of exciting engagement experiences for Honors undergraduates…including robust support for Honors internships and professional development experiences, both in Tucson and beyond; a team-based civic engagement experience that features partnerships with local non-profits; a mentoring program that pairs incoming students with experienced Honors students; and several Honors clubs and organizations that engage Honors students in leadership and service.

"UA Honors has a First Year Experience that includes both academic and non-curricular components. Our Common Reading program is a key dimension, with all first-year students receiving the same book during summer Orientation. This book and its themes are the focal point for a variety of activities through students' first year and we invite the book author, or someone with expertise in its themes, to be our featured speaker at Family Weekend Convocation in the fall.

"We feature a variety of special events throughout the year, including the Honors Engagement Expo in April that showcases a range of student work across internships, study abroad, research, and student leadership experiences. We have a new Elevator Pitch competition that enables students who have completed a thesis or capstone to submit a two-minute video pitch describing their work to a wide-ranging audience. The top video pitches are selected and those students are invited to give a live elevator pitch that demonstrates the relevance of student work."

**Undergraduate Research:** "Three main components to our formal research program: the First Year Project, the Spirit of Inquiry Research Program (SIRP), and the First Year Project and the thesis experience. The First Year Project is for first year students to gain experience in research during the spring semester. Students earn one unit of Honors credit for projects they design with the assistance of a faculty mentor. These projects are featured at the First Year Project Expo, with students vying for cash prizes in multiple categories (including the 'Best Overall Project').

"The SIRP enables Honors students across all colleges and majors to apply for up to $1,500 to fund research projects that will be completed over the summer and/or during the academic year. The projects, which require a faculty mentor, are showcased at the end-of-year Honors Engagement Expo."

**Honors Study Abroad:** "The UA Honors College offers Honors-specific study abroad opportunities that adopt a 'City as Text' model in introducing Honors students to a pair of international locations and the global issues and questions that can be addressed there. Most Honors Trips take place in the summer after students' first year, and most student participants have never been abroad before. These Honors Trips are taught by some of the very best faculty at the UA. The Honors College works closely with the Office of Global Initiatives to keep the cost of attendance as low as possible, and also offers grants in variable amounts that help to defray the overall cost. The Honors College is also developing signature study abroad programs, most notably the Easter Island trip led by Dean Terry Hunt, as well as a few others in development."

**Financial Aid:** "The University of Arizona offers generous merit-based financial aid. The base range for Fall 2018 admitted students are:

- Arizona Residents – "Wildcat Excellence Award": $3,000 - $12,000/yr.

- Non-Residents – "Arizona Excellence Award": $2,000 - $35,000/yr.

"A student matriculating in Fall 2018 with the average Honors enrollee profile would receive an award of $10,000 (resident) or $25,000 (non-resident).

"There are also specific awards for National Scholars as follows:
- Resident National Merit Semi-Finalist (does not advance to Finalist): $13,500/yr.

- Resident National Merit Finalist or National Hispanic Scholar: $18,000/yr. + $1,500 study abroad stipend

- Non-Resident National Merit Semi-Finalist (does not advance to Finalist): Base Arizona Excellence Award + additional $2,000/yr.

- Non-Resident National Merit Finalist or National Hispanic Scholar: Base Arizona Excellence Award + additional $5,000/yr. + $1,500 study abroad stipend.

The Honors College also offers its own awards, including but not limited to:

- The Giue Family Scholarship: Multiple awards of $2,500/yr.

- The Laura & Arch Brown Scholarship: Multiple awards of up to $500/yr.

- The Elizabeth Read Taylor Scholarship: Multiple awards of up to $2,500/yr.

- Honors Fee Assistance Scholarship: Many awards to cover up to the full Honors fee of $500/yr.

- The Richard Kissling Spirit of Inquiry Scholarship: Multiple awards of varying amounts

- The Andria Ligas Memorial Scholarship: Multiple awards of varying amounts

The Honors College also offers grants of up to $1,500 for Honors students to support independent research, study abroad, and professional development.

**Honors Fees:** There is an Honors program fee of $500/yr. There is no additional cost for Honors residence halls or Honors class sections.

**Placement of Honors Graduates:** "May 2018 Honors graduates were accepted to graduate and professional programs at University of Cambridge, Notre Dame, University of Colorado at Boulder, University of Chicago, Duke University, Emory, SUNY College of Optometry, University of Michigan, UC Berkeley, UC Davis, University of Iowa, Georgia Tech, St. Louis University, Washington State, Stanford, UC San Francisco, UCLA, Case Western Reserve, NYU, Georgetown, and Johns Hopkins among many more.

"May 2018 Honors graduates have accepted positions with Deutsche Bank, Apple, Boston Consulting Group, IBM, Ernst & Young, Siemens, Vanguard, W.L. Gore, Teach for America, the Peace Corps, Northrup Grumman, General Dynamics, Barrow Neurological Institute, Microsoft, Farrar Strauss & Giroux Publishing, Goldman Sachs, the CIA, and Amazon among many others."

**Degree of Difference**: This is difference between (1) the average SAT scores for recently enrolled honors students (1403) and (2) the average test scores for all students in the university (1170) as a whole. The difference may be an indication of how "elite" honors students may be perceived as compared to students in the university as a whole. **Please keep in mind that neither the high nor low selectivity of an honors program determines how effective the program may be.**

**NAME**: BARRETT, THE HONORS COLLEGE AT ARIZONA STATE UNIVERSITY

**Date Established:** 1988

**Location**: Temple, Arizona (main campus)

**University Full-time Undergraduate Enrollment (2017):** 42,477

**Honors Members in Good Standing**: 7,228; (mean size of all programs is 2,030).

**Honors Average Admission Test Score(s)**: ACT, 29; SAT, 1340.

**Average High School GPA/Class Rank:** 3.87, unweighted; 87% in top 10% of high school class.

**Basic Admission Requirements:** "Barrett has no 'basic score or GPA requirement'. We make a *subjective* decision on admissions based on the opinions of a 25-person admissions committee reading 9 – page independent admissions applications that students fill out \*after\* they are accepted into ASU. In this sense, we are exactly like a private college."

**Application Deadline(s):** *Please verify with each program, as some deadlines could change.* Early action deadline—November 1, 2018 (notification December 19). Regular decision deadline—January 6, 2019 (notification February 22). Late consideration I, February 24, 2019 (notification April 5). Late consideration II, March 31, 2019 (notification May 10).

**Honors Programs with SAT scores from 1332—1365:** Arizona State, Arkansas, Colorado State, Nevada Reno, Oklahoma State, Oregon, Oregon State.

**Administrative Staff:** 112.

**RATINGS AT A GLANCE:** For all mortarboard ratings immediately below, a score of 5 is the maximum and represents a comparison with all rated honors colleges and programs. More detailed explanations follow the "mortarboard" ratings.

**PERCEPTION\* OF UNIVERSITY AS A WHOLE, NOT OF HONORS:** 🎓🎓🎓🎓

\*Perception is based on the university's ranking among public universities in the 2018 U.S. News Best Colleges report. Please bear in mind that the better the U.S. News ranking, the more difficult it is for an honors college or program to have a rating that equals or improves on the magazine ranking.

**OVERALL HONORS RATING:** 🎓🎓🎓🎓🎓

**Curriculum Requirements:** 🎓🎓🎓🎓🎓

**Number of Honors Classes Offered:** 🎓🎓🎓 1/2

**Number of Honors Classes in Key Disciplines:** 🎓🎓🎓

**Extent of Honors Enrollment:** ⬛⬛⬛⬛¹/²

**Honors-only Class Size:** ⬛⬛⬛¹/²

**Overall Class Size (Honors-only plus mixed, contract):** ⬛⬛⬛

**Honors Grad Rate Adjusted to SAT:** ⬛⬛⬛⬛⬛

**Grad Rate Adjusted to Freshman Retention Rate:** ⬛⬛⬛⬛⬛

**Ratio of Staff to Students:** ⬛⬛⬛⬛⬛

**Priority Registration: Yes,** honors students register two days earlier than all other students.

**Honors Housing Amenities:** ⬛⬛⬛⬛⬛

**Honors Housing Availability:** ⬛⬛⬛⬛⬛

**Prestigious Awards:** ⬛⬛⬛⬛⬛

## RATING SCORES AND EXPLANATIONS:

**Curriculum Requirements (5.0):** The most important rating category, the curriculum completion requirement (classes required to complete honors) defines not only what honors students should learn but also the extent to which honors students and faculty are connected in the classroom. If there is a thesis or capstone requirement, it reinforces the individual contact and research skills so important to learning.

The average number of honors semester hours required for completion across all programs is 30.0.

For first-year students, Barrett Honors College requires 36 honors credits for completion. Students can earn up to 27 credits in honors contract courses, in which the contract with the instructor of a regular class section to do extra work for honors credit. The thesis requirement varies from 3-6 credits. By far, most Barrett students complete this option.

A hybrid option is available to sophomore students beginning in honors. It requires 27 honors credits, and allows up to 18 credits in honors contracts. The thesis again varies from 3-6 credits.

Finally, there is a transfer option for students entering Barrett as juniors. They must complete 21 credits, of which 15 may be by honors contract. The thesis requirement is the same as for other options.

**AP/IB credits** are **not** counted as replacements for honors courses.

**No. Honors Classes Offered (3.5):** This is a measure of the total **adjusted** honors main sections available in the term reported, not including labs and thesis. An adjusted main section has 3 or more semester credits, or equivalent, and sections with fewer credits receive a lower prorated value.

Barrett honors offered a section for every **19.9** enrolled students. The average for all programs was **15.0**. The lower the number, the better.

In the term reported, **45.9%** of honors enrollment was **in honors-only sections; 14.1% was in mixed sections; and 40.0% was in contract sections.** This is a slight increase in contract sections since 2016. For all programs under review, enrollment by type of honors section was 75.8% honors-only, 15.4 % mixed, and 8.8% contract.

**No. Honors Classes in Key Disciplines (3.0):** The 15 "key" disciplines are biological sciences; business (all); chemistry; communications (especially public speaking); computer science; economics; engineering (all); English; history; math (all); philosophy; physics; political science; psychology; and sociology, anthropology, and gender studies. Interdisciplinary sections, such as those often taken for General Education credit in the first two years, do receive a lesser, prorated discipline "credit" because they introduce students to multiple disciplines in an especially engaging way, often with in-depth discussion.

For this measure, mixed and contract sections are not counted as a section in a key discipline unless students taking the sections for honors credit make up at least 10% of the total section enrollment.

In the term reported, the honors college offered a section in a key discipline for every **33.9 honors students.** The average for all programs is **24.7.** The lower the number, the better.

Out of **157 adjusted sections in key disciplines**, **59 were honors-only sections**. The most sections were in English, biology, math, computer science, and engineering, although many of these sections were honors by contract, with at least 10% honors enrollment.

The college also offered more than 150 interdisciplinary sections, many of them in the "Human Event" sequence. In these courses, "students examine human thought and imagination from various perspectives, including philosophy, history, literature, religion, science, and art. Coursework emphasizes critical thinking, discussion, and argumentative writing." The honors college is a **blended** program, with a good mix of interdisciplinary courses and classes in the disciplines.

**Extent of Honors Enrollment (4.5):** Not all honors students take an honors class each term, especially after the first two years. Programs that have fewer honors classes and thesis options for upper-division honors students will *generally* have fewer total members in good standing who are actually enrolled in a given term. (Please be aware, however, that honors students not enrolled in a class for a term are still tied to the honors community through residential and extracurricular activities.) Our research shows that this measure is closely related to honors completion rates, i.e., the number of students who complete honors requirements by the time they graduate.

For example, if a program has 1,800 individual students enrolled in a given term, and 3,000 students in good standing, the level of enrollment was .67, an indication that honors class enrollment is somewhat below average, especially in upper-division classes. Barrett **has a ratio of 1.59**, significantly above the average of 1.30 for all programs.

**Average Class Size, Honors-only Sections (3.5):** Offered mostly in the first two years, honors-only classes tend to be smaller and, as the name implies, have no or very few students other than those in the honors program. These class sections always are much smaller than mixed or contract sections or regular non-honors class sections in the university.

The average honors-only class size at the honors college is **18.3 students**. The average for all programs is **17.5 students.**

**Average Class Size, Overall (3.0):** The overall class calculation is based on the *proportion* of honors students in each type of class (honors-only, mixed honors, and honors contract sections). Thus it is not a raw average. The overall honors-credit class size at Barrett is **49.5 students**, versus the average for all programs of **24.9 students**. Even though the average is high, it is a significant improvement compared with the average in 2016, which was 64.1.

These class size averages also do not correspond to the number of students per honors section ratings above. The reason is that, in computing average class size metrics, we include enrollment in each 1-2-credit section, not just sections with 3 or more credits.

Along with an honors-only class size of 18.3 students (listed above), at Barrett the mixed honors sections average **33.8 students,** and the contract sections with honors credit for individual honors students average **90.7 students.** Across all programs, the average mixed honors section has 68.6 students, and the average contract section has 56.6 students.

**Honors Grad Rate Adjusted to SAT (5.0):** The rating is the based on the actual grad rate for students who entered the program six years earlier, whether or not the students remained in honors. The **actual rate of 90.0%** is also compared to the rates of other programs with the same test score entry requirement range, and then adjusted upward if the program is performing above other programs in the same range, or downward if the performance is less than other programs in the same range. The rate here is upward, to **91.5%.**

**Grad Rate Adjusted to Freshman Retention Rate (5.0):** This rate compares the actual grad rate above to a predicted grade rate when freshman retention rates are considered. The actual grad rate is **3.68 points higher** than the predicted rate. For all programs, the actual grad rate is **.33 points lower** than the predicted rate.

**Ratio of Staff to Honors Students (5.0):** There is 1 staff member for every **64.5** students. (Mean ratio for all programs is 1 staff member for every **127.9** students.)

**Honors Residence Halls, Amenities (5.0):** "It is difficult to compare Barrett housing to any other university honors college at the moment. We are the only university in the nation with our own entire 9-acre, $140 million, 600,000 square feet honors campus at Tempe, complete with everything a private college campus would have, besides things like the university health service and the student recreation center. In addition to this campus, we have added another entire campus at Tempe in the last three years directly across the street from us; it is called the 'Vista del Sol' campus and is another 20 acres and 1800 beds in apartment-style living, with its own community center, swimming pool, fitness center and retail area.

"*We thus now have 3,500 honors students living in honors-specified spaces on the ASU campus in Tempe alone.* On top of this, we have Barrett living communities on each of the other three of ASU's campuses in the Phoenix Valley, though the one described just above is at Tempe, the biggest campus of ASU. The other three Barrett communities—at the ASU West, ASU Downtown Phoenix, and ASU Polytechnic campuses—have honors headquarter space with classrooms, computer labs, advising offices, social lounges, conference rooms and faculty offices. Also at each of the other campuses, there is separate honors residential housing that is usually several floors or wings of a larger residential hall that also houses non-honors students. Each of these housing units has a dining hall, laundry, kitchens at least 'down the hall,' honors lounges, a choice of suite-like rooms, they are co-ed by room but not by hall and have special honors RAs (or 'CAs' as we call them at ASU). *We require honors students to live on campus in honors residences at all four of ASU's Barrett campuses and communities for two years.* Several at each campus stay for all four years, and they are encouraged to do so if they wish."

**Honors Residence Halls, Availability (5.0):** This rating compares the number of occupants in honors residence halls to the number of honors freshman and sophomore members in good standing. The ratio for the college is **1.09** places for each first- and second-year student. The *median* for all programs is .49 places.

**Prestigious Awards (5.0):** The awards that we track and include are listed in the section titled "Prestigious Scholarships." The awards are sometimes won by students who are not in an honors college or program, but increasingly many are enrolled in honors programs. It is also a trend that honors colleges and programs help to prepare their students for the awards competitions.

ASU—and Barrett students, in particular—have an outstanding record of achievement in this category: 60 Goldwater Scholars (tied for 10th among all public universities); 35 Udall Scholars, again one of the best totals; 18 Marshall Scholars, 21 Truman Scholars, 5 Rhodes Scholars; a national leader in Fulbright student awards; high achievement in Boren and Gilman foreign study awards; and a solid, growing number of National Science Foundation Graduate Research winners. This kind of success strongly indicates the highest level of Barrett and university support for aspiring scholars.

**UNRATED FEATURES**

**Continuation and Honors Graduation GPA Requirement: 3.25.**

**Academic Strengths, National Rankings:** This is based on national rankings of *graduate* programs in all but engineering and business, where undergraduate rankings are used. One of the weaknesses of the *U.S. News* rankings is that they focus on too many wealth-related metrics while ignoring their own assessments of academic departments. The *average* department ranking at ASU is better than 47th in the nation. The rankings listed below are for all universities, public or private.

The top nationally ranked academic departments at ASU are education (15); earth sciences (15); undergrad business (24); psychology (39); undergrad engineering (40); economics (42); computer science (43); physics (44); political science (51); and chemistry (52).

**Internships, Professional Development, Community Engagement:** "Barrett has a full-time employee who runs an "Internship and Research Office" and helps honors students obtain these experiences.

"Barrett students engage in cutting-edge research with distinguished ASU faculty or through special partnerships with the Mayo Clinic, the Biodesign Institute, and Intel. Students are developing iPhone applications, building robots, designing games, or developing tools to improve healthcare, meet global energy needs, provide clean water, or secure data and information privacy. There are over six hundred internship opportunities developed exclusively for Barrett students. Barrett students secure internships in the governor's office, local congressional districts, and the United States Senate, as well as with Goldman Sachs, Microsoft, Google, and The American Heart Institute.

"ASU Career and Professional Development Services is an invaluable partner with Barrett, The Honors College, providing comprehensive services in all areas of career advising, career events and fairs, educational programs, and partnerships with local, state, regional, and national employers."

**Undergraduate Research:** The Barrett Dean tells us that "close to 100% [of students do research] because they must carry out a thesis to graduate, and as I have said earlier most honors students 'do' graduate from the honors college at Barrett. Barrett has a full-time person in an office of Internships and Research Experiences that arranges both internships and research experiences for any honors student who asks, and in fifteen years at Barrett and ASU I am not aware of 'any' honors student who has wished to do the kind of formal 'lab-type' research…who has not found that kind of research to do. For this reason, we do not advertise in our admissions material that we 'guarantee' a research experience, since every Barrett student who wants one gets one anyway!"

**Honors Study Abroad:** "Barrett has its own summer study-abroad courses each summer, taking between 150 and 250 students on 3 to 6 trips each summer," the Dean reports. The trips go all over the world (Paris and Berlin, London/Dublin/Edinburgh, Spain, Costa Rica, Greece and Italy are the most recent in the last two years). The trips are led by Barrett faculty, take only Barrett students, and the students get credit for one or two full honors courses on each trip since they both take the courses and visit the countries that are the subjects of the courses in each case. In addition to these trips, there are over 30 summer study abroad trips from ASU open to all students each summer, and honors students can take those too, gaining honors credit for courses taught on those trips by completing an honors contract during the trip.

"We have close to $250,000 per year in scholarship funds, given out on a need basis, to help send students on these trips from all socioeconomic backgrounds.

"We have formal exchanges with the National University of Singapore and the University of Groningen in the Netherlands each academic year, and one still developing with Beihang University in Beijing. During each of these around four students from each institution travel to the other for a semester."

**Financial Aid:** "The financial aid office of ASU handles all scholarships, including those for honors students. ASU gives out many levels of merit aid, and then of course has need-based aid. *95% of Barrett students have merit aid, but 40% also have need-based aid on top of their merit aid.* The merit aid is dispensed using a formulaic combination of high school GPA, rank in class, and ACT or SAT scores, and is tiered as you would expect by decreasing dollar amounts as this combination decreases. The university also has *uncapped* national scholar awards that are the same amount for National Merit, Hispanic and Achievement Scholars. These are **full out of state tuition and college fees** for all OOS national scholars, even if it increases as they are at ASU, and **$16,000 per year** for in-state national scholars. Both in-state and out-of-state national scholars also receive $1,500 towards research costs for research they do, and $1,000 for any honors travel they carry out while at ASU.

**Honors Fees:** Each Barrett student pays a fee of $1,500 per year to be an honors student. There is extra financial aid and a fee waiver system set up for financially needy students specifically to address this fee.

**Placement of Honors Graduates:** Law schools include Stanford, Chicago, Michigan, Virginia, Duke, Cal Berkeley, UCLA, Northwestern, Cornell, and Georgetown.

Grad school acceptances include Dartmouth, Harvard Medical School, Princeton, Caltech, Cal Berkeley, Johns Hopkins, Stanford, Oxford, NYU, Columbia, Washington, UT Austin, and Baylor College of Medicine.

Employment placements include Google, Microsoft, Bloomberg, Facebook, Pricewaterhouse Cooper, Amazon, Goldman Sachs, Dell, Deloitte, Raytheon, Yelp, Snapchat, and Intel.

**Degree of Difference**: This is difference between (1) the average SAT scores for recently enrolled honors students (1340) and (2) the average test scores for all students in the university (1210) as a whole. The difference may be an indication of how "elite" honors students may be perceived as compared to students in the university as a whole. **Please keep in mind that neither the high nor low selectivity of an honors program determines how effective the program may be.**

**NAME**: UNIVERSITY OF ARKANSAS HONORS COLLEGE

**Date Established:** 2002. Preceded by Arts & Sciences honors program (1954) and College of Business honors program (1999).

**Location**: Fayetteville, Arkansas

**University Full-time Undergraduate Enrollment (2017):** 22,548

**Honors Members in Good Standing**: 3,340; (mean size of all programs is 2,030).

**Honors Average Admission Test Score(s)**: ACT, 30; SAT 1356.

**Average High School GPA/Class Rank:** 4.0, weighted.

**Basic Admission Requirements:** ACT 28; SAT 1310; GPA 3.50-3.75.

**Application Deadline(s):** *Please verify with each program, as some deadlines could change.* November 1, 2018 for priority application; for scholarships, priority deadline is November 15, 2018; for financial aid, priority deadline is January 1, 2019, and final deadline is February 1, 2019; final Fall application deadline is August 1, 2019, but this might be too late for the honors college.

**Honors Programs with SAT scores from 1332-1365:** Arizona State, Arkansas, Colorado State, Nevada Reno, Oklahoma State, Oregon, Oregon State.

**Administrative Staff:** 31 plus three graduate assistants.

**RATINGS AT A GLANCE:** For all mortarboard ratings immediately below, a score of 5 is the maximum and represents a comparison with all rated honors colleges and programs. More detailed explanations follow the "mortarboard" ratings.

**PERCEPTION\* OF UNIVERSITY AS A WHOLE, NOT OF HONORS:** 🎓🎓🎓1/2

\*Perception is based on the university's ranking among public universities in the 2018 U.S. News Best Colleges report. Please bear in mind that the better the U.S. News ranking, the more difficult it is for an honors college or program to have a rating that equals or improves on the magazine ranking.

**OVERALL HONORS RATING:** 🎓🎓🎓🎓

**Curriculum Requirements:** 🎓🎓🎓🎓1/2

**Number of Honors Classes Offered:** 🎓🎓🎓1/2

**Number of Honors Classes in Key Disciplines:** 🎓🎓🎓

**Extent of Honors Enrollment:** 🎓🎓🎓🎓

**Honors-only Class Size:** 🎓🎓🎓

**Overall Class Size (Honors-only plus mixed, contract):** 🎓🎓🎓1/2

**Honors Grad Rate Adjusted to SAT:** 🎓🎓🎓1/2

**Grad Rate Adjusted to Freshman Retention Rate:** 🎓🎓🎓🎓

**Ratio of Staff to Students:** 🎓🎓🎓

**Priority Registration: Yes,** honors students register with the class year ahead.

**Honors Housing Amenities:** 🎓🎓🎓1/2

**Honors Housing Availability:** 🎓🎓🎓

**Prestigious Awards:** 🎓🎓🎓🎓


**RATING SCORES AND EXPLANATIONS:**

**Curriculum Requirements (4.5):** The most important rating category, the curriculum completion requirement (classes required to complete honors) defines not only what honors students should learn but also the extent to which honors students and faculty are connected in the classroom. If there is a thesis or capstone requirement, it reinforces the individual contact and research skills so important to learning.

The average number of honors semester hours required for completion across all programs is 30.0.

The honors college coordinates the honors programs in the J. William Fulbright College of Arts and Sciences; the Fay Jones School of Architecture; the College of Education and Health Professions; the Sam M. Walton College of Business; the College of Engineering; and the Dale Bumpers School of Agricultural, Food, and Life Sciences.

The credit hours required for honors completion vary significantly, with the College of Arts and Sciences having the most extensive requirements, **32-34 credits, minimum.** The departmental honors option requires 12 credits. Both include a 6-credit thesis.

Architecture, Education and Health Professions, and Agricultural, Food, and Life Sciences all require 18 credit hours.

Business honors requires 29 credit hours for one option and 21 for departmental honors; engineering honors requires 12 credit hours. There is an **honors thesis or capstone** requirement for **all honors students.**

**AP/IB credits** may be counted as replacements for honors courses, up to 6 credits.

**No. Honors Classes Offered (3.5):** This is a measure of the total **adjusted** honors main sections available in the term reported, not including labs and thesis. An adjusted main section has 3 or more semester credits, or equivalent, and sections with fewer credits receive a lower prorated value.

The Honors College offered a section for every **19.2** enrolled students. The average for all programs was **15.0**. The lower the number, the better.

In the term reported, **73.0%** of honors enrollment was **in honors-only sections; 27% was in mixed sections; and none was in contract sections.** For all programs under review, enrollment by type of honors section was 75.8% honors-only, 15.4 % mixed, and **8.8%** contract.

**No. Honors Classes in Key Disciplines (3.0):** The 15 "key" disciplines are biological sciences; business (all); chemistry; communications (especially public speaking); computer science; economics; engineering (all); English; history; math (all); philosophy; physics; political science; psychology; and sociology, anthropology, and gender studies. Interdisciplinary sections, such as those often taken for General Education credit in the first two years, do receive a lesser, prorated discipline "credit" because they introduce students to multiple disciplines in an especially engaging way, often with in-depth discussion.

For this measure, mixed and contract sections are not counted as a section in a key discipline unless students taking the sections for honors credit make up at least 10% of the total section enrollment.

In the term reported, the honors college offered a section in a key discipline for every **34.1 honors students.** The average for all programs is **24.7.** The lower the number, the better.

Of **79 adjusted sections in key disciplines, 64 were honors-only sections**. The most sections were in communications and public speaking, along with at least six sections in business, engineering, English, history, philosophy, and sociology/anthropology. Biology, chemistry, and psychology each had four sections, and math three.

The Dean tells us that in Spring 2017, "we began to offer a series of Honors College Signature Seminars on cutting-edge topics taught by top professors. Students must apply to participate and are designated Dean's Signature Scholar in the Honors College." In Fall 2017, these included "Race: Rediscovered, Unresolved," taught Charles Robinson, Vice Chancellor for the Division of Student Affairs and a professor of history at the University of Arkansas; and "Cancer: A Constellation of Disease," taught by Timothy Muldoon, Honors College Distinguished Faculty Award Recipient and professor of Biomedical Engineering.

Another feature is the Retro Readings series. "In these courses students receive a 'Great Books' experience, the hallmark of a liberal arts education. Faculty experts partner with honors students from all colleges in a 75-minute, seminar-style discussion in which they view classic works through a contemporary lens."

**Extent of Honors Enrollment (4.0):** Not all honors students take an honors class each term, especially after the first two years. Programs that have fewer honors classes and thesis options for upper-division honors students will *generally* have fewer total members in good standing who are actually enrolled in a given term. (Please be aware, however, that honors students not enrolled in a class for a term are still tied to the honors community through residential and extracurricular activities.) Our research shows that this measure is closely related to honors completion rates, i.e., the number of students who complete honors requirements by the time they graduate.

For example, if a program has 1,800 individual students enrolled in a given term, and 3,000 students in good standing, the level of enrollment was .67, an indication that honors class enrollment is somewhat below average, especially in upper-division classes. **Arkansas honors has a ratio of 1.39**, above the average of 1.30 for all programs.

**Average Class Size, Honors-only Sections (3.0):** Offered mostly in the first two years, honors-only classes tend to be smaller and, as the name implies, have no or very few students other than those in the honors program. These class sections always are much smaller than mixed or contract sections, or regular non-honors class sections in the university.

The average honors-only class size at the honors college is **23.0 students**. The average for all programs is **17.5 students.**

**Average Class Size, Overall (3.5):** The overall class calculation is based on the *proportion* of honors students in each type of class (honors-only, mixed honors, and honors contract sections). Thus it is not a raw average. The overall honors-credit class size is **29.8 students**, versus the average for all programs of **24.9 students**.

These class size averages also do not correspond to the number of students per honors section ratings above. The reason is that, in computing average class size metrics, we include enrollment in each 1-2-credit section, not just sections with 3 or more credits.

Along with an honors-only class size of 23.0 students (listed above), the college's mixed honors sections have an average size of **48.3 students.** Honors contracts sections are not offered. Across all programs, the average mixed honors section has 68.6 students.

**Honors Grad Rate Adjusted to SAT (3.5):** The rating is the based on the actual grad rate for students who entered the program six years earlier, whether or not the students remained in honors. The **actual rate of 82.5%** is also compared to the rates of other programs with the same test score entry requirement range, and then adjusted upward if the program is performing above other programs in the same range, or downward if the performance is less than other programs in the same range. The rate here is downward, to **81.5%.**

**Grad Rate Adjusted to Freshman Retention Rate (4.0):** This rate compares the actual grad rate above to a predicted grade rate when freshman retention rates are considered. The actual grad rate is **.19 points higher** than the predicted rate. For all programs, the actual grad rate is **.33 points lower** than the predicted rate.

**Ratio of Staff to Honors Students (3.0):** There is 1 staff member for every **106.4** students. (Mean ratio for all programs is 1 staff member for every **127.9** students.)

**Honors Residence Halls, Amenities (3.5):** Most first-year honors students living on campus reside in Hotz Hall, which has traditional rooms and hall baths. Upperclassmen can live in Gatewood Hall, Northwest Quad, or Futrall Hall. Gatewood and Northwest Quad feature suite-style rooms. All are air-conditioned. Our amenities rating, where suite-type rooms and in-house dining count for a lot, does not do justice to all of the facilities related to the Honors College:

The Dean writes that "our staff is coordinating the honors student programming in Hotz Honors Hall and other nearby residences with activities in the recently renovated and expanded Gearhart Hall (formerly Ozark Hall), a historic building in the center of the campus, which became the home of the Honors College in 2013. The facilities are open through the evenings to better serve honors students' study needs. Conference rooms serve as meeting spaces for group study and projects, recruitment visits, and a variety of honors classes. A shared auditorium downstairs is host to presentations and large lectures.

"We also offer dinners with deans from each of the academic colleges as well as the chancellor, and numerous faculty mixers to engage students in the research process. Gearhart Hall is now the place where honors students and faculty from all disciplines can come together to socialize, to share big ideas, and to address big problems. The opening of Gearhart Hall in 2013, made possible through the strong support of the university's chancellor and other senior leaders, puts the Honors College in the center of the campus physically and symbolically."

**Honors Residence Halls, Availability (3.0):** This rating compares the number of occupants in honors residence halls to the number of honors freshman and sophomore members in good standing. The ratio for the college is **.33** places for each first- and second-year student. The median for all programs is .49 places.

**Prestigious Awards (4.0):** The awards that we track and include are listed in the section titled "Prestigious Scholarships." The awards are sometimes won by students who are not in an honors college or program, but increasingly many are enrolled in honors programs. It is also a trend that honors colleges and programs help to prepare their students for the awards competitions.

"The Office of Nationally Competitive Awards (ONCA), founded by Dr. Suzanne McCray, became part of the Honors College at its inception," the Dean tells us. "Dr. McCray is a founder and past president of the National Association of Fellowship Advisors and has published four volumes of NAFA conference proceedings and two additional books…almost all University of Arkansas students who compete for the awards listed above are honors students.

"Last year was extraordinary for our students. In 2017 we had two Truman scholars, Sam Harris and Ryann Alonso. The University of Arkansas is ranked #1 in Truman Scholars in the SEC, #9 among public universities, and #21 among all public and private institutions in the nation. Additionally, the University of Arkansas is #2 in the Marshall Scholarship among SEC schools and #23 among all public institutions."

**UNRATED FEATURES**

**Continuation and Honors Graduation GPA Requirement:** 3.50.

**Academic Strengths, National Rankings:** This is based on national rankings of *graduate* programs in all but engineering and business, where undergraduate rankings are used. One of the weaknesses of the *U.S. News* rankings is that they focus on too many wealth-related metrics while ignoring their own assessments of academic departments. The rankings listed below are for all universities, public or private.

The academic departments at the university that are in the top 100 nationwide are business (45); education (46); psychology (90); history (98); and engineering (99).

**Internships, Professional Development, Community Engagement:** "The Honors College awards competitive International Internship Grants to students participating in unpaid internships abroad with research components or professional skills in a spring, summer, or fall semester. Students can receive up to $2,500 to support an internship that is beneficial to their academic program or honors research requirements.

**"The Honors College Ambassador** program provides students a chance to become more involved with the Honors College while adding a service item to their resume. Students accepted to the Ambassador program volunteer with the Honors College in a variety of ways, including assisting at large events and programs, sharing their honors experiences with prospective students, and participating in honors focus groups.

**"The Honors College Advisory Council** offers a select group of honors student leaders an opportunity to plan new programs, bring in speakers, manage honors ambassadors, and spread the word about the honors experience. Each member plays an active role in one of the following committees:

- **The Programming Committee** assists in executing academic, social, service, and professional development programs for freshman and upperclassman honors students. The committee is in charge of choosing and inviting guest lecturers, artists, and musicians to our campus.

- **The Service Committee** helps increase the service and social justice initiatives of the Honors College. This includes developing new volunteer events for Ambassadors and the entire Honors College that benefit the larger Northwest Arkansas community."

**Undergraduate Research:** The Dean is understandably proud that "100% of honors students who complete the program complete a thesis in their field of study consisting of traditional research or other forms of creative work that are directed by a professor and, in most of the colleges, evaluated by a faculty committee."

"Competitive Honors College Research Grants and Honors College Conference Travel Grants provide funds for students to present research at conferences or to help pay expenses associated with their research. In the 2016- 2017 academic years, the Honors College provided $446,455 from our endowment in support of undergraduate research, including over $281,250 in student stipends and $120,750 in faculty mentor funds, and $44,455 in conference travel not covered by other funds, including fellowships and scholarships, State Undergraduate Research Fellowships, and NSF REU grants.

"Funding and support for honors research can help students reach impressive career goals. An example is Rachel Ungar, who, as sophomore biology major won a summer internship in the Clinical Genetics Branch, Division of Cancer Epidemiology and Genetics, at the National Cancer Institute. "She was later selected to participate in the DAAD Research in Science and Engineering (RISE) program and conducted original genetic research at the German Cancer Research Center in Heidelberg. She received offers from Cambridge, Harvard, Stanford, Duke and Dartmouth and chose to pursue graduate study at Stanford, which has the #1 ranked Ph.D. program in translational/clinical genetics in the world."

**Honors Study Abroad:** "Over the past 10 years, the Honors College has awarded more than $5.25 million in study-abroad grants using endowment funds from the 2002 Walton Foundation gift that helped create the Honors College. The Honors College Study-Abroad Grants help students pay for international study experiences ranging from two weeks to one year in length. Last year, 240 students received a total of $838,250 in grant funding. *For many of our students, raised in a poor Southern state, the study-abroad grants provide a first chance to see the larger world and experience other cultures in a meaningful way. Of the Honors College students who were awarded a study abroad grant in 2017, 25% had never traveled outside of the United States; 85% had never studied abroad before.*

"The University of Arkansas owns the University of Arkansas Rome Center, recently ranked among the 50 Best Study-Abroad Programs by Best College Reviews. The U of A Rome Center offers courses in several fields of study to our own students in several fields of study as well as students from other Southeastern Conference universities. The U. of A. has active exchange programs with 18 universities in Austria, Belgium, Denmark, United Kingdom, France, Germany, Italy, Spain, Sweden, Japan, Hong Kong, South Korea, and Australia, with others in the works in African and Latin American nations."

Under the leadership of Dean Lynda Coon, the Honors College has set an ambitious goal to increase the number of honors graduates who have studied abroad from 50 percent (already more than three times the national average) to 70 percent by 2020.

**Financial Aid:** Each year the Honors College awards up to 90 fellowships to entering freshmen that provide each student with $70,000 over four years, plus non-resident tuition, if applicable. For programs with degree plans of more than four years, extra semesters of funding may be available. The fellowships are renewable annually based on academic performance and personal conduct.

"Most honors students who do not win a fellowship receive other merit-based scholarships offered through the Office of Academic Scholarships. These range from scholarships providing $10,000 per year, renewable for four or five years (depending on course of study), to one-time awards of $1,000."

"In an exciting new update, the National Science Foundation has awarded $999,847 in grant funding to the University of Arkansas' Path to Graduation Program, which aims to increase the number of low-income students, especially those from rural regions of Arkansas, who graduate with a degree in science, technology, engineering, and mathematics- related fields.

"The grant will support two groups of 18 STEM students per year who will receive annually renewable scholarships of up to $4,500, or $5,500 if they participate in the Honors College. The Path to Graduation program is an extension of the Honors College Path Program, established in 2014 to recruit exceptional high school students from underrepresented populations and to help them excel at the University of

Arkansas. *More than 40 percent of Path students have joined the Honors College to date, and an estimated 100 percent of the first group are on schedule to graduate in May 2018."*

**Honors Fees:** None.

**Placement of Honors Graduates:** Each spring, the Honors College sends a "Senior Exit Survey" to graduating seniors. Data from Spring 2017 Honors completers determined the following:

- 47% have been accepted to graduate or professional school

    o 17% of these will attend Law School

    o 14% of these will attend Medical School

- 34% enter the workforce

- 9% are uncertain

- 8% plan to apply to graduate or professional school in the future

- 2% work as a volunteer (e.g. Teach for America, AmeriCorps, Peace Corps, etc.)

**Degree of Difference**: This is difference between (1) the average SAT scores for recently enrolled honors students (1356) and (2) the average test scores for all students in the university (1190) as a whole. The difference may be an indication of how "elite" honors students may be perceived as compared to students in the university as a whole. **Please keep in mind that neither the high nor low selectivity of an honors program determines how effective the program may be.**

**NAME**: THE HONORS COLLEGE AT AUBURN UNIVERSITY

**Date Established:** Honors Program, 1979, Honors College, 1998

**Location**: Auburn, Alabama

**University Full-time Undergraduate Enrollment (2017):** 22,658

**Honors Members in Good Standing**: 1,699; (mean size of all programs is 2,030).

**Honors Average Admission Test Score(s)**: ACT, 31.77; est. SAT 1430.

**Average High School GPA/Class Rank:** 4.29, unweighted.

**Basic Admission Requirements:** ACT 29; SAT 1350; GPA 3.85.

**Application Deadline(s):** *Please verify with each program, as some deadlines could change.* January 16, 2019.

**Honors Programs with SAT scores from 1420—1461:** Auburn, Central Florida, Delaware, Iowa, Kansas, Mississippi, Missouri, New Jersey Inst of Technology, Penn State, South Florida, Vermont, Virginia Commonwealth.

**Administrative Staff:** 11.

**RATINGS AT A GLANCE:** For all mortarboard ratings immediately below, a score of 5 is the maximum and represents a comparison with all rated honors colleges and programs. More detailed explanations follow the "mortarboard" ratings.

**PERCEPTION* OF UNIVERSITY AS A WHOLE, NOT OF HONORS:** 🎓🎓🎓🎓

*Perception is based on the university's ranking among public universities in the 2018 U.S. News Best Colleges report. Please bear in mind that the better the U.S. News ranking, the more difficult it is for an honors college or program to have a rating that equals or improves on the magazine ranking.

**OVERALL HONORS RATING:** 🎓🎓🎓1/2

**Curriculum Requirements:** 🎓🎓🎓🎓

**Number of Honors Classes Offered:** 🎓🎓🎓

**Number of Honors Classes in Key Disciplines:** 🎓🎓🎓🎓

**Extent of Honors Enrollment:** 🎓🎓🎓1/2

**Honors-only Class Size:** 🎓🎓🎓

**Overall Class Size (Honors-only plus mixed, contract):** 🎓🎓🎓

**Honors Grad Rate Adjusted to SAT:** 🎓🎓🎓 1/2

**Grad Rate Adjusted to Freshman Retention Rate:** 🎓🎓🎓

**Ratio of Staff to Students:** 🎓🎓🎓 1/2

**Priority Registration: Yes,** honors students register with the class ahead.

**Honors Housing Amenities:** 🎓🎓🎓 1/2

**Honors Housing Availability:** 🎓🎓🎓 1/2

**Prestigious Awards:** 🎓🎓🎓 1/2

**RATING SCORES AND EXPLANATIONS:**

**Curriculum Requirements (4.0):** The most important rating category, the curriculum completion requirement (classes required to complete honors) defines not only what honors students should learn but also the extent to which honors students and faculty are connected in the classroom. If there is a thesis or capstone requirement, it reinforces the individual contact and research skills so important to learning.

The average number of honors semester hours required for completion across all programs is 30.0.

To earn the designation **University Honors Scholar**, students are required to complete a minimum of 30 hours of Honors College courses, including a minimum of:
- 3 hours of Honors Participation Courses, and

- 6 hours of coursework identified as Senior Year Experiences.

Students must also complete their disciplinary requirements and have a minimum 3.4 cumulative unadjusted Auburn GPA at the time of graduation.

To earn the designation **Honors Scholar**, students are required to complete a minimum of 24 hours of Honors College coursework including a minimum of:

- 3 hours of Honors Participation Courses.

Students must also complete their disciplinary requirements and have a minimum of 3.2 cumulative unadjusted Auburn GPA at the time of graduation.

**AP/IB credits** are **not** counted as replacements for honors courses.

**No. Honors Classes Offered (3.0):** This is a measure of the total **adjusted** honors main sections available in the term reported, not including labs and thesis. An adjusted main section has 3 or more semester credits, or equivalent, and sections with fewer credits receive a lower prorated value.

The Honors College offered a section for every **23.8** enrolled students. The average for all programs was **15.0**. The lower the number, the better.

In the term reported, **67.7%** of honors enrollment was **in honors-only sections; 18.5% was in mixed sections; and 13.8% was in contract sections.** For all programs under review, enrollment by type of honors section was 75.8% honors-only, 15.4 % mixed, and 8.8% contract.

**No. Honors Classes in Key Disciplines (4.0):** The 15 "key" disciplines are biological sciences; business (all); chemistry; communications (especially public speaking); computer science; economics; engineering (all); English; history; math (all); philosophy; physics; political science; psychology; and sociology, anthropology, and gender studies. Interdisciplinary sections, such as those often taken for General Education credit in the first two years, do receive a lesser, prorated discipline "credit" because they introduce students to multiple disciplines in an especially engaging way, often with in-depth discussion.

For this measure, mixed and contract sections are not counted as a section in a key discipline unless students taking the sections for honors credit make up at least 10% of the total section enrollment.

In the term reported, the honors college offered a section in a key discipline for every **22.4 honors students.** The average for all programs is **24.7.** The lower the number, the better.

Out of **69 adjusted sections in key disciplines**, **47 were honors-only sections,** including graduate courses taken for honors credit. Engineering and math had the highest number of sections, followed by English, biology, business, computer science, history, and philosophy.

The college offered more than 20 one-credit sections, including "Honors Book Club," "Sustainability," "Research at Auburn," and "Global Issues." Only a few three-credit interdisciplinary sections were listed, including "Genomics and Personalized Health," "Technology and Culture," and "Sustainability in the Modern World." The Honors College is a discipline-oriented program.

**Extent of Honors Enrollment (3.5):** Not all honors students take an honors class each term, especially after the first two years. Programs that have fewer honors classes and thesis options for upper-division honors students will *generally* have fewer total members in good standing who are actually enrolled in a given term. (Please be aware, however, that honors students not enrolled in a class for a term are still tied to the honors community through residential and extracurricular activities.) Our research shows that this measure is closely related to honors completion rates, i.e., the number of students who complete honors requirements by the time they graduate.

For example, if a program has 1,800 individual students enrolled in a given term, and 3,000 students in good standing, the level of enrollment was .67, an indication that honors class enrollment is somewhat below average, especially in upper-division classes. **The Honors College has a ratio of 1.24**, just a bit below the average of 1.30 for all programs.

**Average Class Size, Honors-only Sections (3.0):** Offered mostly in the first two years, honors-only classes tend to be smaller and, as the name implies, have no or very few students other than those in the honors program. These class sections always are much smaller than mixed or contract sections, or regular non-honors class sections in the university.

The average honors-only class size at the honors college is **21.5 students**. The average for all programs is **17.5 students.**

**Average Class Size, Overall (3.0):** The overall class calculation is based on the *proportion* of honors students in each type of class (honors-only, mixed honors, and honors contract sections). Thus it is not a raw average. The overall honors-credit class size is **36.1 students**, versus the average for all programs of **24.9 students**.

These class size averages also do not correspond to the number of students per honors section ratings above. The reason is that, in computing average class size metrics, we include enrollment in each 1-2-credit section, not just sections with 3 or more credits.

Along with an honors-only class size of 18.3 students (listed above), the program's mixed honors sections have an average size of **33.8 students,** and the contract sections with honors credit for individual honors students average **90.7 students**. Across all programs, the average mixed honors section has 68.6 students, and the average contract section has 56.6 students.

**Honors Grad Rate Adjusted to SAT (3.5):** The rating is the based on the actual grad rate for students who entered the program six years earlier, whether or not the students remained in honors. The **actual rate of 84.5%** is also compared to the rates of other programs with the same test score entry requirement range, and then adjusted upward if the program is performing above other programs in the same range, or downward if the performance is less than other programs in the same range. The rate here is slightly downward, to **84.0%.**

**Grad Rate Adjusted to Freshman Retention Rate (3.0):** This rate compares the actual grad rate above to a predicted grade rate when freshman retention rates are considered. The actual grad rate is **5.8 points lower** than the predicted rate. For all programs, the actual grad rate is **.33 points lower** than the predicted rate.

**Ratio of Staff to Honors Students (3.5):** There is 1 staff member for every **154.5** students. (Mean ratio for all programs is 1 staff member for every **127.9** students.)

**Honors Residence Halls, Amenities (3.5):** About 75% of the honors students who live on campus reside in Aubie Hall, which has suite-style rooms and is, of course, air-conditioned. Village is the nearest dining facility. The other honors dorm is on the Upper Quad—Broun Hall, which double rooms with four students sharing a connecting bath. Dining for the Quad dorms is in Foy Hall.

**Honors Residence Halls, Availability (3.5):** This rating compares the number of occupants in honors residence halls to the number of honors freshman and sophomore members in good standing. The ratio for the college is **.47** places for each first- and second-year student. The average for all programs is .49 places.

**Prestigious Awards (3.5):** The awards that we track and include are listed in the section titled "Prestigious Scholarships." The awards are sometimes won by students who are not in an honors college or program, but increasingly many are enrolled in honors programs. It is also a trend that honors colleges and programs help to prepare their students for the awards competitions.

"Auburn University's Office of National Prestigious Scholarships was established in 2008 and is located within the Honors College. The number of awardees from the last 10 years follows: Rhodes (2), Marshall (2), Truman (2), Gates Cambridge (2), Mitchell (1), National Science Foundation Graduate Fellowships (49), Fulbright teaching or scholar awards (23), Goldwater Scholars (9), Udall Scholars (2), and Gilman Scholars 8.

**UNRATED FEATURES**

**Continuation and Honors Graduation GPA Requirement:** First-year students must attain a minimum of a 3.0 cumulative unadjusted Auburn GPA and second, third, and fourth-year students must maintain a minimum of 3.2 cumulative unadjusted Auburn GPA. A student whose GPA falls below the minimum is given one semester to correct the deficiency or be suspended from the Honors College.

Graduation as a University Honors Scholar, 3.40; Honors Scholar, 3.20.

**Academic Strengths, National Rankings:** This is based on national rankings of *graduate* programs in all but engineering and business, where undergraduate rankings are used. One of the weaknesses of the *U.S. News* rankings is that they focus on too many wealth-related metrics while ignoring their own assessments of academic departments. The rankings listed below are for all universities, public or private.

The academic departments at Auburn ranked in the top 100 nationally are engineering (56); business (64); education (84); chemistry (88); computer science (91); math (94); and psychology (98).

**Internships, Professional Development, Community Engagement:** "The Honors College partnered with the Auburn University Career Center to develop a series of career workshops for Honors College students to enhance readiness for graduate/professional school, internships, coops, and full-time employment. These workshops are offered specifically for Honors College students and are presented each semester.

"In order to gain awareness of poverty in the State of Alabama, nation, and world, first-year Honors students may participate in the Honors College Week of Service before fall classes commence. Students participate in lectures, films, poverty simulation, and three full days of service to experience how intentional service can help alleviate poverty. After the experience, students are able to articulate the root causes of poverty and the propagation of the cycle of poverty.

"Honors College students may also participate in the Honors College Alternative Spring Break. During the experience, students participate in community service in a particular community and repair buildings, work with local school students, and even participate in gardening project."

**Undergraduate Research:** "In order to complete the Senior Year Experience, students may elect to participate in undergraduate research with a departmental professor in their major or minor to complete a project of their choosing with the culminating experience of an Honors thesis or professional podium presentation. A limited number of research grants are available each semester.

"Honors Research Seminars are taught in small discussion groups similar to graduate courses and provides Honors students with a research experience under the close supervision of an Auburn faculty member. The course is designed to enable a faculty member to mentor a number of students who are working on collaborative research. Course topics vary by semester."

**Honors Study Abroad:** "The Honors College offers a number of study and travel courses each year. These courses are designed to enhance the holistic academic experience the Honors College provides. The Honors College Study and Travel courses are slightly different than a typical study abroad program. Students spend a semester in class prior to a 10- to 14-day trip in order to fully immerse themselves into the history and the culture of the location. At the end of the semester participants experience first-hand what they have spent the past few months studying. This method allows for a more in-depth understanding of the location, and an easy transition into different cultures.

"In recent years, Honors College students have studied away with Auburn faculty members in Greece, Turkey, Germany, Costa Rica, Cuba, and India. A limited number of travel grants are available each semester."

**Financial Aid:** National Merit Finalists receive a stipend for four years at $4,000 to $8,000 ($1,000 to $2,000 per year), depending on eligibility as determined by National Merit Scholarship Corporation and financial need as determined through completion of the FAFSA.

University Scholarship In State
- Requires a 28-29 ACT or equivalent SAT score and a minimum 3.5 high school GPA for consideration.

- Awarded at $16,000 over four years ($4,000 per year).

Founders Scholarship In State
- Requires a 30-32 ACT or equivalent SAT score and a minimum 3.5 high school GPA for consideration.

- Awarded at $32,000 over four years ($8,000 per year).

Charter Scholarship Out of State
- Requires a 29-30 ACT or equivalent SAT score and a minimum 3.5 high school GPA for consideration.

- Awarded at $32,000 over four years ($8,000 per year).

Heritage Scholarship Out of State

- Requires a 31-32 ACT or equivalent SAT score and a minimum 3.5 high school GPA for consideration.

- Awarded at $52,000 over four years ($13,000 per year).

Presidential Scholarship Out of State
- Requires a 33-36 ACT or equivalent SAT score and a minimum 3.5 high school GPA for consideration.

- Awarded at $72,000 over four years ($18,000 per year).

**Honors Fees:** The Honors College fee is charged in conjunction with tuition at the beginning of each semester. This fee reflects progress through the Honors College. First- and second-year Honors students are charged slightly more due to the number of Honors classes in which first- and second-year Honors students typically enroll. The Honors fee is broken down as follows:

- First-year Honors student - $250/semester

- Second-year Honors students - $225/semester

- Third-year and beyond Honors student - $200/semester

**Placement of Honors Graduates:** None listed.

**Degree of Difference**: This is difference between (1) the average SAT scores for recently enrolled honors students (1430) and (2) the average test scores for all students in the university (1250) as a whole. The difference may be an indication of how "elite" honors students may be perceived as compared to students in the university as a whole. **Please keep in mind that neither the high nor low selectivity of an honors program determines how effective the program may be.**

**NAME**: CALHOUN HONORS COLLEGE, CLEMSON UNIVERSITY

**Date Established: 1962**

**Location**: Clemson, South Carolina

**University <u>Full-time Undergraduate</u> Enrollment (2017):** 18,599

**Honors Members in Good Standing**: 1,554; (mean size of all programs is 2,030).

**Honors <u>Average</u> Admission Test Score(s)**: ACT, 32; SAT, 1471 superscored.

**Average High School GPA/Class Rank:** 3.90, unweighted. Top 2-4% of high school class.

**<u>Basic</u> Admission Requirements:** ACT, 30; SAT 1320; GPA, 3.70, unweighted.

**Application Deadline(s):** *Please verify with each program, as some deadlines could change.* Priority honors deadline December 1, 2018, with notification February 15, 2019; regular deadline March 1, 2019; after meeting university deadline of February 15, 2019; notification April 1, 2019.

**Honors Programs with SAT scores from 1471—1510:** Clemson, Georgia, Illinois, Minnesota, Oklahoma, Rutgers, South Carolina, UT Austin.

**Administrative Staff:** 14.

**RATINGS AT A GLANCE:** For all mortarboard ratings immediately below, a score of 5 is the maximum and represents a comparison with all rated honors colleges and programs. More detailed explanations follow the "mortarboard" ratings.

**PERCEPTION* OF UNIVERSITY AS A WHOLE, <u>NOT</u> OF HONORS:** 🎓🎓🎓🎓 1/2

*Perception is based on the university's ranking among public universities in the 2018 U.S. News Best Colleges report. Please bear in mind that the better the U.S. News ranking, the more difficult it is for an honors college or program to have a rating that equals or improves on the magazine ranking.

**OVERALL HONORS RATING:** 🎓🎓🎓🎓 1/2

**Curriculum Requirements:** 🎓🎓🎓 1/2

**Number of Honors Classes Offered:** 🎓🎓🎓 1/2

**Number of Honors Classes in Key Disciplines:** 🎓🎓🎓🎓

**Extent of Honors Enrollment:** 🎓🎓🎓🎓

**Honors-only Class Size:** 🎓🎓🎓🎓 1/2

**Overall Class Size (Honors-only plus mixed, contract):** 🎓🎓🎓🎓

**Honors Grad Rate Adjusted to SAT:** 🎓🎓🎓🎓 1/2

**Grad Rate Adjusted to Freshman Retention Rate:** 🎓🎓🎓🎓 1/2

**Ratio of Staff to Students:** 🎓🎓🎓🎓

**Priority Registration: Yes.** "Honors students do receive priority and register earlier than those who are non-honors students and have the same number of credit hours."

**Honors Housing Amenities:** 🎓🎓🎓🎓🎓

**Honors Housing Availability:** 🎓🎓🎓 1/2

**Prestigious Awards:** 🎓🎓🎓 1/2

## RATING SCORES AND EXPLANATIONS:

**Curriculum Requirements (3.5):** The most important rating category, the curriculum completion requirement (classes required to complete honors) defines not only what honors students should learn but also the extent to which honors students and faculty are connected in the classroom. If there is a thesis or capstone requirement, it reinforces the individual contact and research skills so important to learning.

The average number of honors semester hours required for completion across all programs is 30.0.

The Honors College requirement for General Honors is 18 credits. Students who also complete Departmental Honors in their major earn another 9-12 credits, including a 6-credit thesis.

Interdisciplinary Honors Option 1 requires 14 credits, including 8 credits of course work and a 6-credit thesis. Two credits may be earned by honors contract.

Interdisciplinary Honors Option 2 requires 14 credits, including 12 credits of course work and a 2-credit capstone project. Two credits may be earned by honors contract.

**AP/IB credits** are **not** counted as replacements for honors courses.

**No. Honors Classes Offered (3.5):** This is a measure of the total **adjusted** honors main sections available in the term reported, not including labs and thesis. An adjusted main section has 3 or more semester credits, or equivalent, and sections with fewer credits receive a lower prorated value.

honors offered a section for every **16.6** enrolled students. The average for all programs was **15.0**. The lower the number, the better.

In the term reported, an impressive **79.4%** of honors enrollment was **in honors-only sections; 14.3% was in mixed sections; and only 6.3% was in contract sections.** For all programs under review, enrollment by type of honors section was 75.8% honors-only, 15.4 % mixed, and 8.8% contract.

**No. Honors Classes in Key Disciplines (4.0):** The 15 "key" disciplines are biological sciences; business (all); chemistry; communications (especially public speaking); computer science; economics; engineering (all); English; history; math (all); philosophy; physics; political science; psychology; and sociology, anthropology, and gender studies. Interdisciplinary sections, such as those often taken for General Education credit in the first two years, do receive a lesser, prorated discipline "credit" because they introduce students to multiple disciplines in an especially engaging way, often with in-depth discussion.

For this measure, mixed and contract sections are not counted as a section in a key discipline unless students taking the sections for honors credit make up at least 10% of the total section enrollment.

In the term reported, the honors college offered a section in a key discipline for every **24.5 honors students.** The average for all programs is **24.7.** The lower the number, the better.

Out of **54 adjusted sections in key disciplines, 47 were honors-only sections**. The most sections were in English and business, followed by math, communications, physics, and engineering. There were no honors sections in computer science.

The college did offer a good range of interdisciplinary courses including the creatively titled "Hell in Literature." Others, some with an emphasis on one discipline, included the soberly titled "Russian Revolution," "Europe in the Age of Dictators," along with "Imaginary Friends in Fiction," and "Southern Literature."

**Extent of Honors Enrollment (4.0):** Not all honors students take an honors class each term, especially after the first two years. Programs that have fewer honors classes and thesis options for upper-division honors students will *generally* have fewer total members in good standing who are actually enrolled in a given term. (Please be aware, however, that honors students not enrolled in a class for a term are still tied to the honors community through residential and extracurricular activities.) *Our research shows that this measure is closely related to honors completion rates, i.e., the number of students who complete honors requirements by the time they graduate.*

For example, if a program has 1,800 individual students enrolled in a given term, and 3,000 students in good standing, the level of enrollment was .67, an indication that honors class enrollment is somewhat below average, especially in upper-division classes. **honors has a ratio of 1.32**, almost exactly at the mean of 1.30 for all programs.

**Average Class Size, Honors-only Sections (4.5):** Offered mostly in the first two years, honors-only classes tend to be smaller and, as the name implies, have no or very few students other than those in the honors program. These class sections always are much smaller than mixed or contract sections, or regular non-honors class sections in the university.

The average honors-only class size at the honors college is **16.4 students**. The average for all programs is **17.5 students.**

**Average Class Size, Overall (4.0):** The overall class calculation is based on the *proportion* of honors students in each type of class (honors-only, mixed honors, and honors contract sections). Thus it is not a raw average. The overall honors-credit class size is **23.6 students**, versus the average for all programs of **24.9 students**.

These class size averages also do not correspond to the number of students per honors section ratings above. The reason is that, in computing average class size metrics, we include enrollment in each 1-2-credit section, not just sections with 3 or more credits.

Along with an honors-only class size of 16.4 students (listed above), the program's mixed honors sections have an average size of **49.1 students,** and the contract sections with honors credit for individual honors students average **55.9 students.** Across all programs, the average mixed honors section has 68.6 students, and the average contract section has 56.6 students.

**Honors Grad Rate Adjusted to SAT (4.5):** The rating is the based on the actual grad rate for students who entered the program six years earlier, whether or not the students remained in honors. The **actual (very high) grad rate of 94.9%** is also compared to the rates of other programs with the same test score entry requirement range, and then adjusted upward if the program is performing above other programs in the same range, or downward if the performance is less than other programs in the same range. The rate here is upward, to **95.2%.**

**Grad Rate Adjusted to Freshman Retention Rate (4.5):** This rate compares the actual grad rate above to a predicted grade rate when freshman retention rates are considered. The actual grad rate is **1.55 points higher** than the predicted rate. For all programs, the actual grad rate is **.33 points lower** than the predicted rate.

**Ratio of Staff to Honors Students (4.0):** There is 1 staff member for every **111.0** students. (Mean ratio for all programs is 1 staff member for every **127.9** students.)

**Honors Residence Halls, Amenities (5.0):** About 360 honors students, freshmen and upperclassmen, live in the Honors Center at Core Campus, Clemson's first residential college. The complex has suite-style housing, and the Honors College administrative offices, classrooms, study areas, and academic event spaces open to all Honors students (whether or not they live in Core Campus) are housed there. There is an on-site dining hall and other dining options (open to all students on campus). The consolidation of honors administrative functions and student housing in residential honors colleges is an important development, though sometimes one that takes a long time to achieve.

**Honors Residence Halls, Availability (3.5):** This rating compares the number of occupants in honors residence halls to the number of honors freshman and sophomore members in good standing. The ratio for the college is **.46** places for each first- and second-year student. The median for all programs is .49 places.

**Prestigious Awards (3.5):** The awards that we track and include are listed in the section titled "Prestigious Scholarships." The awards are sometimes won by students who are not in an honors college

or program, but increasingly many are enrolled in honors programs. It is also a trend that honors colleges and programs help to prepare their students for the awards competitions.

**In May of 2018, the Honors College initiated its own office of prestigious scholarships, signaling that the university intends to compete strongly in this area.** Our figures show that Clemson students are already above the mean for earning Fulbright and National Science Foundation awards. With 43 Goldwater Scholars, university students rank 17th among public universities in earning this very important scholarship, which is an indication of STEM excellence.

**UNRATED FEATURES**

**Continuation and Honors Graduation GPA Requirement:** 3.40.

**Academic Strengths, National Rankings:** This is based on national rankings of *graduate* programs in all but engineering and business, where undergraduate rankings are used. One of the weaknesses of the *U.S. News* rankings is that they focus on too many wealth-related metrics while ignoring their own assessments of academic departments. The rankings listed below are for all universities, public or private.

The nationally ranked academic departments at Clemson include engineering (56); education (70); economics (72); business (78); computer science (82); math (94); psychology (98).

**Internships, Professional Development, Community Engagement:** "Many students use Educational Enrichment Travel Grants to fund unpaid internships in Washington, DC, and other national and international locations. We have also established our new London internship semester. Students are also encouraged and advised to apply for and participate in various internship programs sponsored by both campus and external programs.

"We offer many opportunities for volunteer activities, mostly organized by Honors Community Service Group, which is run by our students. This group sponsors a variety of service activities on and off campus each month. In April 2018, for example, the group sponsored the following activities: beach cleanup; working with Habitat for Humanity; volunteering at a local homeless shelter; and working with children Helping Hands. Most Honors students also pursue service opportunities through various student clubs and groups not affiliated with Honors, or through their own personal activities."

**Undergraduate Research:** "Departmental Honors programs feature undergraduate research as an essential component. In addition, many Honors students participate in undergraduate research through Clemson's Creative Inquiry Program; some of these creative inquiry groups consist wholly or predominantly of Honors students, and some provide Honors credit. We also sponsor the EUREKA! program, an intensive researched-based experience for entering students held during the summer before their freshman year."

**Honors Study Abroad:** "We offer Educational Enrichment Travel Grants to approximately 100 students every year (maximum $3,000 each) for research, internship, or other educational experiences. We also subsidize our other study abroad programs to reduce student costs. These include a five-week summer

Honors-only program in Europe focusing on the history and politics of the European Union, an innovative online program linking Honors students studying in Europe during the Spring semester, and a Spring semester Honors internship program in London *(NEW)*. In addition, two students are selected each year for a full scholarship to the St. Peter's Summer School at Oxford University, Oxford, England, and the 12 students selected each year as Dixon Global Policy Scholars receive a 12-day educational enrichment travel experience in France and Germany for minimal cost.

"Our National Scholars (recipients of our premier undergraduate scholarship) have additional opportunities for fully funded travel, including a study abroad experience in South Africa and May study trips to the National Parks and various international destinations."

**Financial Aid:** "In addition to the **National Scholars Program, which provides full scholarship (tuition, fees, room, board and books) to approximately 12 students/year [average SAT ~1510],** Honors students at Clemson University are eligible for numerous merit scholarships. Virtually every in-state Honors student qualifies as a freshman for a South Carolina Life or Palmetto Fellows scholarship. Students are also eligible for additional merit- and need-based aid. Most Clemson financial aid is awarded to students without regard to their status as Honors students, but there are some specific Honors scholarships.

**"Out-of-state Honors students** usually qualify for an award of between $7,500 and $17,500 annually--depending on test scores, high school performance and financial need. We also offer a limited but growing number of Honors-based scholarships to students with financial need to defray the cost of the Honors Fee (see below) and other Honors-related expenses, such as living costs associated with the Honors Residential College."

**Honors Fees:** $500 each semester.

**Placement of Honors Graduates:**

"Graduate Schools: 36% of our students entered graduate school in the year immediately after graduation.

"Professional Schools: 18% of our students entered graduate school in the year immediately after graduation.

"Employment: 40% of our students were employed in a position related to their Clemson degree in the year immediately after graduation.

"Our graduates enroll in a wide range of graduate and professional schools and are employed by large and small corporations, government agencies, and non-profit organizations. Professional schools include the Harvard Medical School, the Harvard Business School, Yale Law School, UC Berkeley Law School, the Johns Hopkins Medical School, Emory University School of Medicine, Duke University School of Medicine, the University of South Carolina School of Medicine, and the Medical University of South Carolina. Graduate schools include Stanford, MIT, the University of Michigan, the Georgia Institute of Technology, the London School of Economics, Harvard, Yale, and many others. Corporations include Goldman Sachs, Boeing, Michelin, BMW, BB&T Bank, Adidas, General Electric, and many more."

**Degree of Difference**: This is difference between (1) the average SAT scores for recently enrolled honors students (1471) and (2) the average test scores for all students in the university (1310) as a whole. The difference may be an indication of how "elite" honors students may be perceived as compared to students in the university as a whole. **Please keep in mind that neither the high nor low selectivity of an honors program determines how effective the program may be.**

**NAME**: COLORADO STATE UNIVERSITY HONORS PROGRAM

**Date Established:** 1957

**Location**: Fort Collins, Colorado

**University Full-time Undergraduate Enrollment (2017):** 25,177

**Honors Members in Good Standing**: 1,596; (mean size of all programs is 2,030).

**Honors Average Admission Test Score(s)**: ACT, 30; SAT, 1340.

**Average High School GPA/Class Rank:** 4.16, weighted.

**Basic Admission Requirements:** No listed score requirements. GPA 3.70, top tenth of high school class.

**Application Deadline(s):** *Please verify with each program, as some deadlines could change.* "The Honors application date is February 1. In some cases, we may ask for additional information (such as fall grades) before making a final decision. After the deadline has passed, qualified students may be placed on a waiting list if the program is at capacity."

**Honors Programs with SAT scores from 1332—1365:** Arizona State, Arkansas, Colorado State, Nevada Reno, Oklahoma State, Oregon, Oregon State.

**Administrative Staff: 5.**

**RATINGS AT A GLANCE:** For all mortarboard ratings immediately below, a score of 5 is the maximum and represents a comparison with all rated honors colleges and programs. More detailed explanations follow the "mortarboard" ratings.

**PERCEPTION\* OF UNIVERSITY AS A WHOLE, NOT OF HONORS:** 🎓🎓🎓🎓

\*Perception is based on the university's ranking among public universities in the 2018 U.S. News Best Colleges report. Please bear in mind that the better the U.S. News ranking, the more difficult it is for an honors college or program to have a rating that equals or improves on the magazine ranking.

**OVERALL HONORS RATING:** 🎓🎓🎓 1/2

**Curriculum Requirements:** 🎓🎓🎓 1/2

**Number of Honors Classes Offered:** 🎓🎓🎓🎓

**Number of Honors Classes in Key Disciplines:** 🎓🎓🎓🎓

**Extent of Honors Enrollment:** 🎓🎓🎓🎓

**Honors-only Class Size:** 🎓🎓🎓🎓 1/2

**Overall Class Size (Honors-only plus mixed, contract):** 🎓🎓🎓🎓 1/2

**Honors Grad Rate Adjusted to SAT:** 🎓🎓🎓🎓 1/2

**Grad Rate Adjusted to Freshman Retention Rate:** 🎓🎓🎓🎓

**Ratio of Staff to Students:** 🎓🎓 1/2

**Priority Registration: Yes.** After their first semester, all Honors students can register for all classes for which they are eligible one full day before seniors can register.

**Honors Housing Amenities:** 🎓🎓🎓 1/2

**Honors Housing Availability:** 🎓🎓🎓

**Prestigious Awards:** 🎓🎓🎓

## RATING SCORES AND EXPLANATIONS:

**Curriculum Requirements (3.5):** The most important rating category, the curriculum completion requirement (classes required to complete honors) defines not only what honors students should learn but also the extent to which honors students and faculty are connected in the classroom. If there is a thesis or capstone requirement, it reinforces the individual contact and research skills so important to learning.

The average number of honors semester hours required for completion across all programs is 30.0.

For entering first-year students, CSU Honors requires 26 credits for honors completion, including up to 17 honors contract credits, 6 credits in departmental honors sections, and a 3-credit thesis. About 80% of students pursue this option.

For students entering as transfers or after the first year, the requirement is also 26 credits. But students take 15 credits of departmental honors, 8 credits in honors contracts, and also do a 3-credit thesis.

**AP/IB credits** are **not** counted as replacements for honors courses.

**No. Honors Classes Offered (4.0):** This is a measure of the total **adjusted** honors main sections available in the term reported, not including labs and thesis. An adjusted main section has 3 or more semester credits, or equivalent, and sections with fewer credits receive a lower prorated value.

CSU honors offered a section for every **13.2** enrolled students. The average for all programs was **15.0**. The lower the number, the better.

In the term reported, an extremely impressive **91.0%** of honors enrollment was **in honors-only sections; none was in mixed sections; and 9.0% was in contract sections.** For all programs under review, enrollment by type of honors section was 75.8% honors-only, 15.4 % mixed, and 8.8% contract.

**No. Honors Classes in Key Disciplines (4.0):** The 15 "key" disciplines are biological sciences; business (all); chemistry; communications (especially public speaking); computer science; economics; engineering (all); English; history; math (all); philosophy; physics; political science; psychology; and sociology, anthropology, and gender studies. Interdisciplinary sections, such as those often taken for General Education credit in the first two years, do receive a lesser, prorated discipline "credit" because they introduce students to multiple disciplines in an especially engaging way, often with in-depth discussion.

For this measure, mixed and contract sections are not counted as a section in a key discipline unless students taking the sections for honors credit make up at least 10% of the total section enrollment.

In the term reported, the honors CSU Honors offered a section in a key discipline for every **23.9 honors students.** The average for all programs is **24.7.** The lower the number, the better.

Out of **adjusted sections in key disciplines, all were honors-only sections.** The most sections were in biology or microbiology and business, followed by engineering, math, philosophy, and psychology.

CSU Honors actually offers more seminars and interdisciplinary sections than it does departmental honors courses, almost 70 in all. Among these are multiple sections of the following: "First-Years Seminars," "Honors Seminars," "Knowing in the Arts and Humanities," "Knowing Across Cultures."

One of our favorites from the last group is a section with the full title "Knowing across Cultures: Exploring the Foundations of Moral Reasoning Across Cultures."

Course description: "How do you know right from wrong? Is it right to let children die from preventable diseases in far off countries? Is it wrong to engage in acts of sodomy or homosexuality? Is it right to limit speech that denigrates one's country or blasphemes one's God(s)? Is it wrong to force people to pay taxes or buy health insurance? How would you answer these questions of moral judgment and ethical action? "

CSU Honors is a **blended** program, with an emphasis on interdisciplinary courses, some classes in the disciplines, and a high proportion of students completing theses.

**Extent of Honors Enrollment (4.0):** Not all honors students take an honors class each term, especially after the first two years. Programs that have fewer honors classes and thesis options for upper-division honors students will *generally* have fewer total members in good standing who are actually enrolled in a given term. (Please be aware, however, that honors students not enrolled in a class for a term are still tied to the honors community through residential and extracurricular activities.) *Our research shows that this measure is closely related to honors completion rates, i.e., the number of students who complete honors requirements by the time they graduate.*

For example, if a program has 1,800 individual students enrolled in a given term, and 3,000 students in good standing, the level of enrollment was .67, an indication that honors class enrollment is somewhat below average, especially in upper-division classes. **CSU honors has a ratio of 1.35**, above the average of 1.30 for all programs.

**Average Class Size, Honors-only Sections (4.5):** Offered mostly in the first two years, honors-only classes tend to be smaller and, as the name implies, have no or very few students other than those in the honors program. These class sections always are much smaller than mixed or contract sections, or regular non-honors class sections in the university.

The average honors-only class size at CSU Honors is **16.2 students**. The average for all programs is **17.5 students.**

**Average Class Size, Overall (4.5):** The overall class calculation is based on the *proportion* of honors students in each type of class (honors-only, mixed honors, and honors contract sections). Thus it is not a raw average. The overall honors-credit class size is **19.7 students**, versus the average for all programs of **24.9 students.**

These class size averages also do not correspond to the number of students per honors section ratings above. The reason is that, in computing average class size metrics, we include enrollment in each 1-2-credit section, not just sections with 3 or more credits.

Along with an honors-only class size of 16.2 students (listed above), the program's contract sections with honors credit for individual honors students average **54.8 students.** Across all programs, the average contract section has 56.6 students.

**Honors Grad Rate Adjusted to SAT (4.5):** The rating is the based on the actual grad rate for students who entered the program six years earlier, whether or not the students remained in honors. The **actual rate of 87.4%** is also compared to the rates of other programs with the same test score entry requirement range, and then adjusted upward if the program is performing above other programs in the same range, or downward if the performance is less than other programs in the same range. The rate here is slightly upward, to **88.0%.**

**Grad Rate Adjusted to Freshman Retention Rate (4.0):** This rate compares the actual grad rate above to a predicted grade rate when freshman retention rates are considered. The actual grad rate is **.07 points higher** than the predicted rate. For all programs, the actual grad rate is **.33 points lower** than the predicted rate.

**Ratio of Staff to Honors Students (2.5):** There is 1 staff member for every **319.2** students. (Mean ratio for all programs is 1 staff member for every **127.9** students.)

**Honors Residence Halls, Amenities (3.5):** About 200 first-year honors students live in the Academic Village Residence Hall, with air-conditioned suite-style rooms with shared baths. The nearest dining facility is the Rams Horn located within the Academic Village complex.

The remaining 26% of honors students in honors housing reside in Edwards Residence Hall. The hall has traditional double rooms and hall baths for freshmen and upperclassmen, and does not have air-conditioning. The closest dining is also at the Rams Horn in the Academic Village. Edwards provides students with a more economical housing option.

**Honors Residence Halls, Availability (3.0):** This rating compares the number of occupants in honors residence halls to the number of honors freshman and sophomore members in good standing. The ratio for

the program is **.34** places for each first- and second-year student. The median for all programs is .49 places.

**Prestigious Awards (3.0):** The awards that we track and include are listed in the section titled "Prestigious Scholarships." The awards are sometimes won by students who are not in an honors college or program, but increasingly many are enrolled in honors programs. It is also a trend that honors colleges and programs help to prepare their students for the awards competitions.

CSU students have won 11 Udall scholarships and 17 Goldwater awards, both awarded to undergraduates, the latter for outstanding promise in STEM fields. CSU students have also won an impressive 5 Marshall scholarships for postgraduate study in the U.K. CSU Honors students have most of the Goldwater Scholarships at CSU.

**UNRATED FEATURES**

**Continuation and Honors Graduation GPA Requirement:** 3.00 for continuation. And 3.50 for graduation.

**Academic Strengths, National Rankings:** This is based on national rankings of *graduate* programs in all but engineering and business, where undergraduate rankings are used. One of the weaknesses of the *U.S. News* rankings is that they focus on too many wealth-related metrics while ignoring their own assessments of academic departments. The rankings listed below are for all universities, public or private.

CSU has nationally ranked departments in all key disciplines except English and history.

The leading nationally ranked academic departments at CSU are chemistry (52), biology (62), earth sciences (68), engineering (70), physics (71), math (74), and computer science (75).

**Internships, Professional Development, Community Engagement:** "The Honors Enrichment Program is designed to provide assistance with funding for enhanced educational opportunities for Honors students. Funds are available to support group and individual enrichment opportunities. Opportunities must be academically enriching for the group or the individual student." Some examples are below.

**Alternative Spring/Winter Breaks**
- Catalina Island, California, for environmental preservation and education projects
- Samburu, Kenya to work with survivors of gender-based violence in the women's village
- Washington, D.C. to participate in efforts to eliminate homelessness
- Kanab, Utah to volunteer at the Best Friends Animal Society animal sanctuary

**Volunteer Projects**
- Participate in medical relief projects in India
- Volunteer with medical clinics in Guatemala
- Preservation of the Manzanar National Historic Site in Independence, California
- Interview medical personnel in New Orleans on the effects of natural disasters on the health care system

**Internships and Leadership**
- Training Paul W. Zuccaire Internship at the Pasteur Institute in Paris, France
- Walt Disney World College Program
- U.S. Senator in Washington D.C. office
- Outward Bound Wilderness Course
- Leadershape Leadership Institute

**Undergraduate Research:** "Colorado State University's research programs are among the best in the nation, and there are numerous opportunities for undergraduate students to participate in research activities on the main campus, in the Veterinary Teaching Hospital, and at our foothills campus. *CSU leads the world in such areas as infectious disease research, atmospheric science, and environmental science. CSU is home to an NIH Regional Center of Excellence in Infectious Disease, the world's largest animal cancer center, a world-renown Equine Orthopedic Research Center, among many other excellent facilities.* CSU was the first university in the U.S. to receive funding for two National Science Foundation centers in one round—one in extreme ultraviolet light and the other in atmospheric science. Faculty researchers encourage undergraduates to join their research teams in most laboratories on campus."

**Honors Study Abroad:** "Honors Study Abroad seminars and courses are offered in Oxford, Rome, and Zambia in summers. A new Honors seminar in Seoul, South Korea will be offered summer 2019. These are offered every summer.

"Enrichment Awards (up to $400) and the Spot's Scholarship ($1,250) can be used for Study Abroad. A focus of our fundraising is focused on assisting students in paying for these experiences."

**Financial Aid:** "In addition to other merit and need-based scholarships offered by the University, the University Honors Program awards entering first-year students a $1,000 per year Honors scholarship, renewable each year, for 4 years. There are donor-endowed scholarships awarded to ~10 students per year. Students can receive Enrichment Awards and Thesis Improvement Grants each year ($400 per award)."

Resident Merit Scholarships:

For 2019-2020, $16,000 to $4,000 ($4,000 to $1,000 per year, half paid each semester-fall/spring). Merit scholars who meet the selection and renewal criteria may receive this award for up to a total of eight semesters, or until their degree is complete, whichever comes first.

Non-Resident Merit Scholarships:

For 2019-2020, $40,000 – $20,000 ( $10,000 to $5,000 per year, half paid each semester-fall/spring). Merit scholars who meet the selection and renewal criteria may receive this award for up to a total of eight semesters, or until their degree is complete, whichever comes first.

**Honors Fees:** None.

**Placement of Honors Graduates:** "In graduate surveys, about half (50%) planned to enter post-graduate professional or graduate programs; about 36% had jobs after graduation, and 14% did not specify any plans."

**Degree of Difference**: This is difference between (1) the average SAT scores for recently enrolled honors students (1340) and (2) the average test scores for all students in the university (1210) as a whole. The difference may be an indication of how "elite" honors students may be perceived as compared to students in the university as a whole. **Please keep in mind that neither the high nor low selectivity of an honors program determines how effective the program may be.**

**NAME**: WILLIAM E. MACAULAY HONORS COLLEGE AT THE CITY UNIVERSITY OF NEW YORK

**Date Established:** 2001

**Location**: New York, New York

**University <u>Full-time Undergraduate</u> Enrollment (2017):** Enrollment at 8 consortial campuses, 84,572.

**Honors Members in Good Standing**: 2,001; (mean size of all programs is 2,030).

**Honors <u>Average</u> Admission Test Score(s)**: ACT, not reported; SAT, 1370.

**Average High School GPA/Class Rank:** 93.9 grade average.

**<u>Basic</u> Admission Requirements:** ACT, not reported; SAT, 1270; 90.0 grad average.

**Application Deadline(s):** *Please verify with each program, as some deadlines could change.* December 1, 2018.

**Honors Programs with SAT scores from 1370—1403:** Arizona, CUNY Macaulay, Georgia State, Houston, Indiana, LSU, Massachusetts, New Mexico, Purdue, Texas Tech, UAB.

**Administrative Staff:** 57 FTE.

**RATINGS AT A GLANCE:** For all mortarboard ratings immediately below, a score of 5 is the maximum and represents a comparison with all rated honors colleges and programs. More detailed explanations follow the "mortarboard" ratings.

**PERCEPTION\* OF UNIVERSITY AS A WHOLE, <u>NOT</u> OF HONORS:** 🎓🎓🎓 1/2

\*Perception is based on the university's ranking among public universities in the 2018 U.S. News Best Colleges report. Please bear in mind that the better the U.S. News ranking, the more difficult it is for an honors college or program to have a rating that equals or improves on the magazine ranking.

**OVERALL HONORS RATING:** 🎓🎓🎓🎓🎓

**Curriculum Requirements:** 🎓🎓🎓🎓🎓

**Number of Honors Classes Offered:** 🎓🎓🎓🎓🎓

**Number of Honors Classes in Key Disciplines:** 🎓🎓🎓🎓🎓

**Extent of Honors Enrollment:** 🎓🎓🎓🎓🎓

**Honors-only Class Size:** 🎓🎓🎓🎓

**Overall Class Size (Honors-only plus mixed, contract):** 🎓🎓🎓🎓🎓

**Honors Grad Rate Adjusted to SAT:** 🎓🎓🎓🎓🎓

**Grad Rate Adjusted to Freshman Retention Rate:** 🎓🎓🎓🎓 1/2

**Ratio of Staff to Students:** 🎓🎓🎓🎓🎓

**Priority Registration: Yes,** honors students register for all courses, honors and otherwise, with the first group of students during each year they are in the program

**Honors Housing Amenities:** 🎓🎓🎓

**Honors Housing Availability:** 🎓🎓🎓🎓 1/2

**Prestigious Awards:** 🎓🎓🎓🎓

## RATING SCORES AND EXPLANATIONS:

**Curriculum Requirements (5.0):** The most important rating category, the curriculum completion requirement (classes required to complete honors) defines not only what honors students should learn but also the extent to which honors students and faculty are connected in the classroom. If there is a thesis or capstone requirement, it reinforces the individual contact and research skills so important to learning.

The average number of honors semester hours required for completion across all programs is 30.0.

Macaulay students must complete a minimum of 39 credits for honors graduation. Of these, 12 credits must be from honors seminars and another 12 credits from honors departmental courses. Also required is a 6-credit thesis, an internship or study-abroad experience, and another 6 credits or so if departmental honors are available. Finally, students must perform 30 hours of community service.

**AP/IB credits** are **not** counted as replacements for honors courses.

**No. Honors Classes Offered (5.0):** This is a measure of the total **adjusted** honors main sections available in the term reported, not including labs and thesis. An adjusted main section has 3 or more semester credits, or equivalent, and sections with fewer credits receive a lower prorated value.

Macaulay Honors offered a section for every **6.1** enrolled students. The average for all programs was **15.0**. The lower the number, the better.

In the term reported, an extremely impressive **100%** of honors enrollment was **in honors-only or research sections (no contract or mixed sections).** For all programs under review, enrollment by type of honors section was 75.8% honors-only, 15.4 % mixed, and 8.8% contract.

**No. Honors Classes in Key Disciplines (5.0):** The 15 "key" disciplines are biological sciences; business (all); chemistry; communications (especially public speaking); computer science; economics; engineering (all); English; history; math (all); philosophy; physics; political science; psychology; and sociology, anthropology, and gender studies. Interdisciplinary sections, such as those often taken for General Education credit in the first two years, do receive a lesser, prorated discipline "credit" because they introduce students to multiple disciplines in an especially engaging way, often with in-depth discussion.

For this measure, mixed and contract sections are not counted as a section in a key discipline unless students taking the sections for honors credit make up at least 10% of the total section enrollment.

In the term reported, the honors college offered a section in a key discipline for every **9.8 honors students.** The average for all programs is **24.7.** The lower the number, the better.

Of **98 adjusted sections in key disciplines**, **all were honors-only sections**. The most sections were in business and English, followed by biology, chemistry, and psychology. There were also multiple sections of political science, math, and philosophy. All key disciplines were represented.

The college does offer almost 100 interdisciplinary courses including a core seminar series: "The Arts in New York City," "The People of New York City," "Science Forward," and one of our favorites, "Planning the Future of New York City."

**Extent of Honors Enrollment (5.0):** Not all honors students take an honors class each term, especially after the first two years. Programs that have fewer honors classes and thesis options for upper-division honors students will *generally* have fewer total members in good standing who are actually enrolled in a given term. (Please be aware, however, that honors students not enrolled in a class for a term are still tied to the honors community through residential and extracurricular activities.) *Our research shows that this measure is closely related to honors completion rates, i.e., the number of students who complete honors requirements by the time they graduate.*

For example, if a program has 1,800 individual students enrolled in a given term, and 3,000 students in good standing, the level of enrollment was .67, an indication that honors class enrollment is somewhat below average, especially in upper-division classes. **Macaulay Honors** has a ratio of **1.98**, far above the average of 1.30 for all programs.

**Average Class Size, Honors-only Sections (4.0):** Offered mostly in the first two years, honors-only classes tend to be smaller and, as the name implies, have no or very few students other than those in the honors program. These class sections always are much smaller than mixed or contract sections, or regular non-honors class sections in the university.

The average honors-only class size at the honors college is **17.3 students**. The average for all programs is **17.5 students.**

**Average Class Size, Overall (5.0):** The overall class calculation is based on the *proportion* of honors students in each type of class (honors-only, mixed honors, and honors contract sections). Thus it is not a raw average. The overall honors-credit class size is **17.3 students**, versus the average for all programs of **24.9 students**.

These class size averages also do not correspond to the number of students per honors section ratings above. The reason is that, in computing average class size metrics, we include enrollment in each 1-2-credit section, not just sections with 3 or more credits.

Since all honors sections have honors-only enrollment, we have no mixed or contract enrollment figures to report.

**Honors Grad Rate Adjusted to SAT (5.0):** The rating is the based on the actual grad rate for students who entered the program six years earlier, whether or not the students remained in honors. The **actual rate of 89.0%** is also compared to the rates of other programs with the same test score entry requirement range, and then adjusted upward if the program is performing above other programs in the same range, or downward if the performance is less than other programs in the same range. The rate here is upward, to **90.1%.**

**Grad Rate Adjusted to Freshman Retention Rate (4.5):** This rate compares the actual grad rate above to a predicted grade rate when freshman retention rates are considered. The actual grad rate is **2.7 points higher** than the predicted rate. For all programs, the actual grad rate is **.33 points lower** than the predicted rate.

**Ratio of Staff to Honors Students (5.0):** There is 1 staff member for every **49.3** students. (Mean ratio for all programs is 1 staff member for every **127.9** students.)

**Honors Residence Halls, Amenities (3.0):** "Macaulay students have access to eight residence halls or residences off-site, one each at Baruch College, Brooklyn College, City College, Hunter College, John Jay, Lehman College, Queens College and the College of Staten Island." These residences house about 640 students, including freshmen and upperclassmen.

By far, the Brookdale Residence at Hunter College, in Manhattan, has the most Macaulay students who live in honors housing, about 500. Almost all the rooms at Brookdale, a Health Sciences community, are singles, but with hall baths. The facility houses both freshmen and upperclassmen. The rooms are not air-conditioned. Brookdale is less than three miles northeast of Greenwich Village, and near the East River. **Rooms are "offered free or at major discounts for honors students."**

Only 31 Macaulay students live in the Baruch College Residence, located at 1760 Third Avenue, Upper East Side near Central Park. The rooms are doubles and triples; they are air-conditioned. There are no Macaulay discounts, but honors students have priority.

Only five Macaulay students live in the Brooklyn College Residence. Room configurations vary; rooms are air-conditioned.

The honors residence at Lehman College, in the Bronx, is an off-campus townhouse, housing 20 students.

About 60 Macaulay upperclassmen live at the Summit Residence at Queens College. The rooms are not air-conditioned.

A dozen students live in The Towers at Macaulay Honors College in Manhattan. The Towers are air-conditioned.

The air-conditioned Dolphin Cove residence hall in Staten Island houses seven students, as does the New Yorker residence hall in Staten Island. It is air-conditioned.

**Honors Residence Halls, Availability (4.5):** This rating compares the number of occupants in honors residence halls to the number of honors freshman and sophomore members in good standing. The ratio for the college is **.60** places for each first- and second-year student. The median for all programs is .49 places.

**Prestigious Awards (4.0):** The awards that we track and include are listed in the section titled "Prestigious Scholarships." The awards are sometimes won by students who are not in an honors college or program, but increasingly many are enrolled in honors programs. It is also a trend that honors colleges and programs help to prepare their students for the awards competitions.

CUNY students have won eight Rhodes Scholarships, eight Marshall Scholarships, and 13 Truman Scholarships, in addition to 38 National Science Foundation Fellowships and 31 Fulbright Scholarships in the last three years. CUNY underclassmen have earned 34 Goldwater Scholarships, awarded to promising students in the STEM disciplines.

**UNRATED FEATURES**

**Continuation and Honors Graduation GPA Requirement:** 3.50.

What are the GPA requirements for continuation in the college or program? = 3.50 for graduation; for continuation, 3.30 for the first three semesters and 3.50 thereafter.

**Academic Strengths, National Rankings:** This is based on national rankings of *graduate* programs in all but engineering and business, where undergraduate rankings are used. One of the weaknesses of the *U.S. News* rankings is that they focus on too many wealth-related metrics while ignoring their own assessments of academic departments. The rankings listed below are for all universities, public or private.

As for CUNY, City College is strongest in physics, engineering, and psychology; Baruch for business, especially accounting; Brooklyn for its coordinated engineering program, with transfer opportunities to NYU, and for its graduate program in cinema; Hunter, creative writing and psychology; Queens for psychology, and the Aaron Copland School of Music. Most campuses also have notable programs in the fine arts, as well as solid programs in nursing and health care.

**Internships, Professional Development, Community Engagement:** "Macaulay Honors College students are required to either engage in an internship or study abroad experience during their course of study. A recent survey of graduates from the class of 2017 showed that 79% of the students stated they had engaged in at least one internship during their undergraduate studies, 34% had engaged in three or more. The demand for Career Development opportunities is evident among our students. Macaulay assists students by providing a range of support to carry them through graduation and beyond."

"Civic engagement is an important aspect of the student experience. Students are required to complete at least 30 credits of community service. Students have reported an average of 73 hours (Class of 2016). Macaulay has a number of special projects in which all students engage. These experiential learning activities provide 'learning through reflection on doing.' In addition, these foster a sense of community among students. Three such projects are Night at the Museum, BioBlitz and the STEAM Festival. Since 2012, as part of our innovative first-year seminar 'The Arts in New York City,' Macaulay Honors College welcomes all new students every fall to an evening of conversation, engagement and interaction with the visual arts at New York's spectacular Brooklyn Museum. On this magical fall evening, after the museum is closed to the public, all 500+ students in the incoming class experience workshops and instruction and then, in small groups, explore the museum's world-class collections.

"The BioBlitz is an exciting and unique educational experience that provides every sophomore with an opportunity to collaborate with professional scientists and local naturalists. In a 24-hour, marathon session of data collection, teams of students will tally plants, animals and insects—all day and into the night! Their aim: to thoroughly measure and catalog the biodiversity of a selected New York City park or ecosystem. To date, Macaulay has conducted five BioBlitzes: Central Park (2013), New York Botanical Garden (2014), Freshkills Park (2015), Brooklyn Bridge Park (2016), and AlleyPond Park (2017). The 2018 Bioblitz will be held in Inwood Park. Approximately 450 students participated in the event Sept. 15-16, 2017.

"The STEAM festival celebrates critical inquiry in the arts and sciences, with informal presentations tied to final semester projects for the honors seminars Arts in New York City (first year students), and Science Forward (sophomores). Students have an opportunity to reflect on the similarities and differences between the types of critical inquiry that each Seminar demands."

**Undergraduate Research:** "A cornerstone of the Macaulay experience is undergraduate research. The Macaulay Honors College Research Assistantship Program matches CUNY faculty members pursuing original research in their various disciplines with curious and dedicated Macaulay students who are eager to learn more about a given intellectual field of inquiry. These pairings of scholars and students work together to create new knowledge in a discipline, affording students an opportunity to make valuable contributions to the work of their faculty mentors."

**Honors Study Abroad:** "Students have a wide range of study abroad programs open to them through CUNY—both in location and disciplines and Macaulay. CUNY offers over 50 programs each summer and winter session, and full-semester exchange programs during the regular academic year. In addition, Macaulay's own study abroad programs are designed to provide a community where students live, learn and engage with each other abroad.

"A Macaulay grant from the Opportunities Fund provides financial support for study abroad participation. Students can request to use the Opportunities Fund to cover program costs—including airfare, housing, and meals. Study abroad tuition costs are covered by the College through the Macaulay Tuition Scholarship."

**Special Programs:**

Puerto Rico—Partnering with the San Juan Bay Estuary we offer a service program focused on citizen science, water quality, and reforestation in communities devastated by recent hurricanes.

Galapagos—Partnering with the College of Staten Island and Universidad San Francisco de Quito, students enroll in a 3-credit course to examine theories that have shaped the concept of evolution, and how Darwin's experience in the Galapagos influenced his ideas.

Israel—In partnership with Tel Aviv University's Porter School of Environmental Sciences students enroll in a sustainability course focusing on environmental issues in Israel and around the globe. Students take a second course of their choosing in technology, political science or history.

**Financial Aid:** Full tuition each year for students who meet CUNY/NYS residency requirements for in state tuition.

Students accepted into the Macaulay Honors College are automatically considered for all scholarships.

- Financial Aid: Financial Aid available to Macaulay Honors College students:

- Federal PELL Grant

- TAP (New York State Tuition Assistance Program)

- HESC Scholarships/Grants (E.g. NYS Scholarships for Academic Excellence)

- SEOG

- New York City Council Scholarship

- TheDream.US Scholarship

The eight participating CUNY colleges may offer their own additional financial aid and/or scholarships to University Scholars. The Macaulay scholarship is drawn from a combination of sources: CUNY, TAP, City/State scholarships, and other tuition-only scholarships a student may have received.

**Honors Fees:** None.

**Placement of Honors Graduates:** Macaulay Honors College graduates have a history of successful transition to graduate schools nationwide for advanced study in a diverse range of fields.

**Graduate Schools: (sampling),** Carnegie Mellon University, Columbia University, Cornell, CUNY, Duke, Georgetown, Harvard, Howard, Johns Hopkins, MIT, NYU, Oxford, Princeton, Stanford, UC

Berkeley, UCLA, Chicago, Penn, and Yale. **Law Schools:** Boston University, Columbia, Duke, Georgetown, Harvard, NYU, Penn, Stanford UCLA, Vanderbilt. **Medical Schools:** Albert Einstein School of Medicine, Columbia, George Washington, Harvard, Mount Sinai, Johns Hopkins, NYU, Downstate Medical College, Pitt, Vanderbilt, Cornell. **Dental Schools:** Columbia, Harvard, NYU, Temple, Penn. **Vet Schools:** Cornell, Tufts. **Business Schools:** Cornell, Duke, Chicago, MIT, NYU, Northwestern, Penn.

**Employment: (sampling),** J.P. Morgan Chase, Morgan Stanley, Ernst & Young, Barclays, PricewaterhouseCoopers, Citigroup, Memorial Sloan-Kettering Cancer Center, Credit Suisse, Mount Sinai, Weil Medical Center, Bloomberg, Google.

**Degree of Difference**: This is difference between (1) the average SAT scores for recently enrolled honors students (1370) and (2) the average test scores for all students in the university (1230) as a whole. The difference may be an indication of how "elite" honors students may be perceived as compared to students in the university as a whole. **Please keep in mind that neither the high nor low selectivity of an honors program determines how effective the program may be.**

**NAME**: UNIVERSITY OF DELAWARE HONORS PROGRAM

**Date Established:** 1976

**Location**: Newark, Delaware

**University <u>Full-time Undergraduate</u> Enrollment (2017):** 18,374

**Honors Members in Good Standing**: 1,815; (mean size of all programs is 2,030).

**Honors <u>Average</u> Admission Test Score(s)**: ACT, not listed; SAT, 1437.

**Average High School GPA/Class Rank:** 4.0, weighted.

**<u>Basic</u> Admission Requirements:** No set basic requirements. "Although there are no minimum test scores of GPA requirements, students must have a competitive profile. Students must specify their interest in applying to Honors and must submit an additional essay. SAT Subject Tests are strongly recommended."

**Application Deadline(s):** *Please verify with each program, as some deadlines could change.* Deadline January 15, 2019, including honors essay; (notification mid-March 2019).

**Honors Programs with SAT scores from 1420—1461:** Auburn, Central Florida, Delaware, Iowa, Kansas, Mississippi, Missouri, New Jersey Inst of Technology, Penn State, South Florida, Vermont, Virginia Commonwealth.

**Administrative Staff:** 9.

**RATINGS AT A GLANCE:** For all mortarboard ratings immediately below, a score of 5 is the maximum and represents a comparison with all rated honors colleges and programs. More detailed explanations follow the "mortarboard" ratings.

**PERCEPTION\* OF UNIVERSITY AS A WHOLE, <u>NOT</u> OF HONORS:** 🎓🎓🎓🎓 1/2

\*Perception is based on the university's ranking among public universities in the 2018 U.S. News Best Colleges report. Please bear in mind that the better the U.S. News ranking, the more difficult it is for an honors college or program to have a rating that equals or improves on the magazine ranking.

**OVERALL HONORS RATING:** 🎓🎓🎓🎓 1/2

**Curriculum Requirements:** 🎓🎓🎓🎓

**Number of Honors Classes Offered:** 🎓🎓🎓🎓🎓

**Number of Honors Classes in Key Disciplines:** 🎓🎓🎓🎓🎓

**Extent of Honors Enrollment:** ★★★★ 1/2

**Honors-only Class Size:** ★★★ 1/2

**Overall Class Size (Honors-only plus mixed, contract):** ★★★ 1/2

**Honors Grad Rate Adjusted to SAT:** ★★★★★

**Grad Rate Adjusted to Freshman Retention Rate:** ★★★★ 1/2

**Ratio of Staff to Students:** ★★★

**Priority Registration: Yes.** "Honors Program students register in the first group for their class year (i.e. Honors seniors by credit are first to register before all other seniors, Honors juniors by credit are first to register before all other juniors, and so forth)."

**Honors Housing Amenities:** ★★★

**Honors Housing Availability:** ★★★★ 1/2

**Prestigious Awards:** ★★★★

## RATING SCORES AND EXPLANATIONS:

**Curriculum Requirements (4.0):** The most important rating category, the curriculum completion requirement (classes required to complete honors) defines not only what honors students should learn but also the extent to which honors students and faculty are connected in the classroom. If there is a thesis or capstone requirement, it reinforces the individual contact and research skills so important to learning.

The average number of honors semester hours required for completion across all programs is 30.0.

The *Honors Degree with Distinction* requires at least **30 credits** earned in Honors courses, including a 6-credit thesis. A minimum of 12 credits in 300-level courses or higher are required. No more than 12 credits in honors contract work can be counted toward completion. A 6-credit thesis and a 3-credit capstone are required.

The *Honors Degree* has the same basic 30-credit requirement as the Honors Degree with Distinction, but instead of the thesis, students are required to have 3 credits in an Honors Capstone Course. No more than 12 contract credits can count toward completion.

The *General Honors Award* does not result in an honors degree, but an honors award granted after the sophomore year and completion of 18 honors credits, including the 3-credit colloquium and English honors composition course. To earn the General Honors Award, students must also participate in the Honors Freshman Living Learning Community.

**AP/IB credits** are **not** counted as replacements for honors courses.

**No. Honors Classes Offered (5.0):** This is a measure of the total **adjusted** honors main sections available in the term reported, not including labs and thesis. An adjusted main section has 3 or more semester credits, or equivalent, and sections with fewer credits receive a lower prorated value.

Delaware Honors offered a section for every **9.7** enrolled students. The average for all programs was **15.0**. The lower the number, the better.

In the term reported, **67.3%** of honors enrollment was **in honors-only sections; 31.1% was in mixed sections; and 1.6% was in contract sections.** For all programs under review, enrollment by type of honors section was 75.8% honors-only, 15.4 % mixed, and 8.8% contract.

**No. Honors Classes in Key Disciplines (5.0):** The 15 "key" disciplines are biological sciences; business (all); chemistry; communications (especially public speaking); computer science; economics; engineering (all); English; history; math (all); philosophy; physics; political science; psychology; and sociology, anthropology, and gender studies. Interdisciplinary sections, such as those often taken for General Education credit in the first two years, do receive a lesser, prorated discipline "credit" because they introduce students to multiple disciplines in an especially engaging way, often with in-depth discussion.

For this measure, mixed and contract sections are not counted as a section in a key discipline unless students taking the sections for honors credit make up at least 10% of the total section enrollment.

In the term reported, Delaware Honors offered a section in a key discipline for every **9.6 honors students.** The average for all programs is **24.7.** The lower the number, the better.

Of **138 adjusted sections in key disciplines**, **62 all were honors-only sections**. The most sections were in engineering (unusual), history, English, chemistry, biology, and business, along with economics and biology. Political science and math had at least four sections each. All key disciplines were represented.

Delaware Honors offered 14 seminars, across three main topical areas: Arts/Humanities; History/Culture; Social/Behavior. An example: "American Founders and the First Rowdy Decades of the Early Republic." Another example: "Plagues and Peoples in Human History."

**Extent of Honors Enrollment (4.5):** Not all honors students take an honors class each term, especially after the first two years. Programs that have fewer honors classes and thesis options for upper-division honors students will *generally* have fewer total members in good standing who are actually enrolled in a given term. (Please be aware, however, that honors students not enrolled in a class for a term are still tied to the honors community through residential and extracurricular activities.) *Our research shows that this measure is closely related to honors completion rates, i.e., the number of students who complete honors requirements by the time they graduate.*

For example, if a program has 1,800 individual students enrolled in a given term, and 3,000 students in good standing, the level of enrollment was .67, an indication that honors class enrollment is somewhat below average, especially in upper-division classes. **Delaware honors has a ratio of 1.57**, well above the average of 1.30 for all programs.

**Average Class Size, Honors-only Sections (3.5):** Offered mostly in the first two years, honors-only classes tend to be smaller and, as the name implies, have no or very few students other than those in the honors program. These class sections always are much smaller than mixed or contract sections, or regular non-honors class sections in the university.

The average honors-only class size at Delaware Honors is **20.6 students**. The average for all programs is **17.5 students.**

**Average Class Size, Overall (3.5):** The overall class calculation is based on the *proportion* of honors students in each type of class (honors-only, mixed honors, and honors contract sections). Thus it is not a raw average. The overall honors-credit class size is **26.6 students**, a bit higher than the average for all programs of **24.9 students**.

These class size averages also do not correspond to the number of students per honors section ratings above. The reason is that, in computing average class size metrics, we include enrollment in each 1-2-credit section, not just sections with 3 or more credits.

Along with an honors-only class size of 20.6 students (listed above), the program's mixed honors sections have an average size of **39.7 students,** and the contract sections with honors credit for individual honors students average **19.6 students.** Across all programs, the average mixed honors section has 68.6 students, and the average contract section has 56.6 students.

**Honors Grad Rate Adjusted to SAT (5.0):** The rating is the based on the actual grad rate for students who entered the program six years earlier, whether or not the students remained in honors. The **actual rate of 94.0%** is also compared to the rates of other programs with the same test score entry requirement range, and then adjusted upward if the program is performing above other programs in the same range, or downward if the performance is less than other programs in the same range. The rate here is definitely upward, to **96.6%.**

**Grad Rate Adjusted to Freshman Retention Rate (4.5):** This rate compares the actual grad rate above to a predicted grade rate when freshman retention rates are considered. The actual grad rate is **1.65 points higher** than the predicted rate. For all programs, the actual grad rate is **.33 points lower** than the predicted rate.

**Ratio of Staff to Honors Students (3.0):** There is 1 staff member for every **201.7** students. (Mean ratio for all programs is 1 staff member for every **127.9** students.)

**Honors Residence Halls, Amenities (3.0):** About 530 first-year honors student live in Redding Hall. The residence has traditional double rooms and hall baths. The location is quite good. The nearest dining is in Russell Hall.

"All freshman Honors students are required to live in Honors housing during their first year unless they are living at home with a parent/guardian. Freshman Honors Housing is important because it gives students an opportunity to study together, share their talents and interests with each other, and also have upper-division Honors peer mentors (Munson Fellows) who guide them through their first year. The Munson Fellows are specially trained to assist with academic questions and registration, but are also event planners and community builders to give the freshmen a complete living/learning experience."

As for upperclassmen, Harter and Sharp Halls are the honors residences. About 90 live in Sharp, which is air-conditioned; another 30 or so live in Harter, which is not air-conditioned. The most convenient dining for both is the Caesar Rodney Dining Complex.

**Honors Residence Halls, Availability (4.5):** This rating compares the number of occupants in honors residence halls to the number of honors freshman and sophomore members in good standing. The ratio for the program is **.70** places for each first- and second-year student. The median for all programs is .49 places.

**Prestigious Awards (4.0):** The awards that we track and include are listed in the section titled "Prestigious Scholarships." The awards are sometimes won by students who are not in an honors college or program, but increasingly many are enrolled in honors programs. It is also a trend that honors colleges and programs help to prepare their students for the awards competitions.

An extremely high percentage of prestigious scholarship winners from the University of Delaware have been students or graduates of the honors program. UD students have won 10 Rhodes Scholarships, three Marshall awards, one Gates Cambridge Scholarship, and 20 Truman Scholarships. They have also won 43 Goldwater Scholarships.

**UNRATED FEATURES**

**Continuation GPA Requirement:** After completion of the freshman year = Cumulative GPA of 3.20; after completion of the sophomore and junior year = Cumulative GPA of 3.30.

**What is the GPA for graduation with honors (program honors or university honors, if the latter is a formal outcome for the program)?** Cumulative GPA of 3.40.

**Academic Strengths, National Rankings:** This is based on national rankings of *graduate* programs in all but engineering and business, where undergraduate rankings are used. One of the weaknesses of the *U.S. News* rankings is that they focus on too many wealth-related metrics while ignoring their own assessments of academic departments. The rankings listed below are for all universities, public or private.

Almost all of the academic departments at Delaware are in the top 100 nationally, including education (34), engineering (56), chemistry (59), English and sociology (63), history (64), psychology (66), computer science (68), physics (71), math (74), business (78), and earth sciences (78). Chemical engineering is especially strong.

**Internships, Professional Development, Community Engagement:** "Using funds from generous Honors Program donors, the Honors Program has created Honors Enrichment Awards. These awards are designed to assist students with funding for non-credit bearing enrichment activities related to their academic and professional pursuits. Honors students may request up to $3,000 and we offer a fall semester and spring semester cycle.

"During the Fall 2017 semester, 15 students were awarded funds to participate in a variety of internships, volunteer activities, special projects and independent research. A few of these projects are highlighted below:

1. Historical research in Poland and Germany regarding the Holocaust. This student's grandfather is a holocaust survivor and the student was able to research and visit the concentration camp where he stayed and review historical documents related to his stay. She plans to use this research to write a book.

2. A student traveled to Tanzania to volunteer for a mobile medical clinic. She also participated in workshops with local community members focusing on preventative care.

3. A pre-veterinary science student lived in Denmark on a hog farm for one month learning about their practices and how those might influence or improve practices in the United States.

4. A student traveled to the Angel Island Immigration Station in San Francisco to film the site, conduct interviews with descendants of those who had gone through the center and to film major Asian centers around Francisco in the hopes of creating a media document."

**Undergraduate Research:** "As of graduation this upcoming spring 2018, we have approximately 60 students conducting undergraduate research with a thesis on track to complete an Honors Degree with Distinction. We also have approximately 100 Honors students that conducted undergraduate research this past summer with our Summer Scholars Program."

**Honors Study Abroad:** "The University of Delaware was the first institution to have a study abroad trip (the 1923 trip to Paris). Since then, UD has been a leader in Study Abroad. One reason for UD's success is our winter session (optional 5 week term in January through early February). We have a large variety of study abroad programs in the winter session, allowing our students to travel even if their majors are structured so that they cannot be away for an entire semester. In our study abroad history, we have been to all seven continents. There are merit-based and need-based scholarships for study abroad, ranging from $500 to $4,000.

"UD semester study-abroad programs are available in Japan, Argentina, Spain, England, France, and Austria. Semester exchange programs are available with Bond University, Australia; The German American Federation; Hong Kong Polytechnic, Lisbon University, Portugal; Lyon, France; Seinan, Japan; Soka, Japan; the Swiss School of Tourism and Hospitality; and the University of Pretoria, South Africa.

"The UD Honors Program just completed its fourth winter session Honors-only Study Abroad trip to Italy this year. Students must apply for this trip through a competitive selection process. They take two 300-

level Honors courses: one content course and one service learning course that they plan together as a group the semester before the trip.

"The Honors Program also coordinates the only international Alternative Spring Break Trip to the Dominican Republic. The trip cost is subsidized by the Honors Program."

**Financial Aid:** "*All freshmen admitted to the University of Delaware's Honors Program are also offered a merit scholarship.* These awards vary from $1,000 a year to a full ride that covers tuition, room, board and fees. Merit Awards are offered irrespective of financial need. Awards for non-residents are larger than residents as a result of the tuition difference. The University also sponsors the Distinguished Scholars program, which allows the strongest Honors applicants each year to compete for named awards. These awards range in amounts that cover tuition to those that provide funding for all expenses including a stipend for an enrichment activity."

**Honors Fees:** None.

**Placement of Honors Graduates:**

**Post-Graduate Education**

Columbia University, Duke University, Johns Hopkins University, Harvard University, Massachusetts Institute of Technology, New York University, Stanford University, UC Berkeley University of Michigan, University of Oxford, University of Pennsylvania, Yale University

**Employers**

Deloitte, Ernst & Young, Facebook, GlaxoSmithKline, Google, JPMorgan Chase, National Institutes of Health, Peace Corps, The Vanguard Group, U.S. Army & Air Force

**Degree of Difference**: This is difference between (1) the average SAT scores for recently enrolled honors students (1437) and (2) the average test scores for all students in the university (1290) as a whole. The difference may be an indication of how "elite" honors students may be perceived as compared to students in the university as a whole. **Please keep in mind that neither the high nor low selectivity of an honors program determines how effective the program may be.**

***Editor's Note:*** *The Wilkes Honors College at FAU, in Jupiter, Florida, is unique in that it is physically separated—by 40 miles—from the main university in Boca Raton.* ***"It is the nation's only university-affiliated, free-standing honors college,"*** *to take a quote straight from the college site This means that all classes are honors, so the WHC has several advantages when our methodology is applied.*

**NAME**: HARRIET L. WILKES HONORS COLLEGE OF FLORIDA ATLANTIC UNIVERSITY

**Date Established:** 1999

**Location**: The John D. MacArthur Campus of Florida Atlantic University in Jupiter, Florida

**University Full-time Undergraduate Enrollment (2017):** 25,402, main university in Boca Raton.

**Honors Members in Good Standing**: 432 in Jupiter; (mean size of all programs is 2,030).

**Honors Average Admission Test Score(s)**: ACT, 29; SAT, 1300.

**Average High School GPA/Class Rank:** 4.5, weighted.

**Basic Admission Requirements:** "The WHC does not have a set minimum for board scores or GPA."

**Application Deadline(s):** *Please verify with each program, as some deadlines could change.* To be considered for prestigious WHC scholarships (e.g., Flagler), early application is encouraged. The deadline for applications is May 1 for upcoming academic year. Application via the Common App is recommended.

**Honors Programs with SAT scores from 1286—1300:** Florida Atlantic, Washington State, West Virginia.

**Administrative Staff:** 15.

**RATINGS AT A GLANCE:** For all mortarboard ratings immediately below, a score of 5 is the maximum and represents a comparison with all rated honors colleges and programs. More detailed explanations follow the "mortarboard" ratings.

**PERCEPTION** * **OF UNIVERSITY AS A WHOLE, NOT OF HONORS:** 🎓🎓🎓

*Perception is based on the university's ranking among public universities in the 2018 U.S. News Best Colleges report. Please bear in mind that the better the U.S. News ranking, the more difficult it is for an honors college or program to have a rating that equals or improves on the magazine ranking.

**OVERALL HONORS RATING:** 🎓🎓🎓🎓🎓

**Curriculum Requirements:** 🎓🎓🎓🎓🎓

**Number of Honors Classes Offered:** 🎓🎓🎓🎓🎓

**Number of Honors Classes in Key Disciplines:** 🎓🎓🎓🎓🎓

**Extent of Honors Enrollment:** 🎓🎓🎓🎓🎓

**Honors-only Class Size:** 🎓🎓🎓 1/2

**Overall Class Size (Honors-only plus mixed, contract):** 🎓🎓🎓🎓🎓

**Honors Grad Rate Adjusted to SAT:** 🎓🎓🎓

**Grad Rate Adjusted to Freshman Retention Rate:** 🎓🎓🎓

**Ratio of Staff to Students:** 🎓🎓🎓🎓🎓

**Priority Registration: Yes,** well, the only registration is by honors students.

**Honors Housing Amenities:** 🎓🎓🎓🎓 1/2

**Honors Housing Availability:** 🎓🎓🎓🎓🎓

**Prestigious Awards:** 🎓🎓

## RATING SCORES AND EXPLANATIONS:

**Curriculum Requirements (5.0):** The most important rating category, the curriculum completion requirement (classes required to complete honors) defines not only what honors students should learn but also the extent to which honors students and faculty are connected in the classroom. If there is a thesis or capstone requirement, it reinforces the individual contact and research skills so important to learning.

The average number of honors semester hours required for completion across all programs is 30.0.

"The WHC offers a four-year, all-honors curriculum, taught by its own faculty of 37 full-time members, all of whom hold the highest degree in their field and represent the full range of liberal arts and sciences disciplines. Twenty-two other scholars and scientists hold affiliate faculty status in the College.

"Requirements for the baccalaureate degree include three team-taught interdisciplinary courses, an internship or study abroad experience, and completion of a mentored [6-credit] senior thesis. With a student to faculty ration of 12:1, the WHC offers the intimacy and close faculty attention of a private college, with access to all of the benefits and opportunities of a large public research university. The Jupiter and Boca Raton campuses are linked by a shuttle service that operates throughout the day. The main campus also hosts a small Honors Program and some departments offer students the opportunity to earn honors in the major, but these programs are run separately from the Wilkes Honors College."

**AP/IB credits** are **counted**: Up to 45 credits.

**No. Honors Classes Offered (5.0):** This is a measure of the total **adjusted** honors main sections available in the term reported, not including labs and thesis. An adjusted main section has 3 or more semester credits, or equivalent, and sections with fewer credits receive a lower prorated value.

FAU honors offered a section for every **5.3** enrolled students. The average for all programs was **15.0**. The lower the number, the better.

Naturally, **100%** of honors enrollment was **in honors-only sections.**

**No. Honors Classes in Key Disciplines (5.0):** The 15 "key" disciplines are biological sciences; business (all); chemistry; communications (especially public speaking); computer science; economics; engineering (all); English; history; math (all); philosophy; physics; political science; psychology; and sociology, anthropology, and gender studies. Interdisciplinary sections, such as those often taken for General Education credit in the first two years, do receive a lesser, prorated discipline "credit" because they introduce students to multiple disciplines in an especially engaging way, often with in-depth discussion.

For this measure, mixed and contract sections are not counted as a section in a key discipline unless students taking the sections for honors credit make up at least 10% of the total section enrollment.

In the term reported, the honors college offered a section in a key discipline for every **7.3 honors students.** The average for all programs is **24.7**. The lower the number, the better.

Out of **61 adjusted sections in key disciplines, all were honors-only sections**. The most sections were in biology, followed by English and math. There were four sections each in chemistry, economics, history, philosophy, and psychology. In keeping with the WHC's identity as a true liberal arts and sciences college, there were no sections in computer science or engineering. "However, special pathway programs with other FAU colleges, including engineering and computer science, nursing, and business, allow WHC students to earn a second bachelors or masters degree in just one extra year."

"The college is dedicated to helping students integrate knowledge across fields of study and requires that students take three interdisciplinary seminars (1–3 credits each), which are team taught by two faculty members from different disciplines."

**Extent of Honors Enrollment (5.0):** Across the country, not all honors students take an honors class each term, especially after the first two years. Programs that have fewer honors classes and thesis options for upper-division honors students will *generally* have fewer total members in good standing who are actually enrolled in a given term. (Please be aware, however, that honors students not enrolled in a class for a term are still tied to the honors community through residential and extracurricular activities.) *Our research shows that this measure is closely related to honors completion rates, i.e., the number of students who complete honors requirements by the time they graduate.*

For example, if a program has 1,800 individual students enrolled in a given term, and 3,000 students in good standing, the level of enrollment was .67, an indication that honors class enrollment is somewhat below average, especially in upper-division classes. Given that the entire student body is in honors, WHC **has a ratio of 3.59**, far above the average of 1.30 for all programs.

**Average Class Size, Honors-only Sections (3.5):** Offered mostly in the first two years, honors-only classes tend to be smaller and, as the name implies, have no or very few students other than those in the honors program. These class sections always are much smaller than mixed or contract sections, or regular non-honors class sections in the university.

The average honors-only class size at WHC is **17.9 students**. The average for all programs is **17.5 students.**

**Average Class Size, Overall (5.0):** The overall class calculation is based on the *proportion* of honors students in each type of class (honors-only, mixed honors, and honors contract sections). Thus, it is not a raw average. The overall honors-credit class size at WHC is **17.9 students**, versus the average for all programs of **24.7 students**.

These class size averages also do not correspond to the number of students per honors section ratings above. The reason is that, in computing average class size metrics, we include enrollment in each 1-2-credit section, not just sections with 3 or more credits.

The WHC has no mixed or contract honors sections.

**Honors Grad Rate Adjusted to SAT (3.0):** The rating is the based on the actual grad rate for students who entered the program six years earlier, whether or not the students remained in honors. The **actual rate of 82.0%** is also compared to the rates of other programs with the same test score entry requirement range, and then adjusted upward if the program is performing above other programs in the same range, or downward if the performance is less than other programs in the same range. The rate at WHC is downward, to **80.9%.**

**Grad Rate Adjusted to Freshman Retention Rate (3.0):** This rate compares the actual WHC grad rate above to a predicted grade rate when freshman retention rates are considered. The actual grad rate is **4.32 points lower** than the predicted rate. For all programs, the actual grad rate is **.33 points lower** than the predicted rate.

**Ratio of Staff to Honors Students (5.0):** At the WHC there is 1 staff member for every **28.3** students. (Mean ratio for all programs is 1 staff member for every **127.9** students.)

**Honors Residence Halls, Amenities (4.5):** The MacArthur Campus Residence halls "provide a comfortable living environment where the intellectual and social life of the Wilkes Honors College is extended. Educational and cultural programming complements the classroom experience and underscores the commitment of the College to the development of a vital 'living and learning' community. **Each student has her/his private bedroom within a four-bedroom suite, and residence hall housing is mandatory for the first two years of enrollment.**

"Each bedroom is equipped with unlimited access Ethernet connections and basic cable television service. The residence halls also offer a multipurpose room with large-screen TV and free laundry facilities. Features for each room include an extra-long bed (36" X 80" extra-long twin mattress), desk, chair and dresser. Residents may bring a small refrigerator and/or microwave.

"Enhancing the student experience, the residence halls are located adjacent to the campus recreation field, dining facilities, and the Student Resources building which houses the popular 'Burrow' (named for our Burrowing Owl mascot), which includes a game room, lounge, stage, and the Student Government offices. **Just across the street from the College is the Roger Dean Chevrolet Baseball Stadium (spring training center for the St. Louis Cardinals and Florida Marlins), along with Downtown Abacoa's shops and restaurants."**

**Honors Residence Halls, Availability (5.0):** This rating compares the number of occupants in honors residence halls to the number of honors freshman and sophomore members in good standing. The ratio for the WHC is **1.30** places for each first- and second-year student. The median for all programs is .49 places.

**Prestigious Awards (2.0):** The awards that we track and include are listed in the section titled "Prestigious Scholarships." The awards are sometimes won by students who are not in an honors college or program, but increasingly many are enrolled in honors programs. It is also a trend that honors colleges and programs help to prepare their students for the awards competitions.

The Dean reports the following accomplishments:

"The Wilkes Honors College oversees the University's prestige scholarship committee, which was established in 2008.

"Recent Prestige Scholarship's Awarded at to Wilkes Honors College students include:

| | |
|---|---|
| 2017 | Ernest F. Hollings Undergraduate Scholarship: Samantha Iliff |
| 2013 | Boren: Andrea Bailey |
| 2011 - 2012 | Fulbright for study in Macedonia: Cassidy Henry |
| 2010 | Boren for study in Tanzania: Stephen Jones |
| 2006 | Boren for study in Russia: Daniel Gopman |
| 2007 | Boren for study in Morocco: Heather Chase |
| 2007 | Jack Kent Cooke Graduate Award: Sarah Wiggill |

**UNRATED FEATURES**

**Continuation and Honors Graduation GPA Requirement:** 3.00 to retain scholarships, and 2.00 to graduate.

**Academic Strengths, National Rankings:** The best way to think about the WHC is that it is a liberal arts and sciences college unto itself, with a heavy concentration (70%) of science majors. The WHC has no rated academic departments of its own; the main university does have some ranked programs and, unlike the WHC, offers engineering as a major. The WHC offers 29 "major concentrations." These are listed below, alphabetically:

American Studies, Anthropology, Art;
Biological Anthropology, Biology, Business;
Chemistry;
Economics, English Literature, Environmental Studies;
History;
Interdisciplinary Critical Theory, International Studies;
Latin American Studies, Law and Society;
Marine Biology, Mathematics, Mathematical Sciences (interdisciplinary), Medical Humanities
Neuroscience;
Philosophy, Physics, Political Science, Pre-Med, Psychology;
Spanish;
Women's Studies;
Writing (creative, professional).

**Internships, Professional Development, Community Engagement:** "It is a requirement that all Wilkes Honors College students must complete a mentored internship or study abroad, and almost all of our students (95%) complete at least one internship. Unless special permission is granted, these internships are expected to occur outside the mentorship of our own faculty (WHC faculty mentorship naturally occurs due to our required senior thesis). Internships are as varied as our students' interests, ranging from interning with attorneys and judges, shadowing physicians, interning at El Sol (a local resource center for our large, Spanish-speaking immigrant community), many non-profit organizations, NGOs, charitable foundations, nature sanctuaries, biotechnology companies, science museums, and businesses of all types.

"A full-time staff member advises and supports Wilkes Honors College students with identifying and organizing her/his internship. In addition, this staff member works closely with the University Career Center in identifying new and existing internship opportunities.

"The Wilkes Honors College is also home to the Kenan Social Engagement Program, a scholarship program that combines a course in social entrepreneurship with service learning and start-up funding for social ventures. Each fall, students take a co-taught course on social entrepreneurship and write a business plan for their own social venture. Four plans are selected from the class for scholarship funding. The best plan is awarded a $10,000 grant to start the venture, and up to three others are each awarded $2,500."

**Undergraduate Research:** "The Senior Honors Thesis is required, so all students conduct original, mentored research, and many of our students conduct research for multiple semesters/years leading up to their thesis. Multi-year research is especially common for our **science students (who make up about 70%** of our student population). This is possible for a number of reasons unique to our campus: **two world-renowned research institutes exist on our campus: the Scripps Research Institute – Florida, the only Scripps Institute outside of California, and the Max Planck Florida Institute for Neuroscience, the only Max Planck Institute outside of Europe.**

"In addition, our campus houses FAU's Brain Institute and Jupiter Life Science Initiative, each of which host top NIH-funded scientists. Nearby is FAU's Harbor Branch Oceanographic Institute, providing students interested in marine biology with remarkable research opportunities. Therefore, our undergraduates have unprecedented access to working with scientists in all STEM fields. As a result, **since 2002, sixty-eight publications, most of them in top-tier, peer-reviewed journals, have included a Wilkes Honors College student as a co-author."**

**Honors Study Abroad:** "The college typically offers at least one study abroad program led directly by one or more Wilkes Honors College faculty members. Programs have been offered in Spain, Guatemala, London, the European Union, Ecuador, Israel, and Ireland. Many students also participate in study abroad through other university programs and transfer credit back to the college.

"We have an internal, prestigious scholarship that funds 20 students per year, which was endowed by the Kenan Charitable Trust. These four-year scholarships, known as the Henry Morrison Flagler Scholarships, are awarded to five incoming students each year. Each scholarship includes funding for tuition, room & board, and four experiential summer learning opportunities: an Outward Bound experience, two internships (one at a non-profit and one at a for-profit organization), and an academic study abroad experience. Therefore, each of these students completes a study-abroad experience prior to graduation."

**Financial Aid: "National Merit Finalists receive cost of attendance at FAU.** The University will be recognized as a university sponsor by the National Merit Scholarship Program in 2018.

"Every student admitted to the Wilkes Honors College is offered a merit-based scholarship that is renewable each year until graduation if the student maintains a 3.0 GPA. Need-based scholarships are also awarded. We award about $1.5 million per year for these purposes. The average scholarship we offered in 2017-18 was $4,135. Ninety-five percent of the earnings from the College's endowment go to student scholarships, and we have a number of scholarships named for their donors, including scholarships that support first-generation-in-college students.

*"High-achieving prospective students may apply to FAU's College of Medicine at the same time they apply to the Wilkes Honors College.* Students accepted into this program are known as Wilkes Medical Scholars, and as long as they maintain certain standards, they will matriculate directly into medical school at FAU after finishing their baccalaureate degree.

"Florida residents with at least a 1290 SAT receive the State of Florida's Bright Futures scholarship, which covers the cost of tuition, and for students with at least an 1190 SAT, a reduced Bright Futures scholarship covers 75% of tuition.

"There are some out-of-state tuition waivers available to cover the tuition differential between in-state and out-of-state rates."

**Honors Fees:** "There are no additional fees for being in the Wilkes Honors College. Tuition, room and board are the same at the Wilkes Honors College as for the rest of FAU."

**Placement of Honors Graduates:** "We now have 1,011 alumni. Over 70% of our graduates go on to graduate or professional (primarily medicine and law) schools. Our graduates have earned advanced degrees from universities including: Alabama, Auburn, Baltimore, Baylor, UC Berkeley, Boston University, British Columbia, Brown, Cal Tech, Central Florida, Chicago, Chicago Medical School,

Cleveland Clinic, Colorado, Columbia, Connecticut, Cornell, Emory, Florida, Florida International, Florida State, George Mason, Georgetown, Georgia Tech, Harvard Medical School, Hawaii, Hofstra, Howard, Indiana, Iowa, Johns Hopkins, Kansas, Kent State, King's College (UK), London School of Economics, London University of Durham, Loyola – Chicago, Michigan, Michigan State, Massey (New Zealand), Minnesota, Mississippi, MIT, Nebraska, Northwestern, Nova, NYU, Ohio State, Penn State, Pepperdine, Purdue, Rosalind Franklin, San Jose State, Sarah Lawrence, Scripps-FL, South Carolina, South Florida, Southern California, St. Andrew's (Scotland), St. George's (Grenada), St. Matthew's (West Indies), SUNY-Stony Brook, Syracuse, Tennessee, Texas A&M, Tufts, Tulane, UGA, UNC Chapel Hill, University of Kent, University of Miami, US Naval Academy, UVA, Vanderbilt, Wake Forest, Washington University, West Indies, William and Mary, Wisconsin, and Yale.

**Degree of Difference**: This is difference between (1) the average SAT scores for recently enrolled honors students (1300) and (2) the average test scores for all students in the university (1140, FAU Boca Raton) as a whole. The difference may be an indication of how "elite" honors students may be perceived as compared to students in the university as a whole. **Please keep in mind that neither the high nor low selectivity of an honors program determines how effective the program may be.**

**NAME**: UNIVERSITY OF GEORGIA HONORS PROGRAM

**Date Established:** 1960

**Location**: Athens, Georgia

**University Full-time Undergraduate Enrollment (2017):** 27,951

**Honors Members in Good Standing**: 2,497; (mean size of all programs is 2,030).

**Honors Average Admission Test Score(s)**: ACT, 33.26; SAT, 1490.

**Average High School GPA/Class Rank:** 4.12, weighted.

**Basic Admission Requirements:** ACT, 31; SAT, 1440; GPA, 3.7, weighted.

**Application Deadline(s):** *Please verify with each program, as some deadlines could change.* December 1, 2018 to January 15, 2019.

**Honors Programs with SAT scores from 1471—1510:** Clemson, Georgia, Illinois, Minnesota, Oklahoma, Rutgers, South Carolina, UT Austin.

**Administrative Staff:** 21.

**RATINGS AT A GLANCE:** For all mortarboard ratings immediately below, a score of 5 is the maximum and represents a comparison with all rated honors colleges and programs. More detailed explanations follow the "mortarboard" ratings.

**PERCEPTION\* OF UNIVERSITY AS A WHOLE, NOT OF HONORS:** 🎓🎓🎓🎓🎓

\*Perception is based on the university's ranking among public universities in the 2018 U.S. News Best Colleges report. Please bear in mind that the better the U.S. News ranking, the more difficult it is for an honors college or program to have a rating that equals or improves on the magazine ranking.

**OVERALL HONORS RATING:** 🎓🎓🎓🎓 1/2

**Curriculum Requirements:** 🎓🎓🎓🎓 1/2

**Number of Honors Classes Offered:** 🎓🎓🎓🎓

**Number of Honors Classes in Key Disciplines:** 🎓🎓🎓🎓

**Extent of Honors Enrollment:** 🎓🎓🎓🎓

**Honors-only Class Size:** 🎓🎓🎓🎓

**Overall Class Size (Honors-only plus mixed, contract):** 🎓🎓🎓🎓

**Honors Grad Rate Adjusted to SAT:** 🎓🎓🎓🎓

**Grad Rate Adjusted to Freshman Retention Rate:** 🎓🎓🎓 1/2

**Ratio of Staff to Students:** 🎓🎓🎓🎓

**Priority Registration: Yes,** honors students register for all courses, honors and otherwise, with the first group of students during each year they are in the program.

**Honors Housing Amenities:** 🎓🎓🎓🎓

**Honors Housing Availability:** 🎓🎓 1/2

**Prestigious Awards:** 🎓🎓🎓🎓🎓

## RATING SCORES AND EXPLANATIONS:

**Curriculum Requirements (4.5):** The most important rating category, the curriculum completion requirement (classes required to complete honors) defines not only what honors students should learn but also the extent to which honors students and faculty are connected in the classroom. If there is a thesis or capstone requirement, it reinforces the individual contact and research skills so important to learning.

The average number of honors semester hours required for completion across all programs is 30.0.

For Graduation with **Highest Honors**, students must complete at least 34 credits, including 9 courses of honors credit (about 30 semester hours). These must include at least 1 honors seminar and at least 3 upper-division honors courses. Students must also complete a 6-credit thesis, OR a 6-credit internship with a research component, OR 9-12 credits in graduate courses. *Finally, students must finish with a very high GPA, 3.90.*

A minimum of 9 Honors courses of 3 to 4 credit hours each are required in addition to a 1-hour Introduction to Honors seminar, which is required of all first-term Honors students. (Transfer students accepted to the Honors Program are required to take 6 Honors courses.)

No hours required for Honors contract (option), experiences, or thesis, but courses in these areas can be used to satisfy Honors graduation requirements.

Honors capstone hours= 6 or 9 hours

Approved Capstone Options (CURO = Center for Undergraduate Research Opportunities):

1. Thesis Capstone: Three hours of CURO-approved research (4960H, 4970H, or 4980H) and a CURO-approved thesis (HONS 4990H or Honors version of departmental equivalent)

2. Internship Capstone: CURO-approved research (4960H, 4970H, or 4980H) and Honors Internship (HONS 4800H or Honors version of departmental equivalent)

3. Graduate Coursework Capstone: Three graduate-level courses (6000+)

At least 3 of the courses (9 hours) must be upper division.

Departmental honors hours may be used to satisfy Honors course requirements.

For **Graduation with High Honors**, students must complete the same credit thresholds as above, but the *GPA requirement is 3.70.*

For **Graduation with Honors**, the student must complete 28 credits. There is no thesis or capstone requirement. *The final GPA must be at least 3.40.*

**AP/IB credits** are **not** counted as replacements for honors courses.

**No. Honors Classes Offered (4.0):** This is a measure of the total **adjusted** honors main sections available in the term reported, not including labs and thesis. An adjusted main section has 3 or more semester credits, or equivalent, and sections with fewer credits receive a lower prorated value. Georgia Honors offered a section for every **13.3** enrolled students. The average for all programs is also **15.0**. The lower the number, the better.

In the term reported, an impressive **79.5%** of honors enrollment was **in honors-only sections; 6.6% was in mixed sections; and 13.9% was in contract sections, an improvement over 2016.** For all programs under review, enrollment by type of honors section was 75.8% honors-only, 15.4 % mixed, and 8.8% contract.

**No. Honors Classes in Key Disciplines (4.0):** The 15 "key" disciplines are biological sciences; business (all); chemistry; communications (especially public speaking); computer science; economics; engineering (all); English; history; math (all); philosophy; physics; political science; psychology; and sociology, anthropology, and gender studies. Interdisciplinary sections, such as those often taken for General Education credit in the first two years, do receive a lesser, prorated discipline "credit" because they introduce students to multiple disciplines in an especially engaging way, often with in-depth discussion.

For this measure, mixed and contract sections are not counted as a section in a key discipline unless students taking the sections for honors credit make up at least 10% of the total section enrollment.

In the term reported, the Georgia Honors offered a section in a key discipline for every **22.3 honors students.** The average for all programs is **24.7**. The lower the number, the better.

Out of **80 adjusted sections in key disciplines**, **56 were honors-only sections**. *Every discipline* was well-represented in the distribution of classes, except for engineering, which has very few majors at UGA.

Georgia Honors is all about honors courses in the major disciplines, and does not offer a series of seminars.

**Extent of Honors Enrollment (4.0):** Not all honors students take an honors class each term, especially after the first two years. Programs that have fewer honors classes and thesis options for upper-division honors students will *generally* have fewer total members in good standing who are actually enrolled in a given term. (Please be aware, however, that honors students not enrolled in a class for a term are still tied to the honors community through residential and extracurricular activities.) *Our research shows that this measure is closely related to honors completion rates, i.e., the number of students who complete honors requirements by the time they graduate.*

For example, if a program has 1,800 individual students enrolled in a given term, and 3,000 students in good standing, the level of enrollment was .67, an indication that honors class enrollment is somewhat below average, especially in upper-division classes. **Georgia honors has a ratio of 1.32**, essentially the same as the average of 1.30 for all programs.

**Average Class Size, Honors-only Sections (4.0):** Offered mostly in the first two years, honors-only classes tend to be smaller and, as the name implies, have no or very few students other than those in the honors program. These class sections always are much smaller than mixed or contract sections, or regular non-honors class sections in the university.

The average honors-only class size at UGA Honors is **17.5 students**. The average for all programs was also **17.5 students.**

**Average Class Size, Overall (4.0):** The overall class calculation is based on the *proportion* of honors students in each type of class (honors-only, mixed honors, and honors contract sections). Thus it is not a raw average. The overall honors-credit class size is **24.1 students**, versus the average for all programs of **24.9 students**.

These class size averages also do not correspond to the number of students per honors section ratings above. The reason is that, in computing average class size metrics, we include enrollment in each 1-2-credit section, not just sections with 3 or more credits.

Along with an honors-only class size of 17.5 students (listed above), the program's mixed honors sections have an average size of **69.0 students,** and the contract sections with honors credit for individual honors students average **45.3 students.** Across all programs, the average mixed honors section has 68.6 students, and the average contract section has 56.6 students.

**Honors Grad Rate Adjusted to SAT (4.0):** The rating is the based on the actual grad rate for students who entered the program six years earlier, whether or not the students remained in honors. The **actual rate of 94.25%** is also compared to the rates of other programs with the same test score entry requirement range, and then adjusted upward if the program is performing above other programs in the same range, or downward if the performance is less than other programs in the same range. The rate here is slightly downward, to **94.33%.**

**Grad Rate Adjusted to Freshman Retention Rate (3.5):** This rate compares the actual grad rate above to a predicted grade rate when freshman retention rates are considered. The actual grad rate is **1.1 points**

**lower** than the predicted rate. (UGA has one of the highest freshman retention rates of any public university—95%, a high bar to meet). For all programs, the actual grad rate is **.33 points lower** than the predicted rate.

**Ratio of Staff to Honors Students (4.0):** There is 1 staff member for every **118.9** students. (Mean ratio for all programs is 1 staff member for every **127.9** students.)

**Honors Residence Halls, Amenities (4.0):** "Myers Hall serves as the Honors magnet residence hall at UGA. This beautifully renovated hall is home to 250 first-year Honors students, affording them the opportunity to live and study in a learning community of like-minded peers. An Honors satellite advising office is also conveniently located in Myers Hall. Myers Hall features a large lobby, community space with a working piano, and conference rooms for student use."

About 81% of the rooms at Myers are traditional doubles with hall baths. The remainder are suite-style; all rooms at Myers are air-conditioned, and there is onsite laundry. The nearest dining locations are at Snelling Dining Hall and Oglethorpe Dining Hall. Myers also has a kitchen on each floor.

**UGA Honors encourages as much interaction as possible between honors students and their fellow students at UGA**, so honors students may choose (and most do so) a non-honors residence hall because of location or friendships. Another example of the interaction of UGA Honors and the university community is the Center for Undergraduate Research Opportunities (CURO), initiated and still administered by UGA Honors but now with non-honors students accounting for 60% of participants.

**Honors Residence Halls, Availability (2.5):** This rating compares the number of occupants in honors residence halls to the number of honors freshman and sophomore members in good standing. The ratio for the program is **.20** places for each first- and second-year student. The median for all programs is .49 places. **It should be noted here that Myers meets all of the actual demand for honors residence space, so this rating, while true to the methodology, does not mean UGA Honors fails to meet the needs of its students.**

**Prestigious Awards (5.0):** The awards that we track and include are listed in the section titled "Prestigious Scholarships." The awards are sometimes won by students who are not in an honors college or program, but increasingly many are enrolled in honors programs. It is also a trend that honors colleges and programs help to prepare their students for the awards competitions.

"The Honors Program houses a Major Scholarships Office that processes nationally competitive scholarships and also oversees the most prestigious internal academic scholarship programs at UGA: the Foundation Fellowship and the Ramsey Honors Scholarship.

"During the past decade, **every UGA recipient** of a Rhodes, Marshall, Mitchell, Schwarzman, Gates Cambridge, Beinecke, Truman, Goldwater, and Udall scholarship **was an Honors student**. Honors students, along with non-Honors students, have also been awarded the Fulbright, Boren, NSF GRFP, and Gilman."

The record of UGA students is impressive: 24 Rhodes Scholars, tied with UC Berkeley for 9th place among public universities; seven Gates Cambridge Scholars (5th among public universities); eight

Marshall Scholars; 21 Truman Scholars (12th place among public universities); and higher than the mean for Fulbright and National Science Foundation Scholars.

The record in achieving prestigious Goldwater Scholarships for undergraduate excellence in STEM fields is equally impressive—57 scholarships to date. This ranks 11th among public universities. UGA students have also earned a very high number of Udall Scholarships, 20 so far.

## UNRATED FEATURES

**GPA requirements for continuation in the college or program:** 3.40.

**Graduation with honors (program honors or university honors:** Minimum of 3.40 required for graduation with Honors; minimum of 3.70 required for graduation with High Honors; minimum of 3.90 required for graduation with Highest Honors.

**Academic Strengths, National Rankings:** This is based on national rankings of *graduate* programs in all but engineering and business, where undergraduate rankings are used. One of the weaknesses of the *U.S. News* rankings is that they focus on too many wealth-related metrics while ignoring their own assessments of academic departments. The rankings listed below are for all universities, public or private.

UGA has many nationally ranked academic departments, with an overall departmental ranking of about 63rd in the nation. Among the most recognized departments are business (24), education (37), history (44), political science (45), biology and sociology (46), English (51), economics (55), math (55), chemistry (59) and psychology (75); computer science, earth sciences, and physics are all in the 90s.

**Internships, Professional Development, Community Engagement:** "The Honors Program has three internship programs: one in Savannah, GA at the Office of the U.S. Attorney for the Southern District of Georgia: Honors in Savannah (1 student annually); another at the Greater New York Hospital Association: Honors in New York (2 students annually); **and the signature Honors internship program, Honors in Washington (16 students annually).**

"All Honors in Washington interns live in UGA's DC facility, Delta Hall, in the Capitol Hill neighborhood. The total amount of support provided to Honors students for Honors internships programs during 2017 was $102,000. This represents student stipends only, not additional expenditures such as orientation sessions and group dinners.

"The Honors Program also supports several student organizations that provide local service and civic engagement, including mentoring and tutoring. The annual amount of support averages $25,000-$30,000.

"An additional, individualized recognition is the Ash Service Award, which supplies a $3,000 stipend (typically awarded to three students per year) to cultivate and support a culture of locally focused community service.

"Finally, the Honors Program partners with UGA's Center for Leadership and Service to award up to 10 scholarships of $1,000 each to third-year Honors students with exemplary leadership records on campus and/or in the local community, known as the Crane Leadership Scholars."

**Undergraduate Research:** "The main vehicle to support undergraduate research at UGA is the Center for Undergraduate Research Opportunities, or CURO. CURO was launched by the Honors Program in the late 1990s for Honors students, and it was incubated within the Honors Program in the 2000s. One hallmark of CURO from its beginning is that students can participate in faculty-mentored undergraduate research in any major or discipline for up to a full four years.

"CURO offers several research courses, which are available across campus, as well as a number of undergraduate research programs, including the CURO Honors Scholarship, which provides $3,000 in annual support; the CURO Summer Fellowship, which also provides a $3,000 stipend; and the CURO Symposium, which facilitates the presentation of student research through oral and poster sessions.

"Given the overall success of CURO, in 2010 it was decided to offer participation in CURO to all undergraduate students at UGA regardless of major, discipline, or GPA. CURO continues to be administered and overseen by the Honors Program and to serve Honors students, but it now also features an increasing number of participants who are non-Honors students.

"To briefly illustrate the impact and growth of CURO, as recently as 2013 there were 202 presenters at the annual CURO Symposium, of whom 41% were non-Honors students. At the latest CURO Symposium, in April 2018, there were 575 student presenters, of whom 57% were non-Honors students.

"It should also be noted that since its inception, **every UGA recipient of a major nationally competitive scholarship—such as the Rhodes, Marshall, Mitchell, Beinecke, Gates Cambridge, Goldwater, Truman, and Udall—participated in CURO."**

"To support overall participation in undergraduate research at UGA, a program of CURO Research Assistantships was begun in 2014, which now awards 500 students annually a stipend of $1,000, for a total of $500,000 per annum."

"A new initiative deserves mention—**a [new] UGA living learning community** focused on undergraduate research, known as the R House, which will be launched with 28 student participants this coming fall 2018 and will eventually expand to 40 students. *The director of the R House is Dr. David Williams, who serves as Director of the Honors Program and CURO.* The program will include a tailored 'Introduction to Research' seminar for the R House members to help them identify a faculty mentor. The program will also supply a guaranteed CURO Research Assistantship."

**Honors Study Abroad:** "The Honors Program has its own program of support for study abroad, the Honors International Scholars Program (HISP), which is supported by 12 endowed funds. (Since 2004, the **Honors Program has raised more than $12 million in endowments**, most of which has been in support of study abroad.) During 2017, 59 Honors students were supported at a grand total of $213,000.

"In addition, it should be noted that all first-year Foundation Fellows (the top academic scholarship at UGA, administered by the Honors Program) **study with full financial support at Oxford University** for UGA's Maymester term and reside in UGA's facility on Banbury Road, Oxford."

**Financial Aid:** "In addition to the stipends and grants that are available to Honors students, covered above in relation to study abroad, internships, service, and leadership, the Honors Program oversees and awards **the top merit-based scholarships at UGA: the Foundation Fellowship and the Ramsey Honors Scholarship**.

Combined, the FY 2017 total expenditure for these scholarship programs was $2,602,463. The breakdown for this amount is as follows: $1,243,480 represents scholarship stipends for 87 Foundation Fellows; $195,600 represents scholarship stipends for 26 Ramsey Honors Scholars; programmatic costs for the combined programs were $734,397, which includes dinner seminars, retreats, and individualized travel study and conference grants; and the remainder represents administrative, recruitment, operations, and publishing costs."

**Honors Fees:** None.

**Placement of Honors Graduates:** None listed, but honors program graduates earn admission to the nation's top graduate and professional schools, and gain employment at many of the nation's leading companies and organizations.

**Degree of Difference**: This is difference between (1) the average SAT scores for recently enrolled honors students (1490) and (2) the average test scores for all students in the university (1330) as a whole. The difference may be an indication of how "elite" honors students may be perceived as compared to students in the university as a whole. **Please keep in mind that neither the high nor low selectivity of an honors program determines how effective the program may be.**

**NAME**: GEORGIA STATE UNIVERSITY HONORS COLLEGE

**Date Established:** 2011

**Location**: Atlanta, Georgia

**University Full-time Undergraduate Enrollment (2017):** 25,455

**Honors Members in Good Standing**: 1646; (mean size of all programs is 2,030).

**Honors Average Admission Test Score(s)**: ACT, 31; SAT, 1430.

**Average High School GPA/Class Rank:** 3.90, weighted.

**Basic Admission Requirements:** ACT, 28; SAT, 1320; GPA, 3.5 unweighted.

**Application Deadline(s):** *Please verify with each program, as some deadlines could change.* Early action deadline is November 15, 2018; regular action deadline is March 1, 2019.

**Honors Programs with SAT scores from 1403—1461:** Auburn, Central Florida, Delaware, Iowa, Kansas, Mississippi, Missouri, New Jersey Inst of Technology, Penn State, South Florida, Vermont, Virginia Commonwealth.

**Administrative Staff:** 12.

**RATINGS AT A GLANCE:** For all mortarboard ratings immediately below, a score of 5 is the maximum and represents a comparison with all rated honors colleges and programs. More detailed explanations follow the "mortarboard" ratings.

**PERCEPTION\* OF UNIVERSITY AS A WHOLE, NOT OF HONORS:** 🎓🎓🎓

\*Perception is based on the university's ranking among public universities in the 2018 U.S. News Best Colleges report. Please bear in mind that the better the U.S. News ranking, the more difficult it is for an honors college or program to have a rating that equals or improves on the magazine ranking.

**OVERALL HONORS RATING:** 🎓🎓🎓 1/2

**Curriculum Requirements:** 🎓🎓🎓 1/2

**Number of Honors Classes Offered:** 🎓🎓🎓🎓

**Number of Honors Classes in Key Disciplines:** 🎓🎓🎓🎓 1/2

**Extent of Honors Enrollment:** 🎓🎓🎓

**Honors-only Class Size:** 🎓🎓🎓🎓 1/2

**Overall Class Size (Honors-only plus mixed, contract):** 🎓🎓🎓🎓🎓

**Honors Grad Rate Adjusted to SAT:** 🎓🎓🎓🎓

**Grad Rate Adjusted to Freshman Retention Rate:** 🎓🎓🎓🎓 1/2

**Ratio of Staff to Students:** 🎓🎓🎓 1/2

**Priority Registration: Yes,** honors students register for **all** courses, honors and otherwise, with the first group of students during **each** year they are in the program.

**Honors Housing Amenities:** 🎓🎓🎓 1/2

**Honors Housing Availability:** 🎓🎓🎓

**Prestigious Awards:** 🎓🎓 1/2

## RATING SCORES AND EXPLANATIONS:

**Curriculum Requirements (3.5):** The most important rating category, the curriculum completion requirement (classes required to complete honors) defines not only what honors students should learn but also the extent to which honors students and faculty are connected in the classroom. If there is a thesis or capstone requirement, it reinforces the individual contact and research skills so important to learning.

The average number of honors semester hours required for completion across all programs is 30.0.

Completion of the Advanced and Research Honors level requires a total of 24 honors credits. This includes 18 course credits (including 6 credits in colloquia), and a 6-credit honors thesis. A maximum of 9 course credits may be in the form of honors contract courses.

Completion of Advanced Honors is the same as above, minus the thesis requirement.

General Honors requires 13 credits, six of which must be in honors colloquia.

**AP/IB credits** are **not** counted as replacements for honors courses.

**No. Honors Classes Offered (4.0):** This is a measure of the total **adjusted** honors main sections available in the term reported, not including labs and thesis. An adjusted main section has 3 or more semester credits, or equivalent, and sections with fewer credits receive a lower prorated value.

Georgia State Honors offered a section for every **13.1** enrolled students. The average for all programs was **15.0**. The lower the number, the better.

In the term reported, **75.9%** of honors enrollment was **in honors-only sections; 23.7% was in mixed sections; and .33% was in contract sections.** For all programs under review, enrollment by type of honors section was 75.8% honors-only, 15.4 % mixed, and **8.8%** contract.

**No. Honors Classes in Key Disciplines (4.5):** The 15 "key" disciplines are biological sciences; business (all); chemistry; communications (especially public speaking); computer science; economics; engineering (all); English; history; math (all); philosophy; physics; political science; psychology; and sociology, anthropology, and gender studies. Interdisciplinary sections, such as those often taken for General Education credit in the first two years, do receive a lesser, prorated discipline "credit" because they introduce students to multiple disciplines in an especially engaging way, often with in-depth discussion.

For this measure, mixed and contract sections are not counted as a section in a key discipline unless students taking the sections for honors credit make up at least 10% of the total section enrollment.

In the term reported, the honors college offered a section in a key discipline for every **14.9 honors students.** The average for all programs is **24.7**. The lower the number, the better.

Out of **adjusted sections in key disciplines**, **all were honors-only sections**. The most sections were in English, biology, math, political science, sociology/anthropology, philosophy, and psychology.

The college does offer more than 25 seminars, but most are 1-credit only. But at least seven 3-credit seminars were available, including the timely "Authoritarianisms in the Global Age," "Terrorism and Political Violence," as well as "Employment Law and the Future of Work," and "Technologies of Knowledge." The Honors College is mostly a discipline-oriented program.

**Extent of Honors Enrollment (3.0):** Not all honors students take an honors class each term, especially after the first two years. Programs that have fewer honors classes and thesis options for upper-division honors students will *generally* have fewer total members in good standing who are actually enrolled in a given term. (Please be aware, however, that honors students not enrolled in a class for a term are still tied to the honors community through residential and extracurricular activities.) *Our research shows that this measure is closely related to honors completion rates, i.e., the number of students who complete honors requirements by the time they graduate.*

For example, if a program has 1,800 individual students enrolled in a given term, and 3,000 students in good standing, the level of enrollment was .67, an indication that honors class enrollment is somewhat below average, especially in upper-division classes. **GSU honors has a ratio of .92**, below the average of 1.30 for all programs.

**Average Class Size, Honors-only Sections (4.5):** Offered mostly in the first two years, honors-only classes tend to be smaller and, as the name implies, have no or very few students other than those in the honors program. These class sections always are much smaller than mixed or contract sections, or regular non-honors class sections in the university.

The average honors-only class size at the honors college is **16.2 students**. The average for all programs is **17.5 students.**

**Average Class Size, Overall (5.0):** The overall class calculation is based on the *proportion* of honors students in each type of class (honors-only, mixed honors, and honors contract sections). Thus it is not a raw average. The overall honors-credit class size is **17.0 students**, versus the average for all programs of **24.9 students.**

These class size averages also do not correspond to the number of students per honors section ratings above. The reason is that, in computing average class size metrics, we include enrollment in each 1-2-credit section, not just sections with 3 or more credits.

Along with an honors-only class size of 16.2 students (listed above), the program's mixed honors sections have an average size of **19.5 students,** and the contract sections with honors credit for individual honors students average **18 students.** Across all programs, the average mixed honors section has 68.6 students, and the average contract section has 56.6 students.

**Honors Grad Rate Adjusted to SAT (4.0):** The rating is the based on the actual grad rate for students who entered the program six years earlier, whether or not the students remained in honors. The **actual rate of 85.0%** is also compared to the rates of other programs with the same test score entry requirement range, and then adjusted upward if the program is performing above other programs in the same range, or downward if the performance is less than other programs in the same range. The rate here is the same, **85.0%.**

**Grad Rate Adjusted to Freshman Retention Rate (4.5):** This rate compares the actual grad rate above to a predicted grade rate when freshman retention rates are considered. The actual grad rate is **2.69 points higher** than the predicted rate. For all programs, the actual grad rate is **.33 points lower** than the predicted rate.

**Ratio of Staff to Honors Students (3.5):** There is 1 staff member for every **137.2** students. (Mean ratio for all programs is 1 staff member for every **127.9** students.)

**Honors Residence Halls, Amenities (3.5):** University Commons is the main honors residence, featuring four-bedroom, two-bath apartments. The residence houses about 150 freshmen and upperclassmen. It is air-conditioned. "Georgia State's newest and largest dining hall, at Piedmont Central, is directly across the street."

Patton Hall houses another 75 honors students, and is air-conditioned. It is just north of University Commons and has an adjacent dining facility. About half the rooms are traditional doubles, with the other half being suite style.

**Honors Residence Halls, Availability (3.0):** This rating compares the number of occupants in honors residence halls to the number of honors freshman and sophomore members in good standing. The ratio for the college is **.27** places for each first- and second-year student. The median for all programs is .49 places. **Note:** All honors students are *guaranteed honors housing* if they meet application and payment deadlines.

**Prestigious Awards (2.5):** The awards that we track and include are listed in the section titled "Prestigious Scholarships." The awards are sometimes won by students who are not in an honors college or program, but increasingly many are enrolled in honors programs. It is also a trend that honors colleges and programs help to prepare their students for the awards competitions.

"Since its inception in 2013, the Honors College Office of National Scholarships and Fellowships at Georgia State University has demonstrated a strong showing in the field of nationally competitive scholarships and fellowships. Throughout its evolution, Georgia State and the Office of National Scholarships and Fellowships have produced 26 Fulbright Scholars, 10 Boren Scholars, and 44 Gilman Scholars. Georgia State undergraduates have been recipients of three prestigious Goldwater Scholarships, the Pickering Foreign Affairs Fellowship, the Rangel International Affairs Fellowship, the John Lewis Fellowship, and the Bundestag International Parliament Scholarship. Additionally, three students were acknowledged as Goldwater Honorable Mentions, three students received acceptance to Fulbright UK Summer Institutes, and two students received acceptance to the Rangel Summer Enrichment Program. In the area of major national postgraduate awards, Georgia State has advanced finalists for the Marshall Scholarship, the Mitchell Scholarship, and the Schwarzman Scholarship."

**UNRATED FEATURES**

**Continuation and Honors Graduation GPA Requirement:** 3.00.

**Academic Strengths, National Rankings:** This is based on national rankings of *graduate* programs in all but engineering and business, where undergraduate rankings are used. One of the weaknesses of the *U.S. News* rankings is that they focus on too many wealth-related metrics while ignoring their own assessments of academic departments. The rankings listed below are for all universities, public or private.

The highest nationally ranked academic departments at GSU are economics (59), business (64), sociology, (71), political science (72), English (99), and physics (110).

**Internships, Professional Development, Community Engagement:**

**Internships:** "Students acquire and complete internships in one of three ways. First, capstone project internships are required for students participating in Lead with HONORS, a 3-year cohort program. Internships are selected by a faculty associate who is director of the Lead program and a faculty associate for experiential and service learning.

"Second, we have a fully developed internship/study abroad opportunity, the London Global Experience which allows students from all majors to intern (and obtain academic credit) in London and other parts of the United Kingdom. Available internships span a wide range of industries, including public policy, fashion, the arts, media, sciences, and more."

**"Third, students have access to both a dedicated Honors College Internship Coordinator and a faculty associate for internships and service learning**, who help prepare students for internship and service learning opportunities."

**Volunteer and Peer Leadership Activities:** "Each academic year is kicked-off with our annual service event, Starting with Service. The Honors Student Organization organizes service opportunities for students throughout the academic year, and fosters partnerships with local organizations including Relay for Life, PAWS, Lifeline, and more.

"The Georgia State Honors College Ambassadors are student volunteers who are excited to share their Honors College experience with others. These student leaders are active in recruitment, alumni and campus events where they serve as representatives of the Georgia State University Honors College.

"The GSURC Student Planning Committee is comprised of students from various disciplines that volunteer to support GSURC. Students who participate in the committee contribute to the conference through areas of conference/event planning, public relations, recruitment, and assessment."

**Special Projects:** "The Honors College is home to the Herndon Human Rights Initiative, funded by the Atlanta-based Rich Foundation. The Initiative honors Alonzo Herndon and his son, Norris, who were involved in the long struggle for civil rights beginning in 1905….The Initiative offers scholarships to students whose research, service, or creative works further the interests of civil and human rights….

"The Honors College's Digital Literacy initiative prepares students for professional and post-graduate success by teaching them how to 'think digitally' across a spectrum of Honors courses while providing the technology to support digital learning.

"Our HON 3280 Service Learning seminars offer students experiential courses that include a service component….Students in service learning courses spend a portion of the course engaged in actual service to an organization or individuals seeking services from that organization.

"The LEAD with Honors certificate program is a three-year program that develops small cohorts of Honors College students into tomorrow's change agents through the mastery of leadership principles and group dynamics. Students complete 16 credit-hours and a capstone internship project."

**Undergraduate Research:** "The Honors College offers many signature research experiences for students within the college:

**"Research Skills Workshops:** The Honors College offers nine interactive Research Skills Workshops to introduce students to the research enterprise as an initial step toward building competent undergraduate researchers at Georgia State University.

**"The University Assistantship Program** offers students the opportunity to be matched with a faculty member to work on research, scholarship, or creative work. Through the UAP, students are offered grants in the amount of $2,500/year for their work.

"The **Georgia State Undergraduate Research Conference** is held annually and hosted by the Honors College. Students can present their work in the form of a poster, an oral, artistic, or musical display. Annually, more than 200 students, sponsored by faculty mentors, participate in this conference, and top presenters in all categories are awarded cash prizes.

**"*Discovery*, the Honors College research journal**, offers Honors students the opportunity to submit their work for peer-review and publication. Published electronically by BePress, as well as in printed format, Discovery is a showcase for undergraduate research."

**Honors Study Abroad:** "The Honors College promotes study abroad and student exchange experiences, and Georgia State features a fully-developed Study Abroad office that offers hundreds of for-credit international experiences each academic year. Honors students regularly register for semester-long or year-long study abroad experiences led by Georgia State University professors, and earn honors credit with differentiated Honors experiences. Several faculty affiliates who teach seminars in the college conduct a related student abroad experience, for example, a seminar on Human Rights in Argentina precedes a Maymester study abroad trip."

**"Georgia State has created an International Consortium of Universities, the Global Partnership for Better Cities (GPBC).** It includes faculty from partner universities in South Africa and Hong Kong. The GPBC is founded on joint-research projects taking place in Atlanta, Hong Kong, Johannesburg and Cape Town to advance understanding of western, eastern and southern hemisphere conceptual frameworks for studying cities and addressing their challenges.

"Study abroad and exchange programs require financial resources. The Office of International Initiatives offers many scholarships. Study Abroad Programs award more than $1 million in Georgia State study abroad scholarship support to allow students who have limited opportunities to live and study abroad."

**Financial Aid:** "The Presidential Scholarship provides eight semesters of full tuition and fees, housing, living and textbook expenses, as well as a University Assistantship and a study abroad stipend. The Presidential Scholarship, the most prestigious scholarship offered to entering Georgia State freshmen, was offered to ten outstanding students in fall 2015.

"The University Assistantship, available to both entering freshmen and, by recommendation, to enrolled Honors students, provides $2,500 per academic year to students conducting mentored research.

"Georgia State Foundation scholarships, awarded at admission to all Honors students who are admitted Early Action, provide up to $3,000 per academic year to offset the cost of attendance."

**Honors Fees:** "Beginning July 1, 2019 a fee of not more than $250 per semester (subject to Georgia Board of Regents' approval each year) will be assessed for new participants in the GSU Honors College."

**Placement of Honors Graduates:** "While not exhaustive, we have included a partial list of professional, graduate and professional school placements for recent Honors graduates: Carnegie Mellon, Cornell, Georgetown, Harvard, Medical College of Georgia, Morehouse School of Medicine, NYU, Stanford, UC Berkeley law, Chicago, Michigan, Virginia law, Yale law.

Corporate placements including CNN, Delta Air Lines, KPMG, PWC, Ernst & Young, United Air Lines, Home Depot, UPS, and Google

Public Sector placements including the Federal Reserve Bank, the Carter Center, the Clinton Global Initiative, the CIA, and the Georgia Legislature

**Degree of Difference**: This is difference between (1) the average SAT scores for recently enrolled honors students (1376) and (2) the average test scores for all students in the university (1120) as a whole. The difference may be an indication of how "elite" honors students may be perceived as compared to students in the university as a whole. **Please keep in mind that neither the high nor low selectivity of an honors program determines how effective the program may be.**

**NAME**: THE HONORS COLLEGE

**Date Established:** 1958

**Location**: Houston, Texas

**University Full-time Undergraduate Enrollment (2017):** 35,871

**Honors Members in Good Standing**: 2404; (mean size of all programs is 2,030).

**Honors Average Admission Test Score(s)**: ACT, 29; SAT, 1380.

**Average High School GPA/Class Rank:** No average reported.

**Basic Admission Requirements:** "The Honors College application process does not employ minimum requirements in the admissions review process. Applicants are holistically evaluated—academics (grades, types of classes taken, trend in grades, test scores), writing, and leadership/involvement are considered by the admissions committee."

**Application Deadline(s):** *Please verify with each program, as some deadlines could change.* November 15, 2018, for priority consideration; final deadline April 1, 2019.

**Honors Programs with SAT scores from 1370—1403:** Arizona, CUNY Macaulay, Georgia State, Houston, Indiana, LSU, Massachusetts, New Mexico, Purdue, Texas Tech, UAB.

**Administrative Staff:** 28, plus honors faculty and student assistants.

**RATINGS AT A GLANCE:** For all mortarboard ratings immediately below, a score of 5 is the maximum and represents a comparison with all rated honors colleges and programs. More detailed explanations follow the "mortarboard" ratings.

**PERCEPTION\* OF UNIVERSITY AS A WHOLE, NOT OF HONORS:** 🎓🎓🎓

\*Perception is based on the university's ranking among public universities in the 2018 U.S. News Best Colleges report. Please bear in mind that the better the U.S. News ranking, the more difficult it is for an honors college or program to have a rating that equals or improves on the magazine ranking.

**OVERALL HONORS RATING:** 🎓🎓🎓🎓 1/2

**Curriculum Requirements:** 🎓🎓🎓🎓

**Number of Honors Classes Offered:** 🎓🎓🎓🎓🎓

**Number of Honors Classes in Key Disciplines:** 🎓🎓🎓🎓🎓

**Extent of Honors Enrollment:** 👑👑👑👑

**Honors-only Class Size:** 👑👑👑 1/2

**Overall Class Size (Honors-only plus mixed, contract):** 👑👑👑👑

**Honors Grad Rate Adjusted to SAT:** 👑👑 1/2

**Grad Rate Adjusted to Freshman Retention Rate:** 👑👑

**Ratio of Staff to Students:** 👑👑👑👑👑

**Priority Registration: Yes,** honors students register for all courses, honors and otherwise, with the first group of students during each year they are in the program.

**Honors Housing Amenities:** 👑👑👑👑👑

**Honors Housing Availability:** 👑👑👑👑 1/2

**Prestigious Awards:** 👑👑 1/2

## RATING SCORES AND EXPLANATIONS:

**Curriculum Requirements (5.0):** The most important rating category, the curriculum completion requirement (classes required to complete honors) defines not only what honors students should learn but also the extent to which honors students and faculty are connected in the classroom. If there is a thesis or capstone requirement, it reinforces the individual contact and research skills so important to learning.

The average number of honors semester hours required for completion across all programs is 30.0.

The honors college requires a minimum of 36 credits to complete the University Honors with Honors in the Major. A 6-credit thesis is included.

Graduation with University Honors requires 33 total credits, including a 3-credit capstone.

University Honors in the Major requires 30 total credits, including a 6-credit thesis.

Collegiate Honors requires 18 credits, including a 3-credit capstone.

Collegiate Honors in the Major requires 15 credits, including a 6-credit thesis.

Membership in the Honors College requires the completion of 12 honors credits.

Membership in the Honors College with Honors in the Major requires a 6-credit thesis.

**AP/IB credits** are **not** counted as replacements for honors courses.

**No. Honors Classes Offered (5.0):** This is a measure of the total **adjusted** honors main sections available in the term reported, not including labs and thesis. An adjusted main section has 3 or more semester credits, or equivalent, and sections with fewer credits receive a lower prorated value.

The Honors College offered a section for every **9.7** enrolled students. The average for all was **15.0**. The lower the number, the better.

In the term reported, **69.2%** of honors enrollment was **in honors-only sections; 28.9% was in mixed sections; and 1.9% was in contract sections.** For all programs under review, enrollment by type of honors section was 75.8% honors-only, 15.4 % mixed, and 8.8% contract.

**No. Honors Classes in Key Disciplines (5.0):** The 15 "key" disciplines are biological sciences; business (all); chemistry; communications (especially public speaking); computer science; economics; engineering (all); English; history; math (all); philosophy; physics; political science; psychology; and sociology, anthropology, and gender studies. Interdisciplinary sections, such as those often taken for General Education credit in the first two years, do receive a lesser, prorated discipline "credit" because they introduce students to multiple disciplines in an especially engaging way, often with in-depth discussion.

For this measure, mixed and contract sections are not counted as a section in a key discipline unless students taking the sections for honors credit make up at least 10% of the total section enrollment.

In the term reported, the honors college offered a section in a key discipline for every **11.1 honors students.** The average for all programs is **24.7.** The lower the number, the better.

Of **120 adjusted sections in key disciplines, 85 all were honors-only sections**. The most sections were in English (including about 35 composition sections), followed by political science, history, biology, math, and chemistry.

Houston Honors offered about 35 sections of its signature seminar series, "Human Situation: Antiquity." It is described as "a 10-hour sequence that helps you hone your critical thinking and writing skills while reading great religious, literary, philosophical and political texts. It is interdisciplinary to the core, team-taught in lecture and student-driven in discussion. You will emerge from it a fearless reader, confident in your ability to talk with professors and others about major aspects of being human. You will also be a much stronger writer and critical thinker — skills that transfer to any area of study."

The honors college is a **blended** program, with a good mix of interdisciplinary courses and classes in the disciplines.

**Extent of Honors Enrollment (4.0):** Not all honors students take an honors class each term, especially after the first two years. Programs that have fewer honors classes and thesis options for upper-division honors students will *generally* have fewer total members in good standing who are actually enrolled in a given term. (Please be aware, however, that honors students not enrolled in a class for a term are still tied to the honors community through residential and extracurricular activities.) *Our research shows that this* *measure is closely related to honors completion rates, i.e., the number of students who complete honors requirements by the time they graduate.*

For example, if a program has 1,800 individual students enrolled in a given term, and 3,000 students in good standing, the level of enrollment was .67, an indication that honors class enrollment is somewhat below average, especially in upper-division classes. **Houston Honors has a ratio of 1.43**, above the average of 1.30 for all programs.

**Average Class Size, Honors-only Sections (3.5):** Offered mostly in the first two years, honors-only classes tend to be smaller and, as the name implies, have no or very few students other than those in the honors program. These class sections always are much smaller than mixed or contract sections, or regular non-honors class sections in the university.

The average honors-only class size at the honors college is **20.0 students**. The average for all programs is **17.5 students.**

**Average Class Size, Overall (4.0):** The overall class calculation is based on the *proportion* of honors students in each type of class (honors-only, mixed honors, and honors contract sections). Thus it is not a raw average. The overall honors-credit class size is **22.4 students**, versus the average for all programs of **24.9 students**.

These class size averages also do not correspond to the number of students per honors section ratings above. The reason is that, in computing average class size metrics, we include enrollment in each 1-2-credit section, not just sections with 3 or more credits.

Along with an honors-only class size of 20.0 students (listed above), the program's mixed honors sections have an average size of **25.3 students,** and the contract sections with honors credit for individual honors students average **64.8 students.** Across all programs, the average mixed honors section has 68.6 students, and the average contract section has 56.6 students.

**Honors Grad Rate Adjusted to SAT (2.5):** The rating is the based on the actual grad rate for students who entered the program six years earlier, whether or not the students remained in honors. The **actual rate of 72.0%** is also compared to the rates of other programs with the same test score entry requirement range, and then adjusted upward if the program is performing above other programs in the same range, or downward if the performance is less than other programs in the same range. The rate here is significantly downward, to **67.5%.**

**Grad Rate Adjusted to Freshman Retention Rate (2.0):** This rate compares the actual grad rate above to a predicted grade rate when freshman retention rates are considered. The actual grad rate is **14.3 points below** than the predicted rate. For all programs, the actual grad rate is **.33 points lower** than the predicted rate.

**Ratio of Staff to Honors Students (5.0):** There is 1 staff member for every **63.6** students. (Mean ratio for all programs is 1 staff member for every **127.9** students.)

**Honors Residence Halls, Amenities (5.0):** About 560 honors students, first-year and upperclassmen, live in Cougar Village I. The coed residence has "neighborhoods" to which scholars are assigned according to the scholarship they have been awarded (National Merit Scholars, Tier One, Terry Scholars). All of the air-conditioned rooms are suite style. The nearest dining is at the Fresh Food Company.

Another 172 upperclassmen live in Cougar Place, with features similar to those at Cougar Village I. The most convenient dining is at the Cougar Woods Dining Hall.

**Honors Residence Halls, Availability (4.5):** This rating compares the number of occupants in honors residence halls to the number of honors freshman and sophomore members in good standing. The ratio for the college is **.61** places for each first- and second-year student. The median for all programs is .49 places.

**Prestigious Awards (2.5):** The awards that we track and include are listed in the section titled "Prestigious Scholarships." The awards are sometimes won by students who are not in an honors college or program, but increasingly many are enrolled in honors programs. It is also a trend that honors colleges and programs help to prepare their students for the awards competitions.

"The University of Houston's Honors College actively promotes and encourages students from all academic disciplines to apply for competitive scholarship and internship opportunities. The scholarship program is housed within the Office of Undergraduate Research (OUR), which is located physically and administratively in the Honors College. OUR houses a Director of National Fellowships and Major Awards, who assists students with major award applications, manages the campus nomination process, and coordinates the submission of all supporting documents for a wide range of national and international scholarships. The current director is an alumnus of the Fulbright U.S. Student Program and is focused on increasing awareness for major award opportunities for all currently enrolled students at the University of Houston."

**UNRATED FEATURES**

**Continuation and Honors Graduation GPA Requirement:** 3.25 for both.

**Academic Strengths, National Rankings:** This is based on national rankings of *graduate* programs in all but engineering and business, where undergraduate rankings are used. One of the weaknesses of the *U.S. News* rankings is that they focus on too many wealth-related metrics while ignoring their own assessments of academic departments. The rankings listed below are for all universities, public or private.

The leading nationally ranked academic departments at Houston are political science (51), earth sciences (54), English (77), economics (78), engineering (82), chemistry (88), and business (91).

**Internships, Professional Development, Community Engagement:** "UH Bonner—The Bonner Foundation is a national service organization that seeks to improve the lives of individuals and communities by helping meet the basic needs of nutrition and educational opportunity.

"There are currently 105 active Bonner members this 2017-2018 academic year:

"Campus Kitchen, a food recovery program that repurposes prepared, un-served food in two of the UH dining halls and redistributes it to residents at four low-incoming housing locations that provide life-stabilizing, affordable, permanent housing for people on very limited incomes.

"Cultivate, a gardening initiative that develops sustainable community gardens in economically disadvantaged Houston neighborhoods, with the mission of providing healthy lifestyles, increasing access to fresh produce, and providing green spaces for community engagement.

"ImpACT, a college entrance exam program that provides in-depth ACT tutoring to high school juniors. ImpACT also provides college-going mentorship to students, prepares them for college essays, and helps them work toward and identify financial aid resources for college.

"Lobo Prep, a college entrance exam program that provides in-depth SAT tutoring to high school juniors and seniors. Lobo Prep also provides college-going mentorship to students, prepares them for college essays, and helps them work toward and identify financial aid resources for college.

"Writing to Inspire Successful Education (WISE), a program that utilizes in-person and video feedback tutoring and in-person mentoring to 7th grade students, helping to develop overall writing skills with the goal to provide long-term educational success toward college-going."

Another program is Data Analytics in Student Hands (DASH). **The program "embodies an Honors approach to educating students in a world flooded with data and in need of informed and decisive action.** DASH assembles diverse student teams with different skill sets to accomplish meaningful projects using new technologies. We use a boot camp approach over the summers to immerse students in community relevant tasks, beginning with targeted lessons on the particular technologies we use to create that summer's products."

**Undergraduate Research:**

"Housed within the Honors College, the Office of Undergraduate Research is a clearinghouse for mentored research opportunities, serving the entire UH undergraduate population."

Office of Undergraduate Research's Programs:

"Summer Undergraduate Research Fellowship (SURF)—The 2017 SURF program provided $3,500 awards to students to conduct full-time, 10-week summer research experiences under the guidance of a faculty mentor. Of the 81 participants in summer 2017, 39 students were members of the Honors College.

"Houston Early Research Experience (HERE)—The HERE program is a two-week workshop in May, which freshmen and sophomores learn the basics of research inquiry and methodology. The program culminates with a $1,000 fall scholarship. Of the 30 participants in the May 2017 program, 18 students were members of the Honors College.

"Provost's Undergraduate Research Scholarship (PURS)—The PURS program provides $1,000 awards to juniors and seniors to conduct part-time, semester research projects under the guidance of a faculty mentor. Of the 73 students who participated in the spring 2017 and fall 2017 programs, 36 students were members of the Honors College.

"Mellon Research Scholars Program—In summer 2017, the Office of Undergraduate Research received a $500,000 grant from the Andrew W. Mellon Foundation to establish an undergraduate research program in the humanities. There is funding for 60 students to be distributed over the course of three years. Each recipient receives a $1,100 scholarship for a May graduate school workshop and a $3,900 scholarship for a full-time summer research experience."

**Honors Study Abroad:** "In the past three years, the Honors College has organized and sponsored study and service abroad to Russia, Wales, Ireland, Italy, Greece, India, Israel, Honduras, Haiti, Peru, Ecuador and Galapagos, with three-day, ancillary excursions in Rome, Athens, and Istanbul. Students typically prepare for these two-to-three-week trips by completing a semester-long, three-credit-hour course focused on the literature, history, and culture of the country they will be visiting. Or, in the case of clinical service abroad travel, students prepare by developing cultural awareness, studying medical ethics, and considering actual cases and situations.

"University of Houston Honors College faculty have led studies abroad for three decades, but our focus on international education has grown in frequency, range, and focus over the past 10 years. We typically sponsor five to six learning or service abroad experiences annually, including regular travel to our partner 'Shoulder to Shoulder' clinic in Santa Ana, Honduras, and **life science travel to the Galapagos Islands.**

"Each Honors College student who studies abroad receives at least $500 in scholarship support from the Honors College, and, based on financial need, many receive support up to $3,000. In addition, the University of Houston provides scholarships to students through its Office of Learning Abroad; these scholarships are in the $500-$2,500 range based on length of stay. The Office of Learning Abroad maintains a federal passport office on campus to facilitate travel and study abroad."

**Financial Aid:** "Students are guaranteed to be reviewed for academic/merit scholarships if they have a completed University of Houston application by December 1:

•Academic Excellence Scholarship The Academic Excellence Scholarship is for students who have a competitive academic profile—typically a score of 1200 on the critical reading and math sections of the SAT (26 ACT composite) with a class rank in the top 20 percent. The amount awarded varies from $2,500 to $8,500 per year.

•Tier One Scholarship—The UH Tier One Scholarships were established by President Renu Khator to attract highly qualified students to the University of Houston by **funding four years of tuition and mandatory fees, two years of on-campus room and board, and stipends for research ($1,000) and study abroad ($2,000).** Students must have a score of [at least] 1300 on the SAT (critical reading and math) or 29 [at least] on the ACT and a rank in the top 10% in order to be nominated for the Tier One Scholarship. The Tier One class for fall 2017 consisted of 27 first-year students, who will be receiving approximately $587,223 in scholarship awards, or an average of $21,749 for the year.

•National Merit Scholarship—The University of Houston awards **scholarship support covering the entire cost of tuition and required fees, and includes stipends for research ($1,000) and study abroad ($2,000)** to National Merit Scholarship Finalists who select the University of Houston as their first-choice institution in accordance with the rules and deadlines established by the National Merit Scholarship Corporation. In 2017, 14 new National Merit Scholars joined the University of Houston's class of 2021 and will receive approximately $153,160 in scholarship awards, or an average award of $10,940.

•Provost Service Learning Scholarship The Provost Service Learning Scholarship is awarded contingent upon service completed through the Bonner Program, which supports not only students, but also the University's efforts to serve the community. The Bonner Leaders work with nearby KIPP public charter schools and Cesar E. Chavez high school students in two educational preparation programs, and provides meals for those in need through the Campus Kitchen UH program. Academically excellent incoming students are invited to apply, and in 2017 46 students were awarded $69,500 in PSLS funds.

•Terry Foundation Scholarship A Houston-based foundation providing scholarships to outstanding Texas high school graduates, the Terry Foundation supports academically talented students with financial need and a record of leadership. For 2017-18 academic year, 127 scholars received approximately $2.9 million from the Terry Foundation to fund their undergraduate education, or an average of $22,834 for the year.

•Honors College Scholarships Students in good standing are eligible to apply for Honors College Scholarships ranging form $1,000 to $1,500 annually. In 2017, the College awarded $450,000 to 354 students, 61 of whom were incoming freshmen. Honors College Scholarships are available to incoming freshmen (who participate in the scholarship competition at an Open House/Reception event) and current students (who are eligible to apply after their first year in Honors).

**Honors Fees:** None.

**Placement of Honors Graduates:** "From Honors College surveys of students in their last semester, we learn that approximately a third of graduating students in the Honors College plan to immediately enter a graduate or professional school program and that more than half of graduating seniors plan to immediately enter the workforce. Many Honors College graduates go on to be successful in advanced studies, in graduate, medical, and law schools around the world, and in top companies, in keeping with our motto, 'Success that Lasts a Lifetime.'"

**Degree of Difference**: This is difference between (1) the average SAT scores for recently enrolled honors students (1380) and (2) the average test scores for all students in the university (1220) as a whole. The difference may be an indication of how "elite" honors students may be perceived as compared to students in the university as a whole. **Please keep in mind that neither the high nor low selectivity of an honors program determines how effective the program may be.**

**NAME**: CAMPUS HONORS PROGRAM

**Date Established:** 1986

**Location**: Urbana-Champaign, Illinois

**University <u>Full-time Undergraduate</u> Enrollment (2017):** 33,932

**Honors Members in Good Standing**: 517; (mean size of all programs is 2,030).

**Honors <u>Average</u> Admission Test Score(s)**: Mean ACT, 33.8; median, 35; mean SAT, 1492; median 1520.

**Average High School GPA/Class Rank:** Not listed, but extremely high.

**<u>Basic</u> Admission Requirements:** "The CHP minimum ACT Composite Score generally begins in the low-30's for ACT, yet the minimum ACT Composite Score in certain majors may be closer to 35 (such as Computer Science). What is much harder to show is that our admissions criteria focuses on a student's desire to participate in honors—which is much harder to encapsulate. In our admissions process, we look for genuine enthusiasm and a wide array of interests, as shown by the personal statement and high school activities (both breadth and depth, as well as leadership); **we also conduct a limited reference check**."

**Application Deadline(s):** *Please verify with each program, as some deadlines could change.*

**Honors Programs with SAT scores from 1471—1510:** Clemson, Georgia, Illinois, Minnesota, Oklahoma, Rutgers, South Carolina, UT Austin.

**Administrative Staff:** 4.5 FTE's.

**RATINGS AT A GLANCE:** For all mortarboard ratings immediately below, a score of 5 is the maximum and represents a comparison with all rated honors colleges and programs. More detailed explanations follow the "mortarboard" ratings.

**PERCEPTION\* OF UNIVERSITY AS A WHOLE, <u>NOT</u> OF HONORS:** 🎓🎓🎓🎓🎓

\*Perception is based on the university's ranking among public universities in the 2018 U.S. News Best Colleges report. Please bear in mind that the better the U.S. News ranking, the more difficult it is for an honors college or program to have a rating that equals or improves on the magazine ranking.

**OVERALL HONORS RATING:** 🎓🎓🎓🎓 1/2

**Curriculum Requirements:** 🎓🎓🎓

**Number of Honors Classes Offered:** 🎓🎓🎓🎓 1/2

**Number of Honors Classes in Key Disciplines:** 🎓🎓🎓🎓

**Extent of Honors Enrollment:** 🎓🎓🎓🎓🎓

**Honors-only Class Size:** 🎓🎓🎓1/2

**Overall Class Size (Honors-only plus mixed, contract):** 🎓🎓🎓🎓1/2

**Honors Grad Rate Adjusted to SAT:** 🎓🎓🎓🎓1/2

**Grad Rate Adjusted to Freshman Retention Rate:** 🎓🎓🎓🎓1/2

**Ratio of Staff to Students:** 🎓🎓🎓🎓

**Priority Registration: Yes,** honors students register for all courses, honors and otherwise, with the first group of students during each year they are in the program.

**Honors Housing Amenities:** 🎓🎓🎓🎓

**Honors Housing Availability:** 🎓🎓🎓🎓1/2

**Prestigious Awards:** 🎓🎓🎓🎓🎓

**RATING SCORES AND EXPLANATIONS:**

**Curriculum Requirements (3.0):** The most important rating category, the curriculum completion requirement (classes required to complete honors) defines not only what honors students should learn but also the extent to which honors students and faculty are connected in the classroom. If there is a thesis or capstone requirement, it reinforces the individual contact and research skills so important to learning.

The average number of honors semester hours required for completion across all programs is 30.0.

Enrolled students in the CHP are referred to as Chancellor's Scholars. "There are also honors programs in every college (these individuals are referred to as 'James Scholars'), and in many departments. The James Scholar Programs range from a few dozen students (for example, the College of Media and the College of Fine and Applied Arts) up to the College of Engineering and College of Liberal Arts James Scholar Programs, which usually number more than 1,000. Students can be Chancellor's Scholars and James Scholars if they are accepted by both programs.

CHP completion requires about 18 credits. Chancellor's Scholars must take at least four "regular" CHP classes, or 12-13 credits. They must also complete a 3-credit capstone seminar. "We also have co-curricular requirements: Over their undergraduate career, Chancellor's Scholars must participate in 4

"Scholar Adventurers Series" programs which range from 1.5-3 hours, and 1 Krannert Dress Rehearsal (this fine and applied arts event usually 1 hour of lecture, and up to 3 hours of performance)."

**AP/IB credits** are **not** counted as replacements for honors courses.

**No. Honors Classes Offered (4.5):** This is a measure of the total **adjusted** honors main sections available in the term reported, not including labs and thesis. An adjusted main section has 3 or more semester credits, or equivalent, and sections with fewer credits receive a lower prorated value.

CHP offered a section for every **11.0** enrolled students. The average for all programs was **15.0**. The lower the number, the better.

In the term reported, an extremely impressive **100%** of honors enrollment was **in honors-only sections**. For all programs under review, enrollment by type of honors section was 75.8% honors-only, 15.4 % mixed, and 8.8% contract.

**No. Honors Classes in Key Disciplines (4.0):** The 15 "key" disciplines are biological sciences; business (all); chemistry; communications (especially public speaking); computer science; economics; engineering (all); English; history; math (all); philosophy; physics; political science; psychology; and sociology, anthropology, and gender studies. Interdisciplinary sections, such as those often taken for General Education credit in the first two years, do receive a lesser, prorated discipline "credit" because they introduce students to multiple disciplines in an especially engaging way, often with in-depth discussion.

For this measure, mixed and contract sections are not counted as a section in a key discipline unless students taking the sections for honors credit make up at least 10% of the total section enrollment.

In the term reported, the program offered a section in a key discipline for every **24.3 honors students**. The average for all programs is **24.7**. The lower the number, the better.

Out of **20 adjusted sections in key disciplines**, **all were honors-only sections**. The most sections were in math, biology, microbiology, communications, English, economics, psychology, and sociology.

The CHP offered several interesting interdisciplinary courses: "Ecological Criticism," the "Sociology and Psychology of Physical Activity," "Probability in the Real World," and "Language in Human History." The CHP is a core **blended** program, with a mix of interdisciplinary courses and classes in the disciplines.

**Extent of Honors Enrollment (5.0):** Not all honors students take an honors class each term, especially after the first two years. Programs that have fewer honors classes and thesis options for upper-division honors students will *generally* have fewer total members in good standing who are actually enrolled in a given term. (Please be aware, however, that honors students not enrolled in a class for a term are still tied to the honors community through residential and extracurricular activities.) *Our research shows that this measure is closely related to honors completion rates, i.e., the number of students who complete honors requirements by the time they graduate.*

For example, if a program has 1,800 individual students enrolled in a given term, and 3,000 students in good standing, the level of enrollment was .67, an indication that honors class enrollment is somewhat

below average, especially in upper-division classes. **CHP honors has a ratio of 2.09**, well above the average of 1.30 for all programs.

**Average Class Size, Honors-only Sections (3.5):** Offered mostly in the first two years, honors-only classes tend to be smaller and, as the name implies, have no or very few students other than those in the honors program. These class sections always are much smaller than mixed or contract sections, or regular non-honors class sections in the university.

The average honors-only class size at the CHP is **18.4 students**. The average for all programs is **17.5 students.**

**Average Class Size, Overall (4.5):** The overall class calculation is based on the *proportion* of honors students in each type of class (honors-only, mixed honors, and honors contract sections). Thus it is not a raw average. The overall honors-credit class size is also **18.4 students**, versus the average for all programs of **24.9 students**.

These class size averages also do not correspond to the number of students per honors section ratings above. The reason is that, in computing average class size metrics, we include enrollment in each 1-2-credit section, not just sections with 3 or more credits.

All sections offered by the CHP were honors-only sections, so there are no mixed or contract section class sizes to report.

**Honors Grad Rate Adjusted to SAT (4.5):** The rating is the based on the actual grad rate for students who entered the program six years earlier, whether or not the students remained in honors. The **actual rate of 96.0%** is also compared to the rates of other programs with the same test score entry requirement range, and then adjusted upward if the program is performing above other programs in the same range, or downward if the performance is less than other programs in the same range. The rate here is slightly upward, to **96.7%.**

**Grad Rate Adjusted to Freshman Retention Rate (4.5):** This rate compares the actual grad rate above to a predicted grade rate when freshman retention rates are considered. The actual grad rate is **1.64 points higher** than the predicted rate. For all programs, the actual grad rate is **.33 points lower** than the predicted rate.

**Ratio of Staff to Honors Students (4.0):** There is 1 staff member for every **114.9** students. (Mean ratio for all programs is 1 staff member for every **127.9** students.)

**Honors Residence Halls, Amenities (4.0):** Nugent Hall, the Honors Living/Learning Community, houses 240 first-year students and upperclassmen in traditional (mostly) double rooms with hall baths. Floors 3 and 4 in the residence are for CHP students and James Scholars. Nugent has onsite laundry, a kitchen, and air conditioning. Ikenberry Dining Hall is attached to Nugent, a special convenience in cold winter weather. A lounge for honors students is in an adjacent building.

"Regarding course offerings at the Honors LLC, a one credit 'Uncommon Readings' course for all Honors LLC freshmen is required. Other curricular offerings available for undergraduates align with the Honors LLC pillars (Inquiry, Civic Engagement, Leadership) while serving as general education and/or college honors requirements. Any seats for courses taught at the Honors LLC not taken by Honors LLC students are available to non- Honors LLC James Scholars and CHP students."

**Honors Residence Halls, Availability (4.5):** This rating compares the number of occupants in honors residence halls to the number of honors freshman and sophomore members in good standing. The ratio for the program is **.96** places for each first- and second-year student. The median for all programs is .49 places.

**Prestigious Awards (5.0):** The awards that we track and include are listed in the section titled "Prestigious Scholarships." The awards are sometimes won by students who are not in an honors college or program, but increasingly many are enrolled in honors programs. It is also a trend that honors colleges and programs help to prepare their students for the awards competitions.

UIUC students rank first among students at public universities in winning Churchill Scholarships; tied for 2nd among students from public universities in winning Gates Cambridge Scholarships; 2nd behind only UC Berkeley in Marshall Scholarships; and among the top public university recipients of National Science Foundation fellowships for graduate study.

In addition, UIUC students now rank 1st among public universities in winning Goldwater Scholarships, awarded to outstanding STEM undergraduates.

For 2017 alone, these are the accomplishments of UIUC students:

"Of the 97 students who applied for the 13 major awards administered through our office, 21 were offered funding in excess of $600,000, including 15 of our 50 Fulbright applicants (two more were named alternates).

"Other highlights include: a Marshall (1 of 40 nationally), Truman (1 of 62 nationally), Udall (1 of 50 nationally), and Schwarzman (1 of 129 internationally).

"The overall acceptance rate of these awards is five percent of nominated students; few universities in the country can match Illinois' combined level of success this year."

**UNRATED FEATURES**

**Continuation and Honors Graduation GPA Requirement:** 3.30.

**Academic Strengths, National Rankings:** This is based on national rankings of *graduate* programs in all but engineering and business, where undergraduate rankings are used. One of the weaknesses of the *U.S. News* rankings is that they focus on too many wealth-related metrics while ignoring their own assessments of academic departments. The rankings listed below are for all universities, public or private.

The *average* department ranking at UIUC is a very high 20.07 among all universities.

Among the many nationally ranked academic departments at UIUC are computer science (5), chemistry (6) engineering (6), psychology (7), physics (9), business (15), math (19), history (23), political science (24), English (26), biology and education (27), economics (29), earth sciences (31), and sociology (47).

**Internships, Professional Development, Community Engagement:** "We advise students on accessing internships and service projects, and provide co-curricular programming on resume-writing, interviewing skills, and other important topics. We have also provided programs on service (from on-campus to internationally)."

**Undergraduate Research:** "While we do not collect data with regard to who conducts research in any given time period, most of our students will have undertaken research by the time they graduate.

"We support students through advising with regard to seeking research opportunities and we fund a small number of experiences through the CHP Summer Research Grant Program. A CHP staff member serves on the Office of Undergraduate Research Advisory Board, and all opportunities through that office are publicized to Chancellor's Scholars."

**Honors Study Abroad:** "CHP provides funding through the CHP Summer Travel Grants Program, and provides additional funding to CHP Intercultural Study Tours led by CHP faculty (which have included Peru, Japan, and Ecuador and the Galapagos in recent years).

"The University of Illinois provides extensive study abroad support to students through study abroad exchanges (some which may cost less than a semester's tuition) and many financial aid options, which can be found at http://www.studyabroad.illinois.edu/."

**Financial Aid:** "As of Fall 2018, we are able to provide $1,000 per year up to four years to students who are in good standing as Chancellor's Scholars, unless they have financial aid up to or exceeding tuition costs. This is an increase in our financial aid/scholarship. Previously, students received a one-time award of $2,000 for their first year in the CHP.

"All Chancellor's Scholars in good standing may apply for CHP Summer Research and Travel Grants, of $2,000 and $1,000, respectively.

"Field trips are fully or partially covered for students for CHP classes, which may range from visits to the cultural centers in Chicago to a research study tour in the National Parks.

"Scholarships such as National Merit and those listed above and others are administered externally to the Campus Honors Program." UIUC, along with many other top public universities, does not offer generous merit aid based on National Merit Scholarships."

Some of these are below:

**Illinois Residents**

Illinois Achievement Scholarship

Requirements: Illinois residents with demonstrated need

Amount: $10,000

Renewable: Yes, for 4 years, provided you maintain a 3.0 GPA and full-time status
Number: Variable

Stamps Family Charitable Foundation
Requirements: Incoming freshmen
Amount: Up to the cost of attendance
Renewable: Yes, for 4 years, provided the recipient maintains a 3.0 GPA
Number: 4-6 at any one time in CHP

Provost Scholarship
Requirements: Incoming freshmen
Amount: Full tuition
Renewable: Yes, for 4 years, provided you maintain a 3.0 GPA
Number: 30

President's Award Program
Requirements: Students in historically underrepresented groups who have demonstrated outstanding academic achievement
Amount: $5,000
Renewable: Yes, for 4 years, provided you maintain a 2.0 GPA
Number: Variable
President's Award Program Honors
Requirements: Students who are selected as President's Award recipients with the highest level of achievement
Amount: $10,000
Renewable: Yes, for 4 years, provided you maintain a 2.5 GPA
Number: Variable

**Honors Fees:** "There are no extra fees associated with any student who is a member of the Campus Honors Program, any of the college James Scholar programs, or departmental honors.

"There are additional nominal fees associated with residing in a Living and Learning Community (LLC) that are determined by the Housing Division, which are in addition to other Housing fees."

**Placement of Honors Graduates:** None listed.

**Degree of Difference**: This is difference between (1) the average SAT scores for recently enrolled honors students (1490-1520) and (2) the average test scores for all students in the university (1390) as a whole. The difference may be an indication of how "elite" honors students may be perceived as compared to students in the university as a whole. **Please keep in mind that neither the high nor low selectivity of an honors program determines how effective the program may be.**

**NAME**: HUTTON HONORS COLLEGE

**Date Established:** 1965

**Location**: Bloomington, Indiana

**University <u>Full-time Undergraduate</u> Enrollment (2017):** 39,184

**Honors Members in Good Standing**: 5,532; (mean size of all programs is 2,030).

**Honors <u>Average</u> Admission Test Score(s)**: ACT, 32; SAT, 1380 (superscored).

**Average High School GPA/Class Rank:** 3.98.

**<u>Basic</u> Admission Requirements (New):** 32 ACT or 1440 SAT and 3.90 or top 7.5% class rank; or

34 ACT or 1510 SAT and 3.85 GPA or top 10% class rank.

**Application Deadline(s):** *Please verify with each program, as some deadlines could change.* Deadline for Hutton scholarships November 1, 2018.

**Honors Programs with SAT scores from 1370—1403:** Arizona, CUNY Macaulay, Georgia State, Houston, Indiana, LSU, Massachusetts, New Mexico, Purdue, Texas Tech, UAB.

**Administrative Staff:** 16.

**RATINGS AT A GLANCE:** For all mortarboard ratings immediately below, a score of 5 is the maximum and represents a comparison with all rated honors colleges and programs. More detailed explanations follow the "mortarboard" ratings.

**PERCEPTION* OF UNIVERSITY AS A WHOLE, <u>NOT</u> OF HONORS:** 🎓🎓🎓🎓 1/2

*Perception is based on the university's ranking among public universities in the 2018 U.S. News Best Colleges report. Please bear in mind that the better the U.S. News ranking, the more difficult it is for an honors college or program to have a rating that equals or improves on the magazine ranking.

**OVERALL HONORS RATING:** 🎓🎓🎓

**Curriculum Requirements:** 🎓🎓🎓

**Number of Honors Classes Offered:** 🎓🎓🎓 1/2

**Number of Honors Classes in Key Disciplines:** 🎓🎓🎓 1/2

**Extent of Honors Enrollment:** 🎓🎓🎓

**Honors-only Class Size:** 🎓🎓🎓🎓🎓

**Overall Class Size (Honors-only plus mixed, contract):** 🎓🎓🎓🎓

**Honors Grad Rate Adjusted to SAT:** 🎓🎓🎓🎓🎓

**Grad Rate Adjusted to Freshman Retention Rate:** 🎓🎓🎓🎓 1/2

**Ratio of Staff to Students:** 🎓🎓 1/2

**Priority Registration:** No.

**Honors Housing Amenities:** 🎓🎓🎓

**Honors Housing Availability:** 🎓🎓 1/2

**Prestigious Awards:** 🎓🎓🎓🎓 1/2

## RATING SCORES AND EXPLANATIONS:

**Curriculum Requirements (3.0):** The most important rating category, the curriculum completion requirement (classes required to complete honors) defines not only what honors students should learn but also the extent to which honors students and faculty are connected in the classroom. If there is a thesis or capstone requirement, it reinforces the individual contact and research skills so important to learning.

The average number of honors semester hours required for completion across all programs is 30.0.

**Hutton Honors Notation Requirements:**

•Complete at least 18 hours of honors coursework
•Complete at least two Hutton Honors College courses (HON-H) of three credit hours each
•Complete at least one engaged learning experience that carries credit at IU (including study abroad, research projects, service-learning courses, creative projects, internships, and teaching assistantships)
•Maintain at least a 3.40 GPA for the 18 credit hours applied toward the Hutton Honors Notation with no grade lower than a C
•Submit a Hutton Honors Notation application prior to October 1 for winter graduation or April 1 for spring or summer graduation.
•Graduate with a cumulative GPA of at least 3.40

**AP/IB credits** are **not** counted as replacements for honors courses.

**No. Honors Classes Offered (3.5):** This is a measure of the total **adjusted** honors main sections available in the term reported, not including labs and thesis. An adjusted main section has 3 or more semester credits, or equivalent, and sections with fewer credits receive a lower prorated value.

Hutton Honors offered a section for every **19.7** enrolled students. The average for all programs was **15.0**. The lower the number, the better.

In the term reported, **46.3%** of honors enrollment was **in honors-only sections; 54.7% was in mixed sections; and none was in contract sections.** For all programs under review, enrollment by type of honors section was 75.8% honors-only, 15.4 % mixed, and 8.8% contract.

**No. Honors Classes in Key Disciplines (3.0):** The 15 "key" disciplines are biological sciences; business (all); chemistry; communications (especially public speaking); computer science; economics; engineering (all); English; history; math (all); philosophy; physics; political science; psychology; and sociology, anthropology, and gender studies. Interdisciplinary sections, such as those often taken for General Education credit in the first two years, do receive a lesser, prorated discipline "credit" because they introduce students to multiple disciplines in an especially engaging way, often with in-depth discussion.

For this measure, mixed and contract sections are not counted as a section in a key discipline unless students taking the sections for honors credit make up at least 10% of the total section enrollment.

In the term reported, the honors college offered a section in a key discipline for every **29.8 honors students.** The average for all programs is **24.7.** The lower the number, the better.

Of **100 adjusted sections in key disciplines**, **40 were honors-only sections**. An extremely high percentage of these were in business-related disciplines, reflecting the prominence of the Kelley School of Business on campus. Outside of business, the most sections were in math, English, and computer science.

Perhaps because so many courses in the disciplines are in business, Hutton offers an excellent series of about 40 interdisciplinary sections to provide perspectives from the humanities and social sciences. Most of these fall into one of four categories: "Ideas and Experience," "Great Authors, Composers, and Artists," "Literature of Time and Place," and "The Intricate Human." The combination of these courses and the departmental courses make Hutton a **blended** honors program.

**Extent of Honors Enrollment (3.0):** Not all honors students take an honors class each term, especially after the first two years. Programs that have fewer honors classes and thesis options for upper-division honors students will *generally* have fewer total members in good standing who are actually enrolled in a given term. (Please be aware, however, that honors students not enrolled in a class for a term are still tied to the honors community through residential and extracurricular activities.) *Our research shows that this measure is closely related to honors completion rates, i.e., the number of students who complete honors requirements by the time they graduate.*

For example, if a program has 1,800 individual students enrolled in a given term, and 3,000 students in good standing, the level of enrollment was .67, an indication that honors class enrollment is somewhat below average, especially in upper-division classes. **Hutton has a ratio of .61**, significantly below the average of 1.30 for all programs.

**Average Class Size, Honors-only Sections (5.0):** Offered mostly in the first two years, honors-only classes tend to be smaller and, as the name implies, have no or very few students other than those in the honors program. These class sections always are much smaller than mixed or contract sections, or regular non-honors class sections in the university.

The average honors-only class size at the honors college is **15.8 students**. The average for all programs is **17.5 students.**

**Average Class Size, Overall (4.0):** The overall class calculation is based on the *proportion* of honors students in each type of class (honors-only, mixed honors, and honors contract sections). Thus it is not a raw average. The overall honors-credit class size is **22.7 students**, versus the average for all programs of **24.9 students**.

These class size averages also do not correspond to the number of students per honors section ratings above. The reason is that, in computing average class size metrics, we include enrollment in each 1-2-credit section, not just sections with 3 or more credits.

Along with an honors-only class size of 15.8 students (listed above), the program's mixed honors sections have an average size of **28.1 students.** No contract sections were reported. Across all programs, the average mixed honors section has 68.6 students.

**Honors Grad Rate Adjusted to SAT (5.0):** The rating is the based on the actual grad rate for students who entered the program six years earlier, whether or not the students remained in honors. The **actual rate of 92.2%** is also compared to the rates of other programs with the same test score entry requirement range, and then adjusted upward if the program is performing above other programs in the same range, or downward if the performance is less than other programs in the same range. The rate here is notably upward, to **94.4%.**

**Grad Rate Adjusted to Freshman Retention Rate (4.5):** This rate compares the actual grad rate above to a predicted grade rate when freshman retention rates are considered. The actual grad rate is **1.87 points higher** than the predicted rate. For all programs, the actual grad rate is **.33 points lower** than the predicted rate.

**Ratio of Staff to Honors Students (2.5):** There is 1 staff member for every **329.3** students. (Mean ratio for all programs is 1 staff member for every **127.9** students.)

**Honors Residence Halls, Amenities (3.0):** Hutton assigns honors students to three residence halls, with most students, about 200, living in Teter. The other residences are Forest and Briscoe. All residences are air-conditioned. Forest and Teter have traditional rooms with hall baths; Briscoe has suite-style rooms. The dining hall closest to Forest is Woodlands; dining closest to Teter is Wright Cafeteria; and the most convenient dining hall for Briscoe is Gresham.

**Honors Residence Halls, Availability (2.5):** This rating compares the number of occupants in honors residence halls to the number of honors freshman and sophomore members in good standing. The ratio for the college is **.13** places for each first- and second-year student. The median for all programs is .49 places.

**Prestigious Awards (4.5):** The awards that we track and include are listed in the section titled "Prestigious Scholarships." The awards are sometimes won by students who are not in an honors college or program, but increasingly many are enrolled in honors programs. It is also a trend that honors colleges and programs help to prepare their students for the awards competitions.

IU scholars have an impressive record of winning prestigious scholarships: 15 Rhodes, 17 Marshall, 5 Churchill, and 20 Truman awards so far. They have also earned Fulbrights and National Science Foundation awards at a rate above the norm for the universities under review. In addition, IU students have won 44 Goldwater Scholarships for excellence in STEM fields.

## UNRATED FEATURES

**Continuation and Honors Graduation GPA Requirement:** 3.00.

**Academic Strengths, National Rankings:** This is based on national rankings of *graduate* programs in all but engineering and business, where undergraduate rankings are used. One of the weaknesses of the *U.S. News* rankings is that they focus on too many wealth-related metrics while ignoring their own. The rankings listed below are for all universities, public or private.

For decades, IU has been recognized for the excellence of its faculty. The overall ranking of the key departments we track shows that the average national ranking for IU departments in 2017 was 30.9.

The leading nationally ranked academic departments at IU are business (11), sociology (15), psychology (17), English (20), history (20), political science (29), education (30), chemistry (32), math (34), physics (37), biology (39), and economics (39).

**Internships, Professional Development, Community Engagement:** "Students who wish to graduate with the Hutton Honors Notation must complete at least one engaged learning experience that carries credit at IU (including study abroad, research projects, service-learning courses, creative projects, internships, and teaching assistantships)."

**Undergraduate Research:** "We have 85 Cox Research Scholars (freshmen through seniors) who are all obligated to be engaged in research. The Cox Research Scholars are also members of the Hutton Honors College. Approximately 15-25% of our students (inside and outside of Cox) are involved in research in some way."

**Honors Study Abroad:** "The Hutton Honors College is the proud home of the Edward L. Hutton International Experiences Program (HIEP), originally created in 2000 to support undergraduate students in their international endeavors. The HIEP Grant remains the single largest source of funding for Indiana University Bloomington undergraduate students participating in an international experience. Support is available for a variety of activities, including study abroad, overseas research, international internships, student teaching in another country, and volunteer service abroad. **During 2016-17, the HIEP awarded over $900,000 in grants to 513 students.**

"In addition to providing grants and scholarships for international opportunities, the HIEP offers high-impact honors overseas learning experiences through the Hutton Honors Study Abroad programs. Through these programs, participants focus on topics related to globalism and its effects on societies across the world."

**Financial Aid:** "Honors students who submit a complete admissions application to Indiana University by November 1 receive an automatic IU Academic Scholarship from the university. The amount of the award is based on academic information provided at the time of admission. Amounts range from $1,000-$8,000 for resident students and $1,000-$11,000 for non-resident students.

"Indiana University offers scholarships in recognition of student success in a variety of national scholar programs. National Merit Finalists, National Achievement Finalists, and National Hispanic Recognition students each receive a $1,000 renewal scholarship from IU.

"Additionally, honors students who submit a complete admission application by November 1 are invited to complete the Selective Scholarship Application (SSA) to apply for additional merit scholarship funding from the Hutton Honors College as well as other departmental scholarship programs.

"A committee of Honors College faculty carefully reads each SSA application. 'We are particularly interested in the quality of your high school program, the courses you have taken, the quality of your writing, and the nature of your extracurricular activities.'"

**"Approximately 25 percent of honors applicants are awarded an additional $2,000 to $8,000 from the HHC based on the SSA application.** HHC Scholarships are renewable for four years (eight semesters) by maintaining a 3.4 or above GPA, completing a minimum of three graded honors courses during the first two years, and attending at least one approved cultural/educational event each year.

"The Hutton Honors College seeks to encourage undergraduate students to pursue a number of worthwhile activities outside the classroom. The HHC Undergraduate Grant Program has supported students as far back as the 1970s and offers funding for research, internships, creative activities, and more. Through this program, the Hutton Honors College awards approximately $400,000 to students each year."

**Honors Fees:** "We charge $8.00 a year to be an HHC member. There is a $50.00/semester fee for Hutton Residential communities.

**Placement of Honors Graduates:** None listed, but IU honors graduates, especially those who are also in the Kelley School of Business, are very successful on the job market.

**Degree of Difference:** This is difference between (1) the average SAT scores for recently enrolled honors students (1380) and (2) the average test scores for all students in the university (1240) as a whole. The difference may be an indication of how "elite" honors students may be perceived as compared to students in the university as a whole. **Please keep in mind that neither the high nor low selectivity of an honors program determines how effective the program may be.**

**NAME**: UNIVERSITY OF IOWA HONORS PROGRAM

**Date Established:** 1958

**Location**: Iowa City, Iowa

**University Full-time Undergraduate Enrollment (2017):** 21,222

**Honors Members in Good Standing**: 3184; (mean size of all programs is 2,030).

**Honors Average Admission Test Score(s)**: ACT, 31; SAT, est. 1420.

**Average High School GPA/Class Rank:** 4.13, weighted.

**Basic Admission Requirements:** ACT, 30; SAT, est. 1390; GPA, est. 3.85.

**Application Deadline(s):** *Please verify with each program, as some deadlines could change.* First deadline November 15, 2018, with notification February 1, 2019; final deadline, February 1, 2019, and notification March 1, 2019.

**Honors Programs with SAT scores from 1420—1461:** Auburn, Central Florida, Delaware, Iowa, Kansas, Mississippi, Missouri, New Jersey Inst of Technology, Penn State, South Florida, Vermont, Virginia Commonwealth.

**Administrative Staff:** 8.

**RATINGS AT A GLANCE:** For all mortarboard ratings immediately below, a score of 5 is the maximum and represents a comparison with all rated honors colleges and programs. More detailed explanations follow the "mortarboard" ratings.

**PERCEPTION\* OF UNIVERSITY AS A WHOLE, NOT OF HONORS:** 🎓🎓🎓🎓

\*Perception is based on the university's ranking among public universities in the 2018 U.S. News Best Colleges report. Please bear in mind that the better the U.S. News ranking, the more difficult it is for an honors college or program to have a rating that equals or improves on the magazine ranking.

**OVERALL HONORS RATING:** 🎓🎓🎓

**Curriculum Requirements:** 🎓🎓🎓 1/2

**Number of Honors Classes Offered:** 🎓🎓🎓🎓

**Number of Honors Classes in Key Disciplines:** 🎓🎓🎓🎓 1/2

**Extent of Honors Enrollment:** 🎓🎓🎓

**Honors-only Class Size:** 🎓🎓🎓🎓

**Overall Class Size (Honors-only plus mixed, contract):** 🎓🎓

**Honors Grad Rate Adjusted to SAT:** 🎓🎓🎓🎓

**Grad Rate Adjusted to Freshman Retention Rate:** 🎓🎓🎓 1/2

**Ratio of Staff to Students:** 🎓🎓

**Priority Registration: Yes,** by virtue of receiving scholarships, honors students register early.

**Honors Housing Amenities:** 🎓🎓🎓🎓

**Honors Housing Availability:** 🎓🎓 1/2

**Prestigious Awards:** 🎓🎓🎓🎓 1/2

## RATING SCORES AND EXPLANATIONS:

**Curriculum Requirements (3.5):** The most important rating category, the curriculum completion requirement (classes required to complete honors) defines not only what honors students should learn but also the extent to which honors students and faculty are connected in the classroom. If there is a thesis or capstone requirement, it reinforces the individual contact and research skills so important to learning.

The average number of honors semester hours required for completion across all programs is 30.0.

Completion of the General Honors requirements requires a total of 24 credits, comprised of 12 credits in honors courses and 12 credits in honors experiences. These experiences may include honors in the major, internships, study abroad, the writing fellows program, and work for the Iowa Policy Research Organization, among many other options. Students may complete one honors contract course as part of 12 credits. Completing departmental honors, including a thesis/capstone, may be used to satisfy the honors experience requirement.

The University Honors for Engineering option requires 24 credits as well, including 6-11 credits in honors courses and 13-18 credits of honors experiences, and the option of completing departmental honors to meet 12 credits of the honors experience requirement.

**AP/IB credits** are **not** counted as replacements for honors courses.

**No. Honors Classes Offered (4.0):** This is a measure of the total **adjusted** honors main sections available in the term reported, not including labs and thesis. An adjusted main section has 3 or more semester credits, or equivalent, and sections with fewer credits receive a lower prorated value.

Iowa honors offered a section for every **12.4** enrolled students. The average for all programs was **15.0**. The lower the number, the better.

In the term reported, **61.4%** of honors enrollment was **in honors-only sections; 32.5% was in mixed sections; and 6.1% was in contract sections.** For all programs under review, enrollment by type of honors section was 75.8% honors-only, 15.4 % mixed, and 8.8% contract.

**No. Honors Classes in Key Disciplines (4.5):** The 15 "key" disciplines are biological sciences; business (all); chemistry; communications (especially public speaking); computer science; economics; engineering (all); English; history; math (all); philosophy; physics; political science; psychology; and sociology, anthropology, and gender studies. Interdisciplinary sections, such as those often taken for General Education credit in the first two years, do receive a lesser, prorated discipline "credit" because they introduce students to multiple disciplines in an especially engaging way, often with in-depth discussion.

For this measure, mixed and contract sections are not counted as a section in a key discipline unless students taking the sections for honors credit make up at least 10% of the total section enrollment.

In the term reported, the program offered a section in a key discipline for every **14.4 honors students.** The average for all programs is **24.7.** The lower the number, the better.

Of **116 adjusted sections in key disciplines, 45 were honors-only courses or research sections**. The most sections were in English (38), followed by philosophy and sociology/anthropology. Other disciplines in order of representation were business, biology, chemistry, history, engineering, physics, political science, and psychology.

The program offered the excellent honors "Rhetoric" courses, about 20 sections which we counted as English, although they combine elements of communication in the broader sense. The description: "Analysis and critique to discover, question, explain, and justify positions and claims made in writing and speaking; reading and listening to comprehend and assess arguments; employment of rhetorical concepts (e.g., purpose, audience); understanding research as responsible inquiry for speaking and writing..."

**Extent of Honors Enrollment (3.0):** Not all honors students take an honors class each term, especially after the first two years. Programs that have fewer honors classes and thesis options for upper-division honors students will *generally* have fewer total members in good standing who are actually enrolled in a given term. (Please be aware, however, that honors students not enrolled in a class for a term are still tied to the honors community through residential and extracurricular activities.) *Our research shows that this measure is closely related to honors completion rates, i.e., the number of students who complete honors requirements by the time they graduate.*

For example, if a program has 1,800 individual students enrolled in a given term, and 3,000 students in good standing, the level of enrollment was .67, an indication that honors class enrollment is somewhat below average, especially in upper-division classes. **Iowa honors has a ratio of 1.43**, above the average of 1.30 for all programs.

**Average Class Size, Honors-only Sections (5.0):** Offered mostly in the first two years, honors-only classes tend to be smaller and, as the name implies, have no or very few students other than those in the

honors program. These class sections are commonly much smaller than mixed or contract sections, or regular non-honors class sections in the university.

The average honors-only class size at the honors college is **14.0 students**. The average for all programs is **17.5 students.**

**Average Class Size, Overall (2.0):** The overall class calculation is based on the *proportion* of honors students in each type of class (honors-only, mixed honors, and honors contract sections). Thus it is not a raw average. The overall honors-credit class size is **87.4 students**, versus the average for all programs of **24.7 students**. (Below the reasons for the large overall class size are evident.)

These class size averages also do not correspond to the number of students per honors section ratings above. The reason is that, in computing average class size metrics, we include enrollment in each 1-2-credit section, not just sections with 3 or more credits.

Along with an honors-only class size of 14.0 students (listed above), the program's mixed honors sections have an average size of **235.8 students,** and the contract sections with honors credit for individual honors students average **81.3 students.** Across all programs, the average mixed honors section has 68.6 students, and the average contract section has 56.6 students.

**Honors Grad Rate Adjusted to SAT (4.0):** The rating is the based on the actual grad rate for students who entered the program six years earlier, whether or not the students remained in honors. The **actual rate of 85.0%** is also compared to the rates of other programs with the same test score entry requirement range, and then adjusted upward if the program is performing above other programs in the same range, or downward if the performance is less than other programs in the same range. The rate here was the same, **85.0%.**

**Grad Rate Adjusted to Freshman Retention Rate (3.5):** This rate compares the actual grad rate above to a predicted grade rate when freshman retention rates are considered. The actual grad rate is **1.33 points lower** than the predicted rate. For all programs, the actual grad rate is **.33 points lower** than the predicted rate.

**Ratio of Staff to Honors Students (2.0):** There is 1 staff member for every **398.0** students. (Mean ratio for all programs is 1 staff member for every **127.9** students.)

**Honors Residence Halls, Amenities (4.0):** 100% of honors students in honors housing are freshmen, and about 80% reside in Daum Hall. The residence has a variety of traditional rooms and hall baths. It is air-conditioned and has an excellent location for honors students: a tunnel connects Daum to the dining hall in neighboring Burge Hall, and a covered skywalk connects Daum to the Honors Center, which is the administrative home of the program.

Another 20% of first-year honors students in honors housing live in the newest and largest dorm (12 floors, 1,049 beds) on campus, Catlett Hall, east of, and overlooking, the Iowa River. Named for Elizabeth Catlett, an artist and one of the university's first MFA graduates, the hall features onsite dining at the Marketplace. In this air-conditioned facility, the community restrooms include between six and ten individual bathroom pods. The individual pods contain a sink, shower, toilet and lockable door. Catlett also has its own fitness center.

**Honors Residence Halls, Availability (2.5):** This rating compares the number of occupants in honors residence halls to the number of honors freshman and sophomore members in good standing. The ratio for the program is **.22** places for each first- and second-year student. The median for all programs is .49 places.

**Prestigious Awards (4.5):** The awards that we track and include are listed in the section titled "Prestigious Scholarships." The awards are sometimes won by students who are not in an honors college or program, but increasingly many are enrolled in honors programs. It is also a trend that honors colleges and programs help to prepare their students for the awards competitions.

"Since 2007, the University of Iowa and the Honors Program have supported our students in their successful pursuit of over 100 nationally competitive fellowships including:

•35 Fulbright U.S. Student Grants – The honors program no longer coordinates the Fulbright competition, and this is not representative of the University's full record of Fulbright grant winners. Through Fall 2017, 32 of the 35 had been awarded.
•20 Goldwater Scholars – 19 had been awarded through Fall 2017. We have earned 53 as an institution between 1989-Spring 2017 with another in Spring 2018.
•19 NSF Graduate Research Fellowships – 14 had been awarded between 2007-2017 to both current honors students and honors alumnae; this does not reflect the university's full record.
•12 Critical Language Scholarships – 11 had been awarded through Fall 2017.
•7 Truman Scholars – The university has had a total of 14 successful Truman applicants since 1977, with six consecutive awards from 2008-2013. In 2015, all three University of Iowa nominees were named Truman Finalists.
•4 Churchill Scholarships.
•2 Beinecke Scholarships – 1 had been awarded through Fall 2017.
•2 Rhodes Scholarships – A total of 20 University of Iowa students have been awarded Rhodes Scholarships since its inception, the most recent in Fall 2015.
•4 Gates Cambridge Scholarships – Five total, the most recent in 2015,
•1 Schwarzman Scholarship.
•7 Udall Scholarships – Four students had been awarded 5 Udall scholarships between them through Fall 2017."

**UNRATED FEATURES**

**Continuation and Honors Graduation GPA Requirement:** 3.33 for both.

**Academic Strengths, National Rankings:** This is based on national rankings of *graduate* programs in all but engineering and business, where undergraduate rankings are used. One of the weaknesses of the *U.S. News* rankings is that they focus on too many wealth-related metrics while ignoring their own assessments of academic departments. The rankings listed below are for all universities, public or private.

Iowa has a high overall average departmental ranking of 50.3.

The leading nationally ranked academic departments at Iowa are psychology (26), business (31), sociology (36), political science (37), education (40), economics (42), English (42), history (53), and biology (54).

**Internships, Professional Development, Community Engagement:** "Half of the requirements for graduating with University Honors are made up of experiential learning opportunities, which students choose from a menu of options. They may pursue one type of experience, or they might mix and match.

Options for completing the experiential learning requirement include:

•Honors in a major
•Research
•Completing a guided reflection based on an internship or study abroad experience
•Serving as an Honors Writing Fellow
•Participating in the Iowa Policy Research Organization
•A suite of experiential learning coursework, including independent study, teaching practica, service learning (service-based independent study), as well as specialized courses offered within certain colleges and departments
•Serving as an honors program outreach ambassador to communicate with current and prospective honors students
•Graduate-level coursework.

**Undergraduate Research:** "The Iowa Center for Research by Undergraduates, or ICRU, promotes and provides oversight for undergraduate research at the University of Iowa. ICRU works directly with faculty, research staff, and students to foster mentoring relationships. The center provides nearly $400,000 annually in funding for undergraduates to work with faculty and staff; this is principally stipend support, although travel support is also available for students to perform and present their work. ICRU also supports annual scholar development opportunities for undergraduates to present their work (on campus, at events such as the Fall and Spring Undergraduate Research Festivals, and off campus, such as at Research in the Capitol, where a group of undergraduate researchers present their work at the Iowa Statehouse) and learn the 'soft skills' necessary to succeed as researchers. Students and mentors who have excelled in their efforts are recognized by ICRU on behalf of the University through the Excellence in Undergraduate Research and ICRU Distinguished Mentor awards."

**Honors Study Abroad:** "Another change in the past couple of years is the option of completing a guided reflection process to earn honors credit for an internship or study abroad experience. Previously, students would be required to complete an independent project for these types of experiences, and very few students pursued that honors option (often fewer than a dozen per year). The reflection process was introduced in Fall 2016, and 32 students earned honors credit for either an internship or study abroad during the 2016-17 academic year. In the 2017-18 academic year, that number has reached 140 so far (including Spring 2018; 101 just through the winter). Some of the narratives students have produced can be found on our student-run blog under the tags 'Experience Internships' and 'Experience Study Abroad' (honorsatiowa.wordpress.com/)."

**Financial Aid:** "97.8% of the incoming class of honors students in Fall 2017 received at least one merit scholarship. **Note that the requirements for admissions to honors for Fall 2017 match those for the**

**Old Gold Scholarship, giving all automatically qualified in-state honors students $8,500 per year, and out-of-state (domestic) students $10,000 per year.** (These scholarship amounts and criteria have changed for in-state students beginning Fall 2018 and later. Further, with the advent of a **new honors program admissions process, students no longer automatically qualify for honors membership.**)" Note: We were unable to find the updated information.

"Exceptions to this include students who enter the program through the selective admissions process (an appeal process for incoming first-year students who did not meet the automatic requirements under the past admission process for honors membership), as first-year international students, as transfer students, or as current students, who may have admission scholarships in different amounts. Our 2017 population also includes students who applied after the deadline for merit scholarships, though they had the credentials to qualify for one of the above-mentioned scholarships with an earlier application. There are also many other scholarships that students can qualify for based on more specific criteria within departments.

"Underrepresented minority students are also automatically considered for the Advantage Iowa Scholarship, which has both need- and merit-based criteria and ranges from $2,000-8,000 per academic year. This award is stackable on top of the admissions scholarships mentioned above.

"The Provost Scholarship is available for National Merit finalists, National Achievement finalists, and National Hispanic Scholars. It is $3,000 per year for four years and stacks on top of the admissions scholarships mentioned above.

"Additionally, the honors program provided more than $170,000 in scholarships to currently enrolled (rising sophomores, juniors, and seniors) honors students in FY17."

**Honors Fees:** None.

**Placement of Honors Graduates:** "65% of 2017 honors graduates reported plans to pursue further education through a graduate and/or professional program, while another 27% reported still considering that option for the future. The 2017 honors graduating class included the university's first Schwarzman Scholar as well as several Fulbright recipients. 2017 graduates reported plans to pursue graduate studies at institutions such as the University of Chicago and Imperial College London as well as the University of Iowa's own prestigious medical program, and reported securing jobs at companies such as Google, Procter & Gamble, and Principal Financial Group."

**Degree of Difference**: This is difference between (1) the average SAT scores for recently enrolled honors students (1420) and (2) the average test scores for all students in the university (1220) as a whole. The difference may be an indication of how "elite" honors students may be perceived as compared to students in the university as a whole. **Please keep in mind that neither the high nor low selectivity of an honors program determines how effective the program may be.**

**NAME**: UNIVERSITY HONORS PROGRAM AT THE UNIVERSITY OF KANSAS

**Date Established:** 1968

**Location**: Lawrence, Kansas

**University Full-time Undergraduate Enrollment (2017):** 19,262

**Honors Members in Good Standing**: 1,530; (mean size of all programs is 2,030).

**Honors Average Admission Test Score(s)**: ACT, 32.3; SAT, est. 1450.

**Average High School GPA/Class Rank:** 3.98, weighted. Top 5% of high school class.

**Basic Admission Requirements:** "There are no minimum GPA or test score requirements. We use holistic admissions, examining a student's entire application in making admissions decisions. We equally weigh all five of the following in making admissions decisions: ACT/SAT composite, unweighted GPA, strength of curriculum, extra-curricular activities, and critical writing skills."

**Application Deadline(s):** *Please verify with each program, as some deadlines could change.* November 1, 2018, for admission and scholarships.

**Honors Programs with SAT scores from 1420—1461:** Auburn, Central Florida, Delaware, Iowa, Kansas, Mississippi, Missouri, New Jersey Inst of Technology, Penn State, South Florida, Vermont, Virginia Commonwealth.

**Administrative Staff:** 10.

**RATINGS AT A GLANCE:** For all mortarboard ratings immediately below, a score of 5 is the maximum and represents a comparison with all rated honors colleges and programs. More detailed explanations follow the "mortarboard" ratings.

**PERCEPTION\* OF UNIVERSITY AS A WHOLE, NOT OF HONORS:** 🎓🎓🎓🎓

\*Perception is based on the university's ranking among public universities in the 2018 U.S. News Best Colleges report. Please bear in mind that the better the U.S. News ranking, the more difficult it is for an honors college or program to have a rating that equals or improves on the magazine ranking.

**OVERALL HONORS RATING:** 🎓🎓🎓🎓

**Curriculum Requirements:** 🎓🎓🎓🎓1/2

**Number of Honors Classes Offered:** 🎓🎓🎓🎓🎓

**Number of Honors Classes in Key Disciplines:** 🎓🎓🎓🎓1/2

**Extent of Honors Enrollment:** 🎓🎓🎓🎓

**Honors-only Class Size:** 🎓🎓🎓🎓🎓

**Overall Class Size (Honors-only plus mixed, contract):** 🎓🎓🎓🎓🎓

**Honors Grad Rate Adjusted to SAT:** 🎓🎓🎓🎓 1/2

**Grad Rate Adjusted to Freshman Retention Rate:** 🎓🎓🎓🎓🎓

**Ratio of Staff to Students:** 🎓🎓🎓🎓 1/2

**Priority Registration: Yes,** honors students register for all courses, honors and otherwise, with the first group of students during each year they are in the program.

**Honors Housing Amenities:** 🎓🎓🎓🎓

**Honors Housing Availability:** 🎓🎓🎓 1/2

**Prestigious Awards:** 🎓🎓🎓🎓 1/2

## RATING SCORES AND EXPLANATIONS:

**Curriculum Requirements (4.5):** The most important rating category, the curriculum completion requirement (classes required to complete honors) defines not only what honors students should learn but also the extent to which honors students and faculty are connected in the classroom. If there is a thesis or capstone requirement, it reinforces the individual contact and research skills so important to learning.

The average number of honors semester hours required for completion across all programs is 30.0.

The KU Honors Program requires the equivalent of 31 credits: a minimum of 18 credits (6 honors courses), a 1-credit honors seminar, plus the equivalent of 12 credits in honors experiences. The 18 credits may be met by honors program courses, departmental honors courses, honors by contract, graduate courses, or a limited number from a "less commonly taught language."

The 12 experiential credits are from the following areas: Public Service Enhancement; Cultural Literacy & Social Justice; Global Citizenship; Aesthetic Engagement; Professional Development & Social Entrepreneurship; Leadership; Research Skills & In-Depth Learning; Interdisciplinarity & Breadth of Learning.

Completion of departmental honors is also "one pathway for completion of the University Honors Program honors experiences."

**AP/IB credits** are **not** counted as replacements for honors courses.

**No. Honors Classes Offered (5.0):** This is a measure of the total **adjusted** honors main sections available in the term reported, not including labs and thesis. An adjusted main section has 3 or more semester credits, or equivalent, and sections with fewer credits receive a lower prorated value.

The honors offered a section for every **10.1** enrolled students. The average for all programs was **15.0**. The lower the number, the better.

In the term reported, a very impressive **88%** of honors enrollment was **in honors-only sections or experiential activities; 9.4% was in mixed sections; and 2.6% was in contract sections.** For all programs under review, enrollment by type of honors section was 75.8% honors-only, 15.4 % mixed, and 8.8% contract.

**No. Honors Classes in Key Disciplines (4.5):** The 15 "key" disciplines are biological sciences; business (all); chemistry; communications (especially public speaking); computer science; economics; engineering (all); English; history; math (all); philosophy; physics; political science; psychology; and sociology, anthropology, and gender studies. Interdisciplinary sections, such as those often taken for General Education credit in the first two years, do receive a lesser, prorated discipline "credit" because they introduce students to multiple disciplines in an especially engaging way, often with in-depth discussion.

For this measure, mixed and contract sections are not counted as a section in a key discipline unless students taking the sections for honors credit make up at least 10% of the total section enrollment.

In the term reported, the program offered a section in a key discipline for every **16.6 honors students.** The average for all programs is **24.7.** The lower the number, the better.

Out of **63 adjusted sections in key disciplines**, **52 were honors-only sections**. The most sections were in English, followed by business, sociology/anthropology, math, biology, computer science, psychology, chemistry, communications, and history.

The programs offered about 40 sections of the one-credit "Freshman Honors Seminar." They are required in the first semester, and it "serves as an introduction to the Honors Program, the resources offered by the University of Kansas, and one of their academic areas of interest. While closely examining a specific topic, students develop their skills in research, reading, writing, and in-depth discussion. The instructor of the student's seminar also serves as the academic honors advisor for the enrolled students."

**Extent of Honors Enrollment (4.0):** Not all honors students take an honors class each term, especially after the first two years. Programs that have fewer honors classes and thesis options for upper-division honors students will *generally* have fewer total members in good standing who are actually enrolled in a given term. (Please be aware, however, that honors students not enrolled in a class for a term are still tied to the honors community through residential and extracurricular activities.) *Our research shows that this measure is closely related to honors completion rates, i.e., the number of students who complete honors requirements by the time they graduate.*

For example, if a program has 1,800 individual students enrolled in a given term, and 3,000 students in good standing, the level of enrollment was .67, an indication that honors class enrollment is somewhat

below average, especially in upper-division classes. **Kansas honors has a ratio of 1.33**, just above the average of 1.30 for all programs.

**Average Class Size, Honors-only Sections (5.0):** Offered mostly in the first two years, honors-only classes tend to be smaller and, as the name implies, have no or very few students other than those in the honors program. These class sections always are much smaller than mixed or contract sections, or regular non-honors class sections in the university.

The average honors-only class size at KU Honors was **14.4 students**. The average for all programs is **17.5 students.**

**Average Class Size, Overall (5.0):** The overall class calculation is based on the *proportion* of honors students in each type of class (honors-only, mixed honors, and honors contract sections). Thus it is not a raw average. The overall honors-credit class size was **16.9 students**, versus the average for all programs of **24.9 students**.

These class size averages also do not correspond to the number of students per honors section ratings above. The reason is that, in computing average class size metrics, we include enrollment in each 1-2-credit section, not just sections with 3 or more credits.

Along with an honors-only class size of 14.4 students (listed above), the program's mixed honors sections have an average size of **37.3 students,** and the contract sections with honors credit for individual honors students average **28.8 students.** Across all programs, the average mixed honors section has 68.6 students, and the average contract section has 56.6 students.

**Honors Grad Rate Adjusted to SAT (4.5):** The rating is the based on the actual grad rate for students who entered the program six years earlier, whether or not the students remained in honors. The **actual rate of 88.0%** is also compared to the rates of other programs with the same test score entry requirement range, and then adjusted upward if the program is performing above other programs in the same range, or downward if the performance is less than other programs in the same range. The rate here is slightly upward, to **88.7%.**

**Grad Rate Adjusted to Freshman Retention Rate (5.0):** This rate compares the actual grad rate above to a predicted grade rate when freshman retention rates are considered. The actual grad rate is an extremely impressive **7.7 points higher** than the predicted rate. For all programs, the actual grad rate is **.33 points lower** than the predicted rate.

**Ratio of Staff to Honors Students (4.5):** There is 1 staff member for every **92.2** students. (Mean ratio for all programs is 1 staff member for every **127.9** students.)

**Honors Residence Halls, Amenities (4.0):** "Templin Hall is the most popular dorm on campus for Honors Students for its renovated, suite-style rooms and location. Beginning in 2012, the Department of Housing agreed to turn over the entire hall to the University Honors Program for its students, due to its immediate proximity to Nunemaker Center, the University Honors Program's unique, full-service home. Students are NOT required to live in the Honors hall, but it is recommended.

"Many Honor Students also chose to live in a Scholarship Hall. Students complete 4-6 hours of weekly duties, such as cooking or cleaning for the 50-person community. Students apply to live in the scholarship hall and selection is based on financial need, academic merit and essays demonstrating commitment to the cooperative philosophy and diverse community." There are 12 Scholarship Halls; about half the rooms are traditional doubles with hall baths, while the other half features suite-style rooms.

**Honors Residence Halls, Availability (3.5):** This rating compares the number of occupants in honors residence halls to the number of honors freshman and sophomore members in good standing. The ratio for the program is **.43** places for each first- and second-year student. The median for all programs is .49 places.

**Prestigious Awards (4.5):** The awards that we track and include are listed in the section titled "Prestigious Scholarships." The awards are sometimes won by students who are not in an honors college or program, but increasingly many are enrolled in honors programs. It is also a trend that honors colleges and programs help to prepare their students for the awards competitions.

KU Honors students have won at least 90% of all the prestigious awards earned by KU students and graduates. Total scholarships won by KU students include 27 Rhodes (tied for 6th among public universities); three Gates Cambridge; nine Marshall; and 19 Truman.

The record of winning undergraduate awards is likewise impressive: at least 62 Goldwater Scholarships (in the top 10 among public universities); and 19 Udall Scholarships, also easily in the top 10.

## UNRATED FEATURES

**Continuation and Honors Graduation GPA Requirement:** 3.25 for both.

**Academic Strengths, National Rankings:** This is based on national rankings of *graduate* programs in all but engineering and business, where undergraduate rankings are used. One of the weaknesses of the *U.S. News* rankings is that they focus on too many wealth-related metrics while ignoring their own assessments of academic departments. The rankings listed below are for all universities, public or private.

**All 15 departments** at KU that we track are ranked in the top 100.

The nationally ranked academic departments at KU are education (17), history (41), business (45), psychology (50), earth sciences (54), political science (65), math (66), English (67), economics (72), biology (73), chemistry (73), sociology (75), engineering (78), computer science (91), and physics (91).

**Internships, Professional Development, Community Engagement:** The Honors Director reports that 69% of honors students earn credits by Enhanced Learning Experiences (ELEs) in Public Service. "This ELE enables students to gain self-awareness and a sense of social responsibility through service to others."

And 64% of students participate in an ELE called Professional Development & Social Entrepreneurship.

"This ELE encourages students to prepare for their professional careers through internships, entrepreneurship, or coursework in business."

**Undergraduate Research:** "At least 59% of the 2016-2017 Honors Completers [students who complete all honors requirements by the time of graduation] participated in a significant research experience. Virtually all Honors Graduates will have research experience in one or more classes. "The Honors Program cultivated a university-wide program for undergraduate research until 2012. The program included the Undergraduate Research Symposium, a journal for undergraduate research, and research grants for independent student research. Due to the success of this program, it was spun off as the Center for Undergraduate Research in Fall 2012. Honors students benefit broadly from the expanded program, which has grown in scope, resources and reach.

"At the University of Kansas, honors research and theses are integral to departmental honors. Many University Honors Program students pursue departmental honors in their major(s) and completion of departmental honors is one pathway for completion of the University Honors Program.

"One of our eight Enhanced Learning Experiences is Research Skills & In-Depth Learning. This ELE helps students learn how to locate and evaluate information, solve problems, think creatively, and communicate their findings."

**Honors Study Abroad:** "The University of Kansas is a world leader in study abroad. There are over 130 programs plus an additional 200 ISEP and Mid-American University consortium sites in over 70 countries. The University Honors Program, however, sends students to far more destinations than the standard Office of Study Abroad offerings. Essentially, if there is an academic benefit to be gleaned, we will help students coordinate and fund the study abroad destination they choose."

"One of our eight Enhanced Learning Experiences (students must complete 4 ELEs to graduate) is Global Citizenship. This ELE prepares students to understand, adapt to, and thrive in a culturally diverse, global environment. "

**Financial Aid:** "Virtually all Honors students receive a 4-year, renewable scholarship through the University's scholarship structure. In-state students typically receive packages ranging from $4,000 to approximately $80,000 (full tuition, room and board, fees, etc.). Out-of-state students virtually all have their tuition reduced to a rate of either full in-state tuition or 1.5 times that of in-state students.

"**National Merit Scholars, National Achievement Scholars**, and National Hispanic Recognition students receive packages for full-tuition and fees."

Honors Opportunity Awards: Approximately $250-$1,500, these awards provide financial support to Honors Students to take advantage of opportunities for intellectual and academic growth such as study abroad programs, community service, internships, conferences and off-campus research.

**Honors Fees:** None.

**Placement of Honors Graduates:** KU Honors has a placement rate of 96.4%, distributed as follows:

- 37.1% employed at graduation
- 28.6% graduate school
- 13.4% medical school
- 6.7%   law school
- 10.7% other (e.g., peace corps, internships, travel)
- 3.6%   seeking education or employment

**Degree of Difference**: This is difference between (1) the average SAT scores for recently enrolled honors students (1450) and (2) the average test scores for all students in the university (1160) as a whole. The difference may be an indication of how "elite" honors students may be perceived as compared to students in the university as a whole. **Please keep in mind that neither the high nor low selectivity of an honors program determines how effective the program may be.**

**NAME**: LSU ROGER HADFIELD OGDEN HONORS COLLEGE

**Date Established:** 1992

**Location**: Baton Rouge, Louisiana

**University Full-time Undergraduate Enrollment (2017):** 26,118

**Honors Members in Good Standing**: 1584; (mean size of all programs is 2,030).

**Honors Average Admission Test Score(s)**: ACT, 31.2; SAT, 1382.

**Average High School GPA/Class Rank:** 3.79, unweighted.

**Basic Admission Requirements:** ACT, 30; SAT, 1390; GPA, 3.50.

**Application Deadline(s):** *Please verify with each program, as some deadlines could change.* November 15, 2018; notification on a rolling basis.

**Honors Programs with SAT scores from 1370—1403:** Arizona, CUNY Macaulay, Georgia State, Houston, Indiana, LSU, Massachusetts, New Mexico, Purdue, Texas Tech, UAB.

**Administrative Staff:** 16.

**RATINGS AT A GLANCE:** For all mortarboard ratings immediately below, a score of 5 is the maximum and represents a comparison with all rated honors colleges and programs. More detailed explanations follow the "mortarboard" ratings.

**PERCEPTION* OF UNIVERSITY AS A WHOLE, NOT OF HONORS:** 🎓🎓🎓 1/2

*Perception is based on the university's ranking among public universities in the 2018 U.S. News Best Colleges report. Please bear in mind that the better the U.S. News ranking, the more difficult it is for an honors college or program to have a rating that equals or improves on the magazine ranking.

**OVERALL HONORS RATING:** 🎓🎓🎓🎓 1/2

**Curriculum Requirements:** 🎓🎓🎓🎓 1/2

**Number of Honors Classes Offered:** 🎓🎓🎓🎓🎓

**Number of Honors Classes in Key Disciplines:** 🎓🎓🎓🎓 1/2

**Extent of Honors Enrollment:** 🎓🎓🎓 1/2

**Honors-only Class Size:** 🎓🎓🎓🎓 1/2

**Overall Class Size (Honors-only plus mixed, contract):** 🎓🎓🎓🎓

**Honors Grad Rate Adjusted to SAT:** 🎓🎓🎓 1/2

**Grad Rate Adjusted to Freshman Retention Rate:** 🎓🎓🎓 1/2

**Ratio of Staff to Students:** 🎓🎓🎓🎓 1/2

**Priority Registration: Yes,** honors students register for all courses, honors and otherwise, with the first group of students during each year they are in the program.

**Honors Housing Amenities:** 🎓🎓🎓🎓

**Honors Housing Availability:** 🎓🎓🎓🎓 1/2

**Prestigious Awards:** 🎓🎓🎓 1/2

## RATING SCORES AND EXPLANATIONS:

**Curriculum Requirements (4.5):** The most important rating category, the curriculum completion requirement (classes required to complete honors) defines not only what honors students should learn but also the extent to which honors students and faculty are connected in the classroom. If there is a thesis or capstone requirement, it reinforces the individual contact and research skills so important to learning.

The average number of honors semester hours required for completion across all programs is 30.0.

College Honors, the highest distinction, requires 32 honors credits for completion, including a 6-credit thesis. Contract hours can count for 6-9 credits.

Graduation in Good Standing requires 24 honors credit and no thesis.

Sophomore Honors Distinction requires 20 credits, including a 6-credit thesis.

Upper-Division Honors Distinction requires 12-18 credits, which may include 6-9 contract hours. A 6-credit thesis is required.

**AP/IB credits:** "Only the introductory Chemistry sequence…only 1% of incoming students have this credit."

**No. Honors Classes Offered (5.0):** This is a measure of the total **adjusted** honors main sections available in the term reported, not including labs and thesis. An adjusted main section has 3 or more semester credits, or equivalent, and sections with fewer credits receive a lower prorated value.

The honors offered a section for every **9.0** enrolled students. The average for all programs was **15.0**. The lower the number, the better.

In the term reported, **78.7%** of honors enrollment was **in honors-only sections; essentially none in in mixed sections; and 21.3% was in contract sections.** For all programs under review, enrollment by type of honors section was 75.8% honors-only, 15.4 % mixed, and 8.8% contract.

**No. Honors Classes in Key Disciplines (4.5):** The 15 "key" disciplines are biological sciences; business (all); chemistry; communications (especially public speaking); computer science; economics; engineering (all); English; history; math (all); philosophy; physics; political science; psychology; and sociology, anthropology, and gender studies. Interdisciplinary sections, such as those often taken for General Education credit in the first two years, do receive a lesser, prorated discipline "credit" because they introduce students to multiple disciplines in an especially engaging way, often with in-depth discussion.

For this measure, mixed and contract sections are not counted as a section in a key discipline unless students taking the sections for honors credit make up at least 10% of the total section enrollment.

In the term reported, the honors college offered a section in a key discipline for every **13.7 honors students.** The average for all programs is **24.7.** The lower the number, the better.

Out of **61 adjusted sections in key disciplines, 23 were honors-only sections,** indicating that most work in the disciplines was done in honors contract sections. Most of the sections were in math, sociology-related, biology, communications, business, engineering, chemistry, and physics.

The college offered more than 35 seminar sections including 16 sections of the laudable "Critical Analysis and Social Responsibility," an introduction "to various practices of academic discourse and research methods. Interdisciplinary approach [composition, humanities, social sciences] to a specific topic."

**Extent of Honors Enrollment (3.5):** Not all honors students take an honors class each term, especially after the first two years. Programs that have fewer honors classes and thesis options for upper-division honors students will *generally* have fewer total members in good standing who are actually enrolled in a given term. (Please be aware, however, that honors students not enrolled in a class for a term are still tied to the honors community through residential and extracurricular activities.) *Our research shows that this measure is closely related to honors completion rates, i.e., the number of students who complete honors requirements by the time they graduate.*

For example, if a program has 1,800 individual students enrolled in a given term, and 3,000 students in good standing, the level of enrollment was .67, an indication that honors class enrollment is somewhat below average, especially in upper-division classes. **LSU Honors College has a ratio of 1.17**, below the average of 1.30 for all programs.

**Average Class Size, Honors-only Sections (4.5):** Offered mostly in the first two years, honors-only classes tend to be smaller and, as the name implies, have no or very few students other than those in the

honors program. These class sections always are much smaller than mixed or contract sections, or regular non-honors class sections in the university.

The average honors-only class size at the honors college is **16.9 students**. The average for all programs is **17.5 students.**

**Average Class Size, Overall (4.0):** The overall class calculation is based on the *proportion* of honors students in each type of class (honors-only, mixed honors, and honors contract sections). Thus it is not a raw average. The overall honors-credit class size is **23.4 students**, versus the average for all programs of **24.9 students**.

These class size averages also do not correspond to the number of students per honors section ratings above. The reason is that, in computing average class size metrics, we include enrollment in each 1-2-credit section, not just sections with 3 or more credits.

Along with an honors-only class size of 16.9 students (listed above), the contract sections with honors credit for individual honors students average **47.1 students. No mixed sections.** Across all programs, the average mixed honors section has 68.6 students, and the average contract section has 56.6 students.

**Honors Grad Rate Adjusted to SAT (3.5):** The rating is the based on the actual grad rate for students who entered the program six years earlier, whether or not the students remained in honors. The **actual rate of 83.9%** is also compared to the rates of other programs with the same test score entry requirement range, and then adjusted upward if the program is performing above other programs in the same range, or downward if the performance is less than other programs in the same range. The rate here is slightly downward, to **83.4%.**

**Grad Rate Adjusted to Freshman Retention Rate (3.5):** This rate compares the actual grad rate above to a predicted grade rate when freshman retention rates are considered. The actual grad rate is **.42 points lower** than the predicted rate. For all programs, the actual grad rate is **.33 points lower** than the predicted rate.

**Ratio of Staff to Honors Students (4.5):** There is 1 staff member for every **99.0** students. (Mean ratio for all programs is 1 staff member for every **127.9** students.)

**Honors Residence Halls, Amenities (4.0):** Laville Honors House features traditional double rooms for the most part, with shared hall baths. It is home to more than 600 honors students, making it one of the largest all-honors residence halls. All rooms are air conditioned with room controls. Although the building is coed, men and women are assigned to separate floors. Laville has two kitchens and two laundry rooms. The building has two large lounge/study areas on the first floor and additional study lounges on each floor. In addition, there is a large public lounge area at the entrance to the building, and an outdoor patio/grove that is enclosed on three sides by the building and on the fourth side by the dining hall. Very convenient dining is adjacent, at The 459.

"The Ogden Honors College also occupies The French House—La Maison Française--a Renaissance-style Normandy château built in 1935 as a center for intense study of French language, culture, and literature.

"The French House remains the only non-Quadrangle LSU structure on the National Register of Historic Places. In its prime, the facility was host to formal entertainment and distinguished visitors to campus. Since 1999, it has housed the daily administrative and student life functions of the LSU Honors College. The 16,000 square foot structure currently houses 4 classrooms, 12 administrative offices, a student lounge, and a large public space—The Grand Salon—which is used for events, receptions, concerts, ceremonies, and performances."

**Honors Residence Halls, Availability (4.5):** This rating compares the number of occupants in honors residence halls to the number of honors freshman and sophomore members in good standing. The ratio for the program is **.78** places for each first- and second-year student. The median for programs is .49 places.

**Prestigious Awards (3.5):** The awards that we track and include are listed in the section titled "Prestigious Scholarships." The awards are sometimes won by students who are not in an honors college or program, but increasingly many are enrolled in honors programs. It is also a trend that honors colleges and programs help to prepare their students for the awards competitions.

LSU undergraduates and graduates have won 14 Rhodes Scholarships, one Gates Cambridge, four Marshall, and 11 Truman Scholarships. In addition, they have won 31 Goldwater awards and six Udall. There is an office within the Honors College that coordinates applications for prestigious scholarships.

**UNRATED FEATURES**

**Continuation Requirement:** 3.00.
**Honors Graduation Requirement:** 3.50.

**Academic Strengths, National Rankings:** This is based on national rankings of *graduate* programs in all but engineering and business, where undergraduate rankings are used. One of the weaknesses of the *U.S. News* rankings is that they focus on too many wealth-related metrics while ignoring their own assessments of academic departments. The rankings listed below are for all universities, public or private.

The nationally ranked academic departments at LSU are math (66), physics (71), sociology (75), English (77), economics (78), history (79), chemistry (81), political science (81), earth sciences (91), and engineering (99).

**Internships, Professional Development, Community Engagement:** "Roger Hadfield Ogden Leaders Program invites student proposals for off-campus activities and funds five of these up to $5,000 each. Students with the capacity to conduct a year-long project alongside their academic work are developed and complete a project of impact otherwise impossible but for this program.

"The Ogden Honors College hosts numerous service projects of various duration and scope. An English Language Learners tutoring program with the East Baton Rouge Parish Public School System is of a multi- semester duration, and has earned accolades from the system for our students' efforts. Our internship course is utilized for interdisciplinary internship opportunities and for when departmental internships are unavailable to our students who are working beyond departmental preparations.

"The LASAL (Louisiana Service and Leadership) Program requires an internship experience with relevance to the state of Louisiana. All internship courses are mentored by members of the teaching faculty. These opportunities are coordinated by our Director of Career Development."

**Undergraduate Research:** "Students in the Ogden Honors College are encouraged to participate in a variety of research opportunities:

•Over 110 are current members in LSU's Chancellor's Future Leaders in Research Program, which partners students with faculty research mentors as early as the freshman year.

•Over 80% of Honors College graduating seniors are currently enrolled in thesis coursework.

"The culmination of the Honors curriculum is the Honors Thesis, a two-semester independent study with a professor in the student's major on a topic of the student's choosing. The Honors Thesis is a requirement to graduate with College Honors, the highest distinction the LSU Honors College offers.

"The Ogden Honors College awards special funds towards completing their Honors Thesis in order to pay for supplies, travel, and reimbursement for research participants.

"Additionally, Ogden Honors students present their thesis research at the LSU Discover Day, a conference open to the campus community."

**Honors Study Abroad:** "Ogden Honors College students comprise the largest number of LSU students participating in study abroad opportunities including summer trips, one semester, and full year programs. The Ogden Honors College provides scholarships for students participating in semester and year-long academic programs abroad. In the 2018 academic year, three new abroad scholarship programs were created amounting to a tenfold increase in study abroad scholarship offers.

"The Honors College offers special summer programs for Honors students and from 2006-2010, ran the Gateway to China Program fully funded by the university. This program led to LSU's exchange agreement with Tongji University in Shanghai. In Summer 2011, the Honors College led a service learning trip to South Africa in partnership with the University of California (UCLA, UCSB, UCSD, UC Berkeley). From 2014-2017, the Ogden Honors College has led a summer program in Cuba. In summer 2016 an Ogden Honors summer program in Greece was offered. Finally, an Ogden in Oxford program on the campus of Oxford University was initiated in 2017 and continues in 2018."

**Financial Aid:** "LSU freshman scholarship programs are purposefully aligned with Ogden Honors College admission requirements. While Honors admission is not required for these programs, the design ensures a comprehensive overlap with the Honors entering population.

"Louisiana resident students who meet Honors College criteria receive the state's TOPS scholarship that provides full tuition. These students also receive a $1,500–$2,500 per year stipend at graduated levels, beginning slightly below standardized test score requirements for Honors admission and rising at tiers above that level. A large majority of students also receive a campus job award of $1,550 per year, which may be used for research employment, a distinct academic advantage.

"Non-resident students receive $7,500–$20,500 per year stipends at levels that mirror the in-state student program outlined above. A large majority of non-resident students also receive the campus job award of $1,550 per year.

"LSU is a participating institution with the Stamps Foundation Leadership Scholars Award program. Ten incoming students each year receive full cost of attendance for four years as well as $14,000 of enrichment funding and guidance from our Ogden Honors College Office of Fellowship Advising in the beneficial use of these funds.

"The Ogden Honors College also offers several distinct scholarship programs:

•Named scholarship programs ranging from $36,000 over four years to $1,000 one-time awards, direct support for up to five special projects per year at $5,000 each through our Roger Hadfield Ogden Honors Leaders program,
•support for thesis research at $1,000,
•support for study abroad activity with $500 - $5,000,
•scholarships for underrepresented groups in Engineering and in Business with $4,000 over four years, and
•scholarships through the Shell Honors Student Leaders program at $3,500 over four years including interaction with this major energy company."

**Honors Fees:** None.

**Placement of Honors Graduates:**

"Graduate Schools: Cambridge, Harvard, Stanford, MIT, Columbia, Cornell, University of Amsterdam, University of Bristol, UC Berkeley, Michigan, Vanderbilt, Texas A&M, UT Austin, Rice, Notre Dame.

"Professional Schools: Johns Hopkins Medical School, Columbia University School of Physicians and Surgeons, George Washington University Law School, Harvard Law School, Northwestern University Medical School, Baylor College of Medicine, Emory University School of Medicine, Tulane Medical School, University of Texas Health Sciences Center, Notre Dame Law School, LSU Health Sciences Center

"Employment: Our recent alumni work for Apple, Amazon, Google, GE, Chevron, JPMorgan Chase, Shell, Price Waterhouse Coopers, Nestle, ExxonMobil, Schlumberger, and eBay. They work for the US Senate, in the federal judiciary, and in federal agencies such as the Department of Health and Human Services, the Library of Congress, and the Federal Trade Commission, as well as in service in the Peace Corps and US military. Ogden Honors graduates are influential contributors across a range of industries and comprise a network of passionate alumni."

**Degree of Difference**: This is difference between (1) the average SAT scores for recently enrolled honors students (1382) and (2) the average test scores for all students in the university (1210) as a whole. The difference may be an indication of how "elite" honors students may be perceived as compared to students in the university as a whole. **Please keep in mind that neither the high nor low selectivity of an honors program determines how effective the program may be.**

**NAME**: COMMONWEALTH HONORS COLLEGE

**Date Established:** 1998

**Location**: Amherst, Massachusetts

**University <u>Full-time Undergraduate</u> Enrollment (2017):** 23,373

**Honors Members in Good Standing**: 3,629; (mean size of all programs is 2,030).

**Honors <u>Average</u> Admission Test Score(s)**: ACT, 31; SAT, 1386.

**Average High School GPA/Class Rank:** 4.30, weighted.

**<u>Basic</u> Admission Requirements:** "If you are entering UMass Amherst with an exemplary high school record then you may be considered for admission to the Commonwealth Honors College. There is no separate application process; students are notified of their selection with their general letter of admission."

**Application Deadline(s):** *Please verify with each program, as some deadlines could change.* Early action November 5, 2018, credentials by November 20; regular deadline January 15, 2019, credentials by February 1, 2019. No separate honors application.

**Honors Programs with SAT scores from 1370—1403:** Arizona, CUNY Macaulay, Georgia State, Houston, Indiana, LSU, Massachusetts, New Mexico, Purdue, Texas Tech, UAB.

**Administrative Staff:** 25.

**RATINGS AT A GLANCE:** For all mortarboard ratings immediately below, a score of 5 is the maximum and represents a comparison with all rated honors colleges and programs. More detailed explanations follow the "mortarboard" ratings.

**PERCEPTION* OF UNIVERSITY AS A WHOLE, <u>NOT</u> OF HONORS:** 🎓🎓🎓🎓 1/2

*Perception is based on the university's ranking among public universities in the 2018 U.S. News Best Colleges report. Please bear in mind that the better the U.S. News ranking, the more difficult it is for an honors college or program to have a rating that equals or improves on the magazine ranking.

**OVERALL HONORS RATING:** 🎓🎓🎓🎓

**Curriculum Requirements:** 🎓🎓🎓 1/2

**Number of Honors Classes Offered:** 🎓🎓🎓🎓🎓

**Number of Honors Classes in Key Disciplines:** 🎓🎓🎓🎓

**Extent of Honors Enrollment:** 🎓🎓🎓

**Honors-only Class Size:** 🎓🎓🎓🎓🎓

**Overall Class Size (Honors-only plus mixed, contract):** 🎓🎓🎓🎓

**Honors Grad Rate Adjusted to SAT:** 🎓🎓🎓🎓

**Grad Rate Adjusted to Freshman Retention Rate:** 🎓🎓🎓

**Ratio of Staff to Students:** 🎓🎓🎓 1/2

**Priority Registration: No.** "Many honors sections of courses are restricted to honors students during the pre-registration period, but may be opened to non-honors students when the semester begins on a space available basis with permission of instructor. A sufficient number of sections of honors courses are held for entering first-year honors students to enroll during summer orientation. Approximately 20% of honors freshmen enter with sufficient college credits to give them sophomore standing. By the time spring registration starts in November, 70% of honors freshmen have sufficient credits to give them sophomore or junior standing. Because student registration is prioritized by class standing, most honors students are able to register earlier."

**Honors Housing Amenities:** 🎓🎓🎓🎓🎓

**Honors Housing Availability:** 🎓🎓🎓🎓 1/2

**Prestigious Awards:** 🎓🎓🎓 1/2

## RATING SCORES AND EXPLANATIONS:

**Curriculum Requirements (3.5):** The most important rating category, the curriculum completion requirement (classes required to complete honors) defines not only what honors students should learn but also the extent to which honors students and faculty are connected in the classroom. If there is a thesis or capstone requirement, it reinforces the individual contact and research skills so important to learning.

The average number of honors semester hours required for completion across all programs is 30.0.

Honors completion at the highest level (Commonwealth Honors College Scholar, with Departmental Honors) requires a minimum of about 30 hours of honors credit, of which 5 credits must be honors college classes 6-8 credits in departmental honors course work, 15-20 credits in Gen Ed honors courses (of which 9-12 are General Education honors course hours and 6-8 are in upper level honors course hours in any department or in the honors college), and 6-8 credit hours for research and thesis.

Department Honors completion requires 12-16 total credits, including 6-8 credits in departmental honors courses and a 6-8 credit thesis. Note: the average credits earned for thesis work (in any completion option) is 6.925 credits, higher than most honors programs.

Multidisciplinary Honors completion also requires 12-16 credits, including 6-8 honors credit in any department or Honors College work. A thesis (6-8 credits) is also required.

**AP/IB credits** are **not** counted as replacements for honors courses. "Note: Students who complete some or all of their General Education coursework through AP scores must take other honors courses in place of their Honors College Writing or other honors General Education courses they would otherwise take. Alternative honors coursework must be negotiated with an Honors Advisor and entered as an exception in the student's Academic Requirements Report."

**No. Honors Classes Offered (5.0):** This is a measure of the total **adjusted** honors main sections available in the term reported, not including labs and thesis. An adjusted main section has 3 or more semester credits, or equivalent, and sections with fewer credits receive a lower prorated value.

UMass CHC offered a section for every **9.9** enrolled students. The average for all programs was **15.0**. The lower the number, the better.

In the term reported, a very impressive **89.9%** of honors enrollment was **in honors-only course and research sections; 7.2% was in mixed sections; and 2.9% was in contract sections.** The CHC uses different terminology; "add-on" sections approximate contract sections, and "add-in" sections are similar to mixed sections, except they typically have fewer honors students. For all programs under review, enrollment by type of honors section was 75.8% honors-only, 15.4 % mixed, and 8.8% contract.

**No. Honors Classes in Key Disciplines (4.0):** The 15 "key" disciplines are biological sciences; business (all); chemistry; communications (especially public speaking); computer science; economics; engineering (all); English; history; math (all); philosophy; physics; political science; psychology; and sociology, anthropology, and gender studies. Interdisciplinary sections, such as those often taken for General Education credit in the first two years, do receive a lesser, prorated discipline "credit" because they introduce students to multiple disciplines in an especially engaging way, often with in-depth discussion.

For this measure, mixed and contract sections are not counted as a section in a key discipline unless students taking the sections for honors credit make up at least 10% of the total section enrollment.

In the term reported, UMass CHC offered a section in a key discipline for every **19.4 honors students.** The average for all programs is **24.7**. The lower the number, the better.

Out of **72 adjusted sections in key disciplines**, **59 were honors-only sections**. (The CHC allows a small number of non-honors students to enroll in "honors-only" classes if space permits.) The most sections were in English (a lot of composition) and math, followed by economics, psychology, and history.

The CHC has a signature seminar series: "Ideas That Change the World," one of our favorites. "The course explores dilemmas addressed by the sciences, the arts, and the humanities. In each of these broad areas, the course focuses on questions about human nature, the sources of our knowledge, and the application of that knowledge to the solving of perennial and contemporary problems. The semester begins with inquiries into the nature of truth, of particular relevance in our era of debates over 'alternative facts.' Then the course considers ongoing problems of violence, injustice, and environmental crisis."

**Extent of Honors Enrollment (3.0):** Not all honors students take an honors class each term, especially after the first two years. Programs that have fewer honors classes and thesis options for upper-division honors students will *generally* have fewer total members in good standing who are actually enrolled in a given term. (Please be aware, however, that honors students not enrolled in a class for a term are still tied to the honors community through residential and extracurricular activities.) *Our research shows that this measure is closely related to honors completion rates, i.e., the number of students who complete honors requirements by the time they graduate.*

For example, if a program has 1,800 individual students enrolled in a given term, and 3,000 students in good standing, the level of enrollment was .67, an indication that honors class enrollment is somewhat below average, especially in upper-division classes. **The CHC has a ratio of .98**, below the average of 1.30 for all programs.

**Average Class Size, Honors-only Sections (5.0):** Offered mostly in the first two years, honors-only classes tend to be smaller and, as the name implies, have no or very few students other than those in the honors program. These class sections always are much smaller than mixed or contract sections, or regular non-honors class sections in the university.

The average honors-only class size at the honors college is **14.7 students**. The average for all programs is **17.5 students.**

**Average Class Size, Overall (4.0):** The overall class calculation is based on the *proportion* of honors students in each type of class (honors-only, mixed honors, and honors contract sections). Thus it is not a raw average. The overall honors-credit class size is **22.9 students**, versus the average for all programs of **24.9 students**.

These class size averages also do not correspond to the number of students per honors section ratings above. The reason is that, in computing average class size metrics, we include enrollment in each 1-2-credit section, not just sections with 3 or more credits.

Along with an honors-only class size of 14.7 students (listed above), the program's mixed honors sections have an average size of **97.9 students,** and the contract sections with honors credit for individual honors students average **95.6 students.** Across all programs, the average mixed honors section has 68.6 students, and the average contract section has 56.6 students.

**Honors Grad Rate Adjusted to SAT (4.0):** The rating is the based on the actual grad rate for students who entered the program six years earlier, whether or not the students remained in honors. The **actual rate of 85.9%** is also compared to the rates of other programs with the same test score entry requirement range, and then adjusted upward if the program is performing above other programs in the same range, or downward if the performance is less than other programs in the same range. The rate here is slightly upward, to **86.0%.**

**Grad Rate Adjusted to Freshman Retention Rate (3.0):** This rate compares the actual grad rate above to a predicted grade rate when freshman retention rates are considered. The actual grad rate is **4.4 points**

**lower** than the predicted rate. For all programs, the actual grad rate is **.33 points lower** than the predicted rate.

**Ratio of Staff to Honors Students (3.5):** There is 1 staff member for every **145.2** students. (Mean ratio for all programs is 1 staff member for every **127.9** students.)

**Honors Residence Halls, Amenities (5.0):** The CHC does an excellent job of providing outstanding honors residences *and* getting students to live in them: Almost 1,500 CHC students live in honors housing. "The Commonwealth Honors College Residential Community includes six residence halls: Sycamore, Oak, Elm, Birch, Maple and Linden. Nine classrooms, the Greenbaum Gallery, and additional faculty offices are located in Elm House. Faculty apartments are located on the top floor of Birch House and of Linden House (one in each) with a view of the Mount Holyoke Range.

"The central CHC building contains the Roots Café, CHC Events Hall, Bloom Honors Advising Center, faculty offices, the Deans Office and all honors administrative offices."

All residence halls are part of the new Honors Residential Community that opened in 2013.

About 42% of honors students living in honors housing are freshmen residing in Sycamore Hall (294 students) and Oak Hall (334 students). Both residences have traditional double rooms with corridor baths on the floors. This configuration is thought by many to promote more interactions among new students, and thereby enhance their first year experience. Both dorms are air conditioned with on-site laundry. Living/learning themes in Sycamore are Health Sciences, Leadership, Ideas, Isenberg, and Biology Majors.

Oak Hall has living/learning themes in Creativity, Global Learning, Ideas, Engineering Majors, and Nursing Majors.

Upperclassmen can be assigned to Birch, Linden, Maple, and Elm Halls. All have a mix of apartment and suite-style rooms, the latter with shared baths.

**Honors Residence Halls, Availability (4.5):** This rating compares the number of occupants in honors residence halls to the number of honors freshman and sophomore members in good standing. The ratio for the program is **.82** places for each first- and second-year student. The median for all programs is .49 places.

**Prestigious Awards (3.5):** The awards that we track and include are listed in the section titled "Prestigious Scholarships." The awards are sometimes won by students who are not in an honors college or program, but increasingly many are enrolled in honors programs. It is also a trend that honors colleges and programs help to prepare their students for the awards competitions.

"The Office of National Scholarship Advisement, located in Commonwealth Honors College (CHC), serves all UMass Amherst undergraduate and graduate students applying for national and international prestigious scholarships.

"In 2018:

14 Fulbright U.S. Student Program grants (4 CHC students, 3 CHC alums),
1 Udall Scholarship award (1 CHC student),
5 National Science Foundation Fellowships (2 CHC students) and 6 NSF honorable mentions (1 CHC student),
2 Goldwater Scholarships (2 CHC students) and 1 honorable mention (1 CHC student),
1 Critical Language Scholarship,
1 Nakatani RIES Fellowship (1 CHC student),
1 DAAD Scholarship for study in Germany (1 CHC student),
1 Freeman Asia Scholarship (1 CHC student).

"In 2017, UMass Amherst students were awarded 8 Fulbright U.S. Student Program grants, 4 National Science Foundation (NSF) Fellowships and 2 NSF honorable mentions, 3 Boren Scholarships, 1 Beinecke Scholarship, 1 DAAD Scholarship, 1 Goldwater honorable mention, and 1 Udall honorable mention."

**UNRATED FEATURES**

**Continuation and Honors Graduation GPA Requirement:** 3.40 cumulative GPA for both.

**Academic Strengths, National Rankings:** This is based on national rankings of *graduate* programs in all but engineering and business, where undergraduate rankings are used. One of the weaknesses of the *U.S. News* rankings is that they focus on too many wealth-related metrics while ignoring their own assessments of academic departments. The rankings listed below are for all universities, public or private.

Of the 15 academic departments that we track, UMass Amherst has 14 that are nationally ranked, with a strong overall average ranking of 48.97.

The leading nationally ranked academic departments at UMass are computer science (20), sociology (30), history (44), business (45), earth sciences (46) education (51), chemistry (52), psychology (53), biology (54), math (55), physics (55), political science (55), English (57), and engineering (61).

**Internships, Professional Development, Community Engagement:** "The Seuss Project is collaboration between Commonwealth Honors College and the Springfield Museums that offers a set of independent study and internship opportunities for CHC students. In preparation for the opening of the new Amazing World of Dr. Seuss Museum, students assisted with a variety of projects, including painting wall murals, developing docent guides, preparing a wayfinding plan, engineering for interactive exhibits, scanning archival materials, and other projects.

"Sophomores-Serve is a two-semester program that focuses on the links between science and public policy and introduces CHC students to community engaged research. In the fall of their sophomore year, students take a 4-credit General Education honors course, 'Learning through Community Engagement: A Focus on the Food Environment,' which prepares and places students with a community partner. Students complete 30 hours of community service in the fall semester of their sophomore year. In the spring semester, students take a 2-credit course that investigates the larger contexts and interconnectedness of individual service placements.

"Commonwealth Honors College is **the home of the Bachelor's Degree with Individual Concentration (www.bdic.umass.edu) program** that offers highly motivated and self-directed students the opportunity to design their own major. As an alternative to traditional majors, the BDIC Program allows students to pursue their educational goals in areas not available within an existing departmental curriculum on campus. Students, with the help of a faculty sponsor, focus their major and select courses on the basis of a unifying issue, topic, theme, culture, period, or question, called an area of concentration."

**Undergraduate Research:** "The Commonwealth Honors College (CHC) Fellowship and Grant program provides up to $1,000 per student per semester to support honors student research. Research Assistant Fellowships support students assisting faculty on research projects, while Honors Research Grants support students' own research.

"In Academic Year 2017-2018, CHC awarded $134,378 in research fellowships and grants to 212 CHC students.

"All students who complete Departmental Honors or Multidisciplinary Honors and all those who graduate as Commonwealth Honors College Scholars must complete honors thesis/project. In AY2016-2017, **63.5% (505) of honors college graduates completed an honors thesis/project.**

**"Beginning in Fall 2018, all students entering Commonwealth Honors College (CHC) will be required to complete honors research and thesis/project.**

"CHC sponsors the annual Massachusetts statewide Undergraduate Research Conference in which undergraduate students from any of the 28 undergraduate campuses in the Massachusetts Public System of Higher Education may participate. Over 1,000 students presented their research at the 24th annual conference in April 2018.

"CHC offers travel grants for students presenting their research at national and international conferences."

**Honors Study Abroad:** "Commonwealth Honors College (CHC) provides scholarships for honors students participating in the Oxford Summer Seminar program (www.umass.edu/oxford) and the Alternative Theaters summer honors program in Edinburgh, Scotland.

**"The honors college also offers a 3-year academic program, the International Scholars Program (ISP), which combines academic learning with a period of study abroad in order to provide students with the global competencies they will need to become informed and effective citizens of our ever-expanding world.** The program invites all honors students, regardless of major, to develop a concentration in international studies and cross-cultural communication as a supplement to their regular disciplinary work. Students complete two preparatory classes in their sophomore year and a re-entry seminar in their senior year.

"ISP students receive a scholarship from CHC in support of their study abroad.

"ISP students may also complete the International Scholars Program Certificate. This undergraduate certificate builds on ISP, adding a three-course supplemental curriculum that students design to meet their personal, academic and professional goals. Students who complete the certificate receive an official designation on their final UMass Amherst transcript."

**Financial Aid:** "The University offers merit scholarships to all entering first-year students accepted to Commonwealth Honors College (CHC); $2,000 for Massachusetts residents and approximately $6,000 for out of state students.

"CHC administers Commonwealth Talent Awards academic tuition credits of $1,714 per year for up to 94 students each year. In Academic Year 2017-2018 CHC awarded $394,320 in primarily donor-funded scholarships to 202 students."

**Honors Fees:** $300 each semester.

**Placement of Honors Graduates:** None listed.

**Degree of Difference**: This is difference between (1) the average SAT scores for recently enrolled honors students (1386) and (2) the average test scores for all students in the university (1290) as a whole. The difference may be an indication of how "elite" honors students may be perceived as compared to students in the university as a whole. **Please keep in mind that neither the high nor low selectivity of an honors program determines how effective the program may be.**

**NAME**: UNIVERSITY HONORS PROGRAM, UNIVERSITY OF MINNESOTA TWIN CITIES

**Date Established:** 2008

**Location**: Minneapolis/St. Paul, Minnesota

**University Full-time Undergraduate Enrollment (2017):** 34,871

**Honors Members in Good Standing**: 2282; (mean size of all programs is 2,030).

**Honors Average Admission Test Score(s)**: The program admits top students from each college within the university. Those colleges range from very selective to selective, so the test scores for admitted honors students also vary. The College of Engineering admits have an SAT average of about 1520, while the admits from the Colleges of Design, Education and Human Development, and Food, Agriculture, and Natural Resources Sciences have an average of about 1390. The Carlson School of Management is almost as selective as the engineering school. The College of Liberal Arts admits have an average SAT of about 1440. An overall average would likely be 1490-1510, or ACT 33.

**Average High School GPA/Class Rank:** 94th to 99th percentile.

**Basic Admission Requirements:** "Honors admission is offered to the overall most competitive applicants from each freshman-admitting college." This would appear to be about the top 7%.

**Application Deadline(s):** *Please verify with each program, as some deadlines could change.*

**Honors Programs with SAT scores from 1471—1510:** Clemson, Georgia, Illinois, Minnesota, Oklahoma, Rutgers, South Carolina, UT Austin.

**Administrative Staff:** 22 FTEs.

**RATINGS AT A GLANCE:** For all mortarboard ratings immediately below, a score of 5 is the maximum and represents a comparison with all rated honors colleges and programs. More detailed explanations follow the "mortarboard" ratings.

**PERCEPTION\* OF UNIVERSITY AS A WHOLE, NOT OF HONORS:** 🎓🎓🎓🎓 1/2

\*Perception is based on the university's ranking among public universities in the 2018 U.S. News Best Colleges report. Please bear in mind that the better the U.S. News ranking, the more difficult it is for an honors college or program to have a rating that equals or improves on the magazine ranking.

**OVERALL HONORS RATING:** 🎓🎓🎓 1/2

**Curriculum Requirements:** 🎓🎓🎓🎓 1/2

**Number of Honors Classes Offered:** 🎓🎓🎓

**Number of Honors Classes in Key Disciplines:** 🎓🎓🎓

**Extent of Honors Enrollment:** 🎓🎓🎓1/2

**Honors-only Class Size:** 🎓🎓🎓

**Overall Class Size (Honors-only plus mixed, contract):** 🎓🎓🎓1/2

**Honors Grad Rate Adjusted to SAT:** 🎓🎓🎓

**Grad Rate Adjusted to Freshman Retention Rate:** 🎓🎓🎓1/2

**Ratio of Staff to Students:** 🎓🎓🎓🎓

**Priority Registration:** "No, though our data shows that the vast majority of our students register earlier due to credit totals, i.e. registration is based on the total number of credits, including AP, IB, College in the Schools and Post Secondary credits. Seats are held for 1st-year honors students in order to make sure they have access during orientation. No non-Honors students are allowed to register for these courses until after 1st-year students have a chance to do so. Non-honors students are only admitted by application if there are seats available."

**Honors Housing Amenities:** 🎓🎓🎓🎓

**Honors Housing Availability:** 🎓🎓🎓

**Prestigious Awards:** 🎓🎓🎓🎓🎓

**RATING SCORES AND EXPLANATIONS:**

**Curriculum Requirements (4.5):** The most important rating category, the curriculum completion requirement (classes required to complete honors) defines not only what honors students should learn but also the extent to which honors students and faculty are connected in the classroom. If there is a thesis or capstone requirement, it reinforces the individual contact and research skills so important to learning.

The average number of honors semester hours required for completion across all programs is 30.0.

The requirements for the UMTC University Honors Program have changed, **effective Fall 2018**.

"In brief, all students graduating with Latin Honors must complete the following:

• UHP NEXUS ONE experience [These 'are among the many non-course opportunities offered to UHP students. Together with faculty from across the University, students engage in thought experiments while exploring open-ended programming created specifically to introduce students to various fields of research, scholarship and creative activity.'].
• 3 Honors courses (at least one an honors seminar or a Grand Challenge course)
• 5 additional Honors experiences (course or non-course)
• Senior thesis and supporting thesis course work (one semester of thesis coursework, minimum; thesis coursework amounting to at least 2 credits after the first semester of thesis coursework may count as one of the three Honors courses, above)

The combination of course work, thesis, and experiences is a total requirement of about 30-32 credits.

"We encourage students to complete four or five of their [8] Honors requirements during the first two years in order to pass the mid-program review."

**AP/IB credits** are **not** counted as replacements for honors courses.

**No. Honors Classes Offered (3.0):** This is a measure of the total **adjusted** honors main sections available in the term reported, not including labs and thesis. An adjusted main section has 3 or more semester credits, or equivalent, and sections with fewer credits receive a lower prorated value.

The Minnesota Honors offered a section for every **23.9** enrolled students. The average for all programs was **15.0**. The lower the number, the better.

In the term reported, and extremely impressive **92.0%** of honors enrollment was **in honors-only sections; 5.1% was in mixed sections; and 2.9% was in contract sections.** For all programs under review, enrollment by type of honors section was 75.8% honors-only, 15.4 % mixed, and 8.8% contract.

**No. Honors Classes in Key Disciplines (3.0):** The 15 "key" disciplines are biological sciences; business (all); chemistry; communications (especially public speaking); computer science; economics; engineering (all); English; history; math (all); philosophy; physics; political science; psychology; and sociology, anthropology, and gender studies. Interdisciplinary sections, such as those often taken for General Education credit in the first two years, do receive a lesser, prorated discipline "credit" because they introduce students to multiple disciplines in an especially engaging way, often with in-depth discussion.

For this measure, mixed and contract sections are not counted as a section in a key discipline unless students taking the sections for honors credit make up at least 10% of the total section enrollment.

In the term reported, the program offered a section in a key discipline for every **36.0 honors students.** The average for all programs is **24.7**. The lower the number, the better.

Out of **53 adjusted sections in key disciplines, 47 were honors-only sections**. The most sections were in mathematics (18, very large percentage of sections), followed by sociology, anthropology, women's studies, business, psychology, biology, communications, computer science, English, and physics.

The program offered more than 20 interdisciplinary seminars, including "Statistics and Data Science for Everyone," "Reality 101, A Survey of the Human Predicament," "Think Like A Lawyer, the Law and Adventure of Torts," and, well, "The Sex Talk You Should Have Had."

Minnesota Honors is a **blended** program, with a good mix of interdisciplinary courses and classes in the disciplines.

**Extent of Honors Enrollment (3.5):** Not all honors students take an honors class each term, especially after the first two years. Programs that have fewer honors classes and thesis options for upper-division honors students will *generally* have fewer total members in good standing who are actually enrolled in a given term. (Please be aware, however, that honors students not enrolled in a class for a term are still tied to the honors community through residential and extracurricular activities.) *Our research shows that this measure is closely related to honors completion rates, i.e., the number of students who complete honors requirements by the time they graduate.*

For example, if a program has 1,800 individual students enrolled in a given term, and 3,000 students in good standing, the level of enrollment was .67, an indication that honors class enrollment is somewhat below average, especially in upper-division classes. **Minnesota honors has a ratio of 1.05**, below the average of 1.30 for all programs.

**Average Class Size, Honors-only Sections (3.0):** Offered mostly in the first two years, honors-only classes tend to be smaller and, as the name implies, have no or very few students other than those in the honors program. These class sections always are much smaller than mixed or contract sections, or regular non-honors class sections in the university.

The average honors-only class size is **24.3 students**. The average for all programs is **17.5 students.**

**Average Class Size, Overall (3.5):** The overall class calculation is based on the *proportion* of honors students in each type of class (honors-only, mixed honors, and honors contract sections). Thus it is not a raw average. The overall honors-credit class size is **29.9 students**, versus the average for all programs of **24.9 students**.

These class size averages also do not correspond to the number of students per honors section ratings above. The reason is that, in computing average class size metrics, we include enrollment in each 1-2-credit section, not just sections with 3 or more credits.

Along with an honors-only class size of 24.3 students (listed above), the program's mixed honors sections have an average size of **76.1 students,** and the contract sections with honors credit for individual honors students average **124.5 students.** Across all programs, the average mixed honors section has 68.6 students, and the average contract section has 56.6 students.

**Honors Grad Rate Adjusted to SAT (3.0):** The rating is the based on the actual grad rate for students who entered the program six years earlier, whether or not the students remained in honors. The **actual rate of 90.0%** is also compared to the rates of other programs with the same test score entry requirement range, and then adjusted upward if the program is performing above other programs in the same range, or downward if the performance is less than other programs in the same range. The rate here is slightly downward, to **88.7%.**

**Grad Rate Adjusted to Freshman Retention Rate (3.5):** This rate compares the actual grad rate above to a predicted grade rate when freshman retention rates are considered. The actual grad rate is **2.35 points lower** than the predicted rate. For all programs, the actual grad rate is **.33 points lower** than the predicted rate.

**Ratio of Staff to Honors Students (4.0):** There is 1 staff member for every **109.4** students. (Mean ratio for all programs is 1 staff member for every **127.9** students.)

**Honors Residence Halls, Amenities (4.0):** "Entering freshmen are guaranteed a space in Middlebrook Honors Residential Community should they choose the option. Starting with Fall 2018, all Honors students will be placed in the Middlebrook Honors Residential Community unless they specifically request a different Living Learning Community or living arrangement (e.g., some live at home and commute in). Note that Honors students may reside in Middlebrook with a non-Honors roommate. We are hopeful that these changes will significantly boost the percentage of Honors students living in Middlebrook in coming years."

Almost 400 honors freshmen and some upperclassmen live in Middlebrook, which has a mix of traditional doubles and two- and three-person suites. The residence hall is air conditioned with a kitchen, on-site laundry, and a lounge on each floor. One great feature is that Middlebrook has its own dining hall and music rooms.

"[Middlebrook] is located adjacent to the west bank of the Mississippi River, Ted Mann Concert Hall, Wilson Library, and is near downtown Minneapolis. The west bank Riverside area offers a variety of music clubs, coffee shops, co-ops, historical buildings, and ethnic and vegetarian restaurants. Middlebrook is easily accessible by foot, bike, free campus connector and shuttle system, and light rail. Most west bank classroom buildings are connected by underground tunnels. Middlebrook Tower was built in 1969, and the east wing expansion (where second-year honors students live) was added in 2001."

**Honors Residence Halls, Availability (3.0):** This rating compares the number of occupants in honors residence halls to the number of honors freshman and sophomore members in good standing. The ratio for the program is **.33** places for each first- and second-year student. The median for all fifty programs is .49 places.

**Prestigious Awards (5.0):** The awards that we track and include are listed in the section titled "Prestigious Scholarships." The awards are sometimes won by students who are not in an honors college or program, but increasingly many are enrolled in honors programs. It is also a trend that honors colleges and programs help to prepare their students for the awards competitions.

"The Office of National and International Scholarships at the University of Minnesota is housed within the University Honors Program and works with students to develop applications for competitive undergraduate and post-graduate scholarships The University of Minnesota has a strong record of success with these awards, especially in the natural sciences and engineering. The University has graduated 24 American and 1 Canadian Rhodes Scholars, 4 Marshall Scholars, 2 Gates-Cambridge Scholars, and 20 Truman Scholars. Among awards specifically related to STEM scholarship, students at the University of Minnesota have been awarded 64 Goldwater Scholarships and 11 Churchill Scholarships, a record among the best of public universities.

"In addition, 31 undergraduates have been awarded NSF Graduate Research Fellowships since 2000, and another 123 graduates have won after beginning graduate study. Minnesota students have also won 7 Udall Scholarships, and over 100 have received Fulbright awards since 2000. **Since the consolidation of honors education into the University Honors Program in 2008, nearly all of these scholarship winners have come from the ranks of Honors students.**"

## UNRATED FEATURES

**Continuation Requirement:** 3.50.

**Graduation with Honors:** "All students must meet the GPA requirements mandated by University policy for the appropriate level of Latin Honors:

| | |
|---|---|
| *cum laude* | 3.500–3.665 GPA for last 60 graded credits |
| *magna cum laude* | 3.666–3.749 GPA for last 60 graded credits |
| *summa cum laude* | 3.75–4.0 GPA for last 60 graded credits |

"The GPA of the last 60 graded credits and the nature of the senior-year project will be the determining factors as to the student's level of Latin Honors."

**Academic Strengths, National Rankings:** This is based on national rankings of *graduate* programs in all but engineering and business, where undergraduate rankings are used. One of the weaknesses of the *U.S. News* rankings is that they focus on too many wealth-related metrics while ignoring their own assessments of academic departments. The rankings have consistently ranked UMTC far lower than the excellence of the university's academic departments would indicate. The rankings listed below are for all universities, public or private.

The *average* national academic department ranking at UMTC is 24.2, higher than the overall department rankings at many elite private universities.

The leading nationally ranked academic departments at UMTC are psychology (8), business (15), economics (16), sociology (17), math (19), chemistry (24), earth sciences (24), education (24), engineering (25), physics (25), computer science (29), history (32), biology (39), and English (42).

**Internships, Professional Development, Community Engagement:** "An internship may count as an Honors Experience if it is:

"Associated with an organization relevant to your academic or career interests and/or future career goals, with an opportunity to connect learning in the classroom to real-world projects; and

"Comprised of clearly-defined, value-added projects benefiting the organization as well as your own growth and learning; and

"At least one semester in duration (or equivalent), representing a minimum time commitment of 45 hours to one organization or business over the course of the semester; and

"Paid, volunteer, or for credit*; and

"Supervised by a mentor within the host organization; and

"Designed to include a mid-point and end-of-term evaluation."

*Credit-bearing internships may count as non-course experiences, but may not count as honors courses.

**Undergraduate Research:** "An undergraduate research project may count as an Honors Experience if it is:

"A learning experience that contributes to your understanding of how knowledge is created through the application of theories and investigative methods in any discipline or field.

"Supervised by a University of Minnesota faculty mentor holding any type of appointment (including clinical, emeritus, adjunct, research associate, assistant or associate professor, etc.), or by the leader of a government, industry, or academic or non-profit research group; and

"One semester in duration (or equivalent), representing a minimum time commitment of 45 hours over the course of the semester; and

"Paid or unpaid; for-credit or non-credit; completed under the auspices of the Undergraduate Research Opportunities Program (UROP) or not; and

"Not a term paper or other regular requirement for a lecture course or seminar.

"Directed Study and Directed Research…can fulfill an Honors Experience requirement but not an Honors course requirement.

"Any Directed Research offered at the Honors level…and taken as required preparation for the student's Honors thesis will count as an Honors course requirement."

**Honors Study Abroad:** "Study, research, or internships abroad may be used to fulfill Honors Experience requirements as follows:

- Full-term learning abroad experiences (fall semester, spring semester, May session or summer session) with registration in coursework earn students two Honors Experiences—coursework counts as an Honors course and the cultural experience counts as a non-course Honors Experience.
- Students completing two terms of study abroad in one academic year (with registration in coursework for both terms) will earn four Honors Experiences—two for the coursework and two for the cultural experience. This enables students to complete UHP's Honors Experience requirements for an entire academic year through learning abroad.

- Global seminars (including freshman seminars abroad) that include an abroad experience count as an Honors course and earn students one Honors Experience.

"An approved credit-bearing semester of learning abroad to complete a research or internship experience earns two Honors Experiences—one for the research or internship and one for the cultural experience."

**Financial Aid:** Most students invited into the University Honors Program are eligible for some form of merit-based scholarships.

Merit scholarships at UMTC that give preference to National Merit Finalists include the Gold Scholar Award of up to $10,000 per year for four years. To qualify, applicants must list UMTC as their first-choice college by the National Merit Scholarship Corporation deadline.

The Maroon and Gold Scholarship awards up to $12,000 to Minnesota residents or students eligible for the Dream Act who are in the top 1-3% of their high school class.

**Honors Fees:** None.

**Placement of Honors Graduates:** None listed.

**Degree of Difference**: This is difference between (1) the average SAT scores for recently enrolled honors students (1490-1510) and (2) the average test scores for all students in the university (1360) as a whole. The difference may be an indication of how "elite" honors students may be perceived as compared to students in the university as a whole. **Please keep in mind that neither the high nor low selectivity of an honors program determines how effective the program may be.**

**NAME**: SALLY MCDONNELL BARKSDALE HONORS COLLEGE

**Date Established:** 1952 as an honors program; 1997 as an honors college.

**Location**: Oxford, Mississippi

**University Full-time Undergraduate Enrollment (2017):** 19,213

**Honors Members in Good Standing**: 1512; (mean size of all programs is 2,030).

**Honors Average Admission Test Score(s)**: ACT, 31; SAT, 1420.

**Average High School GPA/Class Rank:** 3.97, weighted.

**Basic Admission Requirements:** ACT, 28; SAT, 1310; GPA, 3.50. "Applications are read holistically, and GPA and test scores are only two criteria. The committee considers the rigor of the high school courses, given what the individual school offers; community service; involvement and leadership in school and in the community; the quality of the student's essays; and letters of recommendation from two teachers and the high school counselor. The ACT and SAT scores are not minimums, and a score higher than those numbers does not guarantee admission."

**Application Deadline(s):** *Please verify with each program, as some deadlines could change.* Early action November 1, 2018, notification December 20, 2018; regular deadline is January 5, 2019, notification by early March 2019.

**Honors Programs with SAT scores from 1420—1461:** Auburn, Central Florida, Delaware, Iowa, Kansas, Mississippi, Missouri, New Jersey Inst of Technology, Penn State, South Florida, Vermont, Virginia Commonwealth.

**Administrative Staff:** 10.

**RATINGS AT A GLANCE:** For all mortarboard ratings immediately below, a score of 5 is the maximum and represents a comparison with all rated honors colleges and programs. More detailed explanations follow the "mortarboard" ratings.

**PERCEPTION\* OF UNIVERSITY AS A WHOLE, NOT OF HONORS:** 🎓🎓🎓 1/2

\*Perception is based on the university's ranking among public universities in the 2018 U.S. News Best Colleges report. Please bear in mind that the better the U.S. News ranking, the more difficult it is for an honors college or program to have a rating that equals or improves on the magazine ranking.

**OVERALL HONORS RATING:** 🎓🎓🎓🎓 1/2

**Curriculum Requirements:** 🎓🎓🎓🎓

**Number of Honors Classes Offered:** 🎓🎓🎓🎓🎓

**Number of Honors Classes in Key Disciplines:** 🎓🎓🎓🎓 1/2

**Extent of Honors Enrollment:** 🎓🎓🎓🎓 1/2

**Honors-only Class Size:** 🎓🎓🎓🎓🎓

**Overall Class Size (Honors-only plus mixed, contract):** 🎓🎓🎓🎓

**Honors Grad Rate Adjusted to SAT:** 🎓🎓🎓 1/2

**Grad Rate Adjusted to Freshman Retention Rate:** 🎓🎓🎓 1/2

**Ratio of Staff to Students:** 🎓🎓🎓 1/2

**Priority Registration: Yes,** honors students register for all courses, honors and otherwise, with the first group of students during each year they are in the program.

**Honors Housing Amenities:** 🎓🎓🎓🎓

**Honors Housing Availability:** 🎓🎓🎓 1/2

**Prestigious Awards:** 🎓🎓🎓 1/2

## RATING SCORES AND EXPLANATIONS:

**Curriculum Requirements (4.0):** The most important rating category, the curriculum completion requirement (classes required to complete honors) defines not only what honors students should learn but also the extent to which honors students and faculty are connected in the classroom. If there is a thesis or capstone requirement, it reinforces the individual contact and research skills so important to learning.

The average number of honors semester hours required for completion across all programs is 30.0.

The completion requirement for entering first-year students is 30 credits, including about 6 credits for thesis and/or capstone.

For students entering as juniors, the requirement is 12 credits, including a thesis and/or capstone.

**AP/IB credits** are **not** counted as replacements for honors courses.

**No. Honors Classes Offered (5.0):** This is a measure of the total **adjusted** honors main sections available in the term reported, not including labs and thesis. An adjusted main section has 3 or more semester credits, or equivalent, and sections with fewer credits receive a lower prorated value.

The SMBHC offered a section for every **9.4** enrolled students. The average for all programs was **15.0**. The lower the number, the better.

In the term reported, **72.1%** of honors enrollment was **in honors-only sections; 27.9% was in mixed sections; and none was in contract sections.** For all programs under review, enrollment by type of honors section was 75.8% honors-only, 15.4 % mixed, and 8.8% contract.

**No. Honors Classes in Key Disciplines (4.5):** The 15 "key" disciplines are biological sciences; business (all); chemistry; communications (especially public speaking); computer science; economics; engineering (all); English; history; math (all); philosophy; physics; political science; psychology; and sociology, anthropology, and gender studies. Interdisciplinary sections, such as those often taken for General Education credit in the first two years, do receive a lesser, prorated discipline "credit" because they introduce students to multiple disciplines in an especially engaging way, often with in-depth discussion.

For this measure, mixed and contract sections are not counted as a section in a key discipline unless students taking the sections for honors credit make up at least 10% of the total section enrollment.

In the term reported, the SMBHC offered a section in a key discipline for every **15.3 honors students.** The average for all programs is **24.7**. The lower the number, the better.

Out of **55 adjusted sections in key disciplines**, **32 were honors-only sections**. The most sections were in math (10), followed by English, chemistry, psychology, biology, economics, history, philosophy, physics, and sociology or related disciplines.

SMBHC offered almost 30 sections of a seminar series with the very straightforward title of "Freshman Honors I." These are similar to seminar series offered by other programs, emphasizing rhetoric and writing while studying great works. SMBHC is a **blended** program, with a good mix of interdisciplinary courses and classes in the disciplines.

**Extent of Honors Enrollment (4.5):** Not all honors students take an honors class each term, especially after the first two years. Programs that have fewer honors classes and thesis options for upper-division honors students will *generally* have fewer total members in good standing who are actually enrolled in a given term. (Please be aware, however, that honors students not enrolled in a class for a term are still tied to the honors community through residential and extracurricular activities.) *Our research shows that this measure is closely related to honors completion rates, i.e., the number of students who complete honors requirements by the time they graduate.*

For example, if a program has 1,800 individual students enrolled in a given term, and 3,000 students in good standing, the level of enrollment was .67, an indication that honors class enrollment is somewhat below average, especially in upper-division classes. **SMBHC has a ratio of 1.53**, significantly above the average of 1.30 for all programs.

**Average Class Size, Honors-only Sections (5.0):** Offered mostly in the first two years, honors-only classes tend to be smaller and, as the name implies, have no or very few students other than those in the honors program. These class sections always are much smaller than mixed or contract sections, or regular non-honors class sections in the university.

The average honors-only class size at SMBHC is **15.4 students**. The average for all programs is **17.5 students.**

**Average Class Size, Overall (4.0):** The overall class calculation is based on the *proportion* of honors students in each type of class (honors-only, mixed honors, and honors contract sections). Thus it is not a raw average. The overall honors-credit class size is **23.9 students**, versus the average for all programs of **24.9 students**.

These class size averages also do not correspond to the number of students per honors section ratings above. The reason is that, in computing average class size metrics, we include enrollment in each 1-2-credit section, not just sections with 3 or more credits.

Along with an honors-only class size of 15.4 students (listed above), the program's mixed honors sections have an average size of **45.9 students,** and the college does not offer contract sections. Across all programs, the average mixed honors section has 68.6 students.

**Honors Grad Rate Adjusted to SAT (3.5):** The rating is the based on the actual grad rate for students who entered the program six years earlier, whether or not the students remained in honors. The **actual rate of 84.3%** is also compared to the rates of other programs with the same test score entry requirement range, and then adjusted upward if the program is performing above other programs in the same range, or downward if the performance is less than other programs in the same range. The rate here is slightly downward, to **83.7%.**

**Grad Rate Adjusted to Freshman Retention Rate (3.5):** This rate compares the actual grad rate above to a predicted grade rate when freshman retention rates are considered. The actual grad rate is **2.02 points lower** than the predicted rate. For all programs, the actual grad rate is **.33 points lower** than the predicted rate.

**Ratio of Staff to Honors Students (3.5):** There is 1 staff member for every **115.2** students. (Mean ratio for all programs is 1 staff member for every **127.9** students.)

**Honors Residence Halls, Amenities (4.0):** About 340 first-year honors students live in Pittman Hall. Pittman is air-conditioned and features suite-style rooms with shared baths. The nearest dining is at the Rebel Market.

**Honors Residence Halls, Availability (3.5):** This rating compares the number of occupants in honors residence halls to the number of honors freshman and sophomore members in good standing. The ratio for the program is **.45** places for each first- and second-year student. The median for all programs is .49 places. "While we have the option to live in honors housing, we allow students to self-select where they want to live. Some choose to live in traditional dorms, and others may be part of other special programs (like our early-entry pharmacy program or the Luckyday Scholarship program) and are required to live in those living-learning communities."

**Prestigious Awards (3.5):** The awards that we track and include are listed in the section titled "Prestigious Scholarships." The awards are sometimes won by students who are not in an honors college or program, but increasingly many are enrolled in honors programs. It is also a trend that honors colleges and programs help to prepare their students for the awards competitions.

"The Office of National Scholarship Advisement is housed in the Honors College and is part of the SMBHC budget. Our records are not complete before 1997, when the Honors College began coordinating University involvement with the national scholarships. Since that time, the University can claim 2 Rhodes, 1 Marshall, 1 Mitchell, 2 Gates Cambridge, 8 Trumans, 3 Udalls, 10 Goldwaters, and 19 Fulbright U.S. Student awards. Of these 46 scholarship recipients, 37 were honors students.

"All told, University of Mississippi students have received 25 Rhodes, 2 Marshalls, 1 Mitchell, 2 Gates Cambridge, 15 Trumans, 3 Udalls, 13 Goldwaters, and 19 Fulbrights."

## UNRATED FEATURES

**Continuation and Honors Graduation GPA Requirement:** 3.20 by the end of the first year, 3.40 by the end of the second year, 3.50 by the end of the third year and beyond, and for graduation.

**Academic Strengths, National Rankings:** This is based on national rankings of *graduate* programs in all but engineering and business, where undergraduate rankings are used. One of the weaknesses of the *U.S. News* rankings is that they focus on too many wealth-related metrics while ignoring their own assessments of academic departments. The rankings listed below are for all universities, public or private.

The nationally ranked academic departments at Ole Miss are English (67), history (69), education (89), political science (89), business (109), physics (124), math (127), and chemistry (145).

**Internships, Professional Development, Community Engagement:** "Many honors students intern or co-op, primarily as part of their majors. Honors College fellowships are available to support students participating in unpaid internships. Some examples of internships for which the Honors College provided support in 2016-17 are a Kaiser Edge externship in San Francisco, an internship with JAX Media in New York City, an internship with the Cook County Medical Examiner in Chicago, and an internship with a U.S. senator's office in Washington, D.C."

**Undergraduate Research:** "All honors students must complete a capstone and thesis in order to graduate from the Honors College. Most are involved in capstone and thesis work in spring of their junior year and both semesters of senior year, so in Fall 2017, 26% of honors students were involved in research. In this case, research is defined broadly to include creative and capstone work in the arts and engineering."

**Honors Study Abroad:** "The Honors College has fellowships for which honors students can apply. We prioritize full-year or semester abroad experiences, with lesser amounts awarded to students in summer programs. In 2016-17, the Honors College awarded $37,000 to 25 students studying abroad."

**Financial Aid:** "The University of Mississippi offers generous financial aid packages based on ACT/SAT test scores and high school GPAs. **In addition, National Merit Semifinalists are eligible for scholarships that cover the cost of tuition and the cost of a standard double-occupancy room in a residence hall on campus. National Merit Finalists may receive additional awards.** Applicants to the Honors College are often competitive for major University scholarships, including the Stamps, which covers the cost of attendance after other awards have been made and provides funds for enrichment opportunities; and the Newman, Carrier, and Hill Scholarships.

"The application for admission to the Honors College is also an application for scholarships awarded by the Sally McDonnell Barksdale Honors College. These are very competitive scholarships, with 14-15 students a year out of a freshman class of 420 students receiving an Honors College scholarship. Honors College students may also be competitive for scholarships from other departments at the University of Mississippi, particularly in international studies, public policy leadership, business, accounting, and engineering. Scholarships from the Honors College or from a department can stack with the academic excellence scholarships and other aid up to the cost of attendance."

**Honors Fees:** "Students who accept the offer of admission to the Honors College pay a $250 deposit. Those who are still with the Honors College in early October of freshman year receive a refund of the deposit through their Bursar account. Students who show financial need as determined by the Financial Aid office can receive a waiver of the deposit."

**Placement of Honors Graduates:** Information for the Class of 2017:

Law School—University of Mississippi, Georgetown, University of Virginia, William & Mary, University of Texas, University of Georgia;

Medical School—University of Mississippi, The Mayo Clinic, University of Virginia, University of Alabama-Birmingham, University of Arkansas;

Employment: Amazon, Nike, Cisco, Ford, U.S. Dept. of Justice, St. Jude's Children's Hospital, Federal Reserve Board of Governors, C Spire, Southern Pine Electric.

**Degree of Difference**: This is difference between (1) the average SAT scores for recently enrolled honors students (1420) and (2) the average test scores for all students in the university (1160) as a whole. The difference may be an indication of how "elite" honors students may be perceived as compared to students in the university as a whole. **Please keep in mind that neither the high nor low selectivity of an honors program determines how effective the program may be.**

**NAME**: UNIVERSITY OF MISSOURI HONORS COLLEGE

**Date Established:** 1958, and it is **"the first and oldest honors college in the United States."**

**Location**: Columbia, Missouri

**University <u>Full-time Undergraduate</u> Enrollment (2017):** 25,898

**Honors Members in Good Standing**: 1,889 (mean size of all programs is 2,030); "7.6% of students on campus."

**Honors <u>Average</u> Admission Test Score(s)**: ACT, 31.3; SAT, est. SAT equivalent, 1420.

**Average High School GPA/Class Rank:** 3.96 weighted; top 7%.

**<u>Basic</u> Admission Requirements:** "Beginning Fall 2018, MUHC is holistic in its admissions process and will review every applicant on the basis of their academic and co-curricular accomplishments. Applicants must submit an official ACT/SAT score report, official transcripts, a resume, and one essay for consideration (two additional essays are required if a student wishes to apply for any honors scholarships or scholars and fellows programs).

"MU does not 'superscore' the ACT or SAT; **SAT scores are accepted but internally converted to their ACT equivalent.**"

**Application Deadline(s):** *Please verify with each program, as some deadlines could change.* The college's Stamps Scholars deadline is December 1, 2018. The university scholarship (including all Honors College scholarships) deadline is December 15, 2018. Final application deadline, March 1, 2019.

**Honors Programs with SAT scores from 1420—1461:** Auburn, Central Florida, Delaware, Iowa, Kansas, Mississippi, Missouri, New Jersey Inst of Technology, Penn State, South Florida, Vermont, Virginia Commonwealth.

**Administrative Staff:** 11.5.

**RATINGS AT A GLANCE:** For all mortarboard ratings immediately below, a score of 5 is the maximum and represents a comparison with all rated honors colleges and programs. More detailed explanations follow the "mortarboard" ratings.

**PERCEPTION\* OF UNIVERSITY AS A WHOLE, <u>NOT</u> OF HONORS:** 🎓🎓🎓🎓

\*Perception is based on the university's ranking among public universities in the 2018 U.S. News Best Colleges report. Please bear in mind that the better the U.S. News ranking, the more difficult it is for an honors college or program to have a rating that equals or improves on the magazine ranking.

**OVERALL HONORS RATING:** 🎓🎓🎓 1/2

**Curriculum Requirements:** 🎓🎓🎓 1/2

**Number of Honors Classes Offered:** 🎓🎓🎓

**Number of Honors Classes in Key Disciplines:** 🎓🎓🎓

**Extent of Honors Enrollment:** 🎓🎓🎓

**Honors-only Class Size:** 🎓🎓🎓 1/2

**Overall Class Size (Honors-only plus mixed, contract):** 🎓🎓🎓🎓

**Honors Grad Rate Adjusted to SAT:** 🎓🎓🎓🎓 1/2

**Grad Rate Adjusted to Freshman Retention Rate:** 🎓🎓🎓🎓

**Ratio of Staff to Students:** 🎓🎓🎓 1/2

**Priority Registration: Yes,** honors students register for all courses, honors and otherwise, with the first group of students during each year they are in the program.

**Honors Housing Amenities:** 🎓🎓🎓🎓🎓

**Honors Housing Availability:** 🎓🎓🎓 1/2

**Prestigious Awards:** 🎓🎓🎓🎓

## RATING SCORES AND EXPLANATIONS:

**Curriculum Requirements (3.5):** The most important rating category, the curriculum completion requirement (classes required to complete honors) defines not only what honors students should learn but also the extent to which honors students and faculty are connected in the classroom. If there is a thesis or capstone requirement, it reinforces the individual contact and research skills so important to learning.

The average number of honors semester hours required for completion across all programs is 30.0.

Mizzou Honors requires 24 credits to complete honors requirements. "There are no set or required courses for Honors; a student may select from any of the General Honors or Departmental Honors courses to fulfill their required program hours. They are limited to not more than 8 hours Learning-by-Contract credits, 8 hours approved graduate credits, 6 hours approved Study Abroad credits, and up to 9 transfer hours for Honors credit. **Students must achieve a C or better for regular Honors credit or graduate courses and a B or better for Study Abroad and Honors Learning-by-Contract courses.**

"Students must take at least two courses a year (or at least one a semester if they are a part of one of our Scholars & Fellows programs or a scholarship and award recipient).

"Students can design their Honors Certificate program to include any type and format of courses, from 1 credit Tutorials to 5 credit language and lab science courses, all of which are General Honors and specifically designed and approved by the Honors Faculty and the Honors College Curriculum Committee."

**AP/IB credits** are **not** counted as replacements for honors courses.

**No. Honors Classes Offered (3.0):** This is a measure of the total **adjusted** honors main sections available in the term reported, not including labs and thesis. An adjusted main section has 3 or more semester credits, or equivalent, and sections with fewer credits receive a lower prorated value.

The program offered a section for every **21.9** enrolled students. The average for all programs was **15.0**. The lower the number, the better.

In the term reported, an extremely impressive **86.1%** of honors enrollment was **in honors-only sections; 8.3% was in mixed sections; and 5.6% was in contract sections.** For all programs under review, enrollment by type of honors section was 75.8% honors-only, 15.4 % mixed, and 8.8% contract.

**No. Honors Classes in Key Disciplines (3.0):** The 15 "key" disciplines are biological sciences; business (all); chemistry; communications (especially public speaking); computer science; economics; engineering (all); English; history; math (all); philosophy; physics; political science; psychology; and sociology, anthropology, and gender studies. Interdisciplinary sections, such as those often taken for General Education credit in the first two years, do receive a lesser, prorated discipline "credit" because they introduce students to multiple disciplines in an especially engaging way, often with in-depth discussion.

For this measure, mixed and contract sections are not counted as a section in a key discipline unless students taking the sections for honors credit make up at least 10% of the total section enrollment.

In the term reported, the Mizzou Honors offered a section in a key discipline for every **37.2 honors students.** The average for all programs is **24.7.** The lower the number, the better.

Out of **33 adjusted sections in key disciplines, 22 were honors-only sections**. The most sections were in business, followed by English, history, philosophy, sociology/anthropology, communications, engineering, political science, and psychology.

"We continue to offer numerous sections of our Series courses—Humanities Series (The Ancient World and The Middle Ages and the Renaissance in 17-18) and the Science Series (Energy: From Particles to Civilizations and Environment: From Molecules to the Cosmos)—which were the original course structure that gave birth to the College. **We also regularly offer a four-course series in Constitutional Democracy consisting of the following courses—Intellectual World of the American Founders; The Revolutionary Transformation of Early America; The Constitutional Debates; and The Young**

**Republic.** Students can add just one more course to the Series to obtain a minor and can simultaneously join the Kinder Institute as a student fellow for more research, programming, internship, and funding opportunities.

"We especially wish to call your attention to the number of courses that are taught by faculty from the **MU School of Medicine**, the **MU Law School**, and the **Truman School of Public Affairs**. We have made a concerted effort to engage our students with the faculty, topics, and facets of study that emerge from these three graduate-only schools here at MU."

**Extent of Honors Enrollment (3.0):** Not all honors students take an honors class each term, especially after the first two years. Programs that have fewer honors classes and thesis options for upper-division honors students will *generally* have fewer total members in good standing who are actually enrolled in a given term. (Please be aware, however, that honors students not enrolled in a class for a term are still tied to the honors community through residential and extracurricular activities.) *Our research shows that this measure is closely related to honors completion rates, i.e., the number of students who complete honors requirements by the time they graduate.*

For example, if a program has 1,800 individual students enrolled in a given term, and 3,000 students in good standing, the level of enrollment was .67, an indication that honors class enrollment is somewhat below average, especially in upper-division classes. **Mizzou honors has a ratio of .99**, below the average of 1.30 for all programs.

**Average Class Size, Honors-only Sections (3.5):** Offered mostly in the first two years, honors-only classes tend to be smaller and, as the name implies, have no or very few students other than those in the honors program. These class sections always are much smaller than mixed or contract sections, or regular non-honors class sections in the university.

The average honors-only class size at Mizzou Honors is **19.2 students**. The average for all programs is **17.5 students.**

**Average Class Size, Overall (4.0):** The overall class calculation is based on the *proportion* of honors students in each type of class (honors-only, mixed honors, and honors contract sections). Thus it is not a raw average. The overall honors-credit class size is **24.3 students**, versus the average for all programs of **24.9 students**.

These class size averages also do not correspond to the number of students per honors section ratings above. The reason is that, in computing average class size metrics, we include enrollment in each 1-2-credit section, not just sections with 3 or more credits.

Along with an honors-only class size of 19.2 students (listed above), the program's mixed honors sections have an average size of **35.0 students,** and the contract sections with honors credit for individual honors students average **88.0 students.** Across all programs, the average mixed honors section has 68.6 students, and the average contract section has 56.6 students.

**Honors Grad Rate Adjusted to SAT (4.5):** The rating is the based on the actual grad rate for students who entered the program six years earlier, whether or not the students remained in honors. The **actual rate of 87.3%** is also compared to the rates of other programs with the same test score entry requirement range, and then adjusted upward if the program is performing above other programs in the same range, or downward if the performance is less than other programs in the same range. The rate here is upward, to **87.7%.**

**Grad Rate Adjusted to Freshman Retention Rate (4.0):** This rate compares the actual grad rate above to a predicted grade rate when freshman retention rates are considered. The actual grad rate is **.98 points higher** than the predicted rate. For all programs, the actual grad rate is **.33 points lower** than the predicted rate.

**Ratio of Staff to Honors Students (3.5):** There is 1 staff member for every **164.3** students. (Mean ratio for all programs is 1 staff member for every **127.9** students.)

**Honors Residence Halls, Amenities (5.0):** "With the closing of Schurz Hall in 2017, we moved the entire Honors Learning Center and Honors College presence into Mark Twain….Thus, this is the final year for College Avenue to have an official Honors presence. We are already in discussions to add a second Honors Learning Center Residence Hall, perhaps by reopening Schurz Hall (site of our former HLC) or by finding a new location on East Campus to add geographical/locational 'balance' to Mark Twain Hall [in West Campus]."

About 370 honors first-year students and upperclassmen live in Mark Twain. The residence hall is air-conditioned and features suite-style rooms. The Mark on 5th Street dining facility is onsite. Among the amenities is free onsite laundry service that uses an app on student phones for scheduling.

Another 40 honors students live in the College Avenue Residence Hall. The Freshmen Interest Groups are Journalism and Social Justice. The air-conditioned residence features several room styles, including suite-style rooms, and has onsite laundry. It is close to Baja Grill, Plaza 900 and Mizzou Market/Pershing Commons.

**Honors Residence Halls, Availability (3.5):** This rating compares the number of occupants in honors residence halls to the number of honors freshman and sophomore members in good standing. The ratio for the program is **.44** places for each first- and second-year student. The median for all programs is .49 places.

**Prestigious Awards (4.0):** "The Fellowships Office, which has a full-time staff of two plus a .5 graduate assistant, is co-located with the Honors College, although it has its own Director. The office is fully integrated into all of the Honors College's fourteen different Scholars & Fellows programs through workshops, presentations, information dissemination, and our Honors Day Awards Ceremony."

Mizzou students have won a total of 18 Rhodes Scholarships, four Marshall Scholarships, four Gates Cambridge Scholarships, and 18 Truman Scholarships including three years in a row (2015, 2016, and 2017). Undergraduates at Mizzou in STEM disciplines have won at least 26 Goldwater Scholarships, including two in 2018. In each of the last two years, Mizzou students have earned one of the new Schwarzman Scholarships for study in China.


**UNRATED FEATURES**

**Continuation and Honors Graduation GPA Requirement:** 3.00.

**Academic Strengths, National Rankings:** This is based on national rankings of *graduate* programs in all but engineering and business, where undergraduate rankings are used. One of the weaknesses of the *U.S. News* rankings is that they focus on too many wealth-related metrics while ignoring their own assessments of academic departments. The rankings listed below are for all universities, public or private.

The leading nationally ranked academic departments at Mizzou are, in addition to its renowned journalism department, are education (45), psychology (45), economics (63), math (65), English (67), political science (72), and business (78).

**Internships, Professional Development, Community Engagement:** "Many of our courses, including those taught as General Honors courses, Career Explorations, and Internships, include internships, volunteer, or experiential opportunities. This includes serving our community, our campus, and our state.

**"The Pre-Med and Pre-Dental Scholars programs** give participating students early exposure to their professions by giving them priority placement for numerous volunteer and shadowing **opportunities** throughout Columbia and the surrounding central Missouri region. This includes our three hospitals (on campus) as well as our own clinics.

"Each year our Stamps Scholars join together with other Stamps Scholars from around the country to undertake a national day of service.

"The University of Missouri also runs the nation's largest and best-known Alternative Break program, called MAB (Mizzou Alternative Breaks) which offers programs over weekend, Thanksgiving, spring, summer, and winter breaks and allows students to undertake volunteer action both domestically and abroad. Students themselves select the sites, organize the trips, make all of the plans, and carry out the break program, all under the guidance of the MAB Office."

**Undergraduate Research:** "We believe that research and artistry is one of the highest-impact practices that a student can undertake. To that end, in just the past three years, we have created additional programs so that we now have twelve programs that provide scholarships for undergraduate research or artistry experiences." Here are two examples:

"National Merit Scholars—While the National Merit Scholarship program is well-known, at Mizzou we don't just provide students with a scholarship, but we also provide them with an additional research stipend to help launch them into the realm of scholarly discourse. *Through the assistance and placement process within the Honors College, these students are placed, in their first year, with a faculty member.*"

"Pre-Med and Pre-Dental Scholars—Each is a group of up to 80 students (twenty from each class year) who engage in preparatory activities related to their pursuit of medical or dental school, through shadowing, mentorships, and programming."

**Honors Study Abroad:** "In 2016-17, 1,184 MU undergraduate students studied abroad in 41 countries, 144 of whom were Honors College students, placing Mizzou in the top six percent of all colleges and universities nationwide.

"The Honors College sponsors numerous Honors-only Study Abroad Programs and partners with nearly forty other MU programs to offer Honors credit for a study abroad learning experience." Two examples are below:

"1. Nairobi, Kenya—Oral Traditions and Luyian Language. Focus on either understanding oral tradition in Africa or in linguistics and language collection in western Kenya. Students will have access a collection of oral literature from three Luyia communities of western Kenya as a baseline data set. Other students will collect language samples and participate in the development of a linguistic compilation of language.

"2. Oxford, England—Seminar at Oxford University, Corpus Christi College. This nine-day program draws upon the knowledge and ideas presented during the spring course 'Global and Transnational History since 1400' taught by Dr. Jay Sexton. The program provides students with the opportunity to study under the faculty at the famed Corpus Christi College at Oxford University, learning about the facets of a global society that have existed and influenced us for hundreds of years."

**Financial Aid:** "In 2017 **we became the forty-second school (and forty-fourth program) to join the Stamps Scholars Program**, a nationally-known program that allows us to provide the University's only full academic scholarship, including all tuition, fees, room, board, and a $16,000 educational enrichment account that allows the students to undertake path-breaking opportunities.

The Brazeal Honors College Endowed Diversity Scholarship is a four-year, $15,000 award (also includes a waiver of out-of-state tuition for non-residents and a $6,000 stipend for a study abroad experience) given to one student each year. Students must have a 32 ACT (or higher), rank in the top 5% of their class, and be invited to apply via the George C. Brooks Award process.

The Dorothy Blatchford Scholarship, for Native American students, is a four-year, $2,000 award (also includes a waiver of out-of-state tuition for non-residents) given to up to one student each year. Students must have a 27 ACT (or higher) and apply for the award.

The Dr. Donald Suggs Scholarship, for St. Louis area residents, is a four-year, $12,500 award (also includes a waiver of out-of-state tuition for non-residents and a $7,000 stipend for a study abroad experience) given to one student each year. Students must have a 27 ACT (or higher) and apply for the award.

The Stamps, Brazeal, Blatchford, and Suggs Scholars are all automatically given a research or artistry placement as a Scholar & Fellow for their first year as well.

**\* IMPORTANT CHANGE: National Merit Scholars**. "Beginning in the Fall 2017 semester, National Merit Finalists who are Missouri residents will now be awarded full tuition and fees, one year of room and board, a $3,500 annual stipend, a $2,000 research grant (one time), and a $1,000 technology enrichment grant (one time). Non-residents will have their non-resident tuition waived and receive up to a $2,000 additional stipend."

**Honors Fees:** "The University of Missouri Honors College remains <u>**fundamentally opposed to the idea that Honors students should have to pay additional course fees, semester charges, or membership assessments to be a part of the Honors College.**</u>" [Emphasis in original.]

**Placement of Honors Graduates:** "A recent survey, released in December 2017, shows that 90.4 percent of University of Missouri graduates have found successful career outcomes, including whether they are involved in public service, in the military or are continuing their education."

**Degree of Difference**: This is difference between (1) the average SAT scores for recently enrolled honors students (1420) and (2) the average test scores for all students in the university (1220) as a whole. The difference may be an indication of how "elite" honors students may be perceived as compared to students in the university as a whole. **Please keep in mind that neither the high nor low selectivity of an honors program determines how effective the program may be.**

**NAME**: UNIVERSITY OF NEVADA, RENO HONORS PROGRAM

**Date Established:** 1962

**Location**: Reno, Nevada

**University Full-time Undergraduate Enrollment (2017):** 18,191

**Honors Members in Good Standing**: 549 (mean size of all programs is 2,030).

**Honors Average Admission Test Score(s)**: ACT, 30; SAT, 1365.

**Average High School GPA/Class Rank:** 3.84, unweighted.

**Basic Admission Requirements:** ACT, 28; SAT, 1320; GPA, 3.65 unweighted.

**Application Deadline(s):** *Please verify with each program, as some deadlines could change.* February 1, 2019, and after that early deadline "strong applications will be considered until the fall Honors class reaches capacity."

**Honors Programs with SAT scores from 1332—1365:** Arizona State, Arkansas, Colorado State, Nevada Reno, Oklahoma State, Oregon, Oregon State.

**Administrative Staff:** 5.

**RATINGS AT A GLANCE:** For all mortarboard ratings immediately below, a score of 5 is the maximum and represents a comparison with all rated honors colleges and programs. More detailed explanations follow the "mortarboard" ratings.

**PERCEPTION\* OF UNIVERSITY AS A WHOLE, NOT OF HONORS:** 🎓🎓🎓

\*Perception is based on the university's ranking among public universities in the 2018 U.S. News Best Colleges report. Please bear in mind that the better the U.S. News ranking, the more difficult it is for an honors college or program to have a rating that equals or improves on the magazine ranking.

**OVERALL HONORS RATING:** 🎓🎓🎓🎓 1/2

**Curriculum Requirements:** 🎓🎓🎓🎓

**Number of Honors Classes Offered:** 🎓🎓🎓🎓 1/2

**Number of Honors Classes in Key Disciplines:** 🎓🎓🎓🎓 1/2

**Extent of Honors Enrollment:** 🎓🎓🎓🎓

**Honors-only Class Size:** 🎓🎓🎓 1/2

**Overall Class Size (Honors-only plus mixed, contract):** 🎓🎓🎓 1/2

**Honors Grad Rate Adjusted to SAT:** 🎓🎓🎓🎓 1/2

**Grad Rate Adjusted to Freshman Retention Rate:** 🎓🎓🎓🎓🎓

**Ratio of Staff to Students:** 🎓🎓🎓🎓

**Priority Registration: Yes,** honors students register for all courses, honors and otherwise, with the first group of students during each year they are in the program.

**Honors Housing Amenities:** 🎓🎓🎓🎓

**Honors Housing Availability:** 🎓🎓 1/2

**Prestigious Awards:** 🎓🎓 1/2

## RATING SCORES AND EXPLANATIONS:

**Curriculum Requirements (4.0):** The most important rating category, the curriculum completion requirement (classes required to complete honors) defines not only what honors students should learn but also the extent to which honors students and faculty are connected in the classroom. If there is a thesis or capstone requirement, it reinforces the individual contact and research skills so important to learning.

The average number of honors semester hours required for completion across all programs is 30.0.

The UNR Honors Program requires 30 credits for honors completion. Students may receive 3 or more credits for honors contracts, but they can be earned only in upper-division courses. They may also take 1-6 honors points in honors experiences (service learning), *but* these do not count for university credit toward graduation. Students must also complete a 6-credit honors thesis or a 6-7 credit capstone; the honors program has a thesis sequence for students whose majors departments do not require a thesis or capstone

**AP/IB credits** are **not** counted as replacements for honors courses.

**No. Honors Classes Offered (4.5):** This is a measure of the total **adjusted** honors main sections available in the term reported, not including labs and thesis. An adjusted main section has 3 or more semester credits, or equivalent, and sections with fewer credits receive a lower prorated value.

UNR Honors offered a section for every **11.1** enrolled students. The average for all programs was **15.0**. The lower the number, the better. In the term reported, an extremely impressive **89.4%** of honors enrollment was **in honors-only sections; none was in mixed sections; and 10.6% was in contract sections.** For all programs under review, enrollment by type of honors section was 75.8% honors-only, 15.4 % mixed, and 8.8% contract.

**No. Honors Classes in Key Disciplines (4.5):** The 15 "key" disciplines are biological sciences; business (all); chemistry; communications (especially public speaking); computer science; economics; engineering (all); English; history; math (all); philosophy; physics; political science; psychology; and sociology, anthropology, and gender studies. Interdisciplinary sections, such as those often taken for General Education credit in the first two years, do receive a lesser, prorated discipline "credit" because they introduce students to multiple disciplines in an especially engaging way, often with in-depth discussion.

For this measure, mixed and contract sections are not counted as a section in a key discipline unless students taking the sections for honors credit make up at least 10% of the total section enrollment.

In the term reported, UNR Honors offered a section in a key discipline for every **15.4 honors students.** The average for all programs is **24.7**. The lower the number, the better.

Out of **16 adjusted sections in key disciplines, all were honors-only sections**. The most sections were in English, followed by math and sociology/anthropology. The small honors program offered one section each in biology, computer science, engineering, physics, political science, and psychology.

Nine sections of "Seminar: The University" were offered. The seminar must be taken within the first two semesters. "This seminar introduces students in the University Honors Program to the rewards and responsibilities associated with earning an undergraduate degree with an emphasis on Honors education. The course orients incoming Honors students to graduate with the best possible college education and greatest opportunities for success." In Fall 2018, the seminar title was "Explorations in Honors: Global Perspectives."

UNR Honors is a **blended** program, with a good mix of interdisciplinary courses and classes in the disciplines.

**Extent of Honors Enrollment (4.0):** Not all honors students take an honors class each term, especially after the first two years. Programs that have fewer honors classes and thesis options for upper-division honors students will *generally* have fewer total members in good standing who are actually enrolled in a given term. (Please be aware, however, that honors students not enrolled in a class for a term are still tied to the honors community through residential and extracurricular activities.) *Our research shows that this measure is closely related to honors completion rates, i.e., the number of students who complete honors requirements by the time they graduate.*

For example, if a program has 1,800 individual students enrolled in a given term, and 3,000 students in good standing, the level of enrollment was .67, an indication that honors class enrollment is somewhat below average, especially in upper-division classes. **UNR Honors has a ratio of 1.36**, above the average of 1.30 for all programs.

**Average Class Size, Honors-only Sections (3.5):** Offered mostly in the first two years, honors-only classes tend to be smaller and, as the name implies, have no or very few students other than those in the honors program. These class sections always are much smaller than mixed or contract sections, or regular non-honors class sections in the university.

The average honors-only class size at UNR Honors is **19.0 students**. The average for all programs is **17.5 students.**

**Average Class Size, Overall (3.5):** The overall class calculation is based on the *proportion* of honors students in each type of class (honors-only, mixed honors, and honors contract sections). Thus it is not a raw average. The overall honors-credit class size is **26.5 students**, versus the average for all programs of **24.9 students**.

These class size averages also do not correspond to the number of students per honors section ratings above. The reason is that, in computing average class size metrics, we include enrollment in each 1-2-credit section, not just sections with 3 or more credits.

Along with an honors-only class size of 19.0 students (listed above), the program's contract sections with honors credit for individual honors students average **89.7 students.** Across all programs, the average contract section had 56.6 students.

**Honors Grad Rate Adjusted to SAT (4.5):** The rating is the based on the actual grad rate for students who entered the program six years earlier, whether or not the students remained in honors. The **actual rate of 87.6%** is also compared to the rates of other programs with the same test score entry requirement range, and then adjusted upward if the program is performing above other programs in the same range, or downward if the performance is less than other programs in the same range. The rate here is slightly upward, to **88.1%.**

**Grad Rate Adjusted to Freshman Retention Rate (5.0):** This rate compares the actual grad rate above to a predicted grade rate when freshman retention rates are considered. The actual grad rate is very impressive **6.29 points higher** than the predicted rate. For all programs, the actual grad rate is **.33 points lower** than the predicted rate.

**Ratio of Staff to Honors Students (4.0):** There is 1 staff member for every **109.8** students. (Mean ratio for all programs is 1 staff member for every **127.9** students.)

**Honors Residence Halls, Amenities (4.0):** About 60 first-year honors students live in the Nevada Living/Learning Community, an air-conditioned, coed dorm featuring suite-style rooms in the northwest part of campus. It is close to the journalism and business schools. The most convenient dining is at Downunder for a quick meal. Right across the street is the Virginia Street Gym. Only three minutes to the south is the Jot Travis Building and only a bit farther on is Manzanita Lake, one of the most scenic areas of campus. Jot Travis was formerly the student union at UNR; now "Jot Travis still offers food and beverage service in the form of The Overlook, a $4 million facility that opened in 2004."

**Honors Residence Halls, Availability (2.5):** This rating compares the number of occupants in honors residence halls to the number of honors freshman and sophomore members in good standing. The ratio for

the program is **.22** places for each first- and second-year student. The median for all programs is .49 places.

**Prestigious Awards (2.5):** The awards that we track and include are listed in the section titled "Prestigious Scholarships." The awards are sometimes won by students who are not in an honors college or program, but increasingly many are enrolled in honors programs. It is also a trend that honors colleges and programs help to prepare their students for the awards competitions.

Here is the information from UNR:

Rhodes 18; Marshall 1 (honors); Truman 7 (4 honors); Fulbright 26 (4 honors); Goldwater 11 (10 honors) Udall 1 (honors).

## UNRATED FEATURES

**Continuation and Honors Graduation GPA Requirement:** 3.25 for both.

**Academic Strengths, National Rankings:** This is based on national rankings of *graduate* programs in all but engineering and business, where undergraduate rankings are used. One of the weaknesses of the *U.S. News* rankings is that they focus on too many wealth-related metrics while ignoring their own assessments of academic departments. The rankings listed below are for all universities, public or private.

The nationally ranked academic departments at UNR include earth sciences (64), education (95), chemistry (122), psychology (131), engineering (137), and physics (139).

**Internships, Professional Development, Community Engagement:** "Experiential learning begins in the First Year Seminar for Honors students. In that course, students complete a 15-hour service-learning project with a community partner approved by the Office of Service-Learning and Civic Engagement [and] a number of Honors students work with their FYS service organizations throughout their four years at the University.

"Another option for first-year Honors students is the Honors Bonner Leader Program. Beginning with a service-focused First Year Seminar experience and providing ongoing training and enrichment over eight semesters, the program guides students in assuming progressively responsible roles within their chosen service organizations and prepares them for employment in the nonprofit, government, and private sectors.

"More generally, the Honors Program promotes civic engagement among its students by offering them an opportunity to earn Honors Points via service throughout their undergraduate careers. Unpaid service activities that are unrelated to course or co-curricular requirements are eligible for Honors Points.

"A majority of students who elect to contract for Honors Points plan to pursue careers in health sciences fields....As a result, area hospitals and adjacent organizations (hospices, mobile clinics, etc.) are popular community partners. In recent years, the number of students who contract for Points in recognition of unpaid work in on-campus research labs has also increased."

**Undergraduate Research:** "All students in the Honors Program are required to conduct original research and participate in an oral defense within the context of the Honors Senior Thesis/Project whether they complete their projects via research/thesis or a capstone sequence in their major. Where appropriate, students are encouraged to incorporate their creative and entrepreneurial activities. For example, fine arts and English writing majors typically produce creative projects accompanied by a critical essay and some business majors elect to produce business plans as their theses.

"Students who participate in the [research/thesis] sequence are required to prepare applications for the Honors Undergraduate Research Award and encouraged to present their research both on and off campus (e.g., at regional and national Honors conferences) whenever possible. All Honors Senior Theses are maintained in the University's ScholarWorks repository and accessible to all scholars on campus."

**Honors Study Abroad:** "Honors Program students study abroad at a higher rate than does the general student population (approximately 20% over four years compared with approximately 16%). Study abroad is extremely accessible at the University of Nevada, Reno because of the presence of the University Studies Abroad Consortium (USAC), which allows students to participate in one of more than 50 programs in 28 countries. Because this organization is headquartered on our campus, students are able to use most of their normal financial aid and scholarships for all USAC programs and all of their normal financial aid and scholarships for many of them. The cost of studying abroad can be less than the cost of remaining on campus for a semester depending upon the choice of program. Courses offered fulfill requirements in all university majors."

**Financial Aid:** Major scholarships available to honors students at the University of Nevada, Reno include:

Redfield National Merit Scholarship ($16,000 annually)
Presidential Scholarship ($8,000 annually)
Governor Guinn Millennium Scholarship ($10,000 over four years)
Nevada Scholars: ($2,500 annually)
Pack Pride: ($1,500 annually)

**Honors Fees:** None.

**Placement of Honors Graduates:** Graduate Schools: 37.4%; Professional Schools: 14.4%; Employment: 32.4%

"The above figures are based on the self-reported post-graduation plans of a random sample of honors graduates between 2011 and 2017."

**Degree of Difference**: This is difference between (1) the average SAT scores for recently enrolled honors students (1365) and (2) the average test scores for all students in the university (1150) as a whole. The difference may be an indication of how "elite" honors students may be perceived as compared to students in the university as a whole. **Please keep in mind that neither the high nor low selectivity of an honors program determines how effective the program may be.**

**NAME**: ALBERT DORMAN HONORS COLLEGE

**Date Established:** 1995

**Location**: Newark, New Jersey

**University <u>Full-time Undergraduate</u> Enrollment (2017):** 8,211

**Honors Members in Good Standing**: 732 (mean size of all programs is 2,030).

**Honors <u>Average</u> Admission Test Score(s)**: ACT, 32; SAT, 1462.

**Average High School GPA/Class Rank:** 3.91, unweighted; top 15% (10% for accelerated students.)

**<u>Basic</u> Admission Requirements:** ACT, 30; SAT, 1370; GPA, 3.60.

**Application Deadline(s):** *Please verify with each program, as some deadlines could change.* February 1, 2019.

**Honors Programs with SAT scores from 1420—1461:** Auburn, Central Florida, Delaware, Iowa, Kansas, Mississippi, Missouri, New Jersey Inst of Technology, Penn State, South Florida, Vermont, Virginia Commonwealth.

**Administrative Staff:** 9.

**RATINGS AT A GLANCE:** For all mortarboard ratings immediately below, a score of 5 is the maximum and represents a comparison with all rated honors colleges and programs. More detailed explanations follow the "mortarboard" ratings.

**PERCEPTION\* OF UNIVERSITY AS A WHOLE, <u>NOT</u> OF HONORS:** 🎓🎓🎓 1/2

\*Perception is based on the university's ranking among public universities in the 2018 U.S. News Best Colleges report. Please bear in mind that the better the U.S. News ranking, the more difficult it is for an honors college or program to have a rating that equals or improves on the magazine ranking.

**OVERALL HONORS RATING:** 🎓🎓🎓🎓 1/2

**Curriculum Requirements:** 🎓🎓🎓🎓🎓

**Number of Honors Classes Offered:** 🎓🎓🎓🎓

**Number of Honors Classes in Key Disciplines:** 🎓🎓🎓🎓 1/2

**Extent of Honors Enrollment:** 🎓🎓🎓🎓 1/2

**Honors-only Class Size:** 🎓🎓🎓 1/2

**Overall Class Size (Honors-only plus mixed, contract):** 🎓🎓🎓 1/2

**Honors Grad Rate Adjusted to SAT:** 🎓🎓🎓

**Grad Rate Adjusted to Freshman Retention Rate:** 🎓🎓🎓 1/2

**Ratio of Staff to Students:** 🎓🎓🎓🎓 1/2

**Priority Registration: Yes,** honors students have priority registration for all courses, in the form of being able to register with the class ahead of them.

**Honors Housing Amenities:** 🎓🎓🎓🎓

**Honors Housing Availability:** 🎓🎓🎓🎓🎓

**Prestigious Awards:** 🎓🎓

## RATING SCORES AND EXPLANATIONS:

**Curriculum Requirements (5.0):** The most important rating category, the curriculum completion requirement (classes required to complete honors) defines not only what honors students should learn but also the extent to which honors students and faculty are connected in the classroom. If there is a thesis or capstone requirement, it reinforces the individual contact and research skills so important to learning.

The average number of honors semester hours required for completion across all programs is 30.0.

The Dorman Honors College offers five honors completion options.

The Course Intensive Option requires a minimum of 33 honors credits for completion. No more than 9 credits in contract sections may be applied. Students must complete 16 honors colloquium credits and 240 community service hours, along with a 3-credit thesis or capstone.

The Research Option requires 24 total credit hours, including 16 colloquium hours. Contract courses are not counted as credit toward completion. At least 3 credits must be in departmental honors work, and a 6-credit research paper or product (e.g., prototype, patent application) is required.

For completion of the Professional Development track, students must take a minimum of 24 total credits hours, including the same colloquium requirement, the service requirement, and 3-credit requirement in a departmental class. Students must also complete a 3-credit capstone project.

The Study Abroad Option requirement is essentially the same as the Professional Development track above, except students must achieve course credit for at least one full semester of studying abroad.

The Grand Challenges Option and the Leadership Option require 24 credits, along with 8 colloquium credits, 3 credits in departmental honors, and a 3-credit capstone.

**"The Dorman Honors College offers both regular and accelerated/combined programs in Medicine, Dentistry, Optometry, Physical Therapy (Doctor of Physical Therapy), and Law.** In accelerated programs, students complete all of their General University requirements and most of the major courses in three years at NJIT. The first year of professional school completes the Bachelors (BA/BS) degree requirements.

"The Albert Dorman Honors College typically considers students who score in the 90+ percentile of test takers on the SAT or ACT exams, have a B+ average, and a history of leadership and service to the community. Exceptionally qualified candidates may apply to an accelerated program of their choice at the same time as they apply to NJIT and the Honors College through the Common Application."

**AP/IB credits** are **not** counted as replacements for honors courses.

**No. Honors Classes Offered (4.0):** This is a measure of the total **adjusted** honors main sections available in the term reported, not including labs and thesis. An adjusted main section has 3 or more semester credits, or equivalent, and sections with fewer credits receive a lower prorated value.

The college offered a section for every **13.8** enrolled students. The average for all programs was **15.0.** The lower the number, the better. In the term reported, **73.0%** of honors enrollment was **in honors-only sections; 24.2% was in mixed sections; and 2.8% was in contract sections.** For all programs under review, enrollment by type of honors section was 75.8% honors-only, 15.4 % mixed, and 8.8% contract.

**No. Honors Classes in Key Disciplines (4.5):** The 15 "key" disciplines are biological sciences; business (all); chemistry; communications (especially public speaking); computer science; economics; engineering (all); English; history; math (all); philosophy; physics; political science; psychology; and sociology, anthropology, and gender studies. Interdisciplinary sections, such as those often taken for General Education credit in the first two years, do receive a lesser, prorated discipline "credit" because they introduce students to multiple disciplines in an especially engaging way, often with in-depth discussion.

For this measure, mixed and contract sections are not counted as a section in a key discipline unless students taking the sections for honors credit make up at least 10% of the total section enrollment.

In the term reported, the program offered a section in a key discipline for every **14.1 honors students.** The average for all programs is **24.7.** The lower the number, the better.

Out of **49 adjusted sections in key disciplines, 34 were honors-only sections**. The most sections were in biology, engineering, computer science, and math, followed by business, communications, history, and physics.

The honors college offered a freshman seminar course (but not for credit) in which "students will develop an academic portfolio which will include personal reflections of their first semester, the development of an individual education plan and the creation of a resume. Discussions will focus on the responsibilities of being a successful college student, the academic honor code and ethics, introduction to college research, and the support network within the university. Leadership skills and group presentations will be emphasized.

Dorman Honors College is a **department-based** program, with a special focus on the STEM disciplines.

**Extent of Honors Enrollment (4.5):** Not all honors students take an honors class each term, especially after the first two years. Programs that have fewer honors classes and thesis options for upper-division honors students will *generally* have fewer total members in good standing who are actually enrolled in a given term. (Please be aware, however, that honors students not enrolled in a class for a term are still tied to the honors community through residential and extracurricular activities.) *Our research shows that this measure is closely related to honors completion rates, i.e., the number of students who complete honors requirements by the time they graduate.*

For example, if a program has 1,800 individual students enrolled in a given term, and 3,000 students in good standing, the level of enrollment was .67, an indication that honors class enrollment is somewhat below average, especially in upper-division classes. **Dorman Honors has a ratio of 1.59**, well above the average of 1.30 for all programs.

**Average Class Size, Honors-only Sections (3.5):** Offered mostly in the first two years, honors-only classes tend to be smaller and, as the name implies, have no or very few students other than those in the honors program. These class sections always are much smaller than mixed or contract sections, or regular non-honors class sections in the university.

The average honors-only class size in the college is **20.7 students**. The average for all programs is **17.5 students.**

**Average Class Size, Overall (3.5):** The overall class calculation is based on the *proportion* of honors students in each type of class (honors-only, mixed honors, and honors contract sections). Thus it is not a raw average. The overall honors-credit class size is **25.1 students**, versus the average for all programs of **24.9 students**.

These class size averages also do not correspond to the number of students per honors section ratings above. The reason is that, in computing average class size metrics, we include enrollment in each 1-2-credit section, not just sections with 3 or more credits.

Along with an honors-only class size of 20.7 students (listed above), the program's mixed honors sections have an average size of **37.2 students,** and the contract sections with honors credit for individual honors students average **34.4 students.** Across all programs, the average mixed honors section has 68.6 students, and the average contract section has 56.6 students.

**Honors Grad Rate Adjusted to SAT (3.0):** The rating is the based on the actual grad rate for students who entered the program six years earlier, whether or not the students remained in honors. The **actual rate of 86.0%** is also compared to the rates of other programs with the same test score entry requirement range, and then adjusted upward if the program is performing above other programs in the same range, or downward if the performance is less than other programs in the same range. The rate here is downward, to

**83.4%.** *Colleges with a high percentage of engineering and computer science majors see those students taking more time to graduate than other students, and NJIT has the highest enrollment percentage of those students of any program reviewed in this edition (~36%).*

**Grad Rate Adjusted to Freshman Retention Rate (3.5):** This rate compares the actual grad rate above to a predicted grade rate when freshman retention rates are considered. The actual grad rate is **1.3 points lower** than the predicted rate. For all programs, the actual grad rate is **.33 points lower** than the predicted rate. The same explanation at the end of the preceding category applies here.

**Ratio of Staff to Honors Students (4.5):** There is 1 staff member for every **77.8** students. (Mean ratio for all programs is 1 staff member for every **127.9** students.)

**Honors Residence Halls, Amenities (4.0):** The honors college offers housing in five residence halls, but about 70% of honors students in honors housing live in the Honors Residence Hall. The co-ed residence features suite-style rooms with shared baths; it is fully air-conditioned. Dining is very convenient at Campus Center, which has 25 dining stations to choose from. Students can have breakfast all day, deli sandwiches, sweets of all kinds, sushi, rotisserie chicken, pizza, or carved beef.

The rest of honors students in honors housing are in Laurel, Oak, Cypress, and Redwood Halls. All have suite-style rooms with air-conditioning. For all, the most convenient dining is also at the Campus Center; Cypress and Redwood are closest to the Campus Center.

"In addition to the Honors Residence Hall, there are designated honors rooms grouped within two other residence halls. There are designated areas in Cypress and Laurel Halls, where honors students are assigned in groups which comprise of half-floors the number of which vary depending up enrollment. For the term reported, there were 3 half-floors in Cypress Hall and 1 half-floor in Laurel Hall. The majority of honors students reside in the Honors Residence Hall."

**Honors Residence Halls, Availability (5.0):** This rating compares the number of occupants in honors residence halls to the number of honors freshman and sophomore members in good standing. The ratio for the program is **1.39** places for each first- and second-year student. The median for all programs is .49 places.

**Prestigious Awards (2.0):** The awards that we track and include are listed in the section titled "Prestigious Scholarships." The awards are sometimes won by students who are not in an honors college or program, but increasingly many are enrolled in honors programs. It is also a trend that honors colleges and programs help to prepare their students for the awards competitions.

"NJIT has also established a National Fellowships and Awards Committee to provide needed structure and support to our students as they enter these competitions. The committee began meeting in spring 2016 and is comprised of members of all our colleges, as well as the Provost's office. It is understood that the very large majority of students who apply for these fellowships will be Honors Scholars, and therefore the Honors College has a large presence on this committee. **The committee is chaired by the Dean of the Honors College, and contains two other members of the Honors College.**

"NJIT has significantly increased its efforts to successfully compete for prestigious national fellowships and scholarships. In recent years our students have received Fulbright study/research awards (2 plus one alternate), **Goldwater scholarships (6 plus one Honorable Mention),** NSF Graduate Research Fellowships (3 plus 1 honorable mention), a Gilman award and a Truman Fellowship. We have also had students win a DOE Computational Sciences Graduate Fellowship, a National Defense Science and Engineering Graduate Fellowship, the Department of Defense SMART award (9), and two Whitaker Fellowships. Most of the students mentioned above have been Honors Scholars."

**UNRATED FEATURES**

**Continuation and Honors Graduation GPA Requirement:** 3.20 for both; 3.50 for students in accelerated programs.

**Academic Strengths, National Rankings:** This is based on national rankings of *graduate* programs in all but engineering and business, where undergraduate rankings are used. One of the weaknesses of the *U.S. News* rankings is that they focus on too many wealth-related metrics while ignoring their own assessments of academic departments. The rankings listed below are for all universities, public or private.

The nationally ranked academic departments at NJIT are engineering (82), computer science (91), math (101), and physics (124).

**Internships, Professional Development, Community Engagement:** "Educational experience provided by programs NJIT Splash and After School All Stars provide foundational knowledge for scholars who find benefits in their training through instructive interaction. Our healthcare path scholars begin their professional understanding of medicine with transferable skills with face-to-face training found in Healthy Heroes, Global Brigades and on-site hospital collaboration in Newark. Community service skills are developed and fomented through programs Extra Mile Feeding, which is supplemented by partnering with the United Community Corporation. Environmental support of our community is enacted through the Alternative Spring Break program, developed through Career Development Services of NJIT with 17 honors scholars providing 3135 hours traveling to clean local parks in Newark and beaches at the New Jersey shore.

"Moreover, Albert Dorman Honors Scholars participate in STEM mentoring in Newark public schools. Other service activities include NJIT's Solar Car team, which holds demonstration workshops in Newark schools, and pre-dental honors scholars volunteer in dental clinics for the annual Give Kids a Smile Day with the New Jersey Dental Association (NJDA). Each year, two interns are selected from the Honors College to assist the NJDA in data collection and other tasks."

**Undergraduate Research:** "Beginning in the second semester of freshman year, students have the option to take a 3-credit honors introduction to research methods, which is taught and coordinated in-house.

"One of the students' final deliverables for this course is a research proposal, which is based on this research exposure and can be subsequently submitted to the university for summer stipend support consideration. If awarded summer stipend support, students have the opportunity to participate in our Honors Summer Research Institute milestone. This milestone involves weekly participation in research-oriented professional development workshops for 8 weeks over the summer. As students begin their second year, they receive intensive and careful advising on how to best leverage their newfound research skills and network to best define and/or achieve both their short-term and long-term professional goals."

**Honors Study Abroad:** "The Honors College recently approved three new curricular tracks that provide students with new options for co-curricular experiences that will enrich their educational opportunities. One of these tracks is the Study Abroad track in which students will receive a two-course reduction in required honors courses if they study abroad for one semester. *The university currently has several agreements with international universities for student exchange with a primary focus on Business courses. As part of the commitment, the university will heavily promote these programs especially in the Honors College, where Business is the second most popular minor.*

"The Dean's Fund for Student Development will provide support up to $1,000 for credit-bearing study abroad opportunities or approved international service activities if the applicant takes on an additional research project while studying abroad (such as assessing systems or cultures of health delivery or researching local current or historic building or urban practices). Funding must be used for activity beyond the student's academic requirements. Proposing a means to publish the research (formal or informal) is encouraged.

"Examples of existing programs—China (Fujian University of Technology, Shanghai Lixin University of Commerce); France (Esdes - Lyon, Kedge Business School, Skema Business School); South Korea (Hanyang University); Spain (Cesine Business School, Universitat Politecnica de Valencia); Sweden (Linkoping University), Ireland (University College)."

**Financial Aid:** "NJIT offers incoming students very generous merit-based faculty scholarships, as well as supplementary Honors Awards. 100% of the Honors Scholars in fall 2017 received significant awards. *88% of the Honors Scholars received scholarships and grants that covered at least full tuition.* Furthermore, 151 (21%) received full tuition, fees, room and board, and an additional 264 (36%) received full tuition, fees and room."

**Honors Fees:** None.

**Placement of Honors Graduates:** "For the class of 2017-18, 35.56% of graduates reported they were attending graduate or professional school immediately upon graduation. Another 34.81% had already accepted offers of employment at the time of the survey (May, 2018)."

**Degree of Difference**: This is difference between (1) the average SAT scores for recently enrolled honors students (1462) and (2) the average test scores for all students in the university (1250) as a whole. The difference may be an indication of how "elite" honors students may be perceived as compared to students in the university as a whole. **Please keep in mind that neither the high nor low selectivity of an honors program determines how effective the program may be.**

**NAME**: UNIVERSITY OF NEW MEXICO HONORS COLLEGE

**Date Established:** "UNM's Honors Program was founded in 1958 and became an autonomous College in 2013."

**Location**: Albuquerque, New Mexico

**University Full-time Undergraduate Enrollment (2017):** 20,215

**Honors Members in Good Standing**: 1,933 (mean size of all programs is 2,030).

**Honors Average Admission Test Score(s)**: ACT, 29.1; SAT, 1390.

**Average High School GPA/Class Rank:** 3.90, weighted.

**Basic Admission Requirements:** ACT, 28; SAT, 1320; GPA, 3.5.

**Application Deadline(s):** *Please verify with each program, as some deadlines could change.* May 1, 2019.

**Honors Programs with SAT scores from 1370—1403:** Arizona, CUNY Macaulay, Georgia State, Houston, Indiana, LSU, Massachusetts, New Mexico, Purdue, Texas Tech, UAB.

**Administrative Staff:** 4.

**RATINGS AT A GLANCE:** For all mortarboard ratings immediately below, a score of 5 is the maximum and represents a comparison with all rated honors colleges and programs. More detailed explanations follow the "mortarboard" ratings.

**PERCEPTION* OF UNIVERSITY AS A WHOLE, NOT OF HONORS:**

*Perception is based on the university's ranking among public universities in the 2018 U.S. News Best Colleges report. Please bear in mind that the better the U.S. News ranking, the more difficult it is for an honors college or program to have a rating that equals or improves on the magazine ranking.

**OVERALL HONORS RATING:**

**Curriculum Requirements:**

**Number of Honors Classes Offered:**

**Number of Honors Classes in Key Disciplines:** 1/2

**Extent of Honors Enrollment:** 1/2

**Honors-only Class Size:** 🎓🎓🎓🎓 1/2

**Overall Class Size (Honors-only plus mixed, contract):** 🎓🎓🎓🎓🎓

**Honors Grad Rate Adjusted to SAT:** 🎓🎓🎓🎓🎓

**Grad Rate Adjusted to Freshman Retention Rate:** 🎓🎓🎓🎓🎓

**Ratio of Staff to Students:** 🎓🎓 1/2

**Priority Registration: Yes,** honors students have priority registration for all courses, in the form of being able to register with the class ahead of them.

**Honors Housing Amenities:** 🎓🎓🎓

**Honors Housing Availability:** 🎓🎓

**Prestigious Awards:** 🎓🎓🎓 1/2

## RATING SCORES AND EXPLANATIONS:

**Curriculum Requirements (5.0):** The most important rating category, the curriculum completion requirement (classes required to complete honors) defines not only what honors students should learn but also the extent to which honors students and faculty are connected in the classroom. If there is a thesis or capstone requirement, it reinforces the individual contact and research skills so important to learning.

The average number of honors semester hours required for completion across all programs is 30.0.

UNM Honors College requires 36 credits for completion of the Honors College Major in Interdisciplinary Studies. Students must complete 30 hours in coursework and a 6-credit thesis. The college does not offer contract course credit. Very few students pursue this option, however.

The Honors College Minor in Interdisciplinary Studies requires 24 credits and no thesis.

One other option is the Honors College Designation in Interdisciplinary Studies, the preferred option, which has a requirement of 15 course credits.

**AP/IB credits** are **not** counted as replacements for honors courses.

**No. Honors Classes Offered (4.0):** This is a measure of the total **adjusted** honors main sections available in the term reported, not including labs and thesis. An adjusted main section has 3 or more semester credits, or equivalent, and sections with fewer credits receive a lower prorated value.

The program offered a section for every **14.9** enrolled students. The average for all programs was **15.0**. The lower the number, the better. In the term reported, a very impressive **100%** of honors enrollment was **in honors-only sections.** For all programs under review, enrollment by type of honors section was 75.8% honors-only, 15.4 % mixed, and 8.8% contract.

**No. Honors Classes in Key Disciplines (3.5):** The 15 "key" disciplines are biological sciences; business (all); chemistry; communications (especially public speaking); computer science; economics; engineering (all); English; history; math (all); philosophy; physics; political science; psychology; and sociology, anthropology, and gender studies. Interdisciplinary sections, such as those often taken for General Education credit in the first two years, do receive a lesser, prorated discipline "credit" because they introduce students to multiple disciplines in an especially engaging way, often with in-depth discussion.

For this measure, mixed and contract sections are not counted as a section in a key discipline unless students taking the sections for honors credit make up at least 10% of the total section enrollment.

In the term reported, the program offered a section in a key discipline for every **29.9 honors students.** The average for all programs is **24.7**. The lower the number, the better.

**All sections in key disciplines, all were honors-only sections**. *The program is centered on interdisciplinary seminars, about 55 in all, to an extent greater than all other programs under review. Unlike a few other programs that have a preponderance of these classes, UNM extends them to upper-division courses in addition to the more typical Gen Ed substitute courses for lower-division students. The 29.9 metric above is based on a percentage of "disciplinary" impact such seminars have. The same percentage is applied to the interdisciplinary courses of all programs being rated.*

Among the wealth of seminars offered in Fall 2016 were "What Good Is Tolerance?" and the Legacy series ("Legacy of Darwin," "Legacy of Dreams," "Legacy of Social Justice"; and, as well, "Individuals in Conflict with the Collective" and "Things that Make Us Smart."

**Extent of Honors Enrollment (2.5):** Not all honors students take an honors class each term, especially after the first two years. Programs that have fewer honors classes and thesis options for upper-division honors students will *generally* have fewer total members in good standing who are actually enrolled in a given term. (Please be aware, however, that honors students not enrolled in a class for a term are still tied to the honors community through residential and extracurricular activities.) *Our research shows that this measure is closely related to honors completion rates, i.e., the number of students who complete honors requirements by the time they graduate.*

For example, if a program has 1,800 individual students enrolled in a given term, and 3,000 students in good standing, the level of enrollment was .67, an indication that honors class enrollment is somewhat below average, especially in upper-division classes. **UNM honors has a ratio of .46**, below the average of 1.30 for all programs.

**Average Class Size, Honors-only Sections (4.5):** Offered mostly in the first two years, honors-only classes tend to be smaller and, as the name implies, have no or very few students other than those in the honors program. These class sections always are much smaller than mixed or contract sections, or regular non-honors class sections in the university.

The average honors-only class size at UNM Honors was **16.2 students**. The average for all programs is **17.5 students.**

**Average Class Size, Overall (5.0):** The overall class calculation is based on the *proportion* of honors students in each type of class (honors-only, mixed honors, and honors contract sections). Thus it is not a raw average. The overall honors-credit class size was also **16.2 students**, versus the average for all programs of **24.9 students**.

These class size averages also do not correspond to the number of students per honors section ratings above. The reason is that, in computing average class size metrics, we include enrollment in each 1-2-credit section, not just sections with 3 or more credits.

**Honors Grad Rate Adjusted to SAT (5.0):** The rating is the based on the actual grad rate for students who entered the program six years earlier, whether or not the students remained in honors. The **actual rate of 92.1%** is also compared to the rates of other programs with the same test score entry requirement range, and then adjusted upward if the program is performing above other programs in the same range, or downward if the performance is less than other programs in the same range. The rate here is significantly higher, **94.3%.**

**Grad Rate Adjusted to Freshman Retention Rate (5.0):** This rate compares the actual grad rate above to a predicted grade rate when freshman retention rates are considered. The actual grad rate was a remarkable **12.8 points higher** than the predicted rate. For all programs, the actual grad rate is **.33 points lower** than the predicted rate.

**Ratio of Staff to Honors Students (2.5):** There is 1 staff member for every **359.5** students. (Mean ratio for all programs is 1 staff member for every **127.9** students.)

**Honors Residence Halls, Amenities (3.0):** Most honors students in honors housing live in Hokona Hall, which has a mix of traditional single and double rooms, mostly the latter, and hall baths. Hokona is not air-conditioned; it houses 40 freshmen and upperclassmen. The nearest dining is at La Posada.

**Honors Residence Halls, Availability (2.0):** This rating compares the number of occupants in honors residence halls to the number of honors freshman and sophomore members in good standing. The ratio for the program is **.04** places for each first- and second-year student. The median for all programs is .49 places.

**Prestigious Awards (3.5):** The awards that we track and include are listed in the section titled "Prestigious Scholarships." The awards are sometimes won by students who are not in an honors college or program, but increasingly many are enrolled in honors programs. It is also a trend that honors colleges and programs help to prepare their students for the awards competitions. Below is a list of UNM scholars and their awards in academic year 2017-2018:

Goldwater Recipients:
•Jonathon Cordova, Biochemistry
•Randy Ko, Biochemistry & East Asian Studies
•Jane Nguyen, Chemical Engineering, Honorable Mention

Fulbright Recipients:
•Nicole Baty, English Teaching Assistantship in Vietnam
•Sierra Ludington, English Teaching Assistantship in Mexico

Churchill Scholarship Recipient:
•Julian Vigil, Chemical Engineering

## UNRATED FEATURES

**Continuation and Honors Graduation GPA Requirement:** 3.20 for both.

**Academic Strengths, National Rankings:** This is based on national rankings of *graduate* programs in all but engineering and business, where undergraduate rankings are used. One of the weaknesses of the *U.S. News* rankings is that they focus on too many wealth-related metrics while ignoring their own assessments of academic departments. The rankings listed below are for all universities, public or private.

UNM has a nationally ranked department in all key disciplines except economics. The average department ranking is 91.43—and so among the top 100 in the nation. The academic departments at UNM in the top 100 are earth sciences (46), history (69), computer science (75), sociology (80), political science (81) engineering (82), physics (83), English (85), math (86), and biology (98).

**Internships, Professional Development, Community Engagement:** "Not at this time, but we will soon."

**Undergraduate Research:** "The annual Undergraduate Research Opportunity Conference features research and creative works by our UNM undergraduate students. All majors and phases of projects are celebrated from proposals to completed work. Participant abstracts are published in the Conference Program, and students can include their presentation on resumes, CVs, and graduate school applications."

"The Honors College Research Institute (HRI) provides support to promote collaborations between faculty and students engaged in research in either scholarly or creative pursuits. Faculty may be from any field—humanities, social sciences, natural sciences, fine arts, and mathematics. Faculty will work with 1-4 undergraduate students on a specific project related to the area of their scholarly interest. Activities may include data collection from a geologic location to archival research in a library collection to installing a visual art exhibit for public display. Research for HRI projects may include national and/or international travel as well as on-campus projects. As a final component of the project, students and faculty are expected to complete a final synthesis of their research in a professional format, such as a research paper or report. This work is encouraged to be presented at a conference or published."

**Honors Study Abroad:** "The University of New Mexico, through the Honors College and the Department of Spanish and Portuguese, presents Conexiones—an intensive program of Culture and Language study at UNM and at the field site of Cuenca, Ecuador. *Conexiones offers students up to ten semester hours of credit, with orientation sessions at UNM and abroad and approximately thirty days of field session.*

"Conexiones offers students an extraordinary and unique experience. Ecuador is a country rich in diversity. It has the greatest biodiversity per area in the world: it occupies the first place in the world regarding species per area. In addition, the geographical diversity includes coastal lowlands, the highland Andes, and the Amazon rainforest, as well as the Galapagos Islands. Ecuador is also home to a rich variety of ethnic groups of indigenous populations, which speak 18 different languages among them. Don't worry, however: we will focus on Spanish!

"The field session will start with arrival in the capitol city of Quito, where we will stay 3 days before continuing the next morning on to our field site in the colonial city of Cuenca nestled among mountains at 8400 feet.

"Students will live with a host family in Cuenca for four weeks. They will attend Spanish classes at the Universidad de Cuenca's Programa de Español para Extranjeros, which is located in the heart of the city. All the families live within walking distance of the university. Weekly excursions are part of the program, including a hike in El Cajas National Park and research field study in indigenous communities."

**Financial Aid:** "UNM offers a number of merit-based scholarships, described below.

**In-State:**

Regents Scholarship—Student qualifies for consideration with a 31 ACT (1390 SAT) and 3.9 unit GPA with a submitted application by December 1. Recipients receive an amount that represents tuition/fees, books/supplies and room/board ($18,803), renewable up to four years. Regents Scholars must participate in the Honors College and live in Hokona Hall as freshmen.

National Scholars—Student qualifies for consideration as a National Merit Finalist. Recipients receive an amount that represents tuition/fees, books/supplies and room/board ($18,803), renewable for four years.

National Hispanic Scholars and National American Indian Scholars—Qualify for consideration if admitted by February 1. Recipients will receive approximately $8,951, renewable.

Presidential Scholarship—Students qualify for consideration with a 25 ACT (1200 SAT) and 3.75 unit GPA with a submitted application by December 1. Recipients receive an amount that represents tuition/fees, and books/supplies ($8,292) renewable.

**Out of State:** The Regents and National Scholars awards, above, have the same requirements and award levels for out-of-state students and in-state students.

**Honors Fees:** None.

**Placement of Honors Graduates:** None listed.

**Degree of Difference**: This is difference between (1) the average SAT scores for recently enrolled honors students (1390) and (2) the average test scores for all students in the university (1160) as a whole. The difference may be an indication of how "elite" honors students may be perceived as compared to students in the university as a whole. **Please keep in mind that neither the high nor low selectivity of an honors program determines how effective the program may be.**

**NAME**: OU HONORS COLLEGE

**Date Established:** 1996 (preceded by Honors Program in 1964)

**Location**: Norman, Oklahoma

**University Full-time Undergraduate Enrollment (2017):** 22,436

**Honors Members in Good Standing**: 2,521 (mean size of all programs is 2,030).

**Honors Average Admission Test Score(s)**: ACT, 33; SAT equivalent, 1490-1500. No superscoring.

**Average High School GPA/Class Rank:** 3.70, unweighted. Top 5% of high school class.

**Basic Admission Requirements:** ACT, 30; SAT, 1390; GPA, 3.75.

**Application Deadline(s):** *Please verify with each program, as some deadlines could change.* University scholarship deadline is December 15, 2018. Final deadline is February 1, 2019. No separate deadline for Honors College.

**Honors Programs with SAT scores from 1471—1510:** Clemson, Georgia, Illinois, Minnesota, Oklahoma, Rutgers, South Carolina, UT Austin.

**Administrative Staff:** 20.

**RATINGS AT A GLANCE:** For all mortarboard ratings immediately below, a score of 5 is the maximum and represents a comparison with all rated honors colleges and programs. More detailed explanations follow the "mortarboard" ratings.

**PERCEPTION* OF UNIVERSITY AS A WHOLE, NOT OF HONORS:** 🎓🎓🎓🎓

*Perception is based on the university's ranking among public universities in the 2018 U.S. News Best Colleges report. Please bear in mind that the better the U.S. News ranking, the more difficult it is for an honors college or program to have a rating that equals or improves on the magazine ranking.

**OVERALL HONORS RATING:** 🎓🎓🎓 1/2

**Curriculum Requirements:** 🎓🎓🎓

**Number of Honors Classes Offered:** 🎓🎓🎓 1/2

**Number of Honors Classes in Key Disciplines:** 🎓🎓🎓 1/2

**Extent of Honors Enrollment:** 🎓🎓🎓

**Honors-only Class Size:** 🎓🎓🎓🎓 1/2

**Overall Class Size (Honors-only plus mixed, contract):** 🎓🎓🎓🎓🎓

**Honors Grad Rate Adjusted to SAT:** 🎓🎓🎓🎓

**Grad Rate Adjusted to Freshman Retention Rate:** 🎓🎓🎓🎓🎓

**Ratio of Staff to Students:** 🎓🎓🎓🎓 1/2

**Priority Registration: Yes,** if they have academic scholarships. Freshmen with academic scholarships enroll early their first three semesters. After that, early enrollment is limited to National Merits, Regents, and National Scholars.

**Honors Housing Amenities:** 🎓🎓🎓🎓

**Honors Housing Availability:** 🎓🎓 1/2

**Prestigious Awards:** 🎓🎓🎓🎓 1/2

## RATING SCORES AND EXPLANATIONS:

**Curriculum Requirements (3.0):** The most important rating category, the curriculum completion requirement (classes required to complete honors) defines not only what honors students should learn but also the extent to which honors students and faculty are connected in the classroom. If there is a thesis or capstone requirement, it reinforces the individual contact and research skills so important to learning.

The average number of honors semester hours required for completion across all programs is 30.0.

The OU Honors College requires 21-25 honors credits for completion, depending on the student's major. Six credits must be in honors college courses taught by honors faculty. Up to 4 credits can be by honors contract, and up to 6 credits for studying abroad. The minimum required for thesis/capstone is 3 credits, but some departments require up to 7 credits.

**AP/IB credits** are **not** counted as replacements for honors courses.

**No. Honors Classes Offered (3.5):** This is a measure of the total **adjusted** honors main sections available in the term reported, not including labs and thesis. An adjusted main section has 3 or more semester credits, or equivalent, and sections with fewer credits receive a lower prorated value.

OU Honors offered a section for every **18.4** enrolled students. The average for all programs was **15.0**. The lower the number, the better. In the term reported, an extremely impressive **88.7%** of honors enrollment was **in honors-only sections; none was in mixed sections; and 12.3% was in contract**

**sections.** For all programs under review, enrollment by type of honors section was 75.8% honors-only, 15.4 % mixed, and 8.8% contract.

**No. Honors Classes in Key Disciplines (3.5):** The 15 "key" disciplines are biological sciences; business (all); chemistry; communications (especially public speaking); computer science; economics; engineering (all); English; history; math (all); philosophy; physics; political science; psychology; and sociology, anthropology, and gender studies. Interdisciplinary sections, such as those often taken for General Education credit in the first two years, do receive a lesser, prorated discipline "credit" because they introduce students to multiple disciplines in an especially engaging way, often with in-depth discussion.

For this measure, mixed and contract sections are not counted as a section in a key discipline unless students taking the sections for honors credit make up at least 10% of the total section enrollment.

In the term reported, OU Honors offered a section in a key discipline for every **27.1 honors students.** The average for all programs is 24.7. The lower the number, the better.

Out of **49 adjusted sections in key disciplines**, **31 were honors-only sections**. The most sections were in math, political science, and economics, followed by biology, business, English, chemistry, physics, psychology, and sociology/anthropology.

An interesting range of interdisciplinary courses including "The Atom in American History," "The Roots of Democracy," "Literature and Medicine," and "America in the Seventies." OU Honors is a **blended** program, with a good mix of interdisciplinary courses and classes in the disciplines.

**Extent of Honors Enrollment (3.0):** Not all honors students take an honors class each term, especially after the first two years. Programs that have fewer honors classes and thesis options for upper-division honors students will *generally* have fewer total members in good standing who are actually enrolled in a given term. (Please be aware, however, that honors students not enrolled in a class for a term are still tied to the honors community through residential and extracurricular activities.) *Our research shows that this measure is closely related to honors completion rates, i.e., the number of students who complete honors requirements by the time they graduate.*

For example, if a program has 1,800 individual students enrolled in a given term, and 3,000 students in good standing, the level of enrollment was .67, an indication that honors class enrollment is somewhat below average, especially in upper-division classes. **OU Honors has a ratio of .61**, below the average of 1.30 for all programs.

**Average Class Size, Honors-only Sections (4.5):** Offered mostly in the first two years, honors-only classes tend to be smaller and, as the name implies, have no or very few students other than those in the honors program. These class sections always are much smaller than mixed or contract sections, or regular non-honors class sections in the university.

The average honors-only class size at OU Honors is **16.1 students**. The average for all programs is **17.5 students.**

**Average Class Size, Overall (5.0):** The overall class calculation is based on the *proportion* of honors students in each type of class (honors-only, mixed honors, and honors contract sections). Thus it is not a raw average. The overall honors-credit class size is **16.4 students**, versus the average for all programs of **24.9 students**.

These class size averages also do not correspond to the number of students per honors section ratings above. The reason is that, in computing average class size metrics, we include enrollment in each 1-2-credit section, not just sections with 3 or more credits.

Along with an honors-only class size of 16.4 students (listed above), the college's contract sections with honors credit for individual honors students average **19.4 students.** Across all programs, the average contract section had 56.6 students.

**Honors Grad Rate Adjusted to SAT (4.0):** The rating is the based on the actual grad rate for students who entered the program six years earlier, whether or not the students remained in honors. The **actual rate of 94.0%** also compared to the rates of other programs with the same test score entry requirement range, and then adjusted upward if the program is performing above other programs in the same range, or downward if the performance is less than other programs in the same range. The rate here is exactly the same, **94.0%.**

**Grad Rate Adjusted to Freshman Retention Rate (5.0):** This rate compares the actual grad rate above to a predicted grade rate when freshman retention rates are considered. The actual grad rate is a remarkable 7**.67 points higher** than the predicted rate. For all programs, the actual grad rate is **.33 points lower** than the predicted rate.

**Ratio of Staff to Honors Students (4.5):** There is 1 staff member for every **86.9** students. (Mean ratio for all programs is 1 staff member for every **127.9** students.)

**Honors Residence Halls, Amenities (4.0):** The principal honors residence halls are David L. Boren Hall and honors floors in Walker Tower. Boren Hall, with mostly freshmen residents, has traditional rooms with hall baths, and the rooms are air-conditioned. Laundry service is not located within the residence. The most convenient dining is in Couch Cafeteria. All freshman are required to live on campus.

Walker Tower features air-conditioned, suite-style rooms with shared baths, and houses both first-year students and upperclassmen. Dining is also in Couch Cafeteria.

**"In addition, new OU Honors Students will benefit from a new plan established in conjunction with our new residential colleges. Specifically:**

"(1) Honors freshman can affiliate with one of our two outstanding Residential Colleges (Headington and Dunham) when coming into the university. This affiliates program allows new honors students to take advantage of special programs and events offered by the colleges.
"(2) Honors affiliates also have preference for signing up for the colleges. First preference goes to students who commit to a two-year on-campus housing contract.
"(3) Students who want to maintain affiliation with a residential college, but who cannot be accommodated due to space, have preference for either of the houses at the brand-new Cross Quad neighborhood or Traditions Square, but they still enjoy the perks of college membership."

**Honors Residence Halls, Availability (2.5):** This rating compares the number of occupants in honors residence halls to the number of honors freshman and sophomore members in good standing. The ratio for the program is **.21** places for each first- and second-year student. The median for all programs is .49 places. But going forward honors residence halls will have space for any student who chooses them.

**Prestigious Awards (4.5):** The awards that we track and include are listed in the section titled "Prestigious Scholarships." The awards are sometimes won by students who are not in an honors college or program, but increasingly many are enrolled in honors programs. It is also a trend that honors colleges and programs help to prepare their students for the awards competitions.

OU undergraduates and graduates have an impressive record in this category, earning 28 Rhodes Scholarships, six Marshall, 16 Truman, and 52 Goldwater Scholarships awarded to promising students in the STEM disciplines (tied for 15th among public universities).

**UNRATED FEATURES**

**Continuation and Honors Graduation GPA Requirement:** 3.00, to continue. To graduate *Cum Laude* = 3.40-3.59; *Magna cum Laude* = 3.60-3.79; *Summa cum Laude* = 3.80-4.00.

**Academic Strengths, National Rankings:** This is based on national rankings of *graduate* programs in all but engineering and business, where undergraduate rankings are used. One of the weaknesses of the *U.S. News* rankings is that they focus on too many wealth-related metrics while ignoring their own assessments of academic departments. The rankings listed below are for all universities, public or private.

The nationally ranked academic departments at OU include earth sciences (54), political science (61), history (63), business (64), math (74), education (75), sociology (75), English (80), engineering (82), chemistry (96), computer science (111), and biology (112).

**Internships, Professional Development, Community Engagement:** "The Honors College at the University of Oklahoma has many opportunities for students to become engaged and intellectually stimulated."

**David Ray PhD Informal Reading Groups.** "Each semester, the Honors College sponsors a program of about 40 informal reading groups. Students read, think, and discuss with other Honors College students on important topics of mutual interest. The groups meet for one hour per week, with 10-15 students and one Honors College faculty member or a pre-qualified student to discuss about 50 pages of reading from specific books. The books cover a very wide range of topics, and most have been recommended by Honors students. Thanks to a generous endowment, the books are free!" These are named after former Dean David Ray, who initiated the program.

**Medical Humanities Program.** "The Honors College and the University of Oklahoma College of Medicine offer this exciting opportunity to 5-8 incoming freshmen each year. *In this sequential BA/MD program, Medical Humanities Scholars design unique interdisciplinary programs that allow them to* *enhance their study of medicine with other areas of academic interest from the humanities, arts, and social sciences.* MH Scholars are expected to develop proficiency in foreign spoken language. Students also engage in service learning and clinical experiences to develop an appreciation for the biopsychosocial dimensions of health and healing."

**Student-To-Professional Mentoring Experience.** "The OU Honors College Student-To-Professional Mentoring Experience (aka STPMX) reaches out to local alumni and community professionals to share their valuable insights and strategic best practices with students to help them plan their next career steps. The professionals typically open their homes and gather many of their colleagues for a catered meal with about 30 students. Students are encouraged to circle among the professionals, seek advice for interviews, gather business cards, and follow up."

**Undergraduate Research:** "The Honors College coordinates five separate undergraduate research programs: (1) the First-Year Research Experience (FYRE), (2) the Undergraduate Research Opportunities Program (UROP), (3) the Honors Undergraduate Research Day (URD), (4) the Honors Research Assistant Program (HRAP), and (5) the Honors Undergraduate Research Journal (THURJ).

"FYRE offers an opportunity for first-year Honors students to participate in faculty-mentored laboratory research each Spring. Students chosen from a competitive application process participate in active laboratory research and receive three hours of Honors credit for successfully completing the course.

"UROP is a competitive grant program for any student at OU, awarding up to $1,000 to support research or creative activity conducted in partnership with a faculty member.

"URD is an annual campus-wide showcase of research and creative activity by undergraduates. In 2018, 15 students received cash awards ranging from $250 to $500.

"HRAP provides Honors students the opportunity to work with professors as research assistants on specific projects that the professor is studying. Participants are expected to work for ten hours a week for ten weeks for $1,000. Honors College students with at least 15 hours of college credit and a 3.4+ GPA are eligible to apply.

"THURJ is an annual publication that celebrates undergraduate research in all academic disciplines. Each spring, THURJ publishes the best undergraduate research papers from the previous year written by Honors students, as determined by an editorial board of their peers."

**Honors Study Abroad:**

"Founded in 1998, our **Honors at Oxford** study abroad program offers students the opportunity to live and work in the oldest university in the English-speaking world. The program is open to all Honors students who will have completed one year of college by the time of the trip. Students may choose from 3- or 6-credit hour options, taught by Honors faculty and Oxford professors. Both options take place in Oxford, England during July.

"Melanie Wright was a longtime advisor in the Honors College, focusing on students entering national award competitions or participating in the Honors at Oxford program. Upon her retirement in 2018 the faculty, staff, and alumni of the Honors College created this scholarship in her honor. This need- and merit-based scholarship helps support students who plan to study abroad at Oxford.

"OU runs highly successful and popular **international study centers** in Arezzo, Italy; Puebla, Mexico; and Rio de Janeiro, Brazil. These centers allow students to engage in classes led by OU professors (including Honors College faculty members) while exploring the culture and language of the host country. Several scholarships are offered to support study abroad students through the College of International Studies."

**Financial Aid:**

From the university: "Our Fall 2017 class of 317 National Merit Scholars includes students from 45 states plus New Zealand."

"OU has multiple academic scholarships available including National Merit Scholars Award, Regents Award, Regents Institutional Nominee, Award of Excellence, Distinguished Scholar, and National Award.

"Recently, the Honors College established the Katharine J. Gross Memorial Scholarship to provide an annual cash award to one outstanding student in the Honors College. The scholarship honors Kathy's life as friend and mentor to students and colleagues and for her contributions to the Honors College."

*"While OU's National Merit scholarship is a wonderful financial package, it will not cover all expenses. However, if your student receives outside scholarships, those cash awards will reduce their out-of-pocket expense.* In addition to our National Merit scholarship, we will allow your student to "stack" cash awards or federal financial aid that they receive.

**OU National Merit Finalist Packages, including other awards:**

In State:

Total *four-year* value of $64,000, including tuition waiver of $24,000; room, board, books $22,000; cash stipend, $10,000; technology and textbooks, $1,500; research and study-abroad stipend, $1,500.

Out of State:

Total *four-year* value of $117,000, including tuition waiver of $77,000; resident tuition waiver, in addition, of $10,000; room, board, books, $22,000; cash stipend, $5,000; technology and textbooks, $1,500; research and study-abroad stipend, $1,500.

These can also be used for a fifth year of study if programs require it.

**Honors Fees:** None.

**Placement of Honors Graduates:** "The Honors College hosts a Next Step series to help students with their post-graduation plans and host workshops for graduate school. The Honors College also works closely with OU's Career Services office which offers assistance with cover letters and resumes and administers 'The Handshake App' to connect students to potential employers."

**Degree of Difference**: This is difference between (1) the average SAT scores for recently enrolled honors students (1490-1500) and (2) the average test scores for all students in the university (1270) as a whole. The difference may be an indication of how "elite" honors students may be perceived as compared to students in the university as a whole. **Please keep in mind that neither the high nor low selectivity of an honors program determines how effective the program may be.**

**NAME**: OKLAHOMA STATE UNIVERSITY HONORS COLLEGE

**Date Established:** "The first class of Honors graduates (three students) earned Bachelor's Degrees with Honors in the 1968-1969 academic year, and the Arts & Sciences Honors Program formed the basis for the university-wide Honors Program that was created in 1989."

**Location**: Stillwater, Oklahoma

**University Full-time Undergraduate Enrollment (2017):** 21,093

**Honors Members in Good Standing**: 2,007 (mean size of all programs is 2,030).

**Honors Average Admission Test Score(s)**: ACT, 29.1; est. SAT equivalent, 1350.

**Average High School GPA/Class Rank:** 3.85, unweighted.

**Basic Admission Requirements:** ACT, 27; SAT, 1280; GPA, 3.75.

**Application Deadline(s):** *Please verify with each program, as some deadlines could change.* Deadline for many scholarships is November 1, 2018. Final deadline is February 1, 2019.

**Honors Programs with SAT scores from 1332—1365:** Arizona State, Arkansas, Colorado State, Nevada Reno, Oklahoma State, Oregon, Oregon State.

**Administrative Staff:** 10.

**RATINGS AT A GLANCE:** For all mortarboard ratings immediately below, a score of 5 is the maximum and represents a comparison with all rated honors colleges and programs. More detailed explanations follow the "mortarboard" ratings.

**PERCEPTION\* OF UNIVERSITY AS A WHOLE, NOT OF HONORS:** 🎓🎓🎓 1/2

\*Perception is based on the university's ranking among public universities in the 2018 U.S. News Best Colleges report. Please bear in mind that the better the U.S. News ranking, the more difficult it is for an honors college or program to have a rating that equals or improves on the magazine ranking.

**OVERALL HONORS RATING:** 🎓🎓🎓🎓

**Curriculum Requirements:** 🎓🎓🎓🎓🎓

**Number of Honors Classes Offered:** 🎓🎓🎓 1/2

**Number of Honors Classes in Key Disciplines:** 🎓🎓🎓

**Extent of Honors Enrollment:** 🎓🎓🎓 1/2

**Honors-only Class Size:** 👑 👑 👑 👑 👑

**Overall Class Size (Honors-only plus mixed, contract):** 👑 👑 👑 1/2

**Honors Grad Rate Adjusted to SAT:** 👑 👑 👑 1/2

**Grad Rate Adjusted to Freshman Retention Rate:** 👑 👑 👑 👑

**Ratio of Staff to Students:** 👑 👑 👑

**Priority Registration: Yes,** honors students register for all courses, honors and otherwise, with the first group of students during each year they are in the program.

**Honors Housing Amenities:** 👑 👑 👑

**Honors Housing Availability:** 👑 👑 👑 👑

**Prestigious Awards:** 👑 👑 👑 1/2

## RATING SCORES AND EXPLANATIONS:

**Curriculum Requirements (5.0):** The most important rating category, the curriculum completion requirement (classes required to complete honors) defines not only what honors students should learn but also the extent to which honors students and faculty are connected in the classroom. If there is a thesis or capstone requirement, it reinforces the individual contact and research skills so important to learning.

The average number of honors semester hours required for completion across all programs is 30.0.

The OSU Honors Degree requires a total of 36 honors credits, including 18 course credits, 9 credits in departmental honors, a 6-credit thesis, and 3 additional credits. Honors contracts may be used for credit.

The General Honors award requires a total of 18 honors credits, which may include a maximum of 9 credits in contract coursework and 3 credits in an honors experience (service learning, study abroad, etc.).

College or Departmental Honors typically requires 15 credits, including 9 department honors credits and a 6-credit thesis.

**AP/IB credits** may be counted for up to 6 honors credits.

**No. Honors Classes Offered (3.5):** This is a measure of the total **adjusted** honors main sections available in the term reported, not including labs and thesis. An adjusted main section has 3 or more semester credits, or equivalent, and sections with fewer credits receive a lower prorated value.

The program offered a section for every **15.4** enrolled students. The average for all programs was **15.0**. The lower the number, the better. In the term reported, **74.2%** of honors enrollment was **in honors-only sections; 5.5% was in mixed sections; and 20.3% was in contract sections.** This represents a large increase in contract options for the honors college. For all programs under review, enrollment by type of honors section was **75.8%** honors-only, **15.4 %** mixed, and **8.8%** contract.

**No. Honors Classes in Key Disciplines (3.0):** The 15 "key" disciplines are biological sciences; business (all); chemistry; communications (especially public speaking); computer science; economics; engineering (all); English; history; math (all); philosophy; physics; political science; psychology; and sociology, anthropology, and gender studies. Interdisciplinary sections, such as those often take for General Education credit in the first two years, do receive a lesser, prorated discipline "credit" because they introduce students to multiple disciplines in an especially engaging way, often with in-depth discussion.

For this measure, mixed and contract sections are not counted as a section in a key discipline unless students taking the sections for honors credit make up at least 10% of the total section enrollment.

In the term reported, the program offered a section in a key discipline for every **37.7 honors students.** The average for all programs is **24.7.** The lower the number, the better.

Out of **38 adjusted sections in key disciplines, 25 were honors-only sections**. The most sections were, by far, in English (critical analysis and composition), followed by engineering, economics, math, and history.

The college offered 11 seminar sections, including a series called "The Early Modern World," which are interdisciplinary studies "of art, history, philosophy and literature from the late Renaissance to the mid19th century." Other seminars included "Ethical Issues across Cultural Perspectives," an introduction to "reasoned methods of evaluating ideas and arguments as they pertain to ethical issues from a global perspective. Concepts include obligation, justice, and ethnicity from Lao Tzu, Maimonides, Kant, and Indian wisdom stories."

OSU Honors is a **department-based** program, with some interesting topical seminars as well.

**Extent of Honors Enrollment (3.5):** Not all honors students take an honors class each term, especially after the first two years. Programs that have fewer honors classes and thesis options for upper-division honors students will *generally* have fewer total members in good standing who are actually enrolled in a given term. (Please be aware, however, that honors students not enrolled in a class for a term are still tied to the honors community through residential and extracurricular activities.) *Our research shows that this measure is closely related to honors completion rates, i.e., the number of students who complete honors requirements by the time they graduate.*

For example, if a program has 1,800 individual students enrolled in a given term, and 3,000 students in good standing, the level of enrollment was .67, an indication that honors class enrollment is somewhat below average, especially in upper-division classes. **OSU Honors has a ratio of 1.17**, below the average of 1.30 for all programs.

**Average Class Size, Honors-only Sections (5.0):** Offered mostly in the first two years, honors-only classes tend to be smaller and, as the name implies, have no or very few students other than those in the

honors program. These class sections always are much smaller than mixed or contract sections, or regular non-honors class sections in the university.

The average honors-only class size at OSU Honors is **14.5 students**. The average for all programs is **17.5 students.**

**Average Class Size, Overall (3.5):** The overall class calculation is based on the *proportion* of honors students in each type of class (honors-only, mixed honors, and honors contract sections). Thus it is not a raw average. The overall honors-credit class size is **28.5 students**, versus the average for all programs of **24.9 students**.

These class size averages also do not correspond to the number of students per honors section ratings above. The reason is that, in computing average class size metrics, we include enrollment in each 1-2-credit section, not just sections with 3 or more credits.

Along with an honors-only class size of 14.5 students (listed above), the program's mixed honors sections have an average size of **124.7 students,** and the contract sections with honors credit for individual honors students average **53.7 students.** Across all programs, the average mixed honors section has 68.6 students, and the average contract section has 56.6 students.

**Honors Grad Rate Adjusted to SAT (3.5):** The rating is the based on the actual grad rate for students who entered the program six years earlier, whether or not the students remained in honors. The **actual rate of 82.6%** is also compared to the rates of other programs with the same test score entry requirement range, and then adjusted upward if the program is performing above other programs in the same range, or downward if the performance is less than other programs in the same range. The rate here is downward, to **81.6%.**

**Grad Rate Adjusted to Freshman Retention Rate (4.0):** This rate compares the actual grad rate above to a predicted grade rate when freshman retention rates are considered. The actual grad rate is **1.28 points higher** than the predicted rate. For all programs, the actual grad rate is **.33 points lower** than the predicted rate.

**Ratio of Staff to Honors Students (3.0):** There is 1 staff member for every **200.7** students. (Mean ratio for all programs is 1 staff member for every **127.9** students.)

**Honors Residence Halls, Amenities (3.0):** About 75% of honors students in honors housing reside in Stout Hall. Stout has traditional rooms with hall baths. It is air-conditioned and houses both freshmen and upperclassmen. The nearest dining hall is the Service Station.

The other honors students living in honors housing reside in West Bennett, which has air-conditioned suite-style rooms and shared baths. Dining is on site.

**Honors Residence Halls, Availability (4.0):** This rating compares the number of occupants in honors residence halls to the number of honors freshman and sophomore members in good standing. The ratio for the program is **.52** places for each first- and second-year student. The median for all programs is .49 places.

**Prestigious Awards (3.5):** The awards that we track and include are listed in the section titled "Prestigious Scholarships." The awards are sometimes won by students who are not in an honors college or program, but increasingly many are enrolled in honors programs. It is also a trend that honors colleges and programs help to prepare their students for the awards competitions.

OSU students have won 1 Rhodes scholarship, 2 Gates Cambridge scholarships, 2 Marshall scholarships, and 17 Truman scholarships. In addition, as for Goldwater scholarships (most won by honors students) OSU students have won 22. The Udall total is 18 scholarships, probably in the top 10 among public universities.

**UNRATED FEATURES**

**Continuation and Graduation Requirements:** second year 3.30; third year 3.40; hereafter 3.50; and 3.50 for graduation.

**Academic Strengths, National Rankings:** This is based on national rankings of *graduate* programs in all but engineering and business, where undergraduate rankings are used. One of the weaknesses of the *U.S. News* rankings is that they focus on too many wealth-related metrics while ignoring their own assessments of academic departments. The rankings listed below are for all universities, public or private.

The nationally ranked academic departments at OSU include engineering (82), math (87), business (91), sociology (96), physics (111), history (114), and chemistry (117).

**Internships, Professional Development, Community Engagement:** "In 2017 we began to develop a new program that will become active in the 2018-19 academic year as it has received approval from the University. This program will allow students to utilize significant experiential learning as part of Honors curriculum in line with our philosophy that profound intellectual experiences are not confined to the traditional classroom. *With the implementation of the new program students will be able to obtain honors credit for significant experiences outside the classroom in the areas of academics, the arts, leadership, service, and study away. This new program will increase the flexibility of the General Honors component of the Honors degree.*"

**Undergraduate Research:** "All students who graduate with an Honors College degree or with a Departmental Honors or College Honors Award must complete research in the form of an honors thesis. *In 2016 the thesis hours were raised from a 3-credit one semester requirement to a 6-credit two semester requirement in recognition of the actual time students were putting into their theses.* Students are required to have two readers and do a public presentation of their thesis work. It is not unusual for Honors students to be presenting at regional and national academic conferences."

OSU also offers scholarships ranging from $1,000 to $8,000 for undergraduate research. Each year, the Niblack Research Scholars program selects 12 students for an $8,000 award. The Lew Wentz Foundation and the university also provide research scholarships valued at $4,500. Freshman Scholars and Life Science Scholars are eligible for awards of $1,000.

**Honors Study Abroad:** "The Oklahoma State University Study Abroad Office coordinate study abroad across the University experiences range from faculty lead one-week programs to year long study abroad experiences. Internationalization is a priority for both the University and the Honors College. Honors students are strongly encouraged to take part in study abroad, and we have policies that allow students to count courses or experiences from such trips as Honors credit. Colleges are also supportive of Honors and study abroad and will frequently set up Honors sections or contracts for such courses as recently occurred for faculty led trips to France and Cuba. Scholarships for study abroad are available from individual Colleges and centrally.

**"Cowboys in Cambridge** is an OSU summer study abroad opportunity with honors sections available. Honors students who participate in the program **receive three honors credits after two weeks of study abroad at Magdalene** College, University of Cambridge, and completion of a course project. Students must apply to the program and it is attended by top OSU students. All students admitted to the program receive significant financial support.

Each year the two-week course explores a new topic. Examples: "England during the time of Charles Dickens"; "Life and Work of Charles Darwin"; "Counter Terrorism in the British Experience"; and "Literature in the Age of Empire: The Anglo-Caribbean Experience."

**Financial Aid:**

**National Merit Scholarship:**

•Description: A five-year full tuition waiver and a combination of state, university, and National Merit funding.
•Value: Up to $67,000.
•Eligibility: The National Merit Scholarship Corporation determines requirements and eligibility. National Merit Finalists must select OSU as their first choice.

**In State:**

New 2017-18—Oklahoma State Scholars Society (OSSS) Scholarship:

•Description: A four-year full tuition waiver, university funding, and a one-time stipend. 20 total awards per year (15 semifinalists and 5 finalists).
•Value: Semifinalists—Varies (guaranteed: President's Distinguished Scholarship, $2,500/year x 4 years; "Semifinalist Scholarship," up to $2,000/year x 4 years; other university assured scholarships and competitive awards will vary).
•Value: Finalists—Full cost of attendance + 1-time $4,500 study abroad stipend.
•Eligibility: Highly competitive selection. Open to Oklahoma residents admitted prior to November 1st Early Opportunity Scholarship Deadline. Minimum 3.8 high school unweighted GPA and 30 ACT/1280 SAT-R. Admitted to The Honors College with submission of Honors College application prior to November 1st Early Opportunity Scholarship Deadline. **Completed Scholarship application includes application essays, leadership & involvement resume, and high school transcript.**

**Honors Fees:** None.

**Placement of Honors Graduates:** Recent placement statistics are below.

Public or Private Employment—43%
Professional School—Medical, Law, etc.—20%
Graduate School—36%
Other—1%

**Degree of Difference**: This is difference between (1) the average SAT scores for recently enrolled honors students (1350) and (2) the average test scores for all students in the university (1160) as a whole. The difference may be an indication of how "elite" honors students may be perceived as compared to students in the university as a whole. **Please keep in mind that neither the high nor low selectivity of an honors program determines how effective the program may be.**

**NAME**: ROBERT D. CLARK HONORS COLLEGE, UNIVERSITY OF OREGON

**Date Established:** 1960

**Location**: Eugene, Oregon

**University Full-time Undergraduate Enrollment (2017):** 20,049

**Honors Members in Good Standing**: 833 (mean size of all programs is 2,030).

**Honors Average Admission Test Score(s)**: ACT, 28; SAT, 1332.

**Average High School GPA/Class Rank:** 3.87, unweighted.

**Basic Admission Requirements:** None listed.

**Application Deadline(s):** *Please verify with each program, as some deadlines could change.* Early action deadline November 1, 2018, with all materials due November 7, 2018; notification December 15, 2018. Regular deadline January 15, 2019, with all materials due February 1, 2019; notification April 1, 2019.

**Honors Programs with SAT scores from 1332—1365:** Arizona State, Arkansas, Colorado State, Nevada Reno, Oklahoma State, Oregon, Oregon State.

**Administrative Staff:** 15.

**RATINGS AT A GLANCE:** For all mortarboard ratings immediately below, a score of 5 is the maximum and represents a comparison with all rated honors colleges and programs. More detailed explanations follow the "mortarboard" ratings.

**PERCEPTION\* OF UNIVERSITY AS A WHOLE, NOT OF HONORS:** 🎓🎓🎓🎓

\*Perception is based on the university's ranking among public universities in the 2018 U.S. News Best Colleges report. Please bear in mind that the better the U.S. News ranking, the more difficult it is for an honors college or program to have a rating that equals or improves on the magazine ranking.

**OVERALL HONORS RATING:** 🎓🎓🎓🎓 1/2

**Curriculum Requirements:** 🎓🎓🎓🎓 1/2

**Number of Honors Classes Offered:** 🎓🎓🎓 1/2

**Number of Honors Classes in Key Disciplines:** 🎓🎓🎓🎓

**Extent of Honors Enrollment:** 🎓🎓🎓 1/2

**Honors-only Class Size:** ⬛⬛⬛⬛⬛

**Overall Class Size (Honors-only plus mixed, contract):** ⬛⬛⬛⬛⬛

**Honors Grad Rate Adjusted to SAT:** ⬛⬛⬛1/2

**Grad Rate Adjusted to Freshman Retention Rate:** ⬛⬛⬛

**Ratio of Staff to Students:** ⬛⬛⬛⬛⬛

**Priority Registration: Yes,** honors students register for all courses, honors and otherwise, with the first group of students during each year they are in the program.

**Honors Housing Amenities:** ⬛⬛⬛⬛⬛

**Honors Housing Availability:** ⬛⬛⬛⬛

**Prestigious Awards:** ⬛⬛⬛1/2

## RATING SCORES AND EXPLANATIONS:

**Curriculum Requirements (4.5):** The most important rating category, the curriculum completion requirement (classes required to complete honors) defines not only what honors students should learn but also the extent to which honors students and faculty are connected in the classroom. If there is a thesis or capstone requirement, it reinforces the individual contact and research skills so important to learning.

The average number of honors semester hours required for completion across all programs is 30.0.

"The Clark Honors College grants diplomas to students admitted to it who complete both the college's required curriculum and the requirements of the student's chosen major(s). Clark Honors College students complete majors in every school and department across campus, throughout the College of Arts and Sciences and in the professional schools of Business, Journalism and Communications, Music and Dance, Design, and Education.

"The Clark Honors College's curriculum, most of which occurs in Clark Honors College-only classes, satisfies/replaces the 'general education' required of all University of Oregon graduates. In addition the Clark Honors College requires a thesis, completed in the student's major. On average undergraduate students complete 45-50 courses for the completion of a bachelor's degree from the university, or 180 credits."

Converted to semester hours, the minimum would be about 30 credits.

**AP/IB credits** are **not** counted as replacements for honors courses. "Four credits in quantitative reasoning, as well as an additional 8 credits in science and/or math courses can be fulfilled via AP/IB credits."

**No. Honors Classes Offered (3.5):** This is a measure of the total **adjusted** honors main sections available in the term reported, not including labs and thesis. An adjusted main section has 3 or more semester credits, or equivalent, and sections with fewer credits receive a lower prorated value.

The program offered a section for every **15.3** enrolled students. The average for all programs was **15.0**. The lower the number, the better. In the term reported, an extremely impressive **100%** of honors enrollment was **in honors-only sections**. For all programs under review, enrollment by type of honors section was 75.8% honors-only, 15.4 % mixed, and 8.8% contract.

**No. Honors Classes in Key Disciplines (4.0):** The 15 "key" disciplines are biological sciences; business (all); chemistry; communications (especially public speaking); computer science; economics; engineering (all); English; history; math (all); philosophy; physics; political science; psychology; and sociology, anthropology, and gender studies. Interdisciplinary sections, such as those often take for General Education credit in the first two years, do receive a lesser, prorated discipline "credit" because they introduce students to multiple disciplines in an especially engaging way, often with in-depth discussion.

For this measure, mixed and contract sections are not counted as a section in a key discipline unless students taking the sections for honors credit make up at least 10% of the total section enrollment.

In the term reported, the program offered a section in a key discipline for every **19.7 honors students.** The average for all programs is **24.7**. The lower the number, the better.

Out of **66 adjusted (quarter unit) sections in key disciplines**, **all were honors-only sections**. Many of these classes are seminars or interdisciplinary with an emphasis on one discipline more than another. The emphasis is on the humanities and social sciences, although "Current Biomedical Research Topics," "Relativity, the Quantum, and Reality," and "Cosmology" certainly have a science focus.

The college offered a wealth of interesting seminars: "Ethical Beginnings," Essentialism in Cognition and Culture," and, one of our favorites, "Loose and Baggy Monsters: Russian Novels of the Nineteenth Century."

Clark Honors College is definitely a **core** program, with almost all classes offered directly by the college.

**Extent of Honors Enrollment (3.5):** Not all honors students take an honors class each term, especially after the first two years. Programs that have fewer honors classes and thesis options for upper-division honors students will *generally* have fewer total members in good standing who are actually enrolled in a given term. (Please be aware, however, that honors students not enrolled in a class for a term are still tied to the honors community through residential and extracurricular activities.) *Our research shows that this measure is closely related to honors completion rates, i.e., the number of students who complete honors requirements by the time they graduate.*

For example, if a program has 1,800 individual students enrolled in a given term, and 3,000 students in good standing, the level of enrollment was .67, an indication that honors class enrollment is somewhat

below average, especially in upper-division classes. **Clark Honors has a ratio of 1.15**, below the average of 1.30 for all programs.

**Average Class Size, Honors-only Sections (5.0):** Offered mostly in the first two years, honors-only classes tend to be smaller and, as the name implies, have no or very few students other than those in the honors program. These class sections always are much smaller than mixed or contract sections, or regular non-honors class sections in the university.

The average honors-only class size at Clark Honors **15.7 students**. The average for all programs is **17.5 students.**

**Average Class Size, Overall (5.0):** The overall class calculation is based on the *proportion* of honors students in each type of class (honors-only, mixed honors, and honors contract sections). Thus it is not a raw average. The overall honors-credit class size is also **15.7 students**, versus the average for all programs of **24.9 students**.

These class size averages also do not correspond to the number of students per honors section ratings above. The reason is that, in computing average class size metrics, we include enrollment in each 1-2-credit section, not just sections with 3 or more credits.

Clark Honors College does not have mixed or contract sections.

**Honors Grad Rate Adjusted to SAT (3.5):** The rating is the based on the actual grad rate for students who entered the program six years earlier, whether or not the students remained in honors. The **actual rate of 84.3%** is also compared to the rates of other programs with the same test score entry requirement range, and then adjusted upward if the program is performing above other programs in the same range, or downward if the performance is less than other programs in the same range. The rate here is slightly downward, to **83.9%.**

**Grad Rate Adjusted to Freshman Retention Rate (3.0):** This rate compares the actual grad rate above to a predicted grade rate when freshman retention rates are considered. The actual grad rate is **3.00 points lower** than the predicted rate. For all programs, the actual grad rate is **.33 points lower** than the predicted rate.

**Ratio of Staff to Honors Students (5.0):** There is 1 staff member for every **55.5** students. (Mean ratio for all programs is 1 staff member for every **127.9** students.)

**Honors Residence Halls, Amenities (5.0):** The Global Scholars Residence Hall houses 200 honors students, both freshmen and upperclassmen. The residence has a mix of singles, doubles, triples, and suite-style rooms, all of which are air-conditioned. A great feature is on-site dining at the Fresh Market Café.

"The Global Scholars Hall is home to students in the Robert D. Clark Honors College who can attend lectures, discussions, film screenings, and academic advising offered right where they live. The Global Scholars community is guided by a team of faculty and staff including a Resident Scholar who lives and teaches in the building. The Center for Undergraduate Research and Engagement is located in the Research Commons on the first floor of the building. Drop-in honors peer advising and dedicated advising for students pursuing nationally distinguished scholarships is also available in the building. Students have access to various classrooms, a multi-use performance space, and study rooms."

In Fall 2018, the newly renovated Bean Hall will house about 80 CHC upperclassmen. Bean is air-conditioned and has traditional double rooms with hall baths. Located close to the Global Scholars Hall, Bean has very convenient dining at the Fresh Market Café.

**Honors Residence Halls, Availability (4.0):** This rating compares the number of occupants in honors residence halls to the number of honors freshman and sophomore members in good standing. The ratio for the program is **.48** places for each first- and second-year student. The median for all programs was .49 places. CHC will have more availability after Bean Hall opens.

**Prestigious Awards (3.5):** The awards that we track and include are listed in the section titled "Prestigious Scholarships." The awards are sometimes won by students who are not in an honors college or program, but increasingly many are enrolled in honors programs. It is also a trend that honors colleges and programs help to prepare their students for the awards competitions.

"Beginning in the 2015-2016 academic year, Clark Honors College hired Dr. Elizabeth Raisanen into the new position of Director of Undergraduate Advising. Dr. Raisanen is focused on increasing student awareness around distinguished scholarships through direct student outreach, workshops, and one-on-one mentoring. Dr. Raisanen also is a first-stop for students within the Clark Honors College, and can connect students to other resources throughout the university that the students may not have been aware of. This includes the Office of National and International Distinguished Scholarships at the University of Oregon that provides application assistance and interview support for distinguished scholarship applicants."

"Of the 47 awards received by Clark Honors College students since 1975, almost half have been awarded in the last ten years, demonstrating an increasing focus on the part of the college towards informing and supporting students through the competitive application process."

**UNRATED FEATURES**

**Continuation and Honors Graduation GPA Requirement:** 3.00 for both.

**Academic Strengths, National Rankings:** This is based on national rankings of *graduate* programs in all but engineering and business, where undergraduate rankings are used. One of the weaknesses of the *U.S. News* rankings is that they focus on too many wealth-related metrics while ignoring their own assessments of academic departments. The rankings listed below are for all universities, public or private.

The University of Oregon has strong academic departments, with an average national ranking of 51.4., and including all departments that we track except engineering, a major not offered at U of O.

The nationally ranked academic departments at Oregon are education (13), earth sciences (31), psychology (45), English (47), sociology (47), history (53), math (55), physics (56), chemistry (59), economics (59), biology (62), business (64), and computer science (64).

**Internships, Professional Development, Community Engagement:** "Clark Honors College has recently established a student internship and mentorship program embedded in the cluster of 'signature' opportunities that currently comprise study abroad, Inside Out, community engagement, and experiential learning. A signature program for CHC signifies an opportunity for academic and/or career development available to Clark Honors College students that is facilitated and evaluated by CHC faculty and staff.

"The founding internship in this program comes from the college's partnership with Oregon Health and Science University (OHSU), a leading nationally-ranked medical teaching school. Each year OHSU hosts an internship program in their department of Cell, Developmental & Cancer Biology. This summer (2018) marks the fourth year of a partnership between the Clark Honors College and OHSU where two intern spots are reserved exclusively for CHC students. This partnership provides invaluable hands-on learning experience for students considering a medical career."

**Speech, Debate and Mock Trial:** "These programs, administratively housed within the Clark Honors College, are open to all undergraduates at the University of Oregon; however program enrollment is generally 50% - 66% honors students. In 2016, the Mock Trial team placed 19th in the country at the National Championship invitational among 48 invited teams. *The speech and debate team regularly competes at the highest collegiate levels nationally, and in 2016 placed first in national competition after 17 consecutive undefeated rounds.*

**Undergraduate Research:** "Every student who graduates from Clark Honors College must research, write and orally defend an undergraduate thesis. This process often takes more than a year, and the experience of defining a unique research question, conducting research, writing, and defending the thesis in front of a committee of faculty members gives Clark Honors College students excellent preparation for graduate school. Many theses have become published articles in refereed journals.

"Students prepare for this self-directed research project through the completion of a 200-level research course in either Arts & Letters or Social Science, most commonly completed at the end of the second year. During this course students learn research methodology, how to access resources on campus, and how to write a research paper, ensuring that students have the tools and skills they need to successfully approach the thesis project.

"Additionally, the University of Oregon holds a campus-wide celebration of undergraduate research, creative and performance works—the Undergraduate Research Symposium—each May. While the Clark Honors College student body represents just under 4% of the UO's undergraduate population, each year Clark Honors College students represent 30% or more of the participants in the Undergraduate Symposium."

**Honors Study Abroad:** "The Clark Honors College frequently awards international thesis research grants to students conducting research for their senior thesis while abroad. The University of Oregon's Office of International Affairs coordinates study abroad programs, offering over 190 programs in more than 90 countries, all of which Clark Honors College students have access to." Examples are below.

•Clark Honors College @ Oxford (16-18 credits total: 8 credits fulfilling two CHC colloquia, and additional credits as electives or fulfilling requirements in your major): Live in the center of Oxford, England. During this spring term program, in parallel with Oxford's Trinity term, you will take two tutorials taught by Oxford faculty. The program and its students are housed at the Centre for Medieval and Renaissance Studies, affiliated with Keble College, Oxford University.

•The Genius of Study Abroad (8 credits fulfilling two CHC colloquia): Take a tour of Dublin, London, Oxford, and Paris. Through lectures, discussions, interactive performance, walking excursions and guest speakers you will engage in activist global learning that considers the international and interdisciplinary aspects of creativity in revolutionary imagination – as seen in architecture, landscape, arts, science and technology, and legislation on human rights and equality on both sides of the Channel.

"Study Abroad Thesis Research Grant: Small grants up to $1,000 are available for students conducting research for a CHC thesis project while studying abroad, either through an official UO program or through a program sponsored by another institution."

**Financial Aid:** "The Clark Honors College incoming class of fall 2017, comprised of 249 students, received over $2 million in scholarship awards. 95% of incoming students received merit and/or need-based awards, and 31% of incoming students received more than one award. *11% received awards that completely cover tuition and fees for all four years.*"

The scholarships with the largest awards are the Stamps Scholarship, Presidential Scholarship, Pathway Oregon, Summit Scholarship, Apex Scholars, Diversity Excellence Scholarship, University Scholarship, *Clark Honors College Tuition Remission,* and Clark Honors College Returning Students Scholarships.

The scholarships with the highest award potential for out-of-state students are the Stamps and Presidential Scholarships.

**Honors Fees:** "The Clark Honors College charges differential tuition, which allows us to maintain small class sizes, and ensures that all classes are taught by faculty and not graduate students.

"For the 2017-2018 academic year differential <u>tuition was</u> $4,194 per year ($1,398 per term). *We are very pleased to be able to reduce differential tuition for the upcoming 2018-19 academic year to $2,700 per year ($900 per term).* Differential tuition is assessed as a flat charge per term for each term that a student is actively enrolled in the honors college; however, students pay no more than 12 terms of differential tuition so that those pursuing a double major or a 5-year major are not disadvantaged.

"The decrease in the cost of differential tuition reflects an increased financial investment by the University of Oregon into the Robert D. Clark Honors College, and will not result in any reduction in honors college courses, student support, or amenities."

**Placement of Honors Graduates:** None listed.

**Degree of Difference**: This is difference between (1) the average SAT scores for recently enrolled honors students (1332) and (2) the average test scores for all students in the university (1190) as a whole. The difference may be an indication of how "elite" honors students may be perceived as compared to students in the university as a whole. **Please keep in mind that neither the high nor low selectivity of an honors program determines how effective the program may be.**

**NAME**: OREGON STATE UNIVERSITY HONORS COLLEGE

**Date Established:** 1995

**Location**: Corvallis, Oregon

**University Full-time Undergraduate Enrollment (2017):** 25,327

**Honors Members in Good Standing**: 1,318 (mean size of all programs is 2,030).

**Honors Average Admission Test Score(s)**: ACT, 30; SAT, 1362.

**Average High School GPA/Class Rank:** 3.92, unweighted.

**Basic Admission Requirements:** ACT, 27; SAT, 1300; GPA, 3.75.

**Application Deadline(s):** *Please verify with each program, as some deadlines could change.* February 1, 2019.

**Honors Programs with SAT scores from 1332—1365:** Arizona State, Arkansas, Colorado State, Nevada Reno, Oklahoma State, Oregon, Oregon State.

**Administrative Staff:** 16.25 FTEs.

**RATINGS AT A GLANCE:** For all mortarboard ratings immediately below, a score of 5 is the maximum and represents a comparison with all rated honors colleges and programs. More detailed explanations follow the "mortarboard" ratings.

**PERCEPTION* OF UNIVERSITY AS A WHOLE, NOT OF HONORS:** 🎓🎓🎓 1/2

*Perception is based on the university's ranking among public universities in the 2018 U.S. News Best Colleges report. Please bear in mind that the better the U.S. News ranking, the more difficult it is for an honors college or program to have a rating that equals or improves on the magazine ranking.

**OVERALL HONORS RATING:** 🎓🎓🎓

**Curriculum Requirements:** 🎓🎓🎓

**Number of Honors Classes Offered:** 🎓🎓🎓

**Number of Honors Classes in Key Disciplines:** 🎓🎓 1/2

**Extent of Honors Enrollment:** 🎓🎓🎓

**Honors-only Class Size:** 🎓🎓🎓🎓🎓

**Overall Class Size (Honors-only plus mixed, contract):** 🎓🎓🎓🎓

**Honors Grad Rate Adjusted to SAT:** 🎓🎓🎓🎓🎓

**Grad Rate Adjusted to Freshman Retention Rate:** 🎓🎓🎓🎓🎓

**Ratio of Staff to Students:** 🎓🎓🎓🎓 1/2

**Priority Registration: Yes.** "Students at Oregon State University register based on class standing, which is determined by credit hours earned (seniors first, juniors second, etc.). Honors students register for all courses in advance of the registration date established for all other students with the same class standing (but not in advance of classes of higher rank). This is the case in all terms except the fall term of students' first years: all students incoming to the university register at summer advising sessions."

**Honors Housing Amenities:** 🎓🎓🎓 1/2

**Honors Housing Availability:** 🎓🎓🎓🎓 1/2

**Prestigious Awards:** 🎓🎓🎓

## RATING SCORES AND EXPLANATIONS:

**Curriculum Requirements (3.0):** The most important rating category, the curriculum completion requirement (classes required to complete honors) defines not only what honors students should learn but also the extent to which honors students and faculty are connected in the classroom. If there is a thesis or capstone requirement, it reinforces the individual contact and research skills so important to learning.

The average number of honors semester hours required for completion across all programs is 30.0.

Graduation as an Honors Scholar requires 30 quarter hours, or the equivalent of about 20 semester hours. As noted in the last edition, the college, like several honors programs that are a part of a university with large numbers of engineering and science majors, has a lower than average credit requirement for honors completion.

Of the 30 quarter hours that are required, 6 credits must be in honors baccalaureate core classes; 6 credits in honors colloquia; 12 credits in honors electives; and 6 credits for the honors thesis or research project.

There is a lesser requirement, called the Honors Associate track, which is for students transferring into OSU, mostly for the last two or three years of work. This track requires 15 quarter credits minimum, including 6 credits in honors colloquia, 6 credits in honors electives, and 3 credits for the honors thesis or research project.

**AP/IB credits** are **not** counted as replacements for honors courses.

**No. Honors Classes Offered (3.0):** This is a measure of the total **adjusted** honors main sections available in the term reported, not including labs and thesis. An adjusted main section has 3 or more semester credits, or equivalent, and sections with fewer credits receive a lower prorated value.

The program offered an adjusted section for every **27.5** enrolled students. The average for all programs was **15.0**. The lower the number, the better. In the term reported, an extremely impressive **85.9%** of honors enrollment was **in honors-only sections; 14.1% was in mixed sections; and none was in contract sections.** For all programs under review, enrollment by type of honors section was 75.8% honors-only, 15.4 % mixed, and 8.8% contract.

**No. Honors Classes in Key Disciplines (2.5):** The 15 "key" disciplines are biological sciences; business (all); chemistry; communications (especially public speaking); computer science; economics; engineering (all); English; history; math (all); philosophy; physics; political science; psychology; and sociology, anthropology, and gender studies. Interdisciplinary sections, such as those often taken for General Education credit in the first two years, do receive a lesser, prorated discipline "credit" because they introduce students to multiple disciplines in an especially engaging way, often with in-depth discussion.

For this measure, mixed and contract sections are not counted as a section in a key discipline unless students taking the sections for honors credit make up at least 10% of the total section enrollment.

In the term reported, the program offered an adjusted section in a key discipline for every **70.4 honors students.** The average for all programs is **24.7**. The lower the number, the better. **Note: An "adjusted section" for rating this category has at least 3 semester credits or 4 quarter credits. OSU Honors has a relatively large number of sections that are 3 quarter credits or less. Considering ALL sections offered, the ratio would be much higher.**

Out of **40 adjusted sections in key disciplines, 32 were honors-only sections**. *OSU Honors has the best selection of honors math classes we have seen,* including six in the Fall Quarter and eight in the Winter Quarter. In Fall, the sections were in differential calculus, integral calculus, and vector calculus. In Winter, they were some of the same calculus sections *and* multiple sections of applied differential equations and one section of matrix and power series methods. Biology, chemistry, engineering, and English were also in the mix.

OSU Honors has a solid range of interdisciplinary sections, though several are in the 2-3 quarter unit range discussed above. Among our favorites are "American Identity in the World," "God, Pain, and the Problem of Evil," "Race and Science," and "Dawn of the Anthropocene."

**Extent of Honors Enrollment (3.0):** Not all honors students take an honors class each term, especially after the first two years. Programs that have fewer honors classes and thesis options for upper-division honors students will *generally* have fewer total members in good standing who are actually enrolled in a given term. (Please be aware, however, that honors students not enrolled in a class for a term are still tied to the honors community through residential and extracurricular activities.) *Our research shows that this measure is closely related to honors completion rates, i.e., the number of students who complete honors requirements by the time they graduate.*

For example, if a program has 1,800 individual students enrolled in a given term, and 3,000 students in good standing, the level of enrollment was .67, an indication that honors class enrollment is somewhat below average, especially in upper-division classes. **OSU Honors has a ratio of 1.15**, below the average of 1.30 for all programs.

**Average Class Size, Honors-only Sections (5.0):** Offered mostly in the first two years, honors-only classes tend to be smaller and, as the name implies, have no or very few students other than those in the honors program. These class sections always are much smaller than mixed or contract sections, or regular non-honors class sections in the university.

The average honors-only class size at OSU Honors is **13.7 students**. The average for all programs is **17.5 students.**

**Average Class Size, Overall (4.0):** The overall class calculation is based on the *proportion* of honors students in each type of class (honors-only, mixed honors, and honors contract sections). Thus it is not a raw average. The overall honors-credit class size is **23.6 students**, versus the average for all programs of **24.9 students**.

These class size averages also do not correspond to the number of students per honors section ratings above. The reason is that, in computing average class size metrics, we include enrollment in each 1-2-credit section, not just sections with 3 or more credits.

Along with an honors-only class size of 13.7 students (listed above), the program's mixed honors sections have an average size of **83.8 students,** and no contract sections. Across all programs, the average mixed honors section has 68.6 students, and the average contract section has 56.6 students.

**Honors Grad Rate Adjusted to SAT (5.0):** The rating is the based on the actual grad rate for students who entered the program six years earlier, whether or not the students remained in honors. The **actual rate of 89.0%** is also compared to the rates of other programs with the same test score entry requirement range, and then adjusted upward if the program is performing above other programs in the same range, or downward if the performance is less than other programs in the same range. The rate here is upward, to **90.1%**.

**Grad Rate Adjusted to Freshman Retention Rate (5.0):** This rate compares the actual grad rate above to a predicted grade rate when freshman retention rates are considered. The actual grad rate is **4.68 points higher** than the predicted rate. For all programs, the actual grad rate is **.33 points lower** than the predicted rate.

**Ratio of Staff to Honors Students (4.5):** There is 1 staff member for every **81.1** students. (Mean ratio for all programs is 1 staff member for every **127.9** students.)

**Honors Residence Halls, Amenities (3.5):** "Honors College students receive priority housing in Sackett Hall and West Hall, which are both honors Living and Learning Communities. In both facilities, students have access to unique academic and social programming, on-site honors advising, and the honors academic partner-in-residence, a graduate assistant. Sackett Hall has double and triple rooms with sleeping porches and walk-in closets, while West Hall features suite-style rooms." The nearest dining is at Marketplace West, a very short walk from West Hall.

"Honors students also receive priority in selecting rooms in the privately-managed GEM apartment complex.

"In addition to Honors College lounges in the residential facilities in West and Sackett Hall, there is a student lounge, computer lab, and study rooms in its administrative and teaching spaces in the Learning Innovation Center."

**Honors Residence Halls, Availability (4.5):** This rating compares the number of occupants in honors residence halls to the number of honors freshman and sophomore members in good standing. The ratio for the program is **.77** places for each first- and second-year student. The median for all programs is .49 places.

**Prestigious Awards (3.0):** The awards that we track and include are listed in the section titled "Prestigious Scholarships." The awards are sometimes won by students who are not in an honors college or program, but increasingly many are enrolled in honors programs. It is also a trend that honors colleges and programs help to prepare their students for the awards competitions.

"The OSU Office of Prestigious Scholarships is housed within the Honors College but is a campus-wide position. The coordinator for prestigious scholarships is supervised by the Honors College Dean. The coordinator works closely with Honors College staff in the identification of candidates and is an accessible, visible resource for honors students."

OSU students have already won an impressive 11 Udall scholarships, 32 Goldwater scholarships, 2 Rhodes scholarships, and Marshall and Gates Cambridge awards (1 each). OSU students have also earned more than 50 Gilman Scholarships in the last three years.

**UNRATED FEATURES**

**Continuation and Honors Graduation GPA Requirement:** 3.25 for both.

**Academic Strengths, National Rankings:** This is based on national rankings of *graduate* programs in all but engineering and business, where undergraduate rankings are used. One of the weaknesses of the *U.S. News* rankings is that they focus on too many wealth-related metrics while ignoring their own assessments of academic departments. The rankings listed below are for all universities, public or private.

The nationally ranked academic departments at OSU are earth sciences, computer science, engineering, math, chemistry, and physics.

**Internships, Professional Development, Community Engagement:**

"Student Archivist—In this collaborative position between the Honors College and OSU Libraries' Special Collection & Archives Research Center (SCARC), two paid student archivists perform a broad range of duties within SCARC, including arrangement and description of archival collections, research and writing support for a wide variety of projects, and reference assistance for patrons.

"Michigan Clinical Outcomes Research and Reporting Program (MCORRP) Summer Internship Opportunity—*This is a 10-week summer internship program at the University of Michigan Medical Center in Ann Arbor;* one honors student is picked to participate each year with full funding. The interns participating in the program are a diverse group of undergraduate, graduate, and medical students from various schools across the country. Students are involved with one or more of the MCORRP databases. In addition to database work, each student spends time developing a project. Using the same data they have helped collect over the course of the summer, students develop a hypothesis, do statistical analysis, and present their results at the end of the program. Students also volunteer at the World Medical Relief in Detroit helping to sort reusable medical supplies to be shipped around the world. Additionally, lectures given by MCORRP faculty, staff, and guests enhance students' understanding of a variety of cardiology and research topics. The OSU Honors College intern receives hourly compensation for time worked within MCORRP and a summer housing and travel allowance.

"Summer and Winter Reads—Each year, the Honors College invites a handful of faculty members and university administrators to select a book to share with a small group of Honors College students. Group members each get a free copy of their group's book to read over the summer or winter break, and then groups meet with their faculty hosts to discuss the book over refreshments at the beginning of fall or winter terms. This is a fantastic way to meet some interesting and influential members of the Oregon State community, as well as connect with fellow HC students, in an informal setting. *In 2017, approximately 250 students participated in Summer Read and 86 in Winter Read."*

**Undergraduate Research:** "All students in the Honors College participate in research as a part of the required honors thesis process. They work with a faculty mentor and committee to conduct research in the academic field of their choice.

"Each term we offer the courses 'HC 408 Stage 1: Plan,' 'HC 408 Stage 2: Explore & Build,' 'HC 408 Stage 3: Commit,' and 'HC 408 Stage 4: Compose & Complete.' These classes bring students through each element in the research and thesis-writing process.

"To facilitate matching students with potential thesis mentors, the Honors College partners with each OSU academic college to hold Student-Faculty Matching Receptions. These are opportunities to connect with faculty members, learn about their research, and potentially get involved in projects that could inform a student's thesis and future research."

**Honors Study Abroad:** "Honors College students can apply for scholarship support of up to $1,000 to assist in funding experiential learning opportunities, including study abroad, international and domestic service learning, research, and professional development. *In the 2016-2017 academic year, the college provided over $122,000 to approximately 165 students to support experiential learning.*

"The Honors College offers several international opportunities each year. One, to London, England, is a summer opportunity for incoming first-year students to learn with upper-class students. Another is a partnership with Habitat for Humanities: students take a colloquia class, 'Building Homes and Hope,' and engage in service learning in places like Nepal, Ethiopia, and Vietnam. And a third opportunity is 'HC Experience: France,' which is 2 weeks during the summer. Students take two colloquia classes in Paris and Lyons."

**Financial Aid:** "The Honors College offers scholarships to select incoming students during the admission process; there is no separate application. Continuing students can also receive scholarships upon review by the honors staff. Most Honors College scholarships are in the amount of $1,000.

"The Honors College Differential Tuition Scholarship is designed to make sure that students who are fully engaged with their honors education are not forced to withdraw due to the cost of enrollment in the college. *Differential Tuition Scholarships cover either the full cost of HC differential tuition or half the cost of HC tuition for one academic year*. Only students with unmet financial need who are making progress toward completion of Honors College degree requirements are eligible to apply for this scholarship.

"The Honors Experience Scholarship provides students with up to $1,000 in support of learning experiences outside of the classroom such as study abroad, research, internships, travel to professional conferences, or service learning. This scholarship is open to all honors students by application.

"OSU participates with the **National Merit Scholarship** Corporation (NMSC) to award merit-based scholarships. Students selected as finalists in the College-Sponsored program who list OSU as their first-choice school on the NMSC application will receive **an additional $8,000 over four years.**

"Students participating in an International Baccalaureate (IB) Diploma program may qualify for the IB Diploma Scholarship. To qualify, entering freshmen must have scored a total of 30 or higher on the IB exam and indicated pursuit of the IB Diploma. Awards are $3,000 annually / $12,000 over four years."

**Honors Fees:** "Honors College differential tuition is currently $500/term (fall, winter, spring). There are no additional costs to live in the residence halls as an honors student. The differential tuition primarily supports the honors curriculum."

**Placement of Honors Graduates:** "In a recent, non-comprehensive and voluntary survey of our alumni, 90% of respondents went to graduate school. The remaining 10% were primarily employed in professions such as engineering."

**Degree of Difference**: This is difference between (1) the average SAT scores for recently enrolled honors students (1362) and (2) the average test scores for all students in the university (1180) as a whole. The difference may be an indication of how "elite" honors students may be perceived as compared to students in the university as a whole. **Please keep in mind that neither the high nor low selectivity of an honors program determines how effective the program may be.**

**NAME**: SCHREYER HONORS COLLEGE AT THE PENNSYLVANIA STATE UNIVERSITY

**Date Established:** Endowed as college in 1997; University Scholars Program established in 1980.

**Location**:  University Park, Pennsylvania

**University Full-time Undergraduate Enrollment (2017):** 41,329

**Honors Members in Good Standing**: 1,969 (mean size of all programs is 2,030). About 94% of Schreyer students are enrolled at the main campus.

**Honors Average Admission Test Score(s)**: ACT, est. 32; SAT, est. 1450.

**Average High School GPA/Class Rank:** Mid-range 4.00-4.33, weighted.

**Basic Admission Requirements:** "For students entering directly from high school as first-year students, the Schreyer Honors College does not set minimum academic requirements for grades or standardized tests. Candidates will be assessed based on the academic and extracurricular documents submitted with the application, as well as responses to essay questions and letters of recommendation. An interview is also an optional component of the application process. For students entering as sophomores or juniors, the application is available starting March 1 of each year. Requirements for this type of admission are a cumulative GPA of 3.7, at least one full-time semester of study completed at Penn State, and a minimum of four full-time semesters of study remaining before graduation."

**Application Deadline(s):** *Please verify with each program, as some deadlines could change.* For first-year students, the priority deadline of November 1, 2018, allows for interviews by December 10, 2018; final deadline is December 3, 2018, with notification by late February, 2019. For students entering as sophomores or juniors, the deadline varies by academic college.

**Honors Programs with SAT scores from 1420—1461:** Auburn, Central Florida, Delaware, Iowa, Kansas, Mississippi, Missouri, New Jersey Inst of Technology, Penn State, South Florida, Vermont, Virginia Commonwealth.

**Administrative Staff:** 27.

**RATINGS AT A GLANCE:** For all mortarboard ratings immediately below, a score of 5 is the maximum and represents a comparison with all rated honors colleges and programs. More detailed explanations follow the "mortarboard" ratings.

**PERCEPTION\* OF UNIVERSITY AS A WHOLE, NOT OF HONORS:** 🎓🎓🎓🎓🎓

\*Perception is based on the university's ranking among public universities in the 2018 U.S. News Best Colleges report. Please bear in mind that the better the U.S. News ranking, the more difficult it is for an honors college or program to have a rating that equals or improves on the magazine ranking.

**OVERALL HONORS RATING:** 🎓🎓🎓🎓🎓

**Curriculum Requirements:** 🎓🎓🎓🎓🎓

**Number of Honors Classes Offered:** 🎓🎓🎓🎓

**Number of Honors Classes in Key Disciplines:** 🎓🎓🎓🎓 1/2

**Extent of Honors Enrollment:** 🎓🎓🎓🎓

**Honors-only Class Size:** 🎓🎓🎓🎓🎓

**Overall Class Size (Honors-only plus mixed, contract):** 🎓🎓🎓 1/2

**Honors Grad Rate Adjusted to SAT:** 🎓🎓🎓🎓🎓

**Grad Rate Adjusted to Freshman Retention Rate:** 🎓🎓🎓

**Ratio of Staff to Students:** 🎓🎓🎓🎓 1/2

**Priority Registration: Yes,** honors students register for all courses, honors and otherwise, with the first group of students during each year they are in the program.

**Honors Housing Amenities:** 🎓🎓🎓

**Honors Housing Availability:** 🎓🎓🎓🎓

**Prestigious Awards:** 🎓🎓🎓🎓 1/2

## RATING SCORES AND EXPLANATIONS:

**Curriculum Requirements (5.0):** The most important rating category, the curriculum completion requirement (classes required to complete honors) defines not only what honors students should learn but also the extent to which honors students and faculty are connected in the classroom. If there is a thesis or capstone requirement, it reinforces the individual contact and research skills so important to learning.

The average number of honors semester hours required for completion across all programs is 30.0.

For first-year entrants, Schreyer requires 35 honors credits, including a thesis with up to 6 credits. Most of the courses will be in the academic disciplines, and students may contract for honors credit in regular class sections.

For sophomore entrants, the requirement is 23 credits, including a thesis of up to 6 credits.

Students entering Schreyer as juniors must complete 14 credits including the thesis requirement.

**AP/IB credits** are **not** counted as replacements for honors courses.

**No. Honors Classes Offered (4.0):** This is a measure of the total **adjusted** honors main sections available in the term reported, not including labs and thesis. An adjusted main section has 3 or more semester credits, or equivalent, and sections with fewer credits receive a lower prorated value.

The program offered a section for every 12.4 enrolled students. The average for all programs was **15.0**. The lower the number, the better. **Note**: Schreyer has very few honors-only classes; a typical honors section will have about 40% honors enrollment with the remaining students taking the class for regular credit. Most of these "mixed" classes have fewer than 25 total students.

In the term reported, only **10.8%** of honors enrollment was **in honors-only sections; 61.6% was in mixed sections, described above; and 27.6% was in contract sections.** For all programs under review, enrollment by type of honors section was 75.8% honors-only, 15.4 % mixed, and 8.8% contract.

**No. Honors Classes in Key Disciplines (4.5):** The 15 "key" disciplines are biological sciences; business (all); chemistry; communications (especially public speaking); computer science; economics; engineering (all); English; history; math (all); philosophy; physics; political science; psychology; and sociology, anthropology, and gender studies. Interdisciplinary sections, such as those often taken for General Education credit in the first two years, do receive a lesser, prorated discipline "credit" because they introduce students to multiple disciplines in an especially engaging way, often with in-depth discussion.

For this measure, mixed and contract sections are not counted as a section in a key discipline unless students taking the sections for honors credit make up at least 10% of the total section enrollment.

In the term reported, the program offered a section in a key discipline for every **13.2 honors students.** The average for all programs is **24.7**. The lower the number, the better.

Out of **149 adjusted sections in key disciplines, 129 were mixed rather than contract-credit sections**. The most sections were in English, engineering, communications/rhetoric, and math, followed by biology, sociology/anthropology, business, political science, history, philosophy, chemistry, and physics. All key disciplines were represented.

Schreyer is almost entirely **department-based**, with a very small number of honors interdisciplinary classes; however, the excellent first-year (and year-long) "Rhetoric and Civic Life" course (majority honors enrollment) "focuses particularly on two critical academic capacities: analyzing and contextualizing. In this semester, students learn to rigorously examine the rhetoric surrounding them, compellingly present their findings in various modes, and thoughtfully contextualize their research."

**Extent of Honors Enrollment (4.0):** Not all honors students take an honors class each term, especially after the first two years. Programs that have fewer honors classes and thesis options for upper-division honors students will *generally* have fewer total members in good standing who are actually enrolled in a given term. (Please be aware, however, that honors students not enrolled in a class for a term are still tied to the honors community through residential and extracurricular activities.) *Our research shows that this measure is closely related to honors completion rates, i.e., the number of students who complete honors requirements by the time they graduate.*

For example, if a program has 1,800 individual students enrolled in a given term, and 3,000 students in good standing, the level of enrollment was .67, an indication that honors class enrollment is somewhat below average, especially in upper-division classes. **Schreyer Honors has a ratio of 1.43**, above the average of 1.30 for all programs.

**Average Class Size, Honors-only Sections (5.0):** Offered mostly in the first two years, honors-only classes tend to be smaller and, as the name implies, have no or very few students other than those in the honors program. These class sections always are much smaller than mixed or contract sections, or regular non-honors class sections in the university.

The average honors-only class size at Schreyer Honors is **9.0 students**. (Schreyer has about 20 sections out of more than 140 that are honors-only.) The average for all programs is **17.5 students.**

**Average Class Size, Overall (3.5):** The overall class calculation is based on the *proportion* of honors students in each type of class (honors-only, mixed honors, and honors contract sections). Thus it is not a raw average. The overall honors-credit class size is **31.0 students**, versus the average for all programs of **24.9 students**.

These class size averages also do not correspond to the number of students per honors section ratings above. The reason is that, in computing average class size metrics, we include enrollment in each 1-2-credit section, not just sections with 3 or more credits.

Along with an honors-only class size of 9.0 students (listed above, very few sections), the program's mixed honors sections have an average size of **23.0 students,** and the contract sections with honors credit for individual honors students average **58.0 students.** Across all programs, the average mixed honors section has 68.6 students, and the average contract section has 56.6 students.

**Honors Grad Rate Adjusted to SAT (5.0):** The rating is the based on the actual grad rate for students who entered the program six years earlier, whether or not the students remained in honors. The **actual rate of 91.0%** is also compared to the rates of other programs with the same test score entry requirement range, and then adjusted upward if the program is performing above other programs in the same range, or downward if the performance is less than other programs in the same range. The rate here is upward, to **92.6%.**

**Grad Rate Adjusted to Freshman Retention Rate (3.0):** This rate compares the actual grad rate above to a predicted grade rate when university-wide freshman retention rates are considered. The actual grad rate is **2.35 points lower** than the predicted rate. For all programs, the actual grad rate is **.33 points lower** than the predicted rate. **Note:** Penn State, like Clemson, Delaware, Georgia, Illinois, Purdue, Rutgers, and UT Austin have freshman retention rates higher than 90%. The rate at Penn State is 93%, making it difficult for the honors graduation rate to match the freshman retention rate.

**Ratio of Staff to Honors Students (4.5):** There is 1 staff member for every **75.7** students. (Mean ratio for all programs is 1 staff member for every **127.9** students.)

**Honors Residence Halls, Amenities (3.0):** Assignment of honors dorm space for freshmen and upperclassmen is about evenly divided between two long-time residences for honors students: Atherton and Simmons. About 95% of the rooms in both halls are traditional doubles with hall baths. Neither dorm is air-conditioned. The most convenient dining for both Atherton and Simmons is Redifer Commons. Both residences are coed. More than 550 honors students live in the two halls.

**Honors Residence Halls, Availability (4.0):** This rating compares the number of occupants in honors residence halls to the number of honors freshman and sophomore members in good standing. The ratio for the program is **.57** places for each first- and second-year student. The median for all programs is .49 places.

**Prestigious Awards (4.5):** The awards that we track and include are listed in the section titled "Prestigious Scholarships." The awards are sometimes won by students who are not in an honors college or program, but increasingly many are enrolled in honors programs. It is also a trend that honors colleges and programs help to prepare their students for the awards competitions.

"Penn State University has an Office of Undergraduate Fellowships, where all Penn State students can explore options for prestigious scholarship/fellowship awards. The honors college works very closely with this office to promote these opportunities to Schreyer Scholars. Recent results have included Schreyer Scholars receiving a Churchill Scholarship, Marshall Scholarship, Gates-Cambridge Scholarship, recognition as Junior Fellow of the Carnegie Endowment for International Peace and numerous Fulbright Scholarship winners."

In all, PSU students have won two Rhodes scholarships, nine Gates Cambridge awards, seven Marshall scholarships, two Churchill scholarships, and eight Truman awards. PSU undergraduates have an outstanding record of winning Udall scholarships (21) and Goldwater scholarships (69). The university is 3rd among public universities in winning Goldwater Scholarships.

**UNRATED FEATURES**

**Continuation and Honors Graduation GPA Requirement:** 3.40 for both.

**Academic Strengths, National Rankings:** This is based on national rankings of *graduate* programs in all but engineering and business, where undergraduate rankings are used. One of the weaknesses of the *U.S. News* rankings is that they focus on too many wealth-related metrics while ignoring their own assessments of academic departments. The rankings listed below are for all universities, public or private.

Penn State has exceptional strength and depth in its academic departments, which have an average department ranking of 27.3 in the nation.

The leading nationally ranked academic departments at Penn State are earth sciences (5), sociology (17), chemistry (20), engineering (20), business (21), economics (25), physics (25), psychology (26), English (27), computer science (30), math (32), political science (33), education (38), history (44), and biology (46).

**Internships, Professional Development, Community Engagement:** "Many Schreyer Scholars participate in internships and coop experiences as part of their college experience. In cases where students are engaged in unpaid internships, the Schreyer Honors College provides internship grants to support the student; in the 2016-17 academic year, we awarded over $60,000 to scholars engaged in unpaid internships around the country.

"Service is one of the primary objectives of the Schreyer experience. Our scholars are known for their community engagement and volunteer spirit. A sampling of their activities includes:

•*Three specific honors teams engaged in THON, the largest student-run philanthropy in the nation, raising funds to support pediatric cancer research at Hershey Medical Center;*

•My Backyard service project: engagement with Penn State Office of Physical Plant to beautify and improve various locations on the Penn State campus;

•Regular visits to local nursing homes for musical performances, game nights, and general conversations;

•Empower Orphans—an international organization supporting children throughout the world: founded by a Schreyer Scholar who established a campus chapter engaging hundreds of Penn State students.

**Undergraduate Research:** "All students are required to complete a research/creative inquiry thesis and submit it to the Schreyer Honors College to complete their requirements."

**Honors Study Abroad:** "Penn State offers nearly 300 programs each year to many different countries spread across six continents. Schreyer Scholars take advantage of these programs to enhance their academic experience and are eligible to receive Schreyer Ambassador Travel Grants to help meet their travel expenses. Over $200,000 in travel grant funds are awarded each year to scholars studying overseas." Examples of study-abroad opportunities are below.

**Colombia**: "(Since 2014)—Also a month long, this program examines contemporary Colombian social, economic, and political issues from the perspective of the capital, Bogotá, and three other regions. This is a three-credit honors course."

**London Study Tour:** "(Since 1984)—Previously offered over winter break, the London Study Tour now is a 17-day Maymester program that includes five days in Edinburgh. In both locations students see a variety of theatrical productions and visit cultural and historical sites. This is a three-credit honors course."

**Freiburg Honors Exchange**: (Since 2015—As part of the overall Penn State - University of Freiburg (Germany) exchange, Schreyer Scholars can spend a semester at University College Freiburg, an interdisciplinary 'liberal arts and sciences' division of the University of Freiburg with courses in English."

**Financial Aid:** "The Schreyer *Honors College offers a $5,000 Academic Excellence Scholarship to all scholars entering the college their first year*. This award is renewable for each of the four years they are enrolled in the honors college.

"Additional need and merit based scholarships are available to Schreyer Scholars. Each academic year, the honors college awards over $1 million to scholars to support their academic studies, research and internship experiences.

"Our development team also conducts an annual campaign with the parents of our current scholars. They raise funds for our emergency scholarship program that supports scholars who find themselves in unanticipated financial crises. This campaign typically raises approximately $50,000 each year, which supports between 15–20 scholars during the academic year."

**Honors Fees:** All Schreyer Scholars are assessed a $25 fee each semester. This fee supports student programming that occurs throughout the academic year. This fee also grants all University Park Scholars access to the residence hall facilities, regardless of where they might live on campus.

**Placement of Honors Graduates:** "The Schreyer Honors College has our very own Director of Career Development who works exclusively with scholars on their career plans and outcomes. She conducts regular surveys of graduating classes and achieves close to 100% completion rate from each class. Our most recent graduating statistics (2016-17):

Graduate and Professional Schools: 39%
Employment: 49%
Other (includes service experiences): 12%

"The Schreyer Honors College also conducts research on our graduates, at the five and ten year anniversary of their graduation. Our most recent results show that after five years, 41% of our graduates have earned an advanced degree; after ten years, that number increases to 54%."

**Degree of Difference**: This is difference between (1) the average SAT scores for recently enrolled honors students (1450) and (2) the average test scores for all students in the university (1270) as a whole. The difference may be an indication of how "elite" honors students may be perceived as compared to students in the university as a whole. **Please keep in mind that neither the high nor low selectivity of an honors program determines how effective the program may be.**

**NAME**: PURDUE HONORS COLLEGE

**Date Established:** 2013

**Location**: West Lafayette, Indiana

**University <u>Full-time Undergraduate</u> Enrollment (2017):** 30,043

**Honors Members in Good Standing**: 2,060 (mean size of all programs is 2,030).

**Honors <u>Average</u> Admission Test Score(s)**: ACT, 31; SAT, 1373.

**Average High School GPA/Class Rank:** 3.92, unweighted.

**<u>Basic</u> Admission Requirements:** "The selection process for the Purdue Honors College is holistic. GPA, test scores, aptitude for interdisciplinary learning, leadership and engagement are all considered."

**Application Deadline(s):** *Please verify with each program, as some deadlines could change.* Priority deadline is November 1, 2018, for admission and scholarships.

**Honors Programs with SAT scores from 1370—1403:** Arizona, CUNY Macaulay, Georgia State, Houston, Indiana, Iowa, LSU, Massachusetts, New Mexico, Purdue, Texas Tech, UAB.

**Administrative Staff:** 24.

**RATINGS AT A GLANCE:** For all mortarboard ratings immediately below, a score of 5 is the maximum and represents a comparison with all rated honors colleges and programs. More detailed explanations follow the "mortarboard" ratings.

**PERCEPTION* OF UNIVERSITY AS A WHOLE, <u>NOT</u> OF HONORS:** 🎓🎓🎓🎓🎓

*Perception is based on the university's ranking among public universities in the 2018 U.S. News Best Colleges report. Please bear in mind that the better the U.S. News ranking, the more difficult it is for an honors college or program to have a rating that equals or improves on the magazine ranking.

**OVERALL HONORS RATING:** 🎓🎓🎓1/2

**Curriculum Requirements:** 🎓🎓🎓1/2

**Number of Honors Classes Offered:** 🎓🎓🎓

**Number of Honors Classes in Key Disciplines:** 🎓🎓🎓

**Extent of Honors Enrollment:** 🎓🎓🎓1/2

**Honors-only Class Size:** 🎓🎓🎓 1/2

**Overall Class Size (Honors-only plus mixed, contract):** 🎓🎓🎓🎓

**Honors Grad Rate Adjusted to SAT:** 🎓🎓🎓🎓

**Grad Rate Adjusted to Freshman Retention Rate:** 🎓🎓 1/2

**Ratio of Staff to Students:** 🎓🎓🎓🎓 1/2

**Priority Registration: Yes,** honors students register with the class ahead of them.

**Honors Housing Amenities:** 🎓🎓🎓🎓🎓

**Honors Housing Availability:** 🎓🎓🎓🎓🎓

**Prestigious Awards:** 🎓🎓🎓🎓

## RATING SCORES AND EXPLANATIONS:

**Curriculum Requirements (3.5):** The most important rating category, the curriculum completion requirement (classes required to complete honors) defines not only what honors students should learn but also the extent to which honors students and faculty are connected in the classroom. If there is a thesis or capstone requirement, it reinforces the individual contact and research skills so important to learning.

The average number of honors semester hours required for completion across all programs is 30.0.

Purdue Honors College requires 24 honors credits for completion, including 5 honors program credits, 5 departmental honors credits, 8 credits in honors contract courses, and a 6-credit thesis.

**AP/IB credits** are **not** counted as replacements for honors courses.

**No. Honors Classes Offered (3.0):** This is a measure of the total **adjusted** honors main sections available in the term reported, not including labs and thesis. An adjusted main section has 3 or more semester credits, or equivalent, and sections with fewer credits receive a lower prorated value.

The program offered a section for every **21.3** enrolled students. The average for all programs was **15.0**. The lower the number, the better. In the term reported, an extremely impressive **91.3%** of honors enrollment was **in honors-only sections; none was in mixed sections; and 8.7% was in contract sections.** For all programs under review, enrollment by type of honors section was 75.8% honors-only, 15.4 % mixed, and 8.8% contract.

**No. Honors Classes in Key Disciplines (3.0):** The 15 "key" disciplines are biological sciences; business (all); chemistry; communications (especially public speaking); computer science; economics; engineering (all); English; history; math (all); philosophy; physics; political science; psychology; and sociology, anthropology, and gender studies. Interdisciplinary sections, such as those often taken for General Education credit in the first two years, do receive a lesser, prorated discipline "credit" because they introduce students to multiple disciplines in an especially engaging way, often with in-depth discussion.

For this measure, mixed and contract sections are not counted as a section in a key discipline unless students taking the sections for honors credit make up at least 10% of the total section enrollment.

In the term reported, the program offered a section in a key discipline for every **38.9 honors students.** The average for all programs is **24.7.** The lower the number, the better.

Out of **28 adjusted sections in key disciplines, all were honors-only sections**. The most sections were in communications, math, and physics, followed by biology, engineering, psychology, chemistry, and history. Compared with 2016, more honors students are receiving departmental honors credit via the honors contract option, and they are considered as a section in a key discipline only of they have at least 10% of honors enrollment (see above).

The college now has an Honors Mentor Program, in which students selected as mentors help to lead sections of "Evolution in Ideas," described below. "Through this program, Honors mentors guide small teams of Honors freshman through an iteration of HONR 19901: The Evolution of Ideas. This follows a transformational leadership model, meaning that mentors cultivate collaboration and leadership skills in their small teams, while refining their own leadership and collaboration skills in the process." Mentors receive two credits for their work and for learning leadership and collaboration skills. There were 10 sections of "Honors Seminars Mentors" in Fall 2018.

The college offered more than 50 seminar sections of 1-3 credits. Most were in the "Evolution of Ideas" series, in which students, over eight weeks, are introduced "to critical thinking, cultural critique, and the history of ideas. Each section of the course focuses on a single 'idea' that is significant for modern life." Purdue Honors is a **blended** program, with a mix of experiential courses and classes in the disciplines.

**Extent of Honors Enrollment (3.5):** Not all honors students take an honors class each term, especially after the first two years. Programs that have fewer honors classes and thesis options for upper-division honors students will *generally* have fewer total members in good standing who are actually enrolled in a given term. (Please be aware, however, that honors students not enrolled in a class for a term are still tied to the honors community through residential and extracurricular activities.) *Our research shows that this measure is closely related to honors completion rates, i.e., the number of students who complete honors requirements by the time they graduate.*

For example, if a program has 1,800 individual students enrolled in a given term, and 3,000 students in good standing, the level of enrollment was .67, an indication that honors class enrollment is somewhat below average, especially in upper-division classes. **Purdue Honors has a ratio of 1.11**, below the average of 1.30 for all programs.

**Average Class Size, Honors-only Sections (3.5):** Offered mostly in the first two years, honors-only classes tend to be smaller and, as the name implies, have no or very few students other than those in the honors program. These class sections always are much smaller than mixed or contract sections, or regular non-honors class sections in the university.

The average honors-only class size at Purdue Honors is **19.5 students**. The average for all programs is **17.5 students.**

**Average Class Size, Overall (4.0):** The overall class calculation is based on the *proportion* of honors students in each type of class (honors-only, mixed honors, and honors contract sections). Thus it is not a raw average. The overall honors-credit class size is **24.9 students**, versus the average for all programs of **24.7 students**.

These class size averages also do not correspond to the number of students per honors section ratings above. The reason is that, in computing average class size metrics, we include enrollment in each 1-2-credit section, not just sections with 3 or more credits.

Along with an honors-only class size of 19.5 students (listed above), the program's contract sections with honors credit for individual honors students average **81.4 students.** Across all programs, the average contract section has 56.6 students.

**Honors Grad Rate Adjusted to SAT (4.0): Note: Purdue Honors has not been operating for six years so we are using an** *estimated* grad rate. The **estimated rate of 85.5%** is also compared to the rates of other programs with the same test score entry requirement range, and then adjusted upward if the program is performing above other programs in the same range, or downward if the performance is less than other programs in the same range. The rate here is the same, **85.5%.**

**Grad Rate Adjusted to Freshman Retention Rate (2.5):** This rate compares the **estimated** grad rate above to a predicted grade rate when freshman retention rates are considered. The estimated grad rate is **6.86 points lower** than the predicted rate. For all programs, the actual grad rate is **.33 points lower** than the predicted rate. **At least three factors contribute to this low rating**: (1) engineering majors make more than 28% of the total at Purdue; (2) the six-year graduation rate for Purdue as a whole is 74%, relatively low because of all the engineering majors; and (3) Purdue has a high freshman retention rate (92%), making it difficult for the honors graduation rate to match the freshman retention rate.

**Ratio of Staff to Honors Students (4.5):** There is 1 staff member for every **85.8** students. (Mean ratio for all programs is 1 staff member for every **127.9** students.)

**Honors Residence Halls, Amenities (5.0):** The new Honors College and Residences complex is home to 821 honors students, and it is surely one of the best honors residences in the nation. The facility combines ready access to college staff with air-conditioned, suite-style rooms and on-site dining. Formerly, freshman honors students lived in Shreve Hall.

An additional 114 upper-division honors women reside in historic Duhme Hall, and 159 upper-division students more live in the Third Street Suites, a coed facility. Both feature air-conditioned, suite-style rooms with shared baths. Dining for Duhme is at Windsor Dining Court; for Third Street Suites, it is Wiley Dining Court, also convenient to the Honors College and Residences.

The new complex opened in 2016. "It houses the Honors College faculty and staff offices, study spaces, a STEAM* lab, a music practice room, art and maker spaces, on-site restaurant (Cosi Café), gardens, and the Innovation Forum to present research and creative projects." *STEAM is an acronym for Science, Technology, Engineering, Arts, and Mathematics.

**Honors Residence Halls, Availability (5.0):** This rating compares the number of occupants in honors residence halls to the number of honors freshman and sophomore members in good standing. The ratio for the program is **1.06** places for each first- and second-year student. The median for all programs is .49 places.

**Prestigious Awards (4.0):** The awards that we track and include are listed in the section titled "Prestigious Scholarships." The awards are sometimes won by students who are not in an honors college or program, but increasingly many are enrolled in honors programs. It is also a trend that honors colleges and programs help to prepare their students for the awards competitions.

Purdue's National and International Scholarships Office (NISO), housed within the Honors College, launched in Fall 2012 to coordinate Purdue's nominations for prestigious scholarships and grants. Purdue has shown consistency in finalists and recipients for prestigious scholarships ever since. While the resources of NISO are available to all Purdue students, the majority of applicants are from the Honors College. Please note that NISO works with Rhodes, Marshall, Truman, Gates Cambridge, Churchill, Fulbright Student, Goldwater, Udall, and Gilman.

Some notable recent scholarships are listed below.

- 2018: Purdue's First Marshall Scholar since 1992 (Scholar-elect in 2017)
- 2017 and 2018: Purdue's First and Second Truman Scholar (3 of the annually allotted 4 nominees were 2017 Finalists / 2 of 4 were Finalists in 2018)
- 2016 and 2017: Purdue's First and Second Gates Cambridge Scholars (2017 in international round of 3,082 applicants / 2018 in US round)
- 2015 and 2017: Purdue's First and Second Churchill Scholar since 1997
- 2017: First Schwarzman Scholar (3 finalists, 1 recipient) 2018: (1 finalist)
- 2014: Four Goldwater Scholars (only four nomination slots per university)
- 2013, 2014, 2016, 2017: Purdue's First through Fourth Udall Scholarships
- 2012 through 2018: 38 Gilman Scholars

**UNRATED FEATURES**

**Continuation and Honors Graduation GPA Requirement:** 3.50 for both.

**Academic Strengths, National Rankings:** This is based on national rankings of *graduate* programs in all but engineering and business, where undergraduate rankings are used. One of the weaknesses of the *U.S. News* rankings is that they focus on too many wealth-related metrics while ignoring their own assessments of academic departments. The rankings listed below are for all universities, public or private.

Purdue is not only exceptionally strong in engineering and computer science, but has an overall average academic department ranking of 40.3 in the nation.

The leading nationally ranked academic departments at Purdue are engineering (8), computer science (20), business (24), chemistry (24), math (26), psychology (39), earth sciences (41), economics (42), education (43), and physics (44).

**Internships, Professional Development, Community Engagement:** "The Student Life Unit of the Honors College exists in tandem with our University Residence partners as an academic residential college. Our college is both a home for student living in the residential facilities and a place for learning and growth within the joint classrooms and open programming spaces. Due to this unique blended community and service to all students of the college, our unit came into existence at the start of the 2017-2018 academic year to build upon those academic and residential connections to offer students a robust and balanced foundation of support." A few examples are listed below.

**Volunteer Activities**

•Community Service Programming Committee service projects—a group of students led service projects throughout the year such as winterization and clean up at the local Wolf Park and preservation area, arranging for a Relay for Life team, and working with a local animal shelter for dog walking and adoption support.

**Special Projects**

•Aronson Family Lecture series—an endowed lecture series inviting guests each year in connection to science and technology to meet with students, guest lecture in classes and give a keynote address which is open to the campus and community; the inaugural guest of the series was Dr. Moira Gunn of NPR's Tech Nation.

•Visiting Scholars events—a series of visiting scholars throughout the year in partnership with various departments and centers on campus; each guest resides in our faculty apartment, provides small-scale workshops for honors student students, guest lectures in classes, and many times offers a large scale event open to the whole campus and local community.

**Undergraduate Research:** "The Honors College curriculum requires that students complete a 'scholarly project' that is either a research or creative project, depending on the student's field and interests. This independent research project pairs the student with a faculty mentor or mentors and takes place outside of traditional coursework. Students are required to present the findings of their project in a public forum (e.g. publication or poster session.).

"All Honors College students may apply for research funding through the college to support their research work. They can use this money to travel to conferences, purchase equipment, or pay for housing during and unpaid research experience, for example. Funds of up to $1,000 may be requested to support expenses related to developing and completing projects. Notably, students at any state in the program may request funds provided they present sufficient justification. Students with a need that exceeds $1,000 may propose a larger amount for consideration. In the 2016-2017 academic year $38,779.84 were allocated via 50 grants."

**Honors Study Abroad:** "There were three study abroad courses held in the spring of 2017 with four planned for 2018. While no Maymester courses were held in the previous year, two are planned for summer of 2018. Details these programs are provided for students through the Honors College website. *With the increase in programs available the HC is targeting having 50% of students to have a study abroad/away experience during their academic career.*" Examples of opportunities are below.

- "Making the Human" in Venice, Italy. How did this multi-cultural port city contribute to the development of humanism we call the Renaissance? What characterizes the human experience in contemporary Venice?
- "Berlin: Modernity and the Metropolitan Muse." Berlin is the quintessential modern city, capital of the twentieth century, center of ideological conflict, cultural migration and political revolution. Morning seminars are followed by guided tours of sites related to assigned readings, from museums and markets to historical neighborhoods and trendy clubs.
- "Food Security in Kenya." This learning experience centers on the operation, future directions, and limitations of food security initiatives in Africa. Students visit major aid organizations in Nairobi, Kenya and then fly to the western city of Eldoret, Kenya, where they lodge at the "IU House" AMPATH-Kenya for several days of learning about research partnerships and farming practices in the area.

**Financial Aid:** "The Honors College administers and manages *two scholarship programs, **Beering and Stamps, which provide up to the standard value of cost of attendance**. The components of the standard value of cost of attendance include regular fees/tuition, housing/food, books/supplies, travel, and miscellaneous expenses. **The Beering scholarship program also provides standard value of cost of attendance for one master's degree and one doctoral or professional degree**, at the Purdue University, West Lafayette campus, OR the pursuit of an MD through IU School of Medicine when accepted to the program at the West Lafayette campus.*

"Honors students are eligible to receive the below scholarships that are centrally administered and managed by Purdue's Enrollment Management:

Emerging Leader scholarship, amount varies $15,000-$20,000/year;
National Merit scholarship, $500/year;
National Hispanic scholarship, $1,000/year
Presidential scholarship, amount varies $2,000-$10,000/year;
Trustees scholarship, amount varies $10,000-$16,000/year."

**Honors Fees:** None.

**Placement of Honors Graduates:** "Beginning in spring of 2016, the college implemented a yearly graduation survey to identify what kinds of opportunities students are moving onto and to establish a final point of contact for future communication with these students as alumni. Graduating students have found employment at a wide range of companies and organizations, including Microsoft, Facebook, IBM, Qualtrics, Memorial Hermann Hospital, U.S. Navy, U.S. Forest Service, American Conservatory Theater, Kraft Heinz Company, Pepsico, and Albemarle.

Further, students seeking higher education have been accepted to into a number of highly ranked and competitive graduate programs, such as Stanford, Princeton, Ohio State, Royal Holloway University of London, University College of London, Michigan, Indiana University School of Medicine and School of Law, University of Missouri School of Medicine, and the UT Southwestern Medical School.

**Degree of Difference**: This is difference between (1) the average SAT scores for recently enrolled honors students (1373) and (2) the average test scores for all students in the university (1300) as a whole. The difference may be an indication of how "elite" honors students may be perceived as compared to students in the university as a whole. **Please keep in mind that neither the high nor low selectivity of an honors program determines how effective the program may be.**

**NAME**: HONORS COLLEGE, RUTGERS UNIVERSITY-NEW BRUNSWICK

**Date Established:** 2015

**Location**: New Brunswick, New Jersey

**University Full-time Undergraduate Enrollment (2017):** 36,168

**Honors Members in Good Standing**: 1,396 (mean size of all programs is 2,030).

**Honors Average Admission Test Score(s)**: ACT, NA; SAT, 1506.

**Average High School GPA/Class Rank:** 90% in top 10% of high school class.

**Basic Admission Requirements:** "We use targeted holistic criteria to assess talent, outstanding contributions, and situational excellence."

**Application Deadline(s):** *Please verify with each program, as some deadlines could change.* December 1, 2018.

**Honors Programs with SAT scores from 1471—1510:** Clemson, Georgia, Illinois, Minnesota, Oklahoma, Rutgers, South Carolina, UT Austin.

**Administrative Staff:** 21.


**RATINGS AT A GLANCE:** For all mortarboard ratings immediately below, a score of 5 is the maximum and represents a comparison with all rated honors colleges and programs. More detailed explanations follow the "mortarboard" ratings.

**PERCEPTION\* OF UNIVERSITY AS A WHOLE, NOT OF HONORS:** 🎓🎓🎓🎓 1/2

\*Perception is based on the university's ranking among public universities in the 2018 U.S. News Best Colleges report. Please bear in mind that the better the U.S. News ranking, the more difficult it is for an honors college or program to have a rating that equals or improves on the magazine ranking.

**OVERALL HONORS RATING:** 🎓🎓🎓🎓 1/2

**Curriculum Requirements:** 🎓🎓🎓 1/2

**Number of Honors Classes Offered:** 🎓🎓🎓🎓🎓

**Number of Honors Classes in Key Disciplines:** 🎓🎓🎓🎓🎓

**Extent of Honors Enrollment:** 🎓🎓🎓🎓🎓

**Honors-only Class Size:** 🎓🎓🎓 1/2

**Overall Class Size (Honors-only plus mixed, contract):** 🎓🎓🎓🎓 1/2

**Honors Grad Rate Adjusted to SAT:** 🎓🎓🎓🎓

**Grad Rate Adjusted to Freshman Retention Rate:** 🎓🎓🎓 1/2

**Ratio of Staff to Students:** 🎓🎓🎓🎓🎓

**Priority Registration:** "All Honors students have exclusive registration for all honors seminars and sections throughout their enrollment. Honors students register with their classes, but many of them, due to advanced standing, are able to register in advance of the year they matriculated."

**Honors Housing Amenities:** 🎓🎓🎓 1/2

**Honors Housing Availability:** 🎓🎓🎓🎓🎓

**Prestigious Awards:** 🎓🎓🎓🎓

## RATING SCORES AND EXPLANATIONS:

**Curriculum Requirements (3.5):** The most important rating category, the curriculum completion requirement (classes required to complete honors) defines not only what honors students should learn but also the extent to which honors students and faculty are connected in the classroom. If there is a thesis or capstone requirement, it reinforces the individual contact and research skills so important to learning.

The average number of honors semester hours required for completion across all programs is 30.0. We estimate that the average number of credits for completion at Rutgers Honors College will be about 27.

"Honors College students will generally complete 21-40 credits of honors related work, including the Interdisciplinary Honors Seminars, department based honors courses, Byrne Seminars, and the Capstone Project. These Honors College requirements fulfill general school-based requirements within the 120-128 credits necessary for graduation from the University.

"The majority of our students will register for at least four 3-4 credit honors- designated courses totaling 12 or more credits. These courses may include interdisciplinary honors courses or department-based honors offerings. We offer a wide range of honors courses to meet the needs of our students across all 6 schools. At least one 3-credit interdisciplinary honors seminar must be taken by the end of the second year. Every student also takes a 1-credit Byrne Family First Year Seminar (not all sections are Honors, but at least one Byrne Seminar is a requirement)."

Honors College students must complete the Honors College Forum, our 3-credit mission course, in the first year. Contract course options are also available.

"The Capstone Project is the culminating academic experience for all Honors College students. Designed to reflect a student's deep engagement with a specific discipline, question, or problem, the Capstone Project involves a substantial, sustained, and original writing, research, or performance requirement leading to at least 6 credits. To reflect the diversity of experiences available through the Honors College and the wide range of disciplinary specializations within the participating schools, there are six options for Capstone Projects available to Honors College students. The six options include:

1-completing a senior thesis project through an academic department;
2-completing a School-based senior project or experience such as the School of Engineering Senior Design Project or the Mason Gross School of the Arts Student performance;
3-completing an Honors College Interdisciplinary Thesis;
4-completing two or more graduate level courses;
5-completing a Rutgers program that combines undergraduate and graduate work and culminates in a graduate degree;
6-completing an approved two-semester experiential capstone such as a professional, certificate or service learning experience."

**AP/IB credits** are **not** counted as replacements for honors courses.

**No. Honors Classes Offered (5.0):** This is a measure of the total **adjusted** honors main sections available in the term reported, not including labs and thesis. An adjusted main section has 3 or more semester credits, or equivalent, and sections with fewer credits receive a lower prorated value.

The program offered a section for every **8.4** enrolled students. The average for all programs was **15.0**. The lower the number, the better. In the term reported, an extremely impressive **99.5%** of honors enrollment was **in honors-only sections; none was in mixed sections; and .5% was in contract sections.** For all programs under review, enrollment by type of honors section was 75.8% honors-only, 15.4 % mixed, and 8.8% contract.

**No. Honors Classes in Key Disciplines (5.0):** The 15 "key" disciplines are biological sciences; business (all); chemistry; communications (especially public speaking); computer science; economics; engineering (all); English; history; math (all); philosophy; physics; political science; psychology; and sociology, anthropology, and gender studies. Interdisciplinary sections, such as those often taken for General Education credit in the first two years, do receive a lesser, prorated discipline "credit" because they introduce students to multiple disciplines in an especially engaging way, often with in-depth discussion.

For this measure, mixed and contract sections are not counted as a section in a key discipline unless students taking the sections for honors credit make up at least 10% of the total section enrollment.

In the term reported, the honors college offered a section in a key discipline for every **11.8 honors students.** The average for all programs is **24.7**. The lower the number, the better.

Out of **59 adjusted sections in key disciplines, all were honors-only sections**. The most sections were in math (18), followed by biology, business, English, and political science. We found no honors sections in computer science, engineering, history, or sociology/anthropology.

The college offered 38 three-credit interdisciplinary seminars, including "Philosophy of Cosmology," "Conspiracy Theory in a Global Context," and "Hard Choices," whose description begins with the truism: "Life is rife with hard choices." The description continues: "Should you become a doctor or a lawyer? How much should you sacrifice in order to help others? Should you marry and have children? This course examines the phenomenon of hard choices by focusing on two questions: (1) what makes a choice hard? and (2) what should/does one do when faced with a hard choice? We explore answers to these questions from a variety of perspectives—philosophical, religious, literary, psychological, and neuroscientific."

The Honors College is a **blended** program, with a good mix of interdisciplinary courses and classes in the disciplines.

**Extent of Honors Enrollment (5.0):** Not all honors students take an honors class each term, especially after the first two years. Programs that have fewer honors classes and thesis options for upper-division honors students will *generally* have fewer total members in good standing who are actually enrolled in a given term. (Please be aware, however, that honors students not enrolled in a class for a term are still tied to the honors community through residential and extracurricular activities.) *Our research shows that this measure is closely related to honors completion rates, i.e., the number of students who complete honors requirements by the time they graduate.*

For example, if a program has 1,800 individual students enrolled in a given term, and 3,000 students in good standing, the level of enrollment was .67, an indication that honors class enrollment is somewhat below average, especially in upper-division classes. **Rutgers Honors has a ratio of 1.67**, well above the average of 1.30 for all programs.

**Average Class Size, Honors-only Sections (3.5):** Offered mostly in the first two years, honors-only classes tend to be smaller and, as the name implies, have no or very few students other than those in the honors program. These class sections always are much smaller than mixed or contract sections, or regular non-honors class sections in the university.

The average honors-only class size at Rutgers Honors is **18.7 students**. The average for all programs is **17.5 students.**

**Average Class Size, Overall (4.5):** The overall class calculation is based on the *proportion* of honors students in each type of class (honors-only, mixed honors, and honors contract sections). Thus it is not a raw average. The overall honors-credit class size is **18.9 students**, versus the average for all programs of **24.9 students**.

These class size averages also do not correspond to the number of students per honors section ratings above. The reason is that, in computing average class size metrics, we include enrollment in each 1-2-credit section, not just sections with 3 or more credits.

Along with an honors-only class size of 18.7 students (listed above), the program's very few contract sections with honors credit for individual honors students average **55.4 students.** Across all programs, the average contract section has 56.6 students.

**Honors Grad Rate Adjusted to SAT (4.0):** The rating is the based on the **estimated** grad rate for students who entered the program six years earlier, whether or not the students remained in honors. **The Honors College has not been in operation long enough for us to use an actual graduation rate.** The **estimated rate of 94.0%** is also compared to the rates of other programs with the same test score entry requirement range, and then adjusted upward if the program is performing above other programs in the same range, or downward if the performance is less than other programs in the same range. The rate here is the same, **94.0%.**

**Grad Rate Adjusted to Freshman Retention Rate (3.5):** This **estimated** rate compares the estimated grad rate above to a predicted grade rate when freshman retention rates are considered. The estimated grad rate is **1.48 points lower** than the predicted rate. For all programs, the actual grad rate is **.33 points lower** than the predicted rate.

**Ratio of Staff to Honors Students (5.0):** There is 1 staff member for every **66.5** students. (Mean ratio for all programs is 1 staff member for every **127.9** students.)

**Honors Residence Halls, Amenities (3.5):** "In their first-year, all Honors College students live in the Honors College facility. In their second and subsequent years, they have the option of a variety of honors-only communities (usually floors of residence halls) located across Rutgers. Honors College students participate in an early, exclusive lottery process. These communities provide students with the opportunity to live with students from across all honors programs on the Rutgers campus. Honors communities are strategically located across the five New Brunswick campuses to provide honors living opportunities for students who may want to live on a particular campus due to the location of courses in their major."

Almost 500 honors students live in The Honors College residence. "The building houses all first-year Honors College students as well as being the home to three faculty fellows (including the Academic Dean of the Honors College), the Honors College administrative and advising offices, and six seminar rooms, one of which includes a mini Maker Space/ Innovation Lab."

More than 350 honors upperclassmen who live on campus reside at the following halls:
The Yard on College Avenue (apartments); Campbell Hall; BEST North (STEM); Thomas Suites; McCormick Suites; Quad Hall; New Gibbons; and Newell Apartments. At Rutgers, location is very important, so after the first year, students seek residences near the classrooms for their major subjects or close to other facilities, such as dining halls.

**Honors Residence Halls, Availability (5.0):** This rating compares the number of occupants in honors residence halls to the number of honors freshman and sophomore members in good standing. The ratio for the program is **1.24** places for each first- and second-year student. The median for all programs is .49 places.

**Prestigious Awards (4.0):** The awards that we track and include are listed in the section titled "Prestigious Scholarships." The awards are sometimes won by students who are not in an honors college

or program, but increasingly many are enrolled in honors programs. It is also a trend that honors colleges and programs help to prepare their students for the awards competitions.

"Rutgers' Office of Distinguished Fellowships (ODF) first began to support undergraduates and alumni applying for national and international fellowships in September, 2007. In the ensuing decade, with advising from ODF, the overall performance of Rutgers candidates in these competitions improved dramatically. In the fifty-eight years before the ODF was established, 97 Rutgers students were awarded the Fulbright U.S. Student Grant, in contrast to the 147 who were named "Fulbrighters" in only the first ten years of ODF's existence. (This number does not include the 26 Rutgers students [a very high number] who were offered the Fulbright Grant this year).

Such an increase in annual average—in this case, from fewer than two a year to nearly fifteen—is not limited to Fulbright, however. *With help from ODF, Rutgers students have also enjoyed comparable success with the Gates Cambridge Scholarship,* one of the most prestigious national scholarships, selecting only thirty five to forty U.S. students annually. In the first seven years of the award, only a single Rutgers student was named a Gates Cambridge Scholar; in the past eleven years, with ODF support, Rutgers candidates have been selected for 10 Gates Cambridge Scholarships [second to UC Berkeley among public universities].

"Rutgers nominees' achievement in the competition for the Goldwater Scholarship has also improved markedly. In the first 18 years of this award, 16 Rutgers students were named Goldwater Scholars; in the 11 years since ODF was established, 23 Rutgers students have received the Goldwater Scholarship. During the same 11-year-period, Rutgers candidates have also been recognized with 4 Luce Scholarships (1 declined), 3 Mitchell Scholarships (1 declined), 3 Truman Scholarships, 2 Churchill Scholarships, 2 Soros Fellowships, 2 Rangel Fellowships and 1 Beinecke Scholarship."

## UNRATED FEATURES

**Continuation and Honors Graduation GPA Requirement:** "It depends on the school of enrollment and ranges from 3.2 to 3.5."

**Academic Strengths, National Rankings:** This is based on national rankings of *graduate* programs in all but engineering and business, where undergraduate rankings are used. One of the weaknesses of the *U.S. News* rankings is that they focus on too many wealth-related metrics while ignoring their own assessments of academic departments. The rankings listed below are for all universities, public or private.

Key academic departments at Rutgers have an overall national ranking of 43.9.

The leading nationally ranked academic departments at Rutgers are English (15), history (22), math (23), physics (28), sociology (28), computer science (37), education (43), political science (45), engineering (45), economics (47), and earth sciences (52).

**Internships, Professional Development, Community Engagement:** "The Honors College has an office and Assistant Dean for Professional Development. This office regularly provides future career development engagements and opportunities: Master Classes with alumni; Mentoring Pods with graduate and doctoral candidates; Networking Soirées and other professional gatherings; Internship and Research placements directly with corporate and industry partners. One such opportunity is a special grant from Johnson and Johnson to help support women in STEM fields through scholarships, research opportunities, and internships.

*"Another special offering is a 4+4 initiative through which selected incoming Honors College students are offered admission to the Robert Wood Johnson Medical School without MCAT after completing four years of undergraduate study,* completion of pre-med requirements, and maintenance of good standing in any major.

"We also have a Director of Innovation to head our onsite Honors College Innovation Lab, which provides students with mentoring for social impact projects, a mini makerspace and enterprise development expertise. Honors College students have launched from the Lab to win regional, national, and international recognition, including advancement toward the Hult Prize—the 'Nobel Prize for college students.'"

**Undergraduate Research:** "The Honors College defines undergraduate research in a number of ways:

--through our students' participation with the Aresty Undergraduate Research Center, which serves all of Rutgers-New Brunswick, by matching faculty research projects with student applications;

--through Summer Science research opportunities for rising sophomores, coordinated by the Aresty Center (30 on average per year);

--through Research Tutorials for students in the School of Environmental and Biological Sciences (data on spreadsheet);

--through individual student outreach and initiative to connect with specific faculty members on research projects, regularly in laboratory work, but also across the disciplines;

--through individual faculty researchers who solicit and form teams for data collection and analysis;

--through students who pursue yearlong Honors Thesis research projects in academic departments, to be recognized as Honors College Capstones (this year, two early graduates, up to 500 potential in coming years);

--through special dedicated seminars, as those developed in cooperation with the department of Neuroscience, and the Cancer Institute of New Jersey (23+18 students involved);

--through direct placements into research internships with corporate and institutional partners."

**Honors Study Abroad:** "We have dedicated scholarships for supporting Honors College students to study abroad (usually $1,000 to $2,000). We also feature a number of interdisciplinary honors seminars each year that have 'embedded' one-credit add-on elements, in which students travel to the country studied for one-week over winter or spring break or immediately following the end of spring semester.

"In past years, these courses traveled, among other places, to Brazil, Spain, Ireland, Poland, and Holland. We help support travel expenses for students in these courses. This year, we have had embedded trips to South Africa, Ireland, and France."

**Financial Aid:** "All Honors College students receive a *merit-based award, usually ranging from $10,000 to $27,400 (comparable to in-state tuition, fees, room, and board)*. Other merit and need-based awards are also available."

**Honors Fees:** None.

**Placement of Honors Graduates:** "We are just now admitting our fourth incoming class."

**Degree of Difference**: This is difference between (1) the average SAT scores for recently enrolled honors students (1506) and (2) the average test scores for all students in the university (1300) as a whole. The difference may be an indication of how "elite" honors students may be perceived as compared to students in the university as a whole. **Please keep in mind that neither the high nor low selectivity of an honors program determines how effective the program may be.**

**NAME**: SOUTH CAROLINA HONORS COLLEGE, UNIVERSITY OF SOUTH CAROLINA

**Date Established:** 1965 as a program, 1978 as a college.

**Location**: Columbia, South Carolina

**University Full-time Undergraduate Enrollment (2017):** 25,556

**Honors Members in Good Standing**: 2,021 (mean size of all programs is 2,030).

**Honors Average Admission Test Score(s)**: ACT, 32.5; SAT, 1481.

**Average High School GPA/Class Rank:** 4.68, weighted. Top 4% of high school class.

**Basic Admission Requirements:** None reported. "Students not accepted into the Honors College initially may apply to transfer into the Honors College after the freshman year. Transfer admission is competitive and is based on GPA, letters of recommendation, an essay, and availability of space."

**Application Deadline(s):** *Please verify with each program, as some deadlines could change.* Preferred deadline for scholarships and honors college admission is October 15, 2018. Test score assignment to university and letters of recommendation, November 15, 2018. First round of notifications in late December, 2018. Final notification in mid-February, 2019.

**Honors Programs with SAT scores from 1471—1510:** Clemson, Georgia, Illinois, Minnesota, Oklahoma, Rutgers, South Carolina, UT Austin.

**Administrative Staff:** 33.

**RATINGS AT A GLANCE:** For all mortarboard ratings immediately below, a score of 5 is the maximum and represents a comparison with all rated honors colleges and programs. More detailed explanations follow the "mortarboard" ratings.

**PERCEPTION\* OF UNIVERSITY AS A WHOLE, NOT OF HONORS:** 🎓🎓🎓🎓

\*Perception is based on the university's ranking among public universities in the 2018 U.S. News Best Colleges report. Please bear in mind that the better the U.S. News ranking, the more difficult it is for an honors college or program to have a rating that equals or improves on the magazine ranking.

**OVERALL HONORS RATING:** 🎓🎓🎓🎓🎓

**Curriculum Requirements:** 🎓🎓🎓🎓🎓

**Number of Honors Classes Offered:** 🎓🎓🎓🎓🎓

**Number of Honors Classes in Key Disciplines:** 🎓🎓🎓🎓🎓

**Extent of Honors Enrollment:** 🎓🎓🎓🎓🎓

**Honors-only Class Size:** 🎓🎓🎓🎓 1/2

**Overall Class Size (Honors-only plus mixed, contract):** 🎓🎓🎓🎓 1/2

**Honors Grad Rate Adjusted to SAT:** 🎓🎓🎓 1/2

**Grad Rate Adjusted to Freshman Retention Rate:** 🎓🎓🎓🎓 1/2

**Ratio of Staff to Students:** 🎓🎓🎓🎓🎓

**Priority Registration: Yes,** honors students register for all courses, honors and otherwise, with the first group of students during each year they are in the program.

**Honors Housing Amenities:** 🎓🎓🎓🎓🎓

**Honors Housing Availability:** 🎓🎓🎓🎓🎓

**Prestigious Awards:** 🎓🎓🎓🎓

## RATING SCORES AND EXPLANATIONS:

**Curriculum Requirements (5.0):** The most important rating category, the curriculum completion requirement (classes required to complete honors) defines not only what honors students should learn but also the extent to which honors students and faculty are connected in the classroom. If there is a thesis or capstone requirement, it reinforces the individual contact and research skills so important to learning.

The average number of honors semester hours required for completion across all programs is 30.0.

The minimum requirement for Graduating with Honors from the South Carolina Honors College is 45 honors credits, but the college has two other options that require 69 honors credits.

The 45-credit requirement includes a minimum of 39 credits in honors courses, a 3-credit thesis, and 3 credits from "Beyond the Classroom" options, such as credits for research, internships, study abroad, or from service-learning credits. "Students on average complete about 54 honors credit hours," the Dean tells us.

A more research-intensive option is the Baccalaureus Artium et Scientiae (BARSC) degree. The degree requires 69 credits, including 51-57 course credits and a research/thesis component of 9-15 credits. Another 3 credits from "Beyond the Classroom" options are required.

**AP/IB credits** are **not** counted as replacements for honors courses.

**No. Honors Classes Offered (5.0):** This is a measure of the total **adjusted** honors main sections available in the term reported, not including labs and thesis. An adjusted main section has 3 or more semester credits, or equivalent, and sections with fewer credits receive a lower prorated value.

The honors college offered a section for every **8.0** enrolled students. The average for all programs was **15.0**. The lower the number, the better. In the term reported, an extremely impressive **89.4%** of honors enrollment was **in honors-only sections; 10.6% was in mixed sections; and none was in contract sections.** For all programs under review, enrollment by type of honors section was 75.8% honors-only, 15.4 % mixed, and **8.8% contract.**

**No. Honors Classes in Key Disciplines (5.0):** The 15 "key" disciplines are biological sciences; business (all); chemistry; communications (especially public speaking); computer science; economics; engineering (all); English; history; math (all); philosophy; physics; political science; psychology; and sociology, anthropology, and gender studies. Interdisciplinary sections, such as those often taken for General Education credit in the first two years, do receive a lesser, prorated discipline "credit" because they introduce students to multiple disciplines in an especially engaging way, often with in-depth discussion.

For this measure, mixed and contract sections are not counted as a section in a key discipline unless students taking the sections for honors credit make up at least 10% of the total section enrollment.

In the term reported, the program offered a section in a key discipline for every **10.0 honors students.** The average for all programs is **24.7.** The lower the number, the better.

Out of **149 adjusted sections in key disciplines, 105 were honors-only sections**. The most sections were in English (22, mainly rhetoric and composition), followed by business, math, sociology/anthropology, chemistry, philosophy, engineering, history, psychology, biology, physics, political science, and computer science.

SCHC featured 37 three-credit interdisciplinary sections, including "The U.S. Constitution, How It Was Created, How It Has Survived," "Religion and Science—Conflict and Compatibility," "Demystifying Elective Office," and our favorite, "Authenticity: How to Live a Good Life and Be True To Yourself."

Here's the description for "Authenticity," taught by the associate honors Dean, now appointed Dean at another honors college: "'This above all: to thine own self be true, And it must follow, as the night the day, Thou canst not then be false to any man.' William Shakespeare, *Hamlet*. From Shakespeare to today we are deeply concerned with being true to ourselves. But what can this mean? How is it that we are creatures who cannot be true to ourselves? Does this require us to be a mystery to ourselves, to discover ourselves? How does the desire to be true to ourselves affect our art? our politics? To be true to ourselves, at least in Polonius' speech quoted above, is an ethical precept, but how is it that we have an ethical obligation toward ourself? And what does all of this have to do with living well?"

SCHC is a **blended** program, with an outstanding combination of interdisciplinary courses and classes in the disciplines.

**Extent of Honors Enrollment (5.0):** Not all honors students take an honors class each term, especially after the first two years. Programs that have fewer honors classes and thesis options for upper-division honors students will *generally* have fewer total members in good standing who are actually enrolled in a given term. (Please be aware, however, that honors students not enrolled in a class for a term are still tied to the honors community through residential and extracurricular activities.) *Our research shows that this measure is closely related to honors completion rates, i.e., the number of students who complete honors requirements by the time they graduate.*

For example, if a program has 1,800 individual students enrolled in a given term, and 3,000 students in good standing, the level of enrollment was .67, an indication that honors class enrollment is somewhat below average, especially in upper-division classes. **SCHC has a ratio of 2.03**, far above the average of 1.30 for all programs.

**Average Class Size, Honors-only Sections (4.5):** Offered mostly in the first two years, honors-only classes tend to be smaller and, as the name implies, have no or very few students other than those in the honors program. These class sections always are much smaller than mixed or contract sections, or regular non-honors class sections in the university.

The average honors-only class size at SCHC is **16.7 students**. The average for all programs is **17.5 students.**

**Average Class Size, Overall (4.5):** The overall class calculation is based on the *proportion* of honors students in each type of class (honors-only, mixed honors, and honors contract sections). Thus it is not a raw average. The overall honors-credit class size is **18.7 students**, versus the average for all programs of **24.7 students**.

These class size averages also do not correspond to the number of students per honors section ratings above. The reason is that, in computing average class size metrics, we include enrollment in each 1-2-credit section, not just sections with 3 or more credits.

Along with an honors-only class size of 16.7 students (listed above), the program's mixed honors sections have an average size of **34.8 students.** Across all programs, the average mixed honors section has 68.6 students.

**Honors Grad Rate Adjusted to SAT (3.5):** The rating is the based on the actual grad rate for students who entered the program six years earlier, whether or not the students remained in honors. The **actual rate of 91.0%** is also compared to the rates of other programs with the same test score entry requirement range, and then adjusted upward if the program is performing above other programs in the same range, or downward if the performance is less than other programs in the same range. The rate here is slightly downward, to **90.0%.**

**Grad Rate Adjusted to Freshman Retention Rate (4.5):** This rate compares the actual grad rate above to a predicted grade rate when freshman retention rates are considered. The actual grad rate is **2.67 points higher** than the predicted rate. For all programs, the actual grad rate is **.33 points lower** than the predicted rate.

**Ratio of Staff to Honors Students (5.0):** There is 1 staff member for every **61.2** students. (Mean ratio for all programs is 1 staff member for every **127.9** students.)

**Honors Residence Halls, Amenities (5.0):** SCHC students are now housed in four coed residence halls. The Honors Residential Hall houses almost 537 of the 1,367 students living in honors housing, with freshmen and upperclassmen sharing the hall. The residence has air-conditioned, suite-style rooms with shared baths, and its own dining hall, The Honeycomb Café.

650 Lincoln serves another 500 honors students, all upperclassmen. It features a kitchen in each suite-style unit and has onsite dining at the Community Table—and a swimming pool onsite.

The 180 residents of the Historic Horseshoe are also upperclassmen. The residence has air-conditioned, apartment-style rooms, with kitchens, bathrooms, and washer/dryers in all apartments. Dining is at McCutcheon House located on the Horseshoe or at Russell House Student Union across the street. Historic Horseshoe has the same living/learning themes as the Honors Residential Hall.

Patterson Hall, on the South Quad, houses 150 freshmen and upperclassmen. It is also suite-style and has a kitchen on each floor. Russell House Student Union is the nearest dining facility.

**Honors Residence Halls, Availability (5.0):** This rating compares the number of occupants in honors residence halls to the number of honors freshman and sophomore members in good standing. The ratio for the program is **1.35** places for each first- and second-year student. The median for all programs is .49 places.

**Prestigious Awards (4.0):** The awards that we track and include are listed in the section titled "Prestigious Scholarships." The awards are sometimes won by students who are not in an honors college or program, but increasingly many are enrolled in honors programs. It is also a trend that honors colleges and programs help to prepare their students for the awards competitions.

"The University of South Carolina was ahead of the national trend when the office to provide national fellowship advising was established in 1994. With an advising philosophy focusing on the developmental and educational benefits of national fellowship processes no matter the outcome of the national competition, USC has generated an impressive and, equally if not more important, consistent track record of national winners. The staff of six reports to the Dean of the South Carolina Honors College and is housed in the same building. In the 2017-2018 academic year, 249 applications were submitted by undergraduates, graduate students, and recent alumni in 47 competitions, with 50 winners earning awards totaling $2,384,710.

"We have had national winners in every scholarship competition tracked, except Churchill, which is of course invitation-only by institution. Our most recent highlights include a 2017 Rhodes Scholar, 2016 and 2018 Gates Cambridge Scholars, 26 consecutive years of Goldwater Scholars (including 2 in 2018), back-to-back Udall Scholars in 2017 and 2018, a 2018 Truman Scholar, and 9 Fulbright Scholars in 2017. We also have had two Marshall Scholars (and are the only institution in SC to have a Marshall Scholar). In the last three years, USC has had 28 Gilman Scholarship winners and 19 Fulbright Finalists. In the last two years, USC has had 18 students and alumni win NSF GRFP awards.

"Additionally, we have 25 Goldwater, Udall, Hollings, Gilman and other current undergraduate national fellowship winners who serve as National Fellowship Peer Mentors, and who help with outreach and recruitment of future applicants. Faculty complete the national fellowship resources team with approximately 65 appointed annually to serve as advisors, on nomination committees, and on practice interview teams."

## UNRATED FEATURES

**Continuation and Honors Graduation GPA Requirement:** "There is a sliding GPA requirement. Students are required to maintain at least a 3.0 in their first two semesters (fall and spring), at least a 3.1 in their second two semesters, at least a 3.2 in their third two semesters, and at least a 3.3 in their final semesters to remain in good standing and graduate "With Honors."

**Academic Strengths, National Rankings:** This is based on national rankings of *graduate* programs in all but engineering and business, where undergraduate rankings are used. One of the weaknesses of the *U.S. News* rankings is that they focus on too many wealth-related metrics while ignoring their own assessments of academic departments. The rankings listed below are for all universities, public or private.

The nationally ranked academic departments at USC include business (45, with international business ranked 1st), history (63), political science (72), sociology (75), economics (83), education (84), English (85), chemistry (88), earth sciences (90), engineering (110), and computer science (111).

**Internships, Professional Development, Community Engagement:**

"The SCHC has three unique internship programs. The Washington Semester Program is a state-wide program open to all South Carolina college/university students. Students selected during the competitive process spend a semester living, working, and taking classes in Washington D.C. Students work in internships in the United States Senate, the House of Representatives, the Smithsonian Museum, and a variety of other institutions and organizations.

"The South Carolina Semester Program provides paid internships to University of South Carolina students working in state government while taking a course taught by a State Senator. The course focuses on state government and public policy issues. The honors college provides $2,000 per student to support state government internships.

"In our general internship program, during spring 2017 and fall 2017, 158 honors college students completed internships for academic credit. Sixty-nine percent of these internships were paid, earning on average $15.06 per hour. During the year, USC Honors College interns worked in 23 states and 5 countries. Students enroll in an online course in conjunction with their internships.

"The South Carolina Honors College supports students' desire to serve their communities in two ways: through a growing curriculum of service-learning classes and four Honors student service organizations.

"Service-learning is one of the four designated Beyond the Classroom experiences. Honors service-learning courses span subjects from environmental conservation to homelessness to marine science. The classes have become an interdisciplinary meeting ground for students of all majors, and students report in end-of-course evaluations that applying their classroom knowledge to real community problems fostered greater understanding of the courses' concepts. The courses leave a lasting impact on students: Honors service-learning classes have shaped the foundation of at least 60 senior theses since 2012.

"One Honors organization, the Waverly After-School Program, was named the top student service organization in the state by the South Carolina Campus Compact. In this program, students work with some of the city's most vulnerable and underserved children to develop literacy and a love of learning."

**Undergraduate Research:** "The Honors College has a Director of Undergraduate Research who administers a program that encourages each student to apply for up to $4,500 in research funding.

"Students are guided through the process of identifying a research mentor and project, making the formal application, and conducting and presenting research. *This past year, the Honors College awarded $351,893 to students to support undergraduate research.* Honors students also have access to funding support for research related to their senior thesis, study abroad, internship, and service learning. In addition, Honors students may apply for up to $3,000 in funding from the university's Office of Undergraduate Research. Other funding is available from various other sources as part of faculty research projects. Finally, specific honors classes are offered that are designed to stimulate research: 'Initiating Research,' 'Asking Questions and Finding Answers—Research as a Leadership Skill,' 'Introduction to Nursing Research Methods,' and 'Qualitative Research Methods,' for example. All students awarded Honors College research funding complete the same CITI Responsible Code of Conduct (RCR) training that is required of researchers funded by the National Institutes of Health and the National Science Foundation."

**Honors Study Abroad:** "The Honors College does offer funding support, based on need, for study abroad.

"Countries that our students have studied in: Argentina, Aruba, Australia, Austria, Belgium, Belize, Bermuda, Bhutan, Brazil, Canada, Chile, China, Colombia, Costa Rica, Croatia, Cuba, Cyprus, Czech Republic, Denmark, Dominican Republic, Ecuador, Egypt, England, Fiji, France, Germany, Ghana, Greece, Honduras, Hong Kong, Hungary, Iceland, India, Ireland, Israel, Italy, Jamaica, Japan, Jordan, Kenya, Mali, Mexico, Morocco, Mozambique, Nepal, New Zealand, Nicaragua, Norway, Palestinian Territory, Peru, Poland, Portugal, Romania, Russia, Rwanda, Saint Lucia, Scotland, Senegal, Slovakia, South Africa, South Korea, Spain, Sweden, Switzerland, Taiwan, Tajikistan, Tanzania, Thailand, The Netherlands, Trinidad and Tobago, Tunisia, Turkey, Uganda, United Arab Emirates, United Kingdom, United States, Uruguay, Virgin Islands, Wales, Zambia.

"Universities: The Honors College and the Moore Business School send students to and have an ongoing relationship with Lady Margaret Hall, Oxford University. We just started a partnership with the Honors College at the American College of Greece in Athens. The University has study-abroad agreements and relationships with many universities.

"College-Sponsored Trips: Faculty lead study-abroad experiences sponsored by the Honors College: This year we have 5 Global Classrooms going abroad (Tracing the Holocaust in Eastern Europe; Social Capital in Rome; Art and Culture in Japan; Language and Culture in Paris), and (in partnership with the Journalism School) When Media Matters, a service-learning course in Malawi."

**Financial Aid:** "All students accepted into the South Carolina Honors College receive an academic merit scholarship awarded by the Office of Undergraduate Admissions. *The most competitive are the Top Scholars awards, which encompass six different scholarships (three categories for in-state students and three for out-of-state). The Top Scholars awards are offered to 96 incoming Honors College freshman students each fall.* For in-state students, the Stamps Scholars, Carolina Scholars, and 1801 Scholars are the most prestigious awards. The Stamps award has a total four-year value of $90,000, the Carolina Scholars $60,000, and the 1801 Scholars $40,000.

"*For out-of-state students, Stamps Scholars, McNair Scholars, and Horseshoe Scholars are the top awards. Recipients qualify for in-state tuition. The total value of the Stamps Scholars award for **out-of-state students** is more than $167,000, the McNair more than $137,000, and the Horseshoe more than $121,000.* Each class competes with itself for the Top Scholars awards: There are no set minimum requirements. All students who apply to the SCHC are considered for the Top Scholars program."

"Additionally, other offices on campus, including the SCHC itself, offer scholarships that can be added to the Admissions awards. ***The most valuable SCHC scholarships are the full-tuition Belser Scholarships. The University awards scholarships to National Merit Finalists and National Hispanic Recognition Program Scholars.*** The Provost Scholars Award can be combined with other Admissions-issued scholarships and is worth up to $10,000 per year for in-state students, and up to $6,000 per year for out-of-state students, renewable for four years. Out-of-state recipients also qualify to pay in-state tuition rates, making the value of their scholarship more than $101,000 over four years of study. Provost Scholars also receive a laptop computer and preferred parking privileges."

**Honors Fees:** $575 per semester.

**Placement of Honors Graduates:** "Consistently about one-third of our students go on to graduate school in just about every possible field. Destinations include Ivy League schools, Oxford, Cambridge, Stanford, and many other top-tier schools. Another third of our students go on to professional training, studying to be doctors, lawyers, physician assistants, veterinarians, pharmacists, etc. Our first-time-applicant admissions rate for medical school has ranged over the past decade from 73 to 84%. The most recent class included acceptances to all three medical schools in the state (USC-Columbia, USC-Greenville, MUSC), as well as Vanderbilt, Drexel, UNC-Chapel Hill, West Virginia, East Carolina, Louisville, Baylor, Indiana, Kansas, Kentucky, and Mercer.

"Approximately another third of our students go to work. Companies joined included most recently Amazon, Bank of America, Boeing, Ernst & Young, Exxon Oil, GE Power, Google, IBM Consulting, J.P. Morgan, McKinsey & Company, Nestle USA, Disney, Manhattan Associates, public schools, religious organizations, government agencies, non-profits, family businesses, and more. Graduates also joined military service, the Peace Corps, and Teach for America."

**Degree of Difference**: This is difference between (1) the average SAT scores for recently enrolled honors students (1481) and (2) the average test scores for all students in the university (1270) as a whole. The difference may be an indication of how "elite" honors students may be perceived as compared to students in the university as a whole. **Please keep in mind that neither the high nor low selectivity of an honors program determines how effective the program may be.**

**NAME**: TEXAS TECH UNIVERSITY HONORS COLLEGE

**Date Established:** 1999

**Location**: Lubbock, Texas

**University Full-time Undergraduate Enrollment (2017):** 29,963

**Honors Members in Good Standing**: 1,503 (mean size of all programs is 2,030).

**Honors Average Admission Test Score(s)**: ACT, 29; SAT, 1380.

**Average High School GPA/Class Rank:** (34 Valedictorians admitted for Fall 2017; 212 students in the top 10% of their high school class)

**Basic Admission Requirements:** ACT, 29; SAT, 1360; top 10% of high school class.

**Application Deadline(s):** *Please verify with each program, as some deadlines could change.* Application period begins July 1, 2018, and ends March 1, 2019.

**Honors Programs with SAT scores from 1370—1403:** Arizona, CUNY Macaulay, Georgia State, Houston, Indiana, Iowa, LSU, Massachusetts, New Mexico Texas Tech, UAB.

**Administrative Staff:** Approximately 17 FTEs.

**RATINGS AT A GLANCE:** For all mortarboard ratings immediately below, a score of 5 is the maximum and represents a comparison with all rated honors colleges and programs. More detailed explanations follow the "mortarboard" ratings.

**PERCEPTION* OF UNIVERSITY AS A WHOLE, NOT OF HONORS:** 🎓🎓🎓 1/2

*Perception is based on the university's ranking among public universities in the 2018 U.S. News Best Colleges report. Please bear in mind that the better the U.S. News ranking, the more difficult it is for an honors college or program to have a rating that equals or improves on the magazine ranking.

**OVERALL HONORS RATING:** 🎓🎓🎓🎓 1/2

**Curriculum Requirements:** 🎓🎓🎓🎓

**Number of Honors Classes Offered:** 🎓🎓🎓🎓 1/2

**Number of Honors Classes in Key Disciplines:** 🎓🎓🎓🎓

**Extent of Honors Enrollment:** 🎓🎓🎓🎓

**Honors-only Class Size:** 🎓🎓🎓🎓🎓

**Overall Class Size (Honors-only plus mixed, contract):** 🎓🎓🎓🎓🎓

**Honors Grad Rate Adjusted to SAT:** 🎓🎓🎓1/2

**Grad Rate Adjusted to Freshman Retention Rate:** 🎓🎓🎓1/2

**Ratio of Staff to Students:** 🎓🎓🎓🎓1/2

**Priority Registration: Yes,** honors students register for all courses, honors and otherwise, with the *second* group of students during each year they are in the program.

**Honors Housing Amenities:** 🎓🎓🎓🎓1/2

**Honors Housing Availability:** 🎓🎓🎓🎓🎓

**Prestigious Awards:** 🎓🎓🎓

## RATING SCORES AND EXPLANATIONS:

**Curriculum Requirements (4.0):** The most important rating category, the curriculum completion requirement (classes required to complete honors) defines not only what honors students should learn but also the extent to which honors students and faculty are connected in the classroom. If there is a thesis or capstone requirement, it reinforces the individual contact and research skills so important to learning.

The average number of honors semester hours required for completion across all programs is 30.0.

The honors college has two completion options (see below), but *also has programs that lead to early acceptance to TTU medical and law schools:*

Graduation with Honors—Students complete a total of 24 hours of honors credits, which must include at least 3 hours of upper-level honors seminar work and a 3-credit capstone requirement. The other 18 credit hours can be from any department, lower or upper-level. A maximum of 6 credits in honors contract* courses can be counted.

Graduation with **Highest** Honors—Completion requires the same 24 honors credits along with an additional 6 credits of research, culminating in a senior honors thesis, for a total of 30 credits. The same 6-credit cap applies to honors contract credit.

*The Honors College is a leader nationwide in crafting policies and requirements for honors contract classes. The College limits the number and level of honors contract courses that can count for honors credit and has well-defined procedures in place that are designed to ensure the highest levels of academic quality and integrity.

**Early Acceptance to TTU Medical and Law Schools:**

**Medical School**—"The joint TTU-TTUHSC Early Acceptance Program offers an exciting opportunity to select Honors College students by allowing them to waive the MCAT (Medical College Admissions Test) and to apply early to the TTUHSC's School of Medicine (SOM), typically in the junior year. Successful Early Acceptance applicants are notified of their acceptance to the School of Medicine in February and complete their baccalaureate degrees prior to admission.

"Students must be officially enrolled in the Honors College; enter Texas Tech University as incoming freshmen (students classified as transfer students upon entering TTU are ineligible); have earned a composite score of 1360 on the SAT (verbal and math portions only) or a 29 on the ACT upon matriculation from high school (the composite score must be earned in one test administration); *be Texas residents and U.S. Citizens or Permanent Residents; graduates of a high school in Texas;* and meet all applicable deadlines."

**Law School**—"The Honors College and the Law School cooperate in an Early Decision Plan, which allows exceptional Law School applicants who are Honors College students in good standing to receive notification of their acceptance to the Law School during their third year at Texas Tech. Enrollment in the Law School would not occur until after the student receives a baccalaureate degree.

"To be eligible to apply for Law School Early Decision, applicants must have a minimum undergraduate GPA of at least 3.50; an LSAT score that places them in the top half nationwide (>152, approximately); an SAT of at least 1300 or an ACT of at least 29; and be enrolled in the Texas Tech University Honors College and making satisfactory progress toward a baccalaureate degree with a diploma designation in Honors studies.

"Students will apply during the fall semester of their third year (or during the fall semester of a year in which they are classified as juniors) and must have taken the LSAT by December of that year. Students who receive and accept an Early Decision must commit to enroll at the Texas Tech University School of Law and may not apply to other law schools."

**AP/IB credits** are **not** counted as replacements for honors courses.

**No. Honors Classes Offered (4.5):** This is a measure of the total **adjusted** honors main sections available in the term reported, not including labs and thesis. An adjusted main section has 3 or more semester credits, or equivalent, and sections with fewer credits receive a lower prorated value.

The program offered a section for every **11.3** enrolled students. The average for all programs was **15.0**. The lower the number, the better. In the term reported, 77.2% of honors enrollment was **in honors-only sections; 21.7% was in mixed sections; and only 1.1% was in contract sections.** For all programs under review, enrollment by type of honors section was 75.8% honors-only, 15.4 % mixed, and 8.8% contract.

**No. Honors Classes in Key Disciplines (4.0):** The 15 "key" disciplines are biological sciences; business (all); chemistry; communications (especially public speaking); computer science; economics; engineering (all); English; history; math (all); philosophy; physics; political science; psychology; and sociology, anthropology, and gender studies. Interdisciplinary sections, such as those often taken for General Education credit in the first two years, do receive a lesser, prorated discipline "credit" because they introduce students to multiple disciplines in an especially engaging way, often with in-depth discussion.

For this measure, mixed and contract sections are not counted as a section in a key discipline unless students taking the sections for honors credit make up at least 10% of the total section enrollment.

In the term reported, the program offered a section in a key discipline for every **19.2 honors students.** The average for all programs is **24.7.** The lower the number, the better.

Out of **51 adjusted sections in key disciplines, 34 were honors-only sections.** The most sections were in math, engineering, chemistry, physics, engineering, English, history, philosophy, business, and communications. We found no sections in computer science or sociology/anthropology.

TTU Honors College featured 25 three-credit interdisciplinary sections, including "Space, Place, and Human Health," "The Western Intellectual Tradition," and, a favorite, "Bones, Botanicals, and Birds." The description is as good as the title: "Dangerous ship crossings, unknown and hostile terrain, starvation, bad weather, bandits, and no communication with loved ones for months or years. The nineteenth-century botanists, biologists, and ornithologists were the original Indiana Jones in their quest to discover new plant and animal species. In this Honors College seminar experience, we will travel with them, too, as we learn by illustrating plants and birds ourselves, using many of their same techniques."

The TTU Honors is a **blended** program, with a good mix of interdisciplinary courses and classes in the disciplines.

**Extent of Honors Enrollment (4.0):** Not all honors students take an honors class each term, especially after the first two years. Programs that have fewer honors classes and thesis options for upper-division honors students will *generally* have fewer total members in good standing who are actually enrolled in a given term. (Please be aware, however, that honors students not enrolled in a class for a term are still tied to the honors community through residential and extracurricular activities.) *Our research shows that this measure is closely related to honors completion rates, i.e., the number of students who complete honors requirements by the time they graduate.*

For example, if a program has 1,800 individual students enrolled in a given term, and 3,000 students in good standing, the level of enrollment was .67, an indication that honors class enrollment is somewhat below average, especially in upper-division classes. **TTU Honors has a ratio of 1.29**, just below the average of 1.30 for all programs.

**Average Class Size, Honors-only Sections (5.0):** Offered mostly in the first two years, honors-only classes tend to be smaller and, as the name implies, have no or very few students other than those in the honors program. These class sections always are much smaller than mixed or contract sections, or regular non-honors class sections in the university.

The average honors-only class size at TTU Honors is **15.1 students**. The average for all programs is **17.5 students.**

**Average Class Size, Overall (5.0):** The overall class calculation is based on the *proportion* of honors students in each type of class (honors-only, mixed honors, and honors contract sections). Thus it is not a raw average. The overall honors-credit class size is **16.6 students**, versus the average for all programs of **24.9 students**.

These class size averages also do not correspond to the number of students per honors section ratings above. The reason is that, in computing average class size metrics, we include enrollment in each 1-2-credit section, not just sections with 3 or more credits.

Along with an honors-only class size of 16.6 students (listed above), the program's mixed honors sections have an average size of **19.9 students,** and the contract sections with honors credit for individual honors students average **52.0 students.** Across all programs, the average mixed honors section has 68.6 students, and the average contract section has 56.6 students.

**Honors Grad Rate Adjusted to SAT (3.5):** The rating is the based on the actual grad rate for students who entered the program six years earlier, whether or not the students remained in honors. The **actual rate of 82.6%** is also compared to the rates of other programs with the same test score entry requirement range, and then adjusted upward if the program is performing above other programs in the same range, or downward if the performance is less than other programs in the same range. The rate here is slightly downward, to **81.6%.**

**Grad Rate Adjusted to Freshman Retention Rate (3.5):** This rate compares the actual grad rate above to a predicted grade rate when freshman retention rates are considered. The actual grad rate is **.71 points lower** than the predicted rate. For all programs, the actual grad rate is **.33 points lower** than the predicted rate.

**Ratio of Staff to Honors Students (4.5):** There is 1 staff member for every **95.1** students. (Mean ratio for all programs is 1 staff member for every **127.9** students.)

**Honors Residence Halls, Amenities (4.5):** Tech honors students are fortunate to have three honors residence halls with suite-style rooms that are air-conditioned, with shared baths. The dorms are coed, with each shared suite all male or all female. Honors Hall houses the most students, 320. Murray Hall, with 156 honors students, offers the option of eating at Sam's Place, on site. Both dorms on the west side of campus. Gordon Hall is on the northeast side, with 252 honors students, has dining on site at the Fresh Plate.

**Honors Residence Halls, Availability (5.0):** This rating compares the number of occupants in honors residence halls to the number of honors freshman and sophomore members in good standing. The ratio for the program is **1.17** places for each first- and second-year student. The median for all programs is .49 places.

**Prestigious Awards (3.0):** The awards that we track and include are listed in the section titled "Prestigious Scholarships." The awards are sometimes won by students who are not in an honors college

or program, but increasingly many are enrolled in honors programs. It is also a trend that honors colleges and programs help to prepare their students for the awards competitions.

"We have an office dedicated to working with students on prestigious awards. Over the past few years, students have earned various prestigious awards. In 2013, we received one Fulbright award and five Gilman awards. In 2014, eight Gilman Scholarships were received and one of those students was an honors student. In 2015, nine Gilman Scholarships were received by Texas Tech Students. In 2016, one honors student was awarded the Goldwater Scholarship, and three students received Goldwater Honorable Mention (one was an honors student). Three Gilman awards have also been received for early 2016 competitions. In addition to these, Texas Tech University had one Rhodes Scholarship finalist (2015), one Truman Scholarship finalist (2016), and one Boren Award for International Study winner (2016).

"For the academic year (2017-2018): one Honors College student was awarded the Goldwater Scholarship, one honors student received Honorable Mention for the Goldwater Scholarship; 3 honors students were awarded the Gilman award; an Honorable Mention for one Honors student for the NSF GRFP; one Truman finalist; and an Honorable Mention for an honors student for the Udall award."

## UNRATED FEATURES

**Continuation and Honors Graduation GPA Requirement:** 3.50 for both.

**Academic Strengths, National Rankings:** This is based on national rankings of *graduate* programs in all but engineering and business, where undergraduate rankings are used. One of the weaknesses of the *U.S. News* rankings is that they focus on too many wealth-related metrics while ignoring their own assessments of academic departments. The rankings listed below are for all universities, public or private.

Texas Tech has nationally ranked departments in 12 of the 15 academic disciplines that we track. The top nationally ranked academic departments at Texas Tech are earth sciences (78), engineering (82), education (95), math (108), business (109), computer science (121), and chemistry (122).

**Internships, Professional Development, Community Engagement:** "The Government & Public Service Internship Programs provide students with a unique opportunity to experience either federal or state government first-hand. The internships provide students with an inside look at how government works and what it takes to make our great nation and state run. The internship opportunities are offered each semester in D.C., Lubbock or Austin. To participate in the program, it is preferred that undergraduate students have a minimum cumulative grade point average of 3.0 and have completed a minimum of 60 semester credit hours before the semester they wish to participate in the internship."

**Undergraduate Research:**

"The Honors College program for undergraduate research is called Undergraduate Research Scholars (URS). URS is a year-long (or longer) program which culminates in the student's participation in the TTU Undergraduate Research Conference and/or thesis. Scholars receive a stipend through an endowment and the University National Research University Fund to participate in research with a faculty mentor. Scholars may participate in URS for one or more years. Financial support is provided for travel to national meetings where URS scholars present their work and findings.

"In Fall 2017, the Honors College and the Office of the Provost created Program in Inquiry and Investigative Thinking (Pi$^2$) to introduce freshman-level students to the basics and expectations of doing inquiry and investigative research work at the college level. Students belong to one of five cohorts and work with a faculty member. Scholars may participate in Pi$^2$ for one or more years.

"For the Fall 2017-Spring 2018 year, nearly 150 Honors students participated in the Honors Undergraduate Research Scholars (URS) program. For the Fall 2017 term, 95 Honors students participated in Program in Inquiry and Investigative Thinking."

**Honors Study Abroad:** The centerpiece of the university's study-abroad programs is the Texas Tech University Center in Sevilla, located on the Guadalquivir River in southern Spain, in the heart of the region known as Andalusia.

"A city of roughly 700,000 inhabitants, Sevilla offers all of the advantages of a big city while still maintaining a small-town feel. In Sevilla, students can still appreciate the splendor of Golden Age Spain as they meander through the nooks and crannies of the medieval city center, whose cathedral holds the tomb of Christopher Columbus, and at the same time take advantage of the modern cultural and leisure activities that this vibrant city has to offer.

"The Center allows students to take catalog TTU classes taught by Texas Tech faculty. The Center has a permanent staff as well as faculty that travel from Lubbock to Sevilla every semester (fall, spring and summer). The Center is located in a building that originally dates back to the 1890s, and today has all of the modern conveniences a university facility needs. It is conveniently situated in a bustling neighborhood, literally steps away from all sorts of eateries and shops.""

**Financial Aid:** The Honors College awarded $344,500 in scholarship funding in Academic Year 2017/2018. Scholarship decisions are based on exceptional performance as a TTU Honors College student. Scholarship considerations include: Honors experiences, overcoming adversity and challenges, work responsibilities, family circumstances, and volunteer experience. Award amounts from the Honors College for current students are between $500-1,000; for incoming freshmen, awards vary between $1,000-$2,000.

**National Merit Finalists:** "Students that reach finalist standing will be notified in February by the National Merit Corporation. *Qualifying students that designate Texas Tech University as their first choice institution are eligible to receive 100% of federally approved cost of attendance including tuition, fees, room, board, books, transportation and a personal/miscellaneous allowance.* National merit awards are funded by a combination of federal, state and institutional gift aid funds including Pell Grant, Federal Supplemental Opportunity Educational Grant, TEXAS Grant, Texas Public Education Grant, Texas Tech Grant and scholarships."

"National Merit Finalists who select Texas Tech University and are not residents of the State of Texas, also qualify for Texas Tech's National Merit Scholars Program."

**Honors Fees:** None.

**Placement of Honors Graduates:** None listed.

**Degree of Difference**: This is difference between (1) the average SAT scores for recently enrolled honors students (1380) and (2) the average test scores for all students in the university (1180) as a whole. The difference may be an indication of how "elite" honors students may be perceived as compared to students in the university as a whole. **Please keep in mind that neither the high nor low selectivity of an honors program determines how effective the program may be.**

**NAME**: UAB HONORS COLLEGE

**Date Established:** 2012

**Location**: Birmingham, Alabama

**University Full-time Undergraduate Enrollment (2017):** 12,267.

**Honors Members in Good Standing**: 1,774; (mean size of all programs is 2,030).

**Honors Average Admission Test Score(s)**: ACT, 30.5; est. SAT equivalent, 1400.

**Average High School GPA/Class Rank:** 4.11, weighted.

**Basic Admission Requirements:** ACT 28; SAT 1310; 3.5 GPA.

**Application Deadline(s):** *Please verify with each program, as some deadlines could change.* March 15, 2019 for Honors College; January 15, 2019 for Specialized Programs.

**Honors Programs with SAT scores from 1370—1403:** 1370—1403: Arizona, CUNY Macaulay, Georgia State, Houston, Indiana, LSU, Massachusetts, New Mexico, Purdue, Texas Tech, UAB.

**Administrative Staff:** 15.5.

**RATINGS AT A GLANCE:** For all mortarboard ratings immediately below, a score of 5 is the maximum and represents a comparison with all rated honors colleges and programs. More detailed explanations follow the "mortarboard" ratings.

**PERCEPTION\* OF UNIVERSITY AS A WHOLE, NOT OF HONORS:** 🎓🎓🎓 1/2

\*Perception is based on the university's ranking among public universities in the 2018 U.S. News Best Colleges report. Please bear in mind that the better the U.S. News ranking, the more difficult it is for an honors college or program to have a rating that equals or improves on the magazine ranking.

**OVERALL HONORS RATING:** 🎓🎓🎓 1/2

**Curriculum Requirements:** 🎓🎓🎓🎓

**Number of Honors Classes Offered:** 🎓🎓🎓 1/2

**Number of Honors Classes in Key Disciplines:** 🎓🎓🎓🎓

**Extent of Honors Enrollment:** 🎓🎓🎓 1/2

**Honors-only Class Size:** 🎓🎓🎓

**Overall Class Size (Honors-only plus mixed, contract):** 🎓🎓🎓1/2

**Honors Grad Rate Adjusted to SAT:** 🎓🎓🎓

**Grad Rate Adjusted to Freshman Retention Rate:** 🎓🎓🎓🎓

**Ratio of Staff to Students:** 🎓🎓🎓🎓

**Priority Registration: Yes,** honors students register in the first group after athletes.

**Honors Housing Amenities:** 🎓🎓🎓1/2

**Honors Housing Availability:** 🎓🎓🎓🎓

**Prestigious Awards:** 🎓🎓🎓

## RATING SCORES AND EXPLANATIONS:

**Curriculum Requirements (4.0):** The most important rating category, the curriculum completion requirement (classes required to complete honors) defines not only what honors students should learn but also the extent to which honors students and faculty are connected in the classroom. If there is a thesis or capstone requirement, it reinforces the individual contact and research skills so important to learning.

The average number of honors semester hours required for completion across all programs is 30.0.

UAB Honors College requires 30 honors credits for completion of the High Distinguished Honors option. The requirement for Distinguished Honors ranges from 18 to 29 credits. There is a thesis option.

Within this basic framework, students can choose a **Personalized Path,** allowing for the widest range of course selection, or apply to one of three Specialized Programs: **Global and Community Leadership Honors Program** (GCL), focusing on human rights issues and social change leadership; **Science and Technology Honors Program** (STH), emphasizing undergraduate research and a STEM-focused education; or the **University Honors Program** (UHP),offering a unique interdisciplinary curriculum that replaces the university's core requirements.

**AP/IB credits** are **not** counted as replacements for honors courses.

**No. Honors Classes Offered (3.5):** This is a measure of the total **adjusted** honors main sections available in the term reported, not including labs and thesis. An adjusted main section has 3 or more semester credits, or equivalent, and sections with fewer credits receive a lower prorated value.

UAB honors offered a section for every **16.2** enrolled students. The average for all programs was **15.0**. The lower the number, the better.

In the term reported, an extremely impressive **100%** of honors enrollment was **in honors-only sections (along with 84 students in tutorials for contract credit).** For all programs under review, enrollment by type of honors section was 75.8% honors-only, 15.4 % mixed, and 8.8% contract.

**No. Honors Classes in Key Disciplines (4.0):** The 15 "key" disciplines are biological sciences; business (all); chemistry; communications (especially public speaking); computer science; economics; engineering (all); English; history; math (all); philosophy; physics; political science; psychology; and sociology, anthropology, and gender studies. Interdisciplinary sections, such as those often taken for General Education credit in the first two years, do receive a lesser, prorated discipline "credit" because they introduce students to multiple disciplines in an especially engaging way, often with in-depth discussion.

For this measure, mixed and contract sections are not counted as a section in a key discipline unless students taking the sections for honors credit make up at least 10% of the total section enrollment.

In the term reported, the honors college offered a section in a key discipline for every **22.2 honors students.** The average for all programs is **24.7**. The lower the number, the better.

Out of **39 adjusted sections in key disciplines**, **all were honors-only sections**. The most sections were in English, along with five sections in chemistry, and four each in biology, communications, engineering, and psychology. Only one section was offered in business, math, history, and physics

The college does offer a solid range of interdisciplinary courses including "Think Like an Entrepreneur", "Things about the Brain," "Tracing the Soul in Literature," and "Ethical Conflicts in Healthcare." The honors college is a **blended** program, with a good mix of interdisciplinary courses and classes in the disciplines.

**Extent of Honors Enrollment (3.5):** Not all honors students take an honors class each term, especially after the first two years. Programs that have fewer honors classes and thesis options for upper-division honors students will *generally* have fewer total members in good standing who are actually enrolled in a given term. (Please be aware, however, that honors students not enrolled in a class for a term are still tied to the honors community through residential and extracurricular activities.) Our research shows that this measure is closely related to honors completion rates, i.e., the number of students who complete honors requirements by the time they graduate.

For example, if a program has 1,800 occupied classroom "seats" in a given term, and 3,000 students in good standing, the level of enrollment was .67, an indication that honors class enrollment is somewhat below average, especially in upper-division classes. **UAB honors has a ratio of 1.13**, below the average of 1.30 for all programs.

**Average Class Size, Honors-only Sections (3.0):** Offered mostly in the first two years, honors-only classes tend to be smaller and, as the name implies, have no or very few students other than those in the honors program. These class sections always are much smaller than mixed or contract sections, or regular non-honors class sections in the university.

The average honors-only class size at the honors college is **25.8 students**. The average for all programs is **17.5 students.**

**Average Class Size, Overall (3.5):** The overall class calculation is based on the *proportion* of honors students in each type of class (honors-only, mixed honors, and honors contract sections). Thus it is not a raw average. The overall honors-credit class size is **25.8 students**, versus the average for all programs of **24.9 students**.

These class size averages also do not correspond to the number of students per honors section ratings above. The reason is that, in computing average class size metrics, we include enrollment in each 1-2-credit section, not just sections with 3 or more credits.

Since the UAB Honors College offers honors-only classes, there are no mixed and contract class sizes to report.

**Honors Grad Rate Adjusted to SAT (3.0):** The rating is the based on the actual grad rate for students who entered the program six years earlier, whether or not the students remained in honors. The **actual rate of 81.8%** is also compared to the rates of other programs with the same test score entry requirement range, and then adjusted upward if the program is performing above other programs in the same range, or downward if the performance is less than other programs in the same range. The rate here is slightly downward, to **80.6%.**

**Grad Rate Adjusted to Freshman Retention Rate (4.0):** This rate compares the actual grad rate above to a predicted grade rate when freshman retention rates are considered. The actual grad rate is **.49 points higher** than the predicted rate. For all programs, the actual grad rate is **.33 points lower** than the predicted rate.

**Ratio of Staff to Honors Students (4.0):** There is 1 staff member for every **115.1** students. (Mean ratio for all programs is 1 staff member for every **127.9** students.)

**Honors Residence Halls, Amenities (3.5):** The New Freshman Residence Hall at UAB has honors floors that house 453 first-year students. The coed residence has air-conditioned, two-person suites with a shared bath for suite occupants. Dining is very convenient at Commons on the Green. Each suite has a small refrigerator and a microwave.

**Honors Residence Halls, Availability (4.0):** This rating compares the number of occupants in honors residence halls to the number of honors freshman and sophomore members in good standing. The ratio for the college is **.51** places for each first- and second-year student. The median for all programs is .49 places.

**Prestigious Awards (3.0):** The awards that we track and include are listed in the section titled "Prestigious Scholarships." The awards are sometimes won by students who are not in an honors college or program, but increasingly many are enrolled in honors programs. It is also a trend that honors colleges and programs help to prepare their students for the awards competitions.

"The UAB Office of National and International Fellowships and Scholarships was established in 2012 to serve all UAB undergraduate and graduate students. It is housed within the UAB Honors College, and the staff includes a Director and Assistant Director. The initial priority was building a pipeline of students applying for nationally-competitive major fellowships, as well as building-block scholarships. In its first year of operation (2013), twenty-eight students applied for these awards. Just five years later (2018), the staff supported 107 applications with twenty-six winners and fifteen finalists, alternates, and/or honorable mentions.

"Since 2000, three UAB honors students have been awarded the Rhodes Scholarship, more than any other institution in the state of Alabama." UAB also has nine Truman Scholars. Since 2002, twenty-five of the university's 26 Goldwater Scholars have been selected, showing the strength of STEM-related programs at UAB. Students are also making gains in earning Fulbright awards for teaching or study abroad and National Science Foundation research grants for graduate work.

## UNRATED FEATURES

**Continuation and Honors Graduation GPA Requirement: 3.00.**

**Academic Strengths, National Rankings:** This is based on national rankings of *graduate* programs in all but engineering and business, where undergraduate rankings are used. One of the weaknesses of the *U.S. News* rankings is that they focus on too many wealth-related metrics while ignoring their own assessments of academic departments. The rankings listed below are for all universities, public or private.

The nationally ranked academic departments at UAB are biology (62); sociology (96); psychology (98); business (109); education (112); chemistry (122); physics (124); and engineering (137).

**Internships, Professional Development, Community Engagement:** "In addition to honors internships, service learning, and independent study, our students participate in a variety of non-credit experiential learning opportunities throughout the year. Our New Student Retreat includes a Day of Service where, in 2018, our 575 freshmen went to more than 20 service sites. Additionally, they participate in a City as Text activity where they explore neighborhoods in the Birmingham metro area. Honors College students join with the entire university community for Into the Streets Day of Service in October and March. Our student-led Honors College Leadership Council organizes a number of special projects and volunteer activities each year including donation drives for Blazer Kitchen and service days working with Jones Valley Urban Farm and Gear Up Alabama."

**Undergraduate Research:** "We offer the **Honors College Presidential Summer Fellowship** program in the summer, which provides stipends for undergraduate research, service-learning, and creative activity. The program also includes professional development workshops for students and culminates with poster and oral presentations at the UAB Summer Undergraduate Research Expo. For summer 2018, 28 students will be receiving fellowships.

- Each spring, the Honors College sponsors a trip to the **National Conference on Undergraduate Research (NCUR)**. 43 students attended the 2017 conference, and 50 students attended the 2018 conference.

- We also sponsor participation in the **National Collegiate Honors Council (NCHC)** and **Southern Regional Honors Council (SRHC)** undergraduate research conferences each year.

- In conjunction with our sister campuses, we participate and host the annual **University of Alabama System Honors Research Day.** This event brings together undergraduate researchers from UAB, The University of Alabama (UA), and The University of Alabama at Huntsville (UAH).

- We co-sponsor the **Honors Neuroscience Summer Research Academy** which offers intensive research experiences to rising junior and senior neuroscience students, providing them with practical skills for a future in research and expert support to apply to competitive graduate programs in biomedical research.

- Students may **earn honors credits for undergraduate research experiences** in the fall, spring, and summer semesters.

- Our Science and Technology Honors Program offers a unique four-year immersive experience focusing on undergraduate research and culminating in an honors thesis"

**Honors Study Abroad:** "In 2017, the UAB Honors College began offering an annual Honors Signature Study Abroad course open to all honors students of any level. In the inaugural year, our Dean taught an honors seminar on socioeconomic and political change in Cuba. In 2018, the seminar focused on sustainability and included a spring break trip to Iceland. Students may apply for need-based scholarships through the Honors College to help offset the costs of studying abroad. Our hope is that exposing students early to a short-term faculty-led study abroad experience will inspire them to seek out longer-term programs in the future."

**Financial Aid:**

*In-State Scholarships for 2018-2019*

**4-year awards based on ACT (or SAT equivalent) score and GPA:**

| In-State Scholarships for 2018-2019 | Annual Amount | Required Test Score | Required GPA |
|---|---|---|---|
| **Presidential Recognition*** | Tuition and fees | 30-36 ACT | 3.5 GPA or higher |
| **Collegiate Honors** | $5,500 | 27-29 ACT | 3.5 GPA or higher |
| | | 30-36 ACT | 3.0-3.49 GPA |
| **UAB Breakthrough** | $3,000 | 24-26 ACT | 3.5 GPA or higher |
| **UAB Academic Achievement** | $2,000 | 20-23 ACT | 3.5 GPA or higher |
| | | 24-29 ACT | |

*Out-of-State Scholarships*

**4-year awards based on ACT composite or redesigned SAT score and GPA:**

| Out-of-State Scholarships for 2018-2019 | Annual Amount | Required Test Score | Required GPA |
|---|---|---|---|
| | | | |
| **Blazer Elite** | $15,000 | 30-36 ACT or 1390+ | 3.5 GPA or higher |
| **Blazer Gold** | **$12,000** | **26-29 ACT or 1240-1380 SAT** | **3.5 GPA or higher** |
| **Blazer Pride** | $10,000 | 24-25 ACT or 1160-1230 SAT | 3.5 GPA or higher |
| | | 26-36 ACT or 1240-1600 SAT | 3.0-3.49 GPA |
| **Blazer Distinction** | $7,500 | 20-23 ACT or 1020-1150 SAT | 3.5 GPA or higher |
| | | 24-25 ACT or 1160-1230 SAT | 3.0-3.49 GPA |

National Merit Finalists and National Hispanic Recognition students receive the UAB Presidential Scholarship, which includes:

- Full tuition and academic fees (up to 15 credit hours per semester), for a total of 8 semesters (fall and spring only)

- A one-year on-campus housing award at the freshman rate for your first year

- A one-time $1,000 technology scholarship for the fall semester of your first year

- A one-time $2,500 stipend to be used for experiential learning, such as education abroad programs, internships, and co-ops.

**Honors Fees:** None.

**Placement of Honors Graduates:** 28% professional school, 38% graduate school, 29% employment, 3% special categories (Fulbright, Teach for America, Peace Corps, etc.), and 2% other/unreported.

**Degree of Difference**: This is difference between (1) the average SAT scores for recently enrolled honors students (1400) and (2) the average test scores for all students in the university (1240) as a whole. The difference may be an indication of how "elite" honors students may be perceived as compared to students in the university as a whole. **Please keep in mind that neither the high nor low selectivity of an honors program determines how effective the program may be.**

**NAME**: THE BURNETT HONORS COLLEGE

**Date Established:** The Honors Program: 1982; the Burnett Honors College: 1998

**Location**: Orlando, Florida

**University <u>Full-time Undergraduate</u> Enrollment (2017):** 55,776

**Honors Members in Good Standing**: 1,847; (mean size of all programs is 2,030).

**Honors <u>Average</u> Admission Test Score(s)**: ACT, 32.1; SAT, 1449.

**Average High School GPA/Class Rank:** 4.41, weighted; 78% in top tenth of high school class.

**<u>Basic</u> Admission Requirements:** None listed.

**Application Deadline(s):** *Please verify with each program, as some deadlines could change.* Priority deadline, postmarked application by January 15, 2019; March 31, 2019, postmark for regular deadline.

**Honors Programs with SAT scores from 1420—1461:** Auburn, Central Florida, Delaware, Iowa, Kansas, Mississippi, Missouri, New Jersey Inst of Technology, Penn State, South Florida, Vermont, Virginia Commonwealth.

**Administrative Staff:** 19 full-time, plus about 20 FTE part-time.

**RATINGS AT A GLANCE:** For all mortarboard ratings immediately below, a score of 5 is the maximum and represents a comparison with all rated honors colleges and programs. More detailed explanations follow the "mortarboard" ratings.

**PERCEPTION\* OF UNIVERSITY AS A WHOLE, <u>NOT</u> OF HONORS:** 🎓🎓🎓 1/2

*Perception is based on the university's ranking among public universities in the 2018 U.S. News Best Colleges report. Please bear in mind that the better the U.S. News ranking, the more difficult it is for an honors college or program to have a rating that equals or improves on the magazine ranking.

**OVERALL HONORS RATING:** 🎓🎓🎓🎓 1/2

**Curriculum Requirements:** 🎓🎓🎓 1/2

**Number of Honors Classes Offered:** 🎓🎓🎓🎓 1/2

**Number of Honors Classes in Key Disciplines:** 🎓🎓🎓🎓 1/2

**Extent of Honors Enrollment:** 🎓🎓🎓🎓

**Honors-only Class Size:** 👑👑👑👑👑

**Overall Class Size (Honors-only plus mixed, contract):** 👑👑👑👑 1/2

**Honors Grad Rate Adjusted to SAT:** 👑👑👑 1/2

**Grad Rate Adjusted to Freshman Retention Rate:** 👑👑👑

**Ratio of Staff to Students:** 👑👑👑👑 1/2

**Priority Registration: Yes,** honors students register with the class ahead.

**Honors Housing Amenities:** 👑👑👑👑👑

**Honors Housing Availability:** 👑👑👑👑

**Prestigious Awards:** 👑👑 1/2

## RATING SCORES AND EXPLANATIONS:

**Curriculum Requirements (3.5):** The most important rating category, the curriculum completion requirement (classes required to complete honors) defines not only what honors students should learn but also the extent to which honors students and faculty are connected in the classroom. If there is a thesis or capstone requirement, it reinforces the individual contact and research skills so important to learning.

The average number of honors semester hours required for completion across all programs is 30.0.

To meet the University Honors requirements at Burnett Honors College, a student must complete a 1-credit honors symposium and at least one 3-credit interdisciplinary seminar. In addition, students must complete 18-24 credits of departmental honors courses.

Honors in the Major requires a 3-credit reading course and a 3-credit thesis.

**AP/IB credits** are **not** counted as replacements for honors courses.

**No. Honors Classes Offered (4.5):** This is a measure of the total **adjusted** honors main sections available in the term reported, not including labs and thesis. An adjusted main section has 3 or more semester credits, or equivalent, and sections with fewer credits receive a lower prorated value.

The program offered a section for every **11.0** enrolled students. The average for all programs was **15.0**. The lower the number, the better.

In the term reported, an extremely impressive **98.4% of honors enrollment was in honors-only sections; only 1.6% was in mixed sections; and there were no contract sections.** For all programs under review, enrollment by type of honors section was 75.8% honors-only, 15.4 % mixed, and 8.8% contract.

**No. Honors Classes in Key Disciplines (4.5):** The 15 "key" disciplines are biological sciences; business (all); chemistry; communications (especially public speaking); computer science; economics; engineering (all); English; history; math (all); philosophy; physics; political science; psychology; and sociology, anthropology, and gender studies. Interdisciplinary sections, such as those often taken for General Education credit in the first two years, do receive a lesser, prorated discipline "credit" because they introduce students to multiple disciplines in an especially engaging way, often with in-depth discussion.

For this measure, mixed and contract sections are not counted as a section in a key discipline unless students taking the sections for honors credit make up at least 10% of the total section enrollment.

In the term reported, the honors college offered a section in a key discipline for every **15.1 honors students.** The average for all programs is **24.7.** The lower the number, the better.

Out of **99 adjusted sections in key disciplines, all but one were honors-only sections**. The most sections were in math, communications, and English, followed by biology, philosophy, physics, and psychology. The many course offerings covered every discipline.

The college is almost a pure example of a discipline-based honors program, with all honors courses other than honors symposia being offered through the academic departments.

**Extent of Honors Enrollment (4.0):** Not all honors students take an honors class each term, especially after the first two years. Programs that have fewer honors classes and thesis options for upper-division honors students will *generally* have fewer total members in good standing who are actually enrolled in a given term. (Please be aware, however, that honors students not enrolled in a class for a term are still tied to the honors community through residential and extracurricular activities.) *Our research shows that this measure is closely related to honors completion rates, i.e., the number of students who complete honors requirements by the time they graduate.*

For example, if a program has 1,800 individual students enrolled in a given term, and 3,000 students in good standing, the level of enrollment was .67, an indication that honors class enrollment is somewhat below average, especially in upper-division classes. Burnett Honors **has a ratio of 1.34**, above the average of 1.30 for all programs.

**Average Class Size, Honors-only Sections (5.0):** Offered mostly in the first two years, honors-only classes tend to be smaller and, as the name implies, have no or very few students other than those in the honors program. These class sections always are much smaller than mixed or contract sections, or regular non-honors class sections in the university.

The average honors-only class size at the honors college is **14.0 students**. The average for all programs is **17.5 students.**

**Average Class Size, Overall (4.5):** The overall class calculation is based on the *proportion* of honors students in each type of class (honors-only, mixed honors, and honors contract sections). Thus it is not a raw average. The overall honors-credit class size is **18.7 students**, versus the average for all programs of **24.9 students**.

These class size averages also do not correspond to the number of students per honors section ratings above. The reason is that, in computing average class size metrics, we include enrollment in each 1-2-credit section, not just sections with 3 or more credits.

Along with an honors-only class size of 14.0 students (listed above), the program's single mixed honors section was quite large, **310 students.** There were no contract sections. Across all programs, the average mixed honors section has 68.6 students.

**Honors Grad Rate Adjusted to SAT (3.5):** The rating is the based on the actual grad rate for students who entered the program six years earlier, whether or not the students remained in honors. The **actual rate of 85.2%** is also compared to the rates of other programs with the same test score entry requirement range, and then adjusted upward if the program is performing above other programs in the same range, or downward if the performance is less than other programs in the same range. The rate here is slightly downward, to **84.9%.**

**Grad Rate Adjusted to Freshman Retention Rate (3.0):** This rate compares the actual grad rate above to a predicted grade rate when freshman retention rates are considered. The actual grad rate is **3.1 points lower** than the predicted rate. For all programs, the actual grad rate is **.33 points lower** than the predicted rate.

**Ratio of Staff to Honors Students (4.5):** There is 1 staff member for every **89.7** students. (Mean ratio for all programs is 1 staff member for every **127.9** students.)

**Honors Residence Halls, Amenities (5.0):** More than 80% of honors students living in honors housing reside in Tower III, with the Towers at Knights Plaza. Tower III features air-conditioned apartments with kitchens, for both freshmen and upperclassmen. Dining is not on site, but it is within the Towers community.

The remaining students (all upperclassmen) who live in honors housing live in the Lake Claire Apartments, air-conditioned with a kitchen in each apartment. The most convenient dining for Lake Claire is Knightros.

**Honors Residence Halls, Availability (4.0):** This rating compares the number of rooms in honors residence halls to the number of honors freshman and sophomore members in good standing. The ratio for the college is **.53** places for each first- and second-year student. The median for all programs is .49 places.

**Prestigious Awards (2.5):** The awards that we track and include are listed in the section titled "Prestigious Scholarships." The awards are sometimes won by students who are not in an honors college or program, but increasingly many are enrolled in honors programs. It is also a trend that honors colleges and programs help to prepare their students for the awards competitions.

UCF students are beginning to win more Fulbright and NSF graduate research fellowships, and Burnett Honors students have two of the university's four Astronaut Scholarships. To date, UCF students have earned seven Goldwater Scholarships for undergraduate excellence in the STEM disciplines.

## UNRATED FEATURES

**Continuation and Honors Graduation GPA Requirement:**

**University Honors:** 3.20 UCF GPA and 3.00 Honors GPA
**Honors in the Major:** 3.40 overall GPA, 3.20 UCF GPA

**Academic Strengths, National Rankings:** This is based on national rankings of *graduate* programs in all but engineering and business, where undergraduate rankings are used. One of the weaknesses of the *U.S. News* rankings is that they focus on too many wealth-related metrics while ignoring their own assessments of academic departments. The rankings listed below are for all universities, public or private.

The nationally ranked academic departments at UCF are physics (61); computer science, and engineering (82); education (89); sociology (102); psychology (112); and chemistry (122).

**Internships, Professional Development, Community Engagement:** The university conducts a survey of students about to graduate. Students list the areas in which they have been most involved. A plurality listed "Participated in Organizations Related to Major," followed by almost as many who listed "Other UCF Clubs and Organizations," "Community Service and Volunteer Work," and "Completed an Internship, Field Experience, or Clinical Assignment." A very sizable percentage also held leadership roles in student government or some other organization.

**Undergraduate Research:** "The Burnett Honors College strongly nurtures and supports undergraduate research. Over $90,000 are awarded annually to Honors students who pursue research projects.

"While the University Honors program does not include a research requirement, Honors students can apply for the Honors in the Major program and other research opportunities on and off campus. The Office of Honors Research oversees and facilitates two structured research programs that focus on student development and enrichment: Honors in the Major and Burnett Research Scholars. Both of these programs are available to students regardless of discipline.

"Honors in the Major is the oldest and most prestigious undergraduate research program at the University of Central Florida. Honors in the Major provides students the opportunity to engage in independent and original research as principal investigators. Over the course of at least two semesters, students research, write, defend, and publish an original Honors thesis that serves as the capstone project of their undergraduate career. Upon completion of the thesis, students earn Honors in the Major distinction on their diplomas and final transcripts."

**Honors Study Abroad:** The Burnett Honors College encourages service learning along with foreign travel. The South Africa Conservation "program focuses on animal conservation at the Kariega Big 5

Game Reserve. For eight days, students will be involved in projects such as elephant impact monitoring, lion prey selection monitoring, rhino monitoring, cataloging birds, game count for age and sex, alien vegetation control, soil erosion control, and game capture. Two days will be spent working with a local school. Weekends will be filled with cultural exploration field trips."

"The South Africa Sustainability Program involves travel to a community center located in the Intabazwe Township just outside of the city of Harrismith. Last year, we constructed a new brick and mortar community center supplied with solar and wind power. This provides a place for young children to come to learn and a place for the hungry to come and eat."

Other special programs involve travel to Brazil, Nicaragua, or Chiapas, Mexico.

Honors students who meet the requirements listed below can apply for the President's Scholarship. This scholarship has two award levels depending on program costs. For South Africa, the scholarship award is $2,000. For Nicaragua and Mexico the scholarship award is $1,000. To be eligible for a President's Scholarship, applicants must meet the following requirements:

- President's Scholarship has not been awarded before.

- No more than 80 credit hours completed by the end of the spring semester prior to travel.

- Minimum overall GPA of 3.6 (freshmen grades will be looked at in December)

- 500 word essay commenting of the following quote from Paul Theroux: "Tourists don't know where they've been, travelers don't know where they're going."

Honors Short-term Study Abroad Scholarships

Honors students who are not eligible for the President's Scholars Program can apply for a $500-$1,000 Honors Spring Study Abroad Scholarship. These scholarships are awarded competitively and the award level depends on program costs. These scholarships can be applied towards any study abroad program.

**Financial Aid:** UCF, like other major universities in Florida, offers the **full ride Benacquisto Scholarship**. "This program will provide funds for 100 percent of the number of credit hours required to complete a baccalaureate degree program, or until completion of a baccalaureate degree program, whichever comes first.

"A student is eligible to receive an award for a maximum of 10 semesters or 15 quarters. A student must maintain enrollment at the institution where the student was initially funded in order to maintain scholarship eligibility.

"Eligible students will receive an annual award equal to the institutional cost of attendance (COA), minus the sum of the Bright Futures (BF) award and National Merit®/Achievement Award® (NM).

"**Out-of-state students** will receive an award equal to the in-state on-campus cost of attendance, minus their National Merit award. These students are exempt from paying the out-of-state fees."

"For an automatic renewal, an award recipient will have:

- Earned credit for **all** hours enrolled by the regular drop/add period **each** term.

- Earned a minimum cumulative GPA of 3.0 on a 4.0 scale."

The Honors College website lists *many* additional scholarships.

"The top scholarships at UCF are awarded to: National Merit Scholars, National Hispanic Scholars, Provost Scholars (fewer than 10% of the entering freshmen), and Freshmen Pegasus Award (fewer than 25% of the entering freshmen)

"The Burnett Honors College awards about 15 Honors Enhancement Scholarships for incoming freshmen for the first year.

"The Burnett Honors College also awards a multitude of grants and scholarships designed to support students' co-curricular pursuits (~ $200,000/year).

**Honors Fees:** None.

**Placement of Honors Graduates:**

**Health/Medical Professional Schools:** University of Florida, University of Pittsburgh, UCF College of Medicine, Johns Hopkins Medical School, University of Tennessee, University of Chicago, Oregon State University, University of South Carolina, Case Western Reserve, University of Miami.

**PhD/Masters Programs:** UCF, Florida State University, Johns Hopkins, North Carolina State University, University of Florida, Indiana University, Texas A&M, University of South Carolina, UCLA, Rutgers University, Rennselaer Polytechnic Institute, George Washington University, University of Colorado, University of Denver, University of Washington, University of Georgia, Virginia Tech.

**Law Schools:** Harvard, College of William and Mary, University of Virginia, Boston University, Florida State University, University of Florida, University of Miami, American University, NYU, Columbia, Duke, Vanderbilt, University of Chicago, University of Pennsylvania, UC Berkeley, Emory, Washington University – St. Louis, University of Georgia, University of Southern California, UT Austin, University of Alabama, Boston College.

**Employment:** Air Force Materiel Command HQ, Microsoft, Northrop Grumman, Lockheed Martin, Texas Instruments, Harris Corporation, Siemens, Mitsubishi Hitachi Power Systems, USPS, Walt Disney World, Orlando Regional Medical Center, Orlando Health, Florida Hospital, Sun Trust Banks.

**Degree of Difference**: This is difference between (1) the average SAT scores for recently enrolled honors students (1449) and (2) the average test scores for all students in the university (1320) as a whole. The difference may be an indication of how "elite" honors students may be perceived as compared to students in the university as a whole. **Please keep in mind that neither the high nor low selectivity of an honors program determines how effective the program may be.**

**NAME**: THE HONORS COLLEGE OF THE UNIVERSITY OF SOUTH FLORIDA

**Date Established:** Program, 1983; College, 2002

**Location**: Tampa, Florida

**University Full-time Undergraduate Enrollment (2017):** 31,461

**Honors Members in Good Standing**: 2,282 (mean size of all programs is 2,030).

**Honors Average Admission Test Score(s)**: ACT, 30.53; SAT, 1461.

**Average High School GPA/Class Rank:** 4.34, weighted.

**Basic Admission Requirements:** ACT, 30; SAT, 1370; GPA, 4.00.

**Application Deadline(s):** *Please verify with each program, as some deadlines could change.* Priority Application Deadline: December 1. Second Application Deadline: March 1. Late Application Deadline: April 1

**Honors Programs with SAT scores from 1420—1461:** Auburn, Central Florida, Delaware, Iowa, Kansas, Mississippi, Missouri, New Jersey Inst of Technology, Penn State, South Florida, Vermont, Virginia Commonwealth.

**Administrative Staff:** 33 plus graduate assistants.

**RATINGS AT A GLANCE:** For all mortarboard ratings immediately below, a score of 5 is the maximum and represents a comparison with all rated honors colleges and programs. More detailed explanations follow the "mortarboard" ratings.

**PERCEPTION\* OF UNIVERSITY AS A WHOLE, NOT OF HONORS:** 🎓🎓🎓 1/2

\*Perception is based on the university's ranking among public universities in the 2018 U.S. News Best Colleges report. Please bear in mind that the better the U.S. News ranking, the more difficult it is for an honors college or program to have a rating that equals or improves on the magazine ranking.

**OVERALL HONORS RATING:** 🎓🎓🎓

**Curriculum Requirements:** 🎓🎓 1/2

**Number of Honors Classes Offered:** 🎓🎓🎓 1/2

**Number of Honors Classes in Key Disciplines:** 🎓🎓 1/2

**Extent of Honors Enrollment:** 🎓🎓🎓

**Honors-only Class Size:** 👒👒👒👒

**Overall Class Size (Honors-only plus mixed, contract):** 👒👒👒👒👒

**Honors Grad Rate Adjusted to SAT:** 👒👒 1/2

**Grad Rate Adjusted to Freshman Retention Rate:** 👒👒 1/2

**Ratio of Staff to Students:** 👒👒👒👒👒

**Priority Registration: Yes,** honors students register for all courses, honors and otherwise, with the first group of students during each year they are in the program.

**Honors Housing Amenities:** 👒👒👒👒 1/2

**Honors Housing Availability:** 👒👒👒

**Prestigious Awards:** 👒👒👒

**RATING SCORES AND EXPLANATIONS:**

**Curriculum Requirements (2.5** The most important rating category, the curriculum completion requirement (classes required to complete honors) defines not only what honors students should learn but also the extent to which honors students and faculty are connected in the classroom. If there is a thesis or capstone requirement, it reinforces the individual contact and research skills so important to learning.

The average number of honors semester hours required for completion across all programs is 30.0.

Completion of the **Discovery Track I** option requires at least 18 honors credits, including 12 credits of coursework and a 6-credit thesis. Students must also complete at least 50 hours of community service. Also required are Two Global Learning experiences, chosen from the options below:
- Levels 1 and 2 of a foreign language through coursework or demonstrated proficiency Levels 3 and 4 of a foreign language
- Any Honors or Ed Abroad international trip
- Participation in Honors International Day as a presenter (this is an annual event where international students share their experiences living/studying in the United States while domestic students can report back about their study abroad experiences)
- Service as a GloBull Ambassador via Ed Abroad for two semester
- 75 hours of globally focused research tracked via the Office of Undergraduate Research (e.g. looking at women's education worldwide)

- Complete one of the following cultural minor or certificate programs: Africana Literatures, Asian Studies, India Studies, International Studies, Italian Studies, Latin American and Caribbean Studies, Linguistics, Religious Studies, or Russian Studies

The **Discovery Track II** option requires 15-18 credits, including 12 honors course credits and 3-6 departmental honors credits, including a thesis. The community service and Global Learning requirements are the same as above.

The **Innovation Track** requires 15 course credits and a 3-credit capstone project including supervised group research. The community service and Global Learning requirements are also the same as the options above.

**AP/IB credits** are **not** counted as replacements for honors courses.

**No. Honors Classes Offered (3.5):** This is a measure of the total **adjusted** honors main sections available in the term reported, not including labs and thesis. An adjusted main section has 3 or more semester credits, or equivalent, and sections with fewer credits receive a lower prorated value.

USF Honors offered a section for every **19.8** enrolled students. The average for all programs was **15.0**. The lower the number, the better. In the term reported, **ALL** honors enrollment was **in honors-only sections or activities.** For all programs under review, enrollment by type of honors section was 75.8% honors-only, 15.4 % mixed, and 8.8% contract.

**No. Honors Classes in Key Disciplines (2.5):** The 15 "key" disciplines are biological sciences; business (all); chemistry; communications (especially public speaking); computer science; economics; engineering (all); English; history; math (all); philosophy; physics; political science; psychology; and sociology, anthropology, and gender studies. Interdisciplinary sections, such as those often taken for General Education credit in the first two years, do receive a lesser, prorated discipline "credit" because they introduce students to multiple disciplines in an especially engaging way, often with in-depth discussion.

For this measure, mixed and contract sections are not counted as a section in a key discipline unless students taking the sections for honors credit make up at least 10% of the total section enrollment.

In the term reported, the program offered a section in a key discipline for every **45.0 honors students.** The average for all programs is **24.7**. The lower the number, the better.

**Note:** USF Honors is focused on four things: interdisciplinary learning, mostly seminars; research and thesis/capstone work; community service experiences; and global learning (see curriculum requirements, above). The program does not offer honors sections in the academic disciplines. This means that, in terms of our methodology, we can only assign a standard percentage to seminar sections (see above). On the other hand, as one can read below, the seminar categories do encompass different ranges of disciplines. Out of **78 seminar sections, all were honors-only sections.**

The interdisciplinary sections include courses in six broad discipline categories: Acquisition of Knowledge (29 sections); Arts/Humanities Honors (7); Natural Sciences Honors (6); Social/Behavioral Sciences Honors (10); Seminar in Applied Ethics (6); and Global Perspectives-Honors (14).

An example of an Acquisition of Knowledge section: "Collectively, these writings [Plato, Descartes, Hume] serve as a strong foundation for further readings and the exploration of more contemporary philosophies and viewpoints from the 19th century to present times. While it is our desire for you to thoroughly understand the fundamentals of each of these philosopher's viewpoints, it is also important that you develop your reading skills, learning how to read critically from original sources while you extract the basic arguments and supporting evidence."

From the Natural Sciences Honors sections, here is another example, the course "Climate Change Science." Part of the course description: "This course is devoted to building a scientific understanding of human-caused climate change that reaches across disciplinary boundaries. What does an informed, educated, and engaged global citizen need to know about the science of climate change? Course topics include fancy-sounding concepts like climate forcings, the greenhouse effect, energy imbalance, feedback, scientific reasoning, and the effects and evidence of climate change across multiple domains."

**In sum, even though USF Honors is "interdisciplinary" and does not have a high score in this rating category, our view is that the Honors College has an outstanding series of seminars that do in fact combine disciplinary perspectives in a well-designed and extremely effective manner. The principal decision for prospective students is do they want the breadth and liveliness of interdisciplinary seminars more than they want honors courses in, say, math, physics, or biology. Of course some programs have a blend of courses, but many emphasize either departmental courses or seminars.**

USF Honors is a classic **core interdisciplinary** program.

**Extent of Honors Enrollment (3.0):** Not all honors students take an honors class each term, especially after the first two years. Programs that have fewer honors classes and thesis options for upper-division honors students will *generally* have fewer total members in good standing who are actually enrolled in a given term. (Please be aware, however, that honors students not enrolled in a class for a term are still tied to the honors community through residential and extracurricular activities.) *Our research shows that this measure is closely related to honors completion rates, i.e., the number of students who complete honors requirements by the time they graduate.*

For example, if a program has 1,800 individual students enrolled in a given term, and 3,000 students in good standing, the level of enrollment was .67, an indication that honors class enrollment is somewhat below average, especially in upper-division classes. **USF Honors has a ratio of .71**, below the average of 1.30 for all programs. **Note: Again, a core interdisciplinary program typically does not receive high ratings in some categories because of the emphasis on seminars in the first two years, followed by non-classroom work (thesis/capstone).**

**Average Class Size, Honors-only Sections (4.0):** Offered mostly in the first two years, honors-only classes tend to be smaller and, as the name implies, have no or very few students other than those in the honors program. These class sections always are much smaller than mixed or contract sections, or regular non-honors class sections in the university.

The average honors-only class size at USF Honors is **17.2 students**. The average for all programs is **17.5 students.**

**Average Class Size, Overall (5.0):** The overall class calculation is based on the *proportion* of honors students in each type of class (honors-only, mixed honors, and honors contract sections). Thus it is not a raw average. The overall honors-credit class size is **17.2 students**, versus the average for all programs of **24.9 students**.

These class size averages also do not correspond to the number of students per honors section ratings above. The reason is that, in computing average class size metrics, we include enrollment in each 1-2-credit section, not just sections with 3 or more credits.

USF Honors has offers honors-only classes exclusive, with an average enrollment of 17.2 students (listed above; there are no mixed honors section (average size, 68.6 students) and no contract sections (average size 56.6 students).

**Honors Grad Rate Adjusted to SAT (2.5):** The rating is the based on the actual grad rate for students who entered the program six years earlier, whether or not the students remained in honors. The **actual rate of 80.8%** is also compared to the rates of other programs with the same test score entry requirement range, and then adjusted upward if the program is performing above other programs in the same range, or downward if the performance is less than other programs in the same range. The rate here is downward, to **76.4%.**

**Grad Rate Adjusted to Freshman Retention Rate (2.5):** This rate compares the actual grad rate above to a predicted grade rate when freshman retention rates are considered. The actual grad rate is **8.54 points lower** than the predicted rate. For all programs, the actual grad rate is **.33 points lower** than the predicted rate.

**Ratio of Staff to Honors Students (5.0):** There is 1 staff member for every **66.7** students. (Mean ratio for all programs is 1 staff member for every **127.9** students.)

**Honors Residence Halls, Amenities (4.5):** "The Honors LLC is a residential experience that offers a close-knit community of high-achieving students while celebrating the intellectual diversity of the Honors College.

"It is housed in Summit Hall, one of two residence halls that opened in Fall 2107 in The Village, a campus residential community. The Village offers state-of-the-art dining and fitness facilities, and a new Publix supermarket is under construction on the site. Summit has traditional- and suite-style rooms where Honors majors from across campus live and learn together.

"Summit also features an Honors Faculty-in-Residence, an Honors programming director, and an Honors Graduate Assistant." The hall, opened in 2017, has 59% traditional double rooms and 41% suite-style rooms. Dining is at The Hub.

"To encourage student development in a broad range of interests, the Honors LLC has created two themed common spaces: Educate and Create, and Build and Innovate. Regardless of major, students can explore everything from film and music education to architecture and software development. "

**Honors Residence Halls, Availability (3.0):** This rating compares the number of occupants in honors residence halls to the number of honors freshman and sophomore members in good standing. The ratio for

the program is **.25** places for each first- and second-year students. The median for all programs is .49 places.

**Prestigious Awards (3.0):** The awards that we track and include are listed in the section titled "Prestigious Scholarships." The awards are sometimes won by students who are not in an honors college or program, but increasingly many are enrolled in honors programs. It is also a trend that honors colleges and programs help to prepare their students for the awards competitions.

"The University of South Florida created an Office of National Scholarships to serve the entire university in 2010; the office is housed in the Honors College and the director and his staff of 5 report to the dean. In its first year of existence, ONS supported 11 student national award winners university-wide; in 2016-17, a total 66 USF students won national awards. Of these 66, 22 were Honors College students.

Since 2010, USF students have won a number of the most prestigious awards, including the Goldwater (16), Marshall (1), Truman (5), Gates Cambridge (1), NSF GRFP (117), Udall (3), and Gilman (115) awards. Of these, 53 have been Honors College students.

*"We have been particularly successful in winning student Fulbright awards; with 10 awarded in 2016-17, USF led the state of Florida and qualified as a national high-producing institution* (although one of our students declined the award for personal reasons, so our official count was 9). [We] would also note that USF led the nation in faculty Fulbrights in 16-17.)"

**UNRATED FEATURES**

**Continuation and Honors Graduation GPA Requirement:** 2.75 to continue; 3.25 to graduate with honors.

**Academic Strengths, National Rankings:** This is based on national rankings of *graduate* programs in all but engineering and business, where undergraduate rankings are used. One of the weaknesses of the *U.S. News* rankings is that they focus on too many wealth-related metrics while ignoring their own assessments of academic departments. The rankings listed below are for all universities, public or private.

The nationally ranked academic departments at USF are industrial and organizational psychology (2); public health (16); audiology (17); criminology (22); library and information studies (28); rehabilitation counseling (24); industrial/manufacturing engineering (39); clinical psychology (50).

**Internships, Professional Development, Community Engagement:** "The Honors College this year appointed a full-time Instructor whose assignment includes developing and managing our growing portfolio of internships and volunteer projects. *Our students want and need these experiences in order to distinguish themselves from other applicants for graduate work and desirable jobs.* They gain valuable experience, demonstrate initiative and drive, and build connections in their chosen fields. These are non-credit activities; some internships are paid, and some are not.

"We work with a wide range of off-campus partners in Florida and across the country to establish these opportunities for our students. Current examples include internships with: the Florida legislature for political science majors; a major biological research station near the Everglades for environmental science majors; a large Tampa law firm for students interested in a legal career; the Institute of Political Journalism in D.C. for mass communication and related majors; the Alzheimer's Association for pre-health and natural science majors; Oak Ridge laboratory for natural science majors; a community health initiative in the Dominican Republic for pre-health students; a firm manufacturing prosthetics for engineering and pre-health majors; health clinics around the Tampa Bay area for students in social work and pre-health programs; the Tampa Museum of Art for art and humanities majors—and many more."

**Undergraduate Research:** "The Office of Undergraduate Research is not part of the Honors College, reporting instead to the Dean of Undergraduate Studies, but the director holds a faculty appointment in the College and works closely with our faculty and advisors to facilitate and promote research among Honors students." The Honors College requires an honors thesis or capstone for all completion options.

**Honors Study Abroad:** "The Honors College believes study abroad is an integral part of developing global citizenship, a part of the University of South Florida's strategic plan. 13% of Honors College students studied abroad at some point in 2016-17.

"In 2017-18 we are sponsoring eight study abroad programs within the Honors College, taught by Honors faculty exclusively for Honors students, in several formats."

> •Beyond the Classroom: In this model, students take a three-hour course during Spring semester on campus, learning about the history, culture, politics, and economy of another country. Then the entire class travels to that country for a three-week cultural immersion after final exams. This allows the lessons learned in class to come alive through personal experience. Current courses focus on Germany, Argentina, Peru, and Japan; previous courses in this format have focused on Britain, France, and India.
> •Summer Programs: Dean Adams travels to London each summer to teach an interdisciplinary course for Honors students for four weeks in the USF in London program. Other summer programs visit Vietnam ("Energy Sustainability in Developing Nations") and Thailand (a service program at a shelter for at-risk girls). In these models, students enroll in Honors courses on site during summer term.
> •Service Breaks: In order to allow every student to fit study abroad into their academic curriculum, we offer service breaks during Spring Break, Summer, and Winter Break. Students travel to Latin America and the Caribbean to work with service organizations and get a taste of another culture. These programs typically include a home-stay so students can integrate into the community as much as possible.

"Honors College study abroad programs are funded 50-75% by generous donors, making study abroad an affordable option for many students. About $417,000 was expended from Foundation accounts in 2016-17 to support student travel internationally.

"In 2017, the Honors College was awarded two Global Achievement Awards by USF World for the work done by academic advisors in support of the university's mission."

**Financial Aid:** "The Honors College provides scholarship incentives to reward students for meeting stated competencies considered integral to an honors education. Students are awarded scholarships for demonstrating competencies in community engagement, global awareness, and research.

"In addition, the College manages about 20 privately-funded scholarships for honors students. The College awards about $165,000 annually to Honors College students through these scholarships, which are based on both merit and financial need.

*"The University of South Florida Office of Admissions, in partnership with the Honors College, provides* **scholarships that cover the full cost of attendance for National Merit Scholars**. National Hispanic Scholars receive $20,000 ($5,000 per year), and a study abroad scholarship."

**Honors Fees:** None.

**Placement of Honors Graduates:** "We have not kept systemic records of placement until very recently. We expect to have more data in this regard for the next publication."

**Degree of Difference**: This is difference between (1) the average SAT scores for recently enrolled honors students (1461) and (2) the average test scores for all students in the university (1230) as a whole. The difference may be an indication of how "elite" honors students may be perceived as compared to students in the university as a whole. **Please keep in mind that neither the high nor low selectivity of an honors program determines how effective the program may be.**

**NAME**: PLAN II HONORS PROGRAM, UNIVERSITY OF TEXAS AT AUSTIN

**Date Established:** 1935

**Location**: Austin, Texas 1440-

**University Full-time Undergraduate Enrollment (2017):** 40,468

**Honors Members in Good Standing**: 730 (mean size of all programs is 2,030).

**Honors Average Admission Test Score(s)**: ACT, 33; SAT, est.1446-1490.

**Average High School GPA/Class Rank:** Top 5%-10% of high school class.

**Basic Admission Requirements:** Plan II definitely applies a "holistic" approach to admissions. The program requires a short answer response, a five-sentence personal statement, and an expanded resume, in addition to test scores, transcripts, etc. Plan II seeks students with special experiences, talents, and insights, and these characteristics likely play a larger role in admissions than in other honors programs.

**Application Deadline(s):** *Please verify with each program, as some deadlines could change.* May apply beginning August 1, 2018; recommended deadline is November 1, 2018, but final deadline is December 1, 2018. Applications are reviewed in the order in which they are accepted.

**Honors Programs with SAT scores 1471—1510:** Clemson, Georgia, Illinois, Minnesota, Oklahoma, Rutgers, South Carolina, UT Austin.

**Administrative Staff:** 9 full-time and 3 part-time.

**RATINGS AT A GLANCE:** For all mortarboard ratings immediately below, a score of 5 is the maximum and represents a comparison with all rated honors colleges and programs. More detailed explanations follow the "mortarboard" ratings.

**PERCEPTION\* OF UNIVERSITY AS A WHOLE, NOT OF HONORS:** 🎓🎓🎓🎓🎓

\*Perception is based on the university's ranking among public universities in the 2018 U.S. News Best Colleges report. Please bear in mind that the better the U.S. News ranking, the more difficult it is for an honors college or program to have a rating that equals or improves on the magazine ranking.

**OVERALL HONORS RATING:** 🎓🎓🎓🎓🎓

**Curriculum Requirements:** 🎓🎓🎓🎓🎓

**Number of Honors Classes Offered:** 🎓🎓🎓🎓

**Number of Honors Classes in Key Disciplines:** 🎓🎓🎓🎓1/2

**Extent of Honors Enrollment:** 🎓🎓🎓🎓1/2

**Honors-only Class Size:** 🎓🎓🎓1/2

**Overall Class Size (Honors-only plus mixed, contract):** 🎓🎓🎓🎓1/2

**Honors Grad Rate Adjusted to SAT:** 🎓🎓🎓1/2

**Grad Rate Adjusted to Freshman Retention Rate:** 🎓🎓🎓

**Ratio of Staff to Students:** 🎓🎓🎓🎓1/2

**Priority Registration: Limited:** "Plan II students are guaranteed to get Plan II classes, with provisions. Although Plan II first-year students are not guaranteed to get in exactly the first-year World Literature class or exactly the first-year Signature course of their choosing, they are guaranteed to get one of each."

**Honors Housing Amenities:** 🎓🎓🎓

**Honors Housing Availability:** 🎓🎓🎓🎓

**Prestigious Awards:** 🎓🎓🎓🎓🎓

## RATING SCORES AND EXPLANATIONS:

**Curriculum Requirements (5.0):** The most important rating category, the curriculum completion requirement (classes required to complete honors) defines not only what honors students should learn but also the extent to which honors students and faculty are connected in the classroom. If there is a thesis or capstone requirement, it reinforces the individual contact and research skills so important to learning.

The average number of honors semester hours required for completion across all programs is 30.0. Completion of the Plan II major requires approximately 42 Plan II course credits and another 3 credits in an elective.

"The Plan II Honors Program is a four-year curriculum, designed to build up a student's skills and expertise from one year to the next, culminating in a senior thesis project that is the capstone of the student's undergraduate career.

*"Typically, a student's semester schedule consists of about one-third Plan II courses, leaving room to pursue courses in a second major, degree, or area of specialization (like pre-med) if the student desires. However, Plan II is a major all on its own, and Plan II students do not have to select a second major or degree.* Being "Purely Plan II" allows students maximum flexibility to customize their course of study and incorporate experiences like Study Abroad."

Below is the official explanation of the curriculum requirements:

**World Literature**—This yearlong course is required of all Plan II first-year students and is of central importance in the curriculum. Students may not place out of this course. It is conducted as a seminar, with emphasis on discussion, and is a writing-intensive course= 6 credits.

**First-Year Plan II**—All freshmen take one Plan II Signature course in the fall or spring. The emphasis in these seminars is on discussion, critical thinking, and writing. Faculty from across the campus are specially selected to teach these courses. Recent seminar topics include "Philosophy and Emotions," "Right and Wrong in Politics," and "Shakespeare and Film"= 3 credits.

**Social Science 301**—This course is offered under several disciplines and is usually taken the second year, first or second semester. The content involves contemporary social issues, and students may select from economics, anthropology, government or psychology= 3 credits.

**Second-Year Philosophy: Problems of Knowledge and Valuation**—This yearlong course is also taken in the second year. Using ancient and modern texts, students usually consider problems in ethics, political theory, metaphysics, and epistemology= 6 credits.

**Non-U.S. History**—Two courses in the same geographical area are required: one from an older period of the area's history and the other from a more recent period. *Many elect to take a Western Civilization sequence which is designed for Plan II students, but students are free to take history sequences from other non-U.S. geographic areas (e.g., Africa, Asia, Europe, Latin America and the Middle East)= 6 credits.*

**Math and Science**—All students in Liberal Arts must take 18 hours of math and science. Twelve of these 18 hours are prescribed as follows for Plan II students:

- Plan II Logic (PHL 313Q) or Plan II Modes of Reasoning (TC 310)

- Mathematics for Plan II students (M 310P), or credit for an approved calculus sequence

- Physics for Plan II students (PHY 321)

- Biology for Plan II students (BIO 301E)

The above count for 12 credits.

**Foreign Language Requirement**—Proficiency through the fourth semester is required. Students may place out of some or all of the requirement.

**Junior Seminars**—Plan II students take two seminars in the junior year. Similar in format and approach to the first-year seminars, the junior seminars often require term papers. Recent seminar topics include "Beauty and Politics," "Freedom of Expression," "Psychology and Religion," and "Lawyers, Ethics and Justice"= 6 credits.

**Humanities/Fine Arts**—One course in one of the following:

- Art History from an approved list

- Music History from an approved list

- Theatre & Dance History from an approved list

**AP/IB credits are counted** as replacements for honors courses, as follows: A score of 5 can count for the first biology class; a score of 4 or 5 can count for one course in western civilization or European history.

**No. Honors Classes Offered (4.0):** This is a measure of the total **adjusted** honors main sections available in the term reported, not including labs and thesis. An adjusted main section has 3 or more semester credits, or equivalent, and sections with fewer credits receive a lower prorated value.

The program offered a section for every **12.8** enrolled students. The average for all programs was **15.0**. The lower the number, the better. In the term reported an extremely impressive, **100%** of Plan II- honors enrollment was **in honors-only sections.** For all programs under review, enrollment by type of honors section was 75.8% honors-only, 15.4 % mixed, and 8.8% contract.

**No. Honors Classes in Key Disciplines (4.5):** The 15 "key" disciplines are biological sciences; business (all); chemistry; communications (especially public speaking); computer science; economics; engineering (all); English; history; math (all); philosophy; physics; political science; psychology; and sociology, anthropology, and gender studies. Interdisciplinary sections, such as those often taken for General Education credit in the first two years, do receive a lesser, prorated discipline "credit" because they introduce students to multiple disciplines in an especially engaging way, often with in-depth discussion.

For this measure, mixed and contract sections are not counted as a section in a key discipline unless students taking the sections for honors credit make up at least 10% of the total section enrollment.

In the term reported, the program offered a section in a key discipline for every **17.0 honors students.** The average for all programs is **24.7**. The lower the number, the better.

Out of **34 adjusted sections in key disciplines, all were honors-only sections**. The most sections were Plan II philosophy, English, and biology, followed by history, calculus, and physics. It should be noted that Plan II majors receive a degree in Plan II, but can also graduate with a Plan II degree in business honors and engineering. The UT Business Honors Program alone offers more than a dozen sections each term, and many Plan II majors also complete the BHP, as many as 55 or 60 in a given term. Neither the BHP courses nor any other courses are included in this metric. Finally, Plan II students can complete honors requirements in most of the university's other honors tracks, including Dean's Scholars, Health Science Scholars, Polymathic Scholars, and Turing Scholars. A very high percentage of Plan II students pursue additional majors.

Plan II students also enrolled in 21 first-year and junior seminars. One example is "Honors Social Science: Economics." Requiring calculus and "probably statistics" as prerequisites, the course provides "an introduction to modern decision theory, in which mathematical methods of statistics and economics are integrated with findings from psychology. The course will offer tools for improving individual decision making, avoiding mistakes when taking calculated risks, and better understanding the decisions of others." Examples of junior seminars included "Law and Ethics of Climate Change," "Doctor, Patient, Society, Culture," and "Understanding Human Evolution."

The combination of seminars and courses in the disciplines makes the program unusual. Mostly it is a core honors program, but its core includes classes in math and the sciences, along with multiple seminars, to much greater extent than other core programs.

**Extent of Honors Enrollment (4.5):** Not all honors students take an honors class each term, especially after the first two years. Programs that have fewer honors classes and thesis options for upper-division honors students will *generally* have fewer total members in good standing who are actually enrolled in a given term. (Please be aware, however, that honors students not enrolled in a class for a term are still tied to the honors community through residential and extracurricular activities.) *Our research shows that this measure is closely related to honors completion rates, i.e., the number of students who complete honors requirements by the time they graduate.*

For example, if a program has 1,800 individual students enrolled in a given term, and 3,000 students in good standing, the level of enrollment was .67, an indication that honors class enrollment is somewhat below average, especially in upper-division classes. **Plan II Honors has a ratio of 1.54**, above the average of 1.30 for all programs.

**Average Class Size, Honors-only Sections (3.5):** Offered mostly in the first two years, honors-only classes tend to be smaller and, as the name implies, have no or very few students other than those in the honors program. These class sections always are much smaller than mixed or contract sections, or regular non-honors class sections in the university.

The average honors-only class size at Plan II Honors is **18.0 students**. The average for all programs is **17.5 students.**

**Average Class Size, Overall (4.5):** The overall class calculation is based on the *proportion* of honors students in each type of class (honors-only, mixed honors, and honors contract sections). Thus it is not a raw average. The overall honors-credit class size is **18.0 students**, versus the average for all programs of **24.9 students**.

These class size averages also do not correspond to the number of students per honors section ratings above. The reason is that, in computing average class size metrics, we include enrollment in each 1-2-credit section, not just sections with 3 or more credits.

Plan II honors courses have all-honors enrollment.

**Honors Grad Rate Adjusted to SAT (3.5):** The rating is the based on the actual grad rate for students who entered the program six years earlier, whether or not the students remained in honors. The **actual rate of 91.0%** is also compared to the rates of other programs with the same test score entry requirement range, and then adjusted upward if the program is performing above other programs in the same range, or downward if the performance is less than other programs in the same range. The rate here is slightly downward, to **90.0%.**

**Grad Rate Adjusted to Freshman Retention Rate (3.0):** This rate compares the actual grad rate above to a predicted grade rate when *university-wide* freshman retention rates are considered. The actual grad rate is **4.36 points lower** than the predicted rate. For all programs, the actual grad rate is **.33 points lower** than the predicted rate. **Note:** As is the case with a few other programs whose parent universities have very high freshman retention rates, the UT Austin freshman retention rate of 95% makes the attainment of an equivalent graduation rate very challenging. Added to that, Plan II has a lot of Plan II engineering majors and double majors, and both groups normally take a bit longer to complete graduation requirements.

**Ratio of Staff to Honors Students (4.5):** There is 1 staff member for every **76.0** students. (Mean ratio for all programs is 1 staff member for every **127.9** students.)

**Honors Residence Halls, Amenities (3.0):** The UT honors housing is still in the Honors "Quad." The rooms are traditional with hall baths, but the location is probably the best on campus. About 40% of Plan II freshmen live on campus, and a much lower percentage of Plan II upperclassmen do so. Freshmen and upperclassmen may live in Andrews, Blanton, Carothers and Littlefield. All rooms are air-conditioned. Dining is in nearby Kinsolving Hall.

**Honors Residence Halls, Availability (4.0):** This rating compares the number of occupants in honors residence halls to the number of honors freshman and sophomore members in good standing. The ratio for the program is **.49** places for each first- and second-year student. The median for all programs is also .49 places.

**Prestigious Awards (5.0):** The awards that we track and include are listed in the section titled "Prestigious Scholarships." The awards are sometimes won by students who are not in an honors college or program, but increasingly many are enrolled in honors programs. It is also a trend that honors colleges and programs help to prepare their students for the awards competitions.

UT Austin is among the top seven public universities in winning major awards for upperclassmen and graduates. Along with 29 Rhodes scholarships, UT students have also won 25 Marshall scholarships and 23 Truman awards. The university is also a national leader in National Science Foundation fellowship grants for graduate school, second among public universities to UC Berkeley for 2015-2017, and for Fulbright student awards. Students have also won 40 Goldwater scholarships for undergraduate excellence in the STEM fields, and a very high number of Boren scholarships for postgraduate study abroad.

Plan II students have won about two-thirds of the UT Truman Scholarships, and more than half of the UT Marshall Scholarships, despite the small size of the honors program.

**UNRATED FEATURES**

**Continuation and Honors Graduation GPA Requirement:** 3.25 for both. Graduation with Plan II Honors degree is not the same as graduation with Latin honors from the university, although many, probably most, Plan II students do graduate with Latin honors.

**Academic Strengths, National Rankings:** This is based on national rankings of *graduate* programs in all but engineering and business, where undergraduate rankings are used. One of the weaknesses of the *U.S. News* rankings is that they focus on too many wealth-related metrics while ignoring their own assessments of academic departments. The rankings listed below are for all universities, public or private.

UT Austin has one of the top faculties in the nation, with an average national department ranking of 14.47, or fourth among public universities (UC Berkeley, UCLA, UW-Madison, UT Austin). These are also the only public universities that have all departments ranked in the top 30 nationally or higher.

The nationally ranked academic departments at UT Austin are business (5), earth sciences (7), psychology (8), computer science (10), education (10), engineering (11), sociology (11), math (14), chemistry (15), history (16), physics (17), political science (19), English (20), biology (27), and economics (27).

**Internships, Professional Development, Community Engagement:** "Plan II Honors has established several internship programs at the following sites on the UT Austin campus:

- Harry Ransom Center
- Teresa Lozano Long Institute of Latin American Studies
- The Blanton Museum of Art
- Annette Strauss Institute for Civic Life
- Dolph Briscoe Center for American History
- Dell Medical School

"Plan II students wishing to earn academic course credit for any internship should explore this option through the Liberal Arts Career Services (LACS) Office."

**Undergraduate Research:** The Plan II 6-credit thesis "is the capstone to the student's undergraduate experience in Plan II. It is typically a two-semester project that results in about 60 pages of original research in a topic approved by the Plan II Associate or Assistant Director. Topics are only approved if the student demonstrates adequate course work or other preparation in the area of interest. The student is free to select two professors from any department who they feel will best guide the research and writing on their topic. Supervisors and second readers may be any level of UT faculty, including adjuncts (provided they have the time needed to supervise the thesis to completion). Frequently, Plan II students propose interdisciplinary theses that bring together several areas of interest and represent topics that might not be possible in a departmental honors program."

The first semester of research culminates with a detailed outline that "should provide a complete sense of the arguments the thesis will make and the evidence that will be used to support them." The second semester the student must complete a draft of the thesis at least one month prior to the due date. "Also in the second semester, all Plan II thesis students must present their work at the Thesis Symposium. Thesis supervisors are strongly encouraged to attend the symposium, both to support their students and to evaluate how well they are able to articulate their research."

**Honors Study Abroad:** "Plan II students can study abroad as early as the summer after their first year. *Second and third year are by far the most common times for Plan II students to study abroad.* Occasionally a fourth year student will go abroad, but working out the timing of the Plan II thesis project as well as getting course credits from abroad posted to a student's record in time for graduation can be tricky.

*"Courses from study abroad programs are most often used to fulfill the Plan II Non-US History, Plan II Fine Arts/Humanities and Foreign Language requirements.* The two Plan II Maymester Programs each award credit for one Junior Seminar course. Tip—keep all course descriptions and syllabi as this documentation may be needed to demonstrate that the content of courses taken abroad are appropriate to fulfill the above requirements."

**Financial Aid:** "You should prepare these three documents in advance so that you can cut and paste them into the electronic system as needed. *Most Plan II students will be able to apply for two or more scholarships and will have to cut and paste the cover letter, financial statement and résumé into multiple electronic applications.*

"Look for the scholarship titled Plan II Honors Continuing & Plan II Honors EPS Scholarships. If the scholarship shows up in your listing, you are eligible and have the option of completing the application. We recommend that you apply for all scholarships for which you are eligible. Plan II Continuing Student scholarships (including the Plan II scholarships awarded through the Texas Exes Association and through the Office of Financial Aid) are awarded primarily on a financial need basis."

"A small number of out-of-state tuition adjustment scholarships may be available. Students in Plan II who are also in Business Honors, Engineering Honors, or other honors programs at UT Austin may also be eligible for scholarships related to those programs.

**Honors Fees:** None.

**Placement of Honors Graduates:** "Plan II students graduate with exceptional writing, communication, and analytical skills that can be applied to virtually any career path (including those that don't even exist yet!). *Whether entering the workforce immediately following graduation or pursuing medical, law, MBA, or graduate studies, Plan II students are highly competitive for whatever path they choose after graduation.* Set yourself up for success after graduation by utilizing the many resources Plan II, the College of Liberal Arts, and UT Austin has to offer current students."

**Degree of Difference:** This is difference between (1) the average SAT scores for recently enrolled honors students (1440-1490) and (2) the average test scores for all students in the university (1350) as a whole. The difference may be an indication of how "elite" honors students may be perceived as compared to students in the university as a whole. **Please keep in mind that neither the high nor low selectivity of an honors program determines how effective the program may be.**

**NAME**: UNIVERSITY OF VERMONT HONORS COLLEGE

**Date Established:** 2003

**Location**: Burlington, Vermont

**University Full-time Undergraduate Enrollment (2017):** 10,513

**Honors Members in Good Standing**: 796 (mean size of all programs is 2,030).

**Honors Average Admission Test Score(s)**: ACT, 32; SAT, 1404.

**Average High School GPA/Class Rank:** 3.80, unweighted; 92nd percentile of high school class.

**Basic Admission Requirements:** ACT, 32; SAT, 1400; GPA; 90th percentile of high school class.

**Application Deadline(s):** *Please verify with each program, as some deadlines could change.* Early action November 1, 2018; regular deadline January 15, 2019. No separate honors application.

**Honors Programs with SAT scores from 1403—1461:** Auburn, Central Florida, Delaware, Iowa, Kansas, Mississippi, Missouri, New Jersey Inst of Technology, Penn State, South Florida, Vermont, Virginia Commonwealth.

**Administrative Staff:** 6 plus 3 who also have other university-wide activities.

**RATINGS AT A GLANCE:** For all mortarboard ratings immediately below, a score of 5 is the maximum and represents a comparison with all rated honors colleges and programs. More detailed explanations follow the "mortarboard" ratings.

**PERCEPTION\* OF UNIVERSITY AS A WHOLE, NOT OF HONORS:** 🎓🎓🎓🎓

\*Perception is based on the university's ranking among public universities in the 2018 U.S. News Best Colleges report. Please bear in mind that the better the U.S. News ranking, the more difficult it is for an honors college or program to have a rating that equals or improves on the magazine ranking.

**OVERALL HONORS RATING:** 🎓🎓🎓

**Curriculum Requirements:** 🎓🎓🎓

**Number of Honors Classes Offered:** 🎓🎓🎓

**Number of Honors Classes in Key Disciplines:** 🎓🎓1/2

**Extent of Honors Enrollment:** 🎓🎓🎓1/2

**Honors-only Class Size:** 🎓🎓🎓1/2

**Overall Class Size (Honors-only plus mixed, contract):** 🎓🎓🎓🎓🎓

**Honors Grad Rate Adjusted to SAT:** 🎓🎓🎓

**Grad Rate Adjusted to Freshman Retention Rate:** 🎓🎓1/2

**Ratio of Staff to Students:** 🎓🎓🎓🎓

**Priority Registration:** "The UVM Honors College has a two-tiered system for priority registration. All HCOL students have at minimum in-class priority registration: they have the opportunity to register for all classes half an hour before the standard registration time for students in their class year (based on credits completed at the end of the previous semester). Students in highly structured majors, primarily in the professional programs and sciences, have overall priority registration status: they register the first day of registration week, before all other undergrads at the university, along with a small number of non-HCOL students who also have overall priority registration (some athletes, students with accommodations, etc)."

**Honors Housing Amenities:** 🎓🎓🎓🎓🎓

**Honors Housing Availability:** 🎓🎓🎓🎓1/2

**Prestigious Awards:** 🎓🎓🎓1/2

## RATING SCORES AND EXPLANATIONS:

**Curriculum Requirements (3.0):** The most important rating category, the curriculum completion requirement (classes required to complete honors) defines not only what honors students should learn but also the extent to which honors students and faculty are connected in the classroom. If there is a thesis or capstone requirement, it reinforces the individual contact and research skills so important to learning.

The average number of honors semester hours required for completion across all programs is 30.0.

Vermont Honors College requires 20-22 honors credits for completion, including a 6-credit thesis.

First Year: two 3-credit "Pursuit of Knowledge" seminars
Sophomore Year: two 3-credit interdisciplinary courses
Junior Year: four credits maximum, average 1-3 credits, in honors contract work
Senior Year: honors thesis, 6 credits
Other: two 1-credit honors electives

**No. Honors Classes Offered (3.0):** This is a measure of the total **adjusted** honors main sections available in the term reported, not including labs and thesis. An adjusted main section has 3 or more semester credits, or equivalent, and sections with fewer credits receive a lower prorated value.

The program offered a section for every **21.0** enrolled students. The average for all programs was **15.0**. The lower the number, the better. In the term reported, an impressive **81.0%** of honors enrollment was **in honors-only sections; none was in mixed sections; and 19.0% was in contract sections.** For all programs under review, enrollment by type of honors section was 75.8% honors-only, 15.4 % mixed, and 8.8% contract.

**No. Honors Classes in Key Disciplines (2.5):** The 15 "key" disciplines are biological sciences; business (all); chemistry; communications (especially public speaking); computer science; economics; engineering (all); English; history; math (all); philosophy; physics; political science; psychology; and sociology, anthropology, and gender studies. Interdisciplinary sections, such as those often taken for General Education credit in the first two years, do receive a lesser, prorated discipline "credit" because they introduce students to multiple disciplines in an especially engaging way, often with in-depth discussion.

For this measure, mixed and contract sections are not counted as a section in a key discipline unless students taking the sections for honors credit make up at least 10% of the total section enrollment.

In the term reported, the program offered a section in a key discipline for every **53.5 honors students.** The average for all programs is **24.7**. The lower the number, the better.

Out of **six adjusted sections in key disciplines, all were honors-only sections.** The sections included two in biology, and one each in engineering, history, philosophy, and political science. These sections with "credit" for emphasizing a key discipline are also interdisciplinary to an extent. Including these, the college has 27 of these courses.

Among them were "Crafting Democratic Institutions," "Shakespeare and the Classical Tradition," and "Challenge of Biological Invasions." The Pursuit of Knowledge seminar series, for first-year students in the Fall term, "draws on the expertise of the university's faculty and visitors to the course in areas such as the natural sciences, mathematics, economics, creative writing, music, medicine, and more." In the Spring term, "students apply some of what they learned in The Pursuit of Knowledge course to one of a series of special topics seminars that are grouped together under the title 'Ways of Knowing.'" This thoughtfully structured series of courses is what makes the Vermont Honors College is a **core** program, with a combination of excellent seminars and a high number of students working on the 6-credit thesis.

**Extent of Honors Enrollment (3.5):** Not all honors students take an honors class each term, especially after the first two years. Programs that have fewer honors classes and thesis options for upper-division honors students will *generally* have fewer total members in good standing who are actually enrolled in a given term. (Please be aware, however, that honors students not enrolled in a class for a term are still tied to the honors community through residential and extracurricular activities.) *Our research shows that this measure is closely related to honors completion rates, i.e., the number of students who complete honors requirements by the time they graduate.*

For example, if a program has 1,800 individual students enrolled in a given term, and 3,000 students in good standing, the level of enrollment was .67, an indication that honors class enrollment is somewhat

below average, especially in upper-division classes. **UVM Honors has a ratio of 1.04**, below the average of 1.30 for all programs.

**Average Class Size, Honors-only Sections (3.5):** Offered mostly in the first two years, honors-only classes tend to be smaller and, as the name implies, have no or very few students other than those in the honors program. These class sections always are much smaller than mixed or contract sections, or regular non-honors class sections in the university.

The average honors-only class size at UVM Honors is **18.7 students**. The average for all programs is **17.5 students.**

**Average Class Size, Overall (5.0):** The overall class calculation is based on the *proportion* of honors students in each type of class (honors-only, mixed honors, and honors contract sections). Thus it is not a raw average. The overall honors-credit class size is **17.9 students**, versus the average for all programs of **24.9 students**.

These class size averages also do not correspond to the number of students per honors section ratings above. The reason is that, in computing average class size metrics, we include enrollment in each 1-2-credit section, not just sections with 3 or more credits.

Along with an honors-only class size of 18.7 students (listed above), the program's contract sections with honors credit for individual honors students average **9.0 students.** Across all programs the average contract section has 56.6 students.

**Honors Grad Rate Adjusted to SAT (3.0):** The rating is the based on the actual grad rate for students who entered the program six years earlier, whether or not the students remained in honors. The **actual rate of 78.0%** is also compared to the rates of other programs with the same test score entry requirement range, and then adjusted upward if the program is performing above other programs in the same range, or downward if the performance is less than other programs in the same range. The rate here is downward, to **75.3%.**

**Grad Rate Adjusted to Freshman Retention Rate (2.5):** This rate compares the actual grad rate above to a predicted grade rate when *university-wide* freshman retention rates are considered. The actual grad rate is **8.32 points lower** than the predicted rate. For all programs, the actual grad rate is **.33 points lower** than the predicted rate.

**Ratio of Staff to Honors Students (4.0):** There is 1 staff member for every **120.6** students. (Mean ratio for all programs is 1 staff member for every **127.9** students.)

**Honors Residence Halls, Amenities (5.0):** "University Heights North is the heart and home of the Honors College. The top four floors are the Honors residence hall, where the majority of the first-year and sophomore Honors College students live, as well as a handful of Honors juniors and seniors. The ground floor of the building houses the Honors College classrooms, where most first-year and sophomore seminar courses are taught. The Honors College administrative and advising offices—including the FOUR Office (Fellowships, Opportunities, and Undergraduate Research) are also on the main floor of the building.

"University Heights North residence hall provides housing for Honors College students in a wide variety of spacious rooms in suite options, as well as single rooms. Because the Honors College classrooms and administrative offices are also located in UHN, students have easy access to advising and support from the staff and faculty."

**Honors Residence Halls, Availability (4.5):** This rating compares the number of occupants in honors residence halls to the number of honors freshman and sophomore members in good standing. The ratio for the program is **1.04** places for each first- and second-year student. The median for all programs is .49 places.

**Prestigious Awards (3.5):** The awards that we track and include are listed in the section titled "Prestigious Scholarships." The awards are sometimes won by students who are not in an honors college or program, but increasingly many are enrolled in honors programs. It is also a trend that honors colleges and programs help to prepare their students for the awards competitions.

"UVM's Office of Fellowships, Opportunities, and Undergraduate Research (FOUR) is housed in the Honors College and available to all undergraduate and graduate students at the university. The office's mission is to provide application and administrative support for University of Vermont (UVM) students and alumni applying for nationally competitive scholarship and fellowship opportunities that will greatly enhance their undergraduate, graduate or postgraduate academic work. Established by the Honors College in July 2009, with a full-time Fellowships Advisor, the office supports and mentors students throughout the application process, manages the university endorsement process and coordinates the on-campus process with the national scholarship and fellowship organizations."

UVM students have won 10 Rhodes scholarships, 10 Truman scholarships, five Udall awards, and nine Goldwater scholarships.

**UNRATED FEATURES**

**Continuation and Honors Graduation GPA Requirement:** "Starting with the Class of 2020, the GPA requirement for good standing is 3.2 for first year and sophomore students, but by the time of Honors thesis proposal a student must have a 3.4 to go forward [and graduate] in Honors (thesis proposal typically happens in spring of a student's junior year or in the fall of a student's senior year)."

**Academic Strengths, National Rankings:** This is based on national rankings of *graduate* programs in all but engineering and business, where undergraduate rankings are used. One of the weaknesses of the *U.S. News* rankings is that they focus on too many wealth-related metrics while ignoring their own assessments of academic departments. The rankings listed below are for all universities, public or private.

The nationally ranked academic departments at UVM include education (66), psychology (66), biology (112), math (117), chemistry (122), and engineering (125).

**Internships, Professional Development, Community Engagement:** At UVM experiential learning is often coordinated by college departments and divisions and not by the honors college.

**Undergraduate Research:** "All Honors College seniors are required to do a senior thesis, the basis of which is undergraduate research. Many students are involved in research prior to embarking on thesis work.

"The Office of Undergraduate Research provides research grants, matches students with faculty conducting research, and co-sponsors an annual research symposium, Student Research Conference."

**Honors Study Abroad:** "The University of Vermont has study abroad options for the summer, a semester, or an academic year. The university offers exchange programs in Japan, Germany, Wales, Ireland, Australia, France, Finland, Mexico, New Zealand, Spain, England, Sweden, Austria, and Russia. In addition, the university enables students to pursue study abroad through many external study abroad programs. Finally, the Honors College has summer research grants that can be used to fund research projects abroad.

"The UVM Honors College has a partnership with two study abroad Honors programs:

- Starting in 2018 the UVM Honors College will have an exchange with University College Maastricht (UCM, the Honors College at Maastricht University in the Netherlands). Up to four UVM Honors College students will be nominated each year to participate in the UCM exchange. In addition, four students from UCM will join the UVM Honors College community during the same semester UVM students are studying at UCM.
- The UVM Honors College also has a special tie to Glasgow University in Scotland as a part of the Principia Consortium. Students who participate in the program can complete a three-credit sophomore seminar requirement.

'Because of the nature of study abroad and the options students have for studying abroad through the university, an external program, a summer program, or through leave-of-absence, it is difficult to track the percentage of Honors College students who study abroad. That said, 31.2% of UVM students study abroad, and we believe that that number is likely a good representation of Honors College students who study abroad."

**Financial Aid:** Most students invited to the Honors College receive the top merit awards from the University of Vermont. This could include the Presidential Scholarship, the Vermont Scholars Award, or others. *Merit scholarships awarded at UVM can be for full tuition, room, and board (such as the Green & Gold Scholarships), or they can offer significant financial support to attend the university (many Honors College students receive the Presidential Scholarship, which can be for as much as $18,000 annually).*

--Presidential Scholarships are awarded to out-of-state first year students who demonstrate the highest academic performance. Recipients are selected based on the application for admission. Presidential Scholars are awarded a four-year (eight semester) merit scholarship that ranges from $15,000 to $18,000 annually. No separate application is required. Students must be enrolled in 12 or more credits per semester and maintain a minimum cumulative grade point average of 3.0.

--Green and Gold Scholars Award is a full in-state tuition, four-year merit scholarship (currently valued at over $62,000) is directed to top-rated seniors attending selected Vermont high schools (including all public high schools and select private high schools in Vermont, and a number of border high schools).

The highest-achieving Vermont resident in each eligible school at the end of the junior year may be considered.

**Honors Fees:** "There are no extra fees associated with the Honors College. Students who choose to live in the private doubles (the top end room) in University Heights North may pay more than a traditional UVM double, but the university offers cost-offset forms for students who need to keep the housing costs in line with the university's room and board fees."

**Placement of Honors Graduates:** "Recent UVM Honors College graduates are now:

- Pursuing medical study at Harvard University, Stanford University, Brown Medical School, and the University of Vermont Medical School, among others.
- Pursuing graduate doctoral study in the sciences at Cal Tech (Chemistry), Vanderbilt University (mathematics), Columbia University (cell and molecular biology), and Brown University (pathobiology), among others.
- Pursuing graduate doctoral study in the humanities, social sciences, and arts at Harvard University, University of California-Berkeley, Johns Hopkins, Duke University, and the University of Warwick, among others.
- Veterinarians (recent Honors College graduates are pursuing vet school Tufts University, Cornell University, University of Pennsylvania, among others).
- Lawyers (recent Honors College graduates are at law school at Duke University, University of Pennsylvania, Georgetown Law, and Harvard School of Law, among others),
- Public health officials (recent graduates are at Columbia University and Yale University, among others)
- Entering the workforce at companies including Google, HBO, Equitas Life Science Consulting, Global Foundries, Fuse Marketing, Flying Plow Farm, W. W. Norton & Company, NextCapital Group, among others.
- Founded their own companies or non-profit organizations, including ReWork, The Whole Human Upgrade, Books 4 Equality, among others.
- Working in the public sector at the U.S. State Department, the Office of the Mayor of Burlington, the Office of Senator Patrick J. Leahy, the State House of Vermont, Amnesty International, Vermont Public Interest Research Group (VPIRG), serving in the U.S Army, among others.
- Doing postgraduate fellowship work through the Gates Cambridge Program, Fulbright U.S. Student Program, the National Institutes of Health, Teach for America, Peacecorps, and Americorps, among others.

**Degree of Difference**: This is difference between (1) the average SAT scores for recently enrolled honors students (1403) and (2) the average test scores for all students in the university (1240) as a whole. The difference may be an indication of how "elite" honors students may be perceived as compared to students in the university as a whole. **Please keep in mind that neither the high nor low selectivity of an honors program determines how effective the program may be.**

**NAME**: VIRGINIA COMMONWEALTH UNIVERSITY HONORS COLLEGE

**Date Established:** 1983 as an honors program.

**Location**: Richmond, Virginia

**University Full-time Undergraduate Enrollment (2017):** 24,212

**Honors Members in Good Standing**: 874 (mean size of all programs is 2,030).

**Honors Average Admission Test Score(s)**: ACT, 31; SAT, 1420.

**Average High School GPA/Class Rank:** 4.33, weighted.

**Basic Admission Requirements:** ACT, 29; SAT, 1330; GPA, 3.50.

**Application Deadline(s):** *Please verify with each program, as some deadlines could change.* "Applications to the Honors College from incoming freshmen are accepted through April 15 of the senior year in high school. However, students are encouraged to apply by our priority deadline of February 1."

**Honors Programs with SAT scores 1403—1461**: Auburn, Central Florida, Delaware, Iowa, Kansas, Mississippi, Missouri, New Jersey Inst of Technology, Penn State, South Florida, Vermont, Virginia Commonwealth.

**Administrative Staff:** 15.

**RATINGS AT A GLANCE:** For all mortarboard ratings immediately below, a score of 5 is the maximum and represents a comparison with all rated honors colleges and programs. More detailed explanations follow the "mortarboard" ratings.

**PERCEPTION\* OF UNIVERSITY AS A WHOLE, NOT OF HONORS:** 🎓🎓🎓 1/2

\*Perception is based on the university's ranking among public universities in the 2018 U.S. News Best Colleges report. Please bear in mind that the better the U.S. News ranking, the more difficult it is for an honors college or program to have a rating that equals or improves on the magazine ranking.

**OVERALL HONORS RATING:** 🎓🎓🎓🎓 1/2

**Curriculum Requirements:** 🎓🎓🎓 1/2

**Number of Honors Classes Offered:** 🎓🎓🎓🎓🎓

**Number of Honors Classes in Key Disciplines:** 🎓🎓🎓🎓

**Extent of Honors Enrollment:** 🎓🎓🎓 1/2

**Honors-only Class Size:** 🎓🎓🎓🎓🎓

**Overall Class Size (Honors-only plus mixed, contract):** 🎓🎓🎓🎓🎓

**Honors Grad Rate Adjusted to SAT:** 🎓🎓🎓🎓1/2

**Grad Rate Adjusted to Freshman Retention Rate:** 🎓🎓🎓🎓

**Ratio of Staff to Students:** 🎓🎓🎓🎓🎓

**Priority Registration: Yes,** honors students register for all courses, honors and otherwise, with the first group of students during each year they are in the program.

**Honors Housing Amenities:** 🎓🎓🎓🎓1/2

**Honors Housing Availability:** 🎓🎓🎓1/2

**Prestigious Awards:** 🎓🎓1/2

**RATING SCORES AND EXPLANATIONS:**

**Curriculum Requirements (3.5):** The most important rating category, the curriculum completion requirement (classes required to complete honors) defines not only what honors students should learn but also the extent to which honors students and faculty are connected in the classroom. If there is a thesis or capstone requirement, it reinforces the individual contact and research skills so important to learning.

The average number of honors semester hours required for completion across all programs is 30.0.

"VCU Honors College requires VCU honors requires a minimum of 24 credits. A thesis is not required.

"Honors Writing Sequence—Students who enter the Honors College directly from high school are required to take an honors version of the university's writing sequence. Honors students take both Rhetoric and Expository Writing. Successful completion of these two honors courses satisfies three university-required courses.

"Honors Core— In addition to the writing sequence, students must complete 18 credits in the honors core, which includes a designated honors course (each) in math, philosophy, physics, and political science. First-year students are also required to take two one-credit courses, Introduction to Community Engagement (HONR160) and Flourishing (HONR150).

"Honors Electives—In addition to the honors core, students have the option of taking honors seminars, honors contract courses and honors independent study.

"Departmental Honors—In conjunction with the Honors College, students have the option of pursuing departmental honors in business and psychology."

**AP/IB credits** are **not** counted as replacements for honors courses.

**No. Honors Classes Offered (5.0):** This is a measure of the total **adjusted** honors main sections available in the term reported, not including labs and thesis. An adjusted main section has 3 or more semester credits, or equivalent, and sections with fewer credits receive a lower prorated value.

The program offered a section for every **7.1** enrolled students. The average for all programs was **15.0**. The lower the number, the better. In the term reported, an extremely impressive **99.6%** of honors enrollment was **in honors-only sections; none was in mixed sections; and .4% was in contract sections.** For all programs under review, enrollment by type of honors section was 75.8% honors-only, 15.4 % mixed, and 8.8% contract.

**No. Honors Classes in Key Disciplines (4.0):** The 15 "key" disciplines are biological sciences; business (all); chemistry; communications (especially public speaking); computer science; economics; engineering (all); English; history; math (all); philosophy; physics; political science; psychology; and sociology, anthropology, and gender studies. Interdisciplinary sections, such as those often taken for General Education credit in the first two years, do receive a lesser, prorated discipline "credit" because they introduce students to multiple disciplines in an especially engaging way, often with in-depth discussion.

For this measure, mixed and contract sections are not counted as a section in a key discipline unless students taking the sections for honors credit make up at least 10% of the total section enrollment.

In the term reported, VCU Honors offered a section in a key discipline for every **18.7 honors students.** The average for all programs is **24.7.** The lower the number, the better.

Out of **44 adjusted sections in key disciplines**, **all were honors-only sections**. The most sections were in math, philosophy, communications/rhetoric, English, physics, political science, and business, along with multiple sections in economics and psychology.

VCU Honors offered seven interdisciplinary sections, among them "Art of the Narrative" and "The Rise of Civilizations." The combination of classes in the academic disciplines and some honors interdisciplinary courses make VCU Honors a **blended** program.

**Extent of Honors Enrollment (3.5):** Not all honors students take an honors class each term, especially after the first two years. Programs that have fewer honors classes and thesis options for upper-division honors students will *generally* have fewer total members in good standing who are actually enrolled in a given term. (Please be aware, however, that honors students not enrolled in a class for a term are still tied to the honors community through residential and extracurricular activities.) *Our research shows that this measure is closely related to honors completion rates, i.e., the number of students who complete honors requirements by the time they graduate.*

For example, if a program has 1,800 individual students enrolled in a given term, and 3,000 students in good standing, the level of enrollment was .67, an indication that honors class enrollment is somewhat

below average, especially in upper-division classes. **VCU Honors has a ratio of 1.25**, below the average of 1.30 for all programs.

**Average Class Size, Honors-only Sections (5.0):** Offered mostly in the first two years, honors-only classes tend to be smaller and, as the name implies, have no or very few students other than those in the honors program. These class sections always are much smaller than mixed or contract sections, or regular non-honors class sections in the university.

The average honors-only class size at VCU Honors is **15.0 students**. The average for all programs is **17.5 students.**

**Average Class Size, Overall (5.0):** The overall class calculation is based on the *proportion* of honors students in each type of class (honors-only, mixed honors, and honors contract sections). Thus it is not a raw average. The overall honors-credit class size is also **15.0 students**, versus the average for all programs of **25.4 students**.

These class size averages also do not correspond to the number of students per honors section ratings above. The reason is that, in computing average class size metrics, we include enrollment in each 1-2-credit section, not just sections with 3 or more credits.

**Honors Grad Rate Adjusted to SAT (4.5):** The rating is the based on the actual grad rate for students who entered the program six years earlier, whether or not the students remained in honors. The **actual rate of 88.7%** is also compared to the rates of other programs with the same test score entry requirement range, and then adjusted upward if the program is performing above other programs in the same range, or downward if the performance is less than other programs in the same range. The rate here is upward, to **89.6%.**

**Grad Rate Adjusted to Freshman Retention Rate (4.0):** This rate compares the actual grad rate above to a predicted grade rate when *university-wide* freshman retention rates are considered. The actual grad rate is **1.37 points higher** than the predicted rate. For all programs, the actual grad rate is **.33 points lower** than the predicted rate.

**Ratio of Staff to Honors Students (5.0):** There is 1 staff member for every **58.3** students. (Mean ratio for all programs is 1 staff member for every **127.9** students.)

**Honors Residence Halls, Amenities (4.5):** "VCU Honors College provides our students with two on-campus housing options. Freshmen can choose to live in the Honors College Residence Hall, a 169-bed all-Honors building. All rooms are single bed and single bath, and each floor has laundry facilities and a shared common space. *This building also houses the Honors College, including faculty and administrative offices, classrooms, and the Honors College Student Lounge, which is open to all students, not just residents.* Upperclass students can choose to live in Honors-specific suites in the Grace and Broad II Residence Hall. *Each suite includes a full residential kitchen, a common space, a shared bathroom, and either single or double bedrooms.*"

About 87% of honors students living in honors housing reside in the Honors Residence, featuring single apartments and private baths. Both freshmen and upperclassmen may live in the residence, which is air-conditioned throughout. The remainder of honors residence space is in Brandt Hall (freshmen only) and

West Grace Hall (upperclassmen only), both air-conditioned with suite-style rooms and shared baths. The Shafer Court Dining Center is the most convenient dining location. The only reason the rating is not 5.0 is that the Honors Residence does not include onsite dining. Otherwise, it is clear that the residence is outstanding.

**Honors Residence Halls, Availability (3.5):** This rating compares the number of occupants in honors residence halls to the number of honors freshman and sophomore members in good standing. The ratio for the program is **.42** places for each first- and second-year student. The median for all programs is .49 places.

**Prestigious Awards (2.5):** The awards that we track and include are listed in the section titled "Prestigious Scholarships." The awards are sometimes won by students who are not in an honors college or program, but increasingly many are enrolled in honors programs. It is also a trend that honors colleges and programs help to prepare their students for the awards competitions.

"Since 2005, all 10 Goldwater Scholars from VCU have been Honors College students. As of April 2018, 22 of our 59 recipients for the Fulbright U.S. Student program have been honors students or honors alumni (three declined). A number of those 59 were graduate students who did their undergraduate work elsewhere. Two of our most recent Boren Scholarship recipients are honors students, and several of our recent NSF GRF recipients are alumni of the Honors College. Virtually all of our Rhodes, Marshall, and Truman nominees have been honors students or recent alumni.

"The National Scholarship Office (NSO) supported 163 completed applications (representing undergraduate and graduate students, as well as alumni, from across VCU's campus, not just within the Honors College)."

**UNRATED FEATURES**

**Continuation and Honors Graduation GPA Requirement:** Cumulative 3.50 for both.

**Academic Strengths, National Rankings:** This is based on national rankings of *graduate* programs in all but engineering and business, where undergraduate rankings are used. One of the weaknesses of the *U.S. News* rankings is that they focus on too many wealth-related metrics while ignoring their own assessments of academic departments. The rankings listed below are for all universities, public or private.

VCU has many highly ranked departments in health care and related fields, as well as fine arts.

The nationally ranked academic departments at VCU include Fine Arts (2nd, but not including theater and dance); healthcare management (3), rehabilitation counseling (4), occupational therapy (17), pharmacy (17), physical therapy (20), nuclear engineering (24), education (26), and social work (30).

**Internships, Professional Development, Community Engagement:** "VCU's urban location provides students with an abundance of opportunities to gain practical, hands-on experience. In addition to thriving non-profit and artistic communities, the Virginia General Assembly, several fortune 500 companies, and the Federal Reserve Bank are located in Richmond. *For students who are interested in health care, there are many hospitals and clinics in the area that provide shadowing experiences to students.*

"All honors freshmen participate in two significant events during their first semester: a full class, offsite, one-day Freshmen Retreat designed to develop community and leadership ability, and a full Day of Service. During the Day of Service, honors students partner with other VCU students to participate in service projects in the Richmond community."

**Undergraduate Research:** "The Honors College offers two undergraduate research programs: Freshman Research Institute and the Honors Summer Undergraduate Research Program.

"The Freshman Research Institute is designed to introduce 20-25 incoming freshmen to the nuances of undergraduate research at VCU. For example, students interact with faculty across disciplines to learn about their research and the qualities they are seeking in research assistants. Additionally, students are introduced community-engaged research which includes a brief introduction the Institutional Review Board process and human subject research. Beyond learning about undergraduate research, this free program is designed to aid students in transitioning to college and building community among honors students.

"The Honors Summer Undergraduate Research Program is a nine-week program designed to engage 20-25 students in faculty mentored research projects. Students are selected through a competitive process and receive on-campus housing, a stipend, and professional development workshops, such as resume writing and interviewing skills."

**Honors Study Abroad:** "The Honors College offers two signature study abroad programs, Discover Medicine in Italy and an Abroad Experience to Northern Ireland. A $2,500 scholarship was available to each student accepted to participate in these programs."

**Financial Aid:** "National Merit Scholars in the Honors College are eligible to receive the VCU Presidential Scholarship *(full in-state level room, board, tuition and fees)*. In addition all Honors College students are eligible to apply for Honors College endowed scholarships each year, which range from $1,000-$3,000 per academic year. The Honors College has also collaborated with the Office of Admissions to offer the Academic Excellence Scholarship, which is a $2,000 four year renewable scholarship to certain honors students who may not receive a larger merit based scholarship."

**Honors Fees:** "The honors fee is $50.00 per semester. The fee is used to fund study abroad scholarships, travel grants, and co-curricular activities."

**Placement of Honors Graduates:** "For the May 2017 graduating class, 43% will be attending graduate or professional school, 40% will be begin their work careers, and the remainder did not report their post-graduation plans

**Degree of Difference**: This is difference between (1) the average SAT scores for recently enrolled honors students (1420) and (2) the average test scores for all students in the university (1180) as a whole. The difference may be an indication of how "elite" honors students may be perceived as compared to students in the university as a whole. **Please keep in mind that neither the high nor low selectivity of an honors program determines how effective the program may be.**

**NAME**: THE HONORS COLLEGE, WASHINGTON STATE UNIVERSITY

**Date Established:** 1960

**Location**: Pullman, Washington

**University Full-time Undergraduate Enrollment (2017):** 24,904

**Honors Members in Good Standing**: 929 (mean size of all programs is 2,030).

**Honors Average Admission Test Score(s)**: ACT, 29; SAT, 1299.

**Average High School GPA/Class Rank:** 3.84, unweighted.

**Basic Admission Requirements:** "We do not require a basic test score and gpa/class rank requirement as we do a holistic review of applications."

**Application Deadline(s):** *Please verify with each program, as some deadlines could change.* January 31, 2019.

**Honors Programs with SAT scores from 1286—1300:** Florida Atlantic, Washington State, West Virginia.

**Administrative Staff:** 9 administrative staff and 4 full-time faculty.

**RATINGS AT A GLANCE:** For all mortarboard ratings immediately below, a score of 5 is the maximum and represents a comparison with all rated honors colleges and programs. More detailed explanations follow the "mortarboard" ratings.

**PERCEPTION\* OF UNIVERSITY AS A WHOLE, NOT OF HONORS:** 🎓🎓🎓 1/2

\*Perception is based on the university's ranking among public universities in the 2018 U.S. News Best Colleges report. Please bear in mind that the better the U.S. News ranking, the more difficult it is for an honors college or program to have a rating that equals or improves on the magazine ranking.

**OVERALL HONORS RATING:** 🎓🎓🎓 1/2

**Curriculum Requirements:** 🎓🎓🎓 1/2

**Number of Honors Classes Offered:** 🎓🎓🎓 1/2

**Number of Honors Classes in Key Disciplines:** 🎓🎓🎓

**Extent of Honors Enrollment:** 🎓🎓🎓 1/2

**Honors-only Class Size:** 🎓🎓🎓 1/2

**Overall Class Size (Honors-only plus mixed, contract):** 🎓🎓🎓🎓 1/2

**Honors Grad Rate Adjusted to SAT:** 🎓🎓🎓🎓 1/2

**Grad Rate Adjusted to Freshman Retention Rate:** 🎓🎓🎓🎓🎓

**Ratio of Staff to Students:** 🎓🎓🎓🎓 1/2

**Priority Registration:** Yes, "there are two early sessions of Summer registration called ALIVE! designated for Honors students."

**Honors Housing Amenities:** 🎓🎓🎓🎓 1/2

**Honors Housing Availability:** 🎓🎓🎓

**Prestigious Awards:** 🎓🎓🎓

## RATING SCORES AND EXPLANATIONS:

**Curriculum Requirements (3.5):** The most important rating category, the curriculum completion requirement (classes required to complete honors) defines not only what honors students should learn but also the extent to which honors students and faculty are connected in the classroom. If there is a thesis or capstone requirement, it reinforces the individual contact and research skills so important to learning.

The average number of honors semester hours required for completion across all programs is 30.0.

Honors completion at WSU Honors College requires about 25 honors credits, including a 1-credit research course and a 3-credit thesis.

At least one honors course is required in each of the following areas: English Writing and Research; Contextual Understanding in the Arts and Humanities; Science as a Way of Knowing; Global Issues in Social Science; Global Issues in Arts and Humanities; and Global Issues in the Sciences.

The college has long been recognized for its emphasis on global study, so there is an additional foreign language requirement. "The foreign language requirement may be satisfied in one of the following ways:

--Satisfactory completion of the STAMP test.
--Satisfactory completion of a foreign language 204 level course.
--Completion of a minor in a foreign language
-- Earning the Honors College Certificate of Global Competencies

"Students whose native language is not English and arrived in the United States after 8th grade will be exempt of this requirement upon discussion with an Honors adviser."

"The Certificate of Global Competencies is a separate option that requires 15 credits and a thesis. It essentially requires study-abroad credits and courses in international studies, in addition to the foreign language requirement."

**AP/IB credits** are **not** counted as replacements for honors courses.

**No. Honors Classes Offered (3.5):** This is a measure of the total **adjusted** honors main sections available in the term reported, not including labs and thesis. An adjusted main section has 3 or more semester credits, or equivalent, and sections with fewer credits receive a lower prorated value.

The program offered a section for every **18.6** enrolled students. The average for all programs was **15.0**. The lower the number, the better. In the term reported, an extremely impressive **96.2%** of honors enrollment was **in honors-only sections; 3.8% was in mixed sections; and none was in contract sections.** For all programs under review, enrollment by type of honors section was 75.8% honors-only, 15.4 % mixed, and 8.8% contract.

**No. Honors Classes in Key Disciplines (3.0):** The 15 "key" disciplines are biological sciences; business (all); chemistry; communications (especially public speaking); computer science; economics; engineering (all); English; history; math (all); philosophy; physics; political science; psychology; and sociology, anthropology, and gender studies. Interdisciplinary sections, such as those often take for General Education credit in the first two years, do receive a lesser, prorated discipline "credit" because they introduce students to multiple disciplines in an especially engaging way, often with in-depth discussion.

For this measure, mixed and contract sections are not counted as a section in a key discipline unless students taking the sections for honors credit make up at least 10% of the total section enrollment.

In the term reported, the WSU Honors offered a section in a key discipline for every **32.0 honors students.** The average for all programs is **24.7.** The lower the number, the better.

Out of **16 adjusted sections in key disciplines, 13 were honors-only sections.** The most sections by far were in English (writing and research), followed by economics and physics, and then by chemistry, math, and political science.

Aside from a series of 1-credit courses in experiential learning, another 21 classes were from these core groups: English Writing and Research; Contextual Understanding in the Arts and Humanities; Science as a Way of Knowing; Global Issues in Social Science; Global Issues in Arts and Humanities; and Global Issues in the Sciences. Many of these have a strong disciplinary focus, and that is certainly the case with one of the Global Issues in the Sciences sections. "The main goal of this course is to help students see the real-world relevance of the various academic disciplines and their comparative strengths and weaknesses by looking at the history of several scientific inventions…We will then turn to modern society and look at several cases where scientists from different disciplines join forces to address complex global issues, such as environmental, ecological, and global health problems."

WSU Honors is a **core** program, and like other core programs, the college offers interdisciplinary courses within specific ranges of academic disciplines. It is unique in its continued emphasis on studying these topics in a global context.

**Extent of Honors Enrollment (3.5):** Not all honors students take an honors class each term, especially after the first two years. Programs that have fewer honors classes and thesis options for upper-division honors students will *generally* have fewer total members in good standing who are actually enrolled in a given term. (Please be aware, however, that honors students not enrolled in a class for a term are still tied to the honors community through residential and extracurricular activities.) *Our research shows that this measure is closely related to honors completion rates, i.e., the number of students who complete honors requirements by the time they graduate.*

For example, if a program has 1,800 individual students enrolled in a given term, and 3,000 students in good standing, the level of enrollment was .67, an indication that honors class enrollment is somewhat below average, especially in upper-division classes. **WSU Honors has a ratio of 1.09**, below the average of 1.30 for all programs.

**Average Class Size, Honors-only Sections (3.5):** Offered mostly in the first two years, honors-only classes tend to be smaller and, as the name implies, have no or very few students other than those in the honors program. These class sections always are much smaller than mixed or contract sections, or regular non-honors class sections in the university.

The average honors-only class size at WSU Honors is **19.9 students**. The average for all programs is **17.5 students.**

**Average Class Size, Overall (4.5):** The overall class calculation is based on the *proportion* of honors students in each type of class (honors-only, mixed honors, and honors contract sections). Thus it is not a raw average. The overall honors-credit class size is **19.7 students**, versus the average for all programs of **24.9 students**.

These class size averages also do not correspond to the number of students per honors section ratings above. The reason is that, in computing average class size metrics, we include enrollment in each 1-2-credit section, not just sections with 3 or more credits.

Along with an honors-only class size of 19.9 students (listed above), the program's mixed honors sections have an average size of **15.3 students.** Across all programs, the average mixed honors section has 68.6 students.

**Honors Grad Rate Adjusted to SAT (4.5):** The rating is the based on the actual grad rate for students who entered the program six years earlier, whether or not the students remained in honors. The **actual rate of 87.0%** is also compared to the rates of other programs with the same test score entry requirement range, and then adjusted upward if the program is performing above other programs in the same range, or downward if the performance is less than other programs in the same range. The rate here is slightly downward, to **87.5%.**

**Grad Rate Adjusted to Freshman Retention Rate (5.0):** This rate compares the actual grad rate above to a predicted grade rate when *university-wide* freshman retention rates are considered. The actual grad rate is **7.70 points higher** than the predicted rate. For all programs, the actual grad rate is **.33 points lower** than the predicted rate.

**Ratio of Staff to Honors Students (4.5):** There is 1 staff member for every **94.8** students. (Mean ratio for all programs is 1 staff member for every **127.9** students.)

**Honors Residence Halls, Amenities (4.5):** "Honors Hall is the home of 118 students in suite-style housing. The 1st floor of the building houses the Honors College and the 1st floor lounge is the meeting place for the Honors Student Advisory Council (HSAC). This allows for much overlapping for programming, discussions, presentations, seminars and events put on by the residence life staff, Honors College, and HSAC. This maintains a strong academic environment within the hall." Dining is at the nearby Hillside Café, a two-minute walk.

"WSU also has another Residence Hall that is considered a Scholars Hall (Scott-Coman), but it is not part of the Honors Hall or College."

**Honors Residence Halls, Availability (3.0):** This rating compares the number of occupants in honors residence halls to the number of honors freshman and sophomore members in good standing. The ratio for the program is **.25** places for each first- and second-year student. The median for all programs is .49 places.

**Prestigious Awards (3.0):** The awards that we track and include are listed in the section titled "Prestigious Scholarships." The awards are sometimes won by students who are not in an honors college or program, but increasingly many are enrolled in honors programs. It is also a trend that honors colleges and programs help to prepare their students for the awards competitions.

"In 2010, a new Distinguished Scholarships Office was created at WSU and, since that time, WSU has worked to encourage high-achieving students to pursue prestigious awards. *Scholarships from the Public University Honors list for which WSU students have competed successfully in the past decade are the Boren, Gilman, Goldwater, Fulbright and Udall scholarships. In most cases, the rate at which WSU students have won these awards has increased in recent years.*

"In 2012, the WSU Honors College appointed a faculty member in the college to serve quarter-time as a coordinator and advisor of distinguished scholarships for WSU honors students and to promote the WSU Distinguished Scholarships Program in the WSU Honors College and recruit honors student applicants for prestigious awards. In recent years, the numbers of Honors College applicants and winners among the total WSU applicants and winners have increased."

In the past 10 years alone, WSU students have won an impressive 14 Goldwater Scholarships, awarded to the most accomplished STEM undergraduates in the nation.

**UNRATED FEATURES**

**Continuation and Honors Graduation GPA Requirement:** 3.20 for both.

**Academic Strengths, National Rankings:** This is based on national rankings of *graduate* programs in all but engineering and business, where undergraduate rankings are used. One of the weaknesses of the *U.S. News* rankings is that they focus on too many wealth-related metrics while ignoring their own assessments of academic departments. The rankings listed below are for all universities, public or private.

WSU had a nationally ranked department in every subject we track except education.

The academic departments at WSU that are ranked nationally in the top 100 are sociology (42), earth sciences (68), engineering (70), computer science (75), economics (78), history (79), political science (81), physics (83), chemistry (88), and English (99).

**Internships, Professional Development, Community Engagement:** "The top incoming freshmen are chosen for the Honors 198 Leadership Course, which is offered in the Fall. This course has sections for Pre-Med and Business and two sections of combined degrees. In the spring semester, students from the 198 cohort are chosen for the Honors 298 Leadership course."

**Undergraduate Research:** "All Honors College students, except those majoring in engineering, are required to complete an Honors thesis that involves research directly under the supervision of a faculty mentor. *The students have to complete a written thesis and defend it orally in front of a faculty committee that includes at least one external examiner (i.e., not from the Honors College) and one faculty member from the Honors College.* For students majoring in engineering (about 20% of our students) their capstone project is counted in lieu of the Honors thesis. However, many of the engineering students in Honors also do undergraduate research. Undergraduate research is encouraged for all students in Honors."

**Honors Study Abroad:** For honors study abroad, there are two Universities in Wales, Aberystwyth and Swansea, and in China, Southeast University in Nanjing.

"We offer 2-3 faculty led trips every summer, led by Honors faculty. Honors has led the university in providing this type of experience since 1996. Scholarships are available specifically for study-abroad programs. These are provided by Honors, the Office of International Programs, and through the academic degree-granting colleges."

**Financial Aid:** "The Honors College at Washington State University is very proud to have many alumni, friends, and programs dedicated to helping our students meet the financial demands as they earn their education in Honors and at WSU. Honors scholarships and awards for Honors College students are awarded based on or to support incoming freshmen, merit for outstanding grades and achievements, financial need as determined by FAFSA, diversity, study-and research-abroad experiences including foreign language immersion programs, undergraduate research, and pursuit of a specific major. Most scholarships go into student accounts and are used for tuition and/or fees. Each of our scholarship awards requires that applicants be current Honors students and have a WSU cumulative grade point average of at least 3.20."

**National Merit Semifinalists:** "You're eligible for this scholarship if you're identified as a semifinalist by the National Merit Corporation and you're admitted to WSU Pullman. *You could earn full tuition for up to four years.* For Washington residents, the award value is based on current in-state tuition rates for

2018–19. For students from outside Washington state, the award value is based on current non-resident tuition rates for 2018–19."

**Honors Fees:** None.

**Placement of Honors Graduates:** None listed.

**Degree of Difference**: This is difference between (1) the average SAT scores for recently enrolled honors students (1299) and (2) the average test scores for all students in the university (1110) as a whole. The difference may be an indication of how "elite" honors students may be perceived as compared to students in the university as a whole. **Please keep in mind that neither the high nor low selectivity of an honors program determines how effective the program may be.**

**NAME**: WEST VIRGINIA UNIVERSITY HONORS COLLEGE

**Date Established:** 1982-1983 academic year.

**Location**: Morgantown, West Virginia

**University Full-time Undergraduate Enrollment (2017):** 22,350

**Honors Members in Good Standing**: 2,681 (mean size of all programs is 2,030).

**Honors Average Admission Test Score(s):** ACT, 28.8; SAT, 1192.

**Average High School GPA/Class Rank:** 4.14, weighted.

**Basic Admission Requirements:** ACT, 26; SAT, 1230; high school GPA 3.7.

**Application Deadline(s):** *Please verify with each program, as some deadlines could change.* "The Honors College reviews all WVU applications for eligibility on a rolling basis, after students have been formally admitted to the University. Applications for the Fall will continue to be evaluated for eligibility through April 1."

**Honors Programs with SAT scores from 1286—1300:** Florida Atlantic, Washington State, West Virginia.

**Administrative Staff:** 13.

**RATINGS AT A GLANCE:** For all mortarboard ratings immediately below, a score of 5 is the maximum and represents a comparison with all rated honors colleges and programs. More detailed explanations follow the "mortarboard" ratings.

**PERCEPTION\* OF UNIVERSITY AS A WHOLE, NOT OF HONORS:** 🎓🎓🎓

\*Perception is based on the university's ranking among public universities in the 2018 U.S. News Best Colleges report. Please bear in mind that the better the U.S. News ranking, the more difficult it is for an honors college or program to have a rating that equals or improves on the magazine ranking.

**OVERALL HONORS RATING:** 🎓🎓🎓

**Curriculum Requirements:** 🎓🎓🎓 1/2

**Number of Honors Classes Offered:** 🎓🎓 1/2

**Number of Honors Classes in Key Disciplines:** 🎓🎓 1/2

**Extent of Honors Enrollment:** 🎓🎓🎓

**Honors-only Class Size:** 🎓🎓🎓 1/2

**Overall Class Size (Honors-only plus mixed, contract):** 🎓🎓🎓

**Honors Grad Rate Adjusted to SAT:** 🎓🎓🎓 1/2

**Grad Rate Adjusted to Freshman Retention Rate:** 🎓🎓🎓🎓🎓

**Ratio of Staff to Students:** 🎓🎓🎓

**Priority Registration: Yes,** honors students register for all courses, honors and otherwise, with the first group of students during each year they are in the program.

**Honors Housing Amenities:** 🎓🎓🎓 1/2

**Honors Housing Availability:** 🎓🎓🎓 1/2

**Prestigious Awards:** 🎓🎓🎓🎓

## RATING SCORES AND EXPLANATIONS:

**Curriculum Requirements (3.5):** The most important rating category, the curriculum completion requirement (classes required to complete honors) defines not only what honors students should learn but also the extent to which honors students and faculty are connected in the classroom. If there is a thesis or capstone requirement, it reinforces the individual contact and research skills so important to learning.

The average number of honors semester hours required for completion across all programs is 30.0.

Presidential Honors requires a total of 25 credits, including a 3-6 credit thesis. Any honors courses and honors contract options can be used to meet the requirement, but all students must complete a 1-credit honors orientation course.

Deans Honors requires a total of 16 credits, including the same thesis and orientation requirements.

Honors Foundation completion requires 13 credits without a thesis or capstone requirement.

**AP/IB credits** may be counted as replacements for 3 honors credits.

**No. Honors Classes Offered (2.5):** This is a measure of the total **adjusted** honors main sections available in the term reported, not including labs and thesis. An adjusted main section has 3 or more semester credits, or equivalent, and sections with fewer credits receive a lower prorated value.

The program offered a section for every **34.4** enrolled students. The average for all programs was **15.0**. The lower the number, the better. In the term reported, **77.4%** of honors enrollment was **in honors-only sections; 18.8% was in mixed sections; and 3.8% was in contract sections.** For all programs under review, enrollment by type of honors section was 75.8% honors-only, 15.4 % mixed, and 8.8% contract.

**No. Honors Classes in Key Disciplines (2.5):** The 15 "key" disciplines are biological sciences; business (all); chemistry; communications (especially public speaking); computer science; economics; engineering (all); English; history; math (all); philosophy; physics; political science; psychology; and sociology, anthropology, and gender studies. Interdisciplinary sections, such as those often taken for General Education credit in the first two years, do receive a lesser, prorated discipline "credit" because they introduce students to multiple disciplines in an especially engaging way, often with in-depth discussion.

For this measure, mixed and contract sections are not counted as a section in a key discipline unless students taking the sections for honors credit make up at least 10% of the total section enrollment.

In the term reported, the program offered a section in a key discipline for every **58.0 honors students.** The average for all programs is **24.7**. The lower the number, the better.

Out of **42 adjusted sections in key disciplines, 25 were honors-only sections**. The most sections were in biology, business, engineering, and math, followed by English, political science, economics, history, and philosophy.

WVU Honors offered 10 interdisciplinary sections. Examples include "Medicine and the Arts," "The Salem Witch Trials," and "The History of Now." WVU Honors is a **blended** program, with a preponderance of classes in the disciplines.

**Extent of Honors Enrollment (3.0):** Not all honors students take an honors class each term, especially after the first two years. Programs that have fewer honors classes and thesis options for upper-division honors students will *generally* have fewer total members in good standing who are actually enrolled in a given term. (Please be aware, however, that honors students not enrolled in a class for a term are still tied to the honors community through residential and extracurricular activities.) *Our research shows that this measure is closely related to honors completion rates, i.e., the number of students who complete honors requirements by the time they graduate.*

For example, if a program has 1,800 individual students enrolled in a given term, and 3,000 students in good standing, the level of enrollment was .67, an indication that honors class enrollment is somewhat below average, especially in upper-division classes. **WVU Honors has a ratio of .73**, below the average of 1.30 for all programs.

**Average Class Size, Honors-only Sections (3.5):** Offered mostly in the first two years, honors-only classes tend to be smaller and, as the name implies, have no or very few students other than those in the honors program. These class sections always are much smaller than mixed or contract sections, or regular non-honors class sections in the university.

The average honors-only class size at WVU Honors is **19.6 students**. The average for all programs is **17.5 students**.

**Average Class Size, Overall (3.0):** The overall class calculation is based on the *proportion* of honors students in each type of class (honors-only, mixed honors, and honors contract sections). Thus it is not a raw average. The overall honors-credit class size is **35.5 students**, versus the average for all programs of **24.9 students**.

These class size averages also do not correspond to the number of students per honors section ratings above. The reason is that, in computing average class size metrics, we include enrollment in each 1-2-credit section, not just sections with 3 or more credits.

Along with an honors-only class size of 19.6 students (listed above), the program's mixed honors sections have an average size of **97.3 students,** and the contract sections with honors credit for individual honors students average **54.4 students.** Across all programs, the average mixed honors section has 68.6 students, and the average contract section has 56.6 students.

**Honors Grad Rate Adjusted to SAT (3.5):** The rating is the based on the actual grad rate for students who entered the program six years earlier, whether or not the students remained in honors. The **actual rate of 82.4%** is also compared to the rates of other programs with the same test score entry requirement range, and then adjusted upward if the program is performing above other programs in the same range, or downward if the performance is less than other programs in the same range. The rate here is slightly downward, to **81.4%.**

**Grad Rate Adjusted to Freshman Retention Rate (5.0):** This rate compares the actual grad rate above to a predicted grade rate when *university-wide* freshman retention rates are considered. The actual grad rate is **4.11 points higher** than the predicted rate. For all programs, the actual grad rate is **.33 points lower** than the predicted rate.

**Ratio of Staff to Honors Students (3.0):** There is 1 staff member for every **206.2** students. (Mean ratio for all programs is 1 staff member for every **127.9** students.)

**Honors Residence Halls, Amenities (3.5):** "The faculty and staff of the Honors College believe that some of the most important interactions a student has with professors and fellow students occur outside of the classroom. The Honors Living-Learning Community enhances our students' experience through small weekly dinners with members of the university's faculty and administration, including West Virginia University's president and provost."

Both honors residence halls are for first-year students. Honors Hall is on the WVU main campus and also is the site for tutoring, mentoring, and leadership programming for WVU. It is air-conditioned with suite-style rooms and has onsite laundry. Dining is across the street at the Summit Café.

Lincoln Hall is at the WVU Evansdale Campus, about 1.5 miles from the main campus downtown. Lincoln Hall has the same features at Honors Hall; dining is across the street at Café Evansdale.

**Honors Residence Halls, Availability (3.5):** This rating compares the number of occupants in honors residence halls to the number of honors freshman and sophomore members in good standing. The ratio for the program is **.44** places for each first- and second-year student. The median for all programs is .49 places.

**Prestigious Awards (4.0):** The awards that we track and include are listed in the section titled "Prestigious Scholarships." The awards are sometimes won by students who are not in an honors college or program, but increasingly many are enrolled in honors programs. It is also a trend that honors colleges and programs help to prepare their students for the awards competitions.

Students at West Virginia University have won 24 Rhodes Scholarships, two Marshall Scholarships, one Gates Cambridge Scholarship, 23 Truman Scholarships, five Udall awards, and 45 Goldwater Scholarships. In the last three years alone, WVU students had won 16 Fulbright Student awards, 13 Boren Scholarships, and three National Science Foundation graduate fellowships. In the last two years, WVU students have won 25.9% of all Gilman Scholarships awarded to WVU students.
Percentage of Gilman awards won in the last two years: 25.9%

**UNRATED FEATURES**

**Continuation and Honors Graduation GPA Requirement:** "To be recognized from West Virginia University's Honors College as a Presidential Scholar students need a 3.5 cumulative GPA, for Dean's Scholar students need a 3.4 cumulative GPA and to complete the Honors Foundation Program students need a 3.0 cumulative GPA and a 3.5 Honors grade point average."

**Academic Strengths, National Rankings:** This is based on national rankings of *graduate* programs in all but engineering and business, where undergraduate rankings are used. One of the weaknesses of the *U.S. News* rankings is that they focus on too many wealth-related metrics while ignoring their own assessments of academic departments. The rankings listed below are for all universities, public or private.

WVU has nationally ranked departments in 13 of the 15 academic departments that we track.

The nationally ranked academic departments at WVU include economics (83), political science (96), history (98), English (99), physics (100), earth sciences (107), engineering (110), and computer science (111).

**Internships, Professional Development, Community Engagement:** The programs listed below are centered at Honors Hall, the principal honors residence.

**"Honors College Mentor Program is designed to provide leadership opportunities for second, third and fourth year Honors students** to serve as mentors for the incoming first year students. Individuals interested in participating in this program need to register for HONR 402: Foundations of Peer Mentoring during the spring semester. The course curriculum consists of best practices in mentoring and teaching. Students must pass this course with a 'B' or better to be an official part of the mentor program. The following fall semester, mentors must return to campus early to assist first year students as they move into residence halls, the Honors Induction Ceremony and Honors Retreat. Mentors will also lead the Orientation to Honors course, an eight-week course, in which they would be paired with another mentor to teach/mentor up to sixteen students together (eight students each). These courses are held within the residence halls. There are approximately 120 mentors in the program who are responsible for approximately 1,000 new Honors students. The Honors College mentor program also provides another opportunity for students to earn Honors credit through 'Foundations of Peer Mentoring' and 'Teaching Practicum [courses].'"

**"Honors College Tutor Program:** "The Honors College cultivates an attitude of service to West Virginia University, the Mountain State, our broader region, and the world. *One way the Honors College demonstrates this and **includes all undergraduate students** at the university is through the Honors College Tutor Program.* Tutors primarily work in the testWELL Learning Center which is a multi-subject learning center providing tutoring services in a wide variety of courses ranging from math and chemistry to political science, foreign languages and provide assistance with the writing of papers. The testWELL Learning Center is located in both Honors residence halls, Lincoln Hall and Honors Hall. The Honors College Tutor Program employs approximately thirty Honors students each year as tutors."

**Undergraduate Research:** "At West Virginia University, we have an Office of Undergraduate Research which is housed in the Honors College. The mission of this office is to enhance academic excellence through undergraduate research and creative endeavors. This office connects undergraduate students, who have strong and committed interests in research and creative endeavors, to faculty members, programs, and research-related opportunities that are aligned with their interests. As the home of the WVU Summer Undergraduate Research Experience (SURE) program, this office fosters a culture of academic engagement by providing unparalleled opportunities for student participation in research."

"The Office of Undergraduate Research at West Virginia University offers to primary research programs for students: Summer Undergraduate Research Experience (SURE) and Research Apprentice Program (RAP).

*"SURE is a summer undergraduate research experience for students interested in graduate school and research/creative work within their discipline or a related discipline.* Selected students complete research at WVU for eight weeks during the summer under the direction of a WVU faculty research mentor and a graduate or post-doctoral mentor. Students are expected to research full-time (minimum of 40 hours per week for eight weeks).

"The Research Apprenticeship Program *(RAP) allows freshman and sophomore level students at West Virginia University to use federal work-study funds or gain course credit for undergraduate research apprenticeships with WVU research faculty.* The goal of this initiative is to expand opportunities for students and facilitate their introduction to the concept of scholarship while learning the research or scholarly methods in their field."

**Honors Study Abroad:** "West Virginia University was awarded the prestigious Heiskell Award for international partnerships. This award recognizes West Virginia University for its international partnerships with its strategic partner in the Middle East, the Royal University for Women in Bahrain.

"West Virginia University's Civil and Environmental Engineering program starting fall 2017 semester at a new location in Bahrain. Students will be enrolled as West Virginia University students and will be eligible to earn their bachelor of science in civil engineering. Newly constructed facilities and classrooms with state-of-the-art laboratory equipment. Courses and labs instructed by West Virginia University affiliated faculty.

"The WVU Bahrain location is coed, and will be hosted at the Royal University for Women, located in Riffa, close to Bahrain's capital, Manama, and international airport. All students admitted to the program will enroll in a preparatory foundation semester in English and mathematics. Career support services are available to assist with job placement upon graduation."

**Financial Aid:** "West Virginia University does not offer any specific scholarships designated for Honors students, but we do offer many opportunities for incoming freshmen students. Below please see a list of the scholarships (and approximate value) that are available to incoming freshman students:

**Freshman Scholarships for Residents of West Virginia**

- Foundation Scholarship - Covers cost of attendance as determined by Student Financial Support and Services, less any other gift aid the student is receiving from the University or other outside agencies (including private, State, and Federal programs).
- Bucklew Scholarship - $10,000 per year for four undergraduate years (or a bachelor's degree - whichever comes first)
- University Merit Scholarship - $7,000 per year for four undergraduate years (or a bachelor's degree - whichever comes first), plus a one-time $3,500 stipend for study abroad/academic enhancement.

**Freshman Scholarships for Non-Residents of West Virginia**

- University Merit Scholarship - $21,000 per year for four undergraduate years (or a bachelor's degree - whichever comes first), plus a one-time $3,500 stipend for study abroad/academic enhancement.
- Scholarship of Distinction Level 1 - $15,000 per year for four undergraduate years (or a bachelor's degree - whichever comes first)
- Scholarship of Distinction Level 2 - $9,000 per year for four undergraduate years (or a bachelor's degree - whichever comes first)
- Scholarship of Distinction Level 3 - $7,000 per year for four undergraduate years (or a bachelor's degree - whichever comes first)

**Honors Fees:** None.

**Placement of Honors Graduates:** WVU Honors graduates have enrolled in graduate and professional school programs at Case Western Reserve, Yale School of Medicine, University of Pittsburgh, Rice University, Ohio State University, University of Maryland, American University, University of Colorado, and many others.

**Degree of Difference**: This is difference between (1) the average SAT scores for recently enrolled honors students (1192-1290) and (2) the average test scores for all students in the university (1120) as a whole. The difference may be an indication of how "elite" honors students may be perceived as compared to students in the university as a whole. **Please keep in mind that neither the high nor low selectivity of an honors program determines how effective the program may be.**

# SUMMARY REVIEWS

The following reviews summarize the admissions information, curriculum requirements, class sizes, graduation rates, honors housing and other perks, along with each university's record of winning prestigious scholarships.

The honors colleges and programs in this section are not rated because (1) they simply did not have all the data that we requested for this edition; (2) they did not submit any data; (3) they had special features that we could not measure, such as allowing students to choose any course for honors credit; or (4) they were in the midst of major program changes or transitioning to an honors college from an honors program.

**NAME**: UNIVERSITY OF ALABAMA HONORS COLLEGE

**Date Established:** 2003

**Location**: Tuscaloosa, Alabama

**University <u>Full-time Undergraduate</u> Enrollment (2015):** 32,563.

**Honors Members in Good Standing**: 9,000 estimated size; (mean size of all rated programs is 2,030). This is the <u>largest honors program in the country.</u>

**Honors <u>Average</u> Admission Statistics (Honors College)**: est. ACT, 30-31; est. SAT, 1400-1410. Randall Scholars (formerly computer-based honors) estimated ACT 33, SAT, 1460. University Fellows estimated ACT 33, SAT, 1460.

**Average High School GPA/Class Rank:** Regular Honors College, 3.77, and 84% are in the top 10% of their class. Randall Scholars, 4.30. University Fellows, 3.90.

**Basic Admission Requirements:** The requirements for admission to the Honors College are a 30 ACT/1360 SAT and a 3.5 high school GPA or higher. Because of our commitment to meeting the needs of students from within the state, Alabama high school graduates have another path to admission if they are within the top 5% of their class and have at a 28 ACT/1310 SAT or higher and a 3.5 or higher GPA.

**Application Deadline(s):** *Please verify with each program, as some deadlines could change.* For Randall Scholars and University Fellows applications, the deadline is December 15, 2018; for other applications there is "no formal deadline," but for housing and orientation purposes, the earlier the better.

**Honors Programs with old SAT scores from 1403—1461:** Auburn, Central Florida, Delaware, Iowa, Kansas, Mississippi, Missouri, New Jersey Inst of Technology, Penn State, South Florida, Vermont, Virginia Commonwealth.

**Administrative Staff:** estimated at 24, not counting several 40-50 affiliated faculty.

**Curriculum Requirements:** The most important rating category, the curriculum completion requirement (classes required to complete honors) defines not only what honors students should learn but also the extent to which honors students and faculty are connected in the classroom. If there is a thesis or capstone requirement, it reinforces the individual contact and research skills so important to learning.

The average number of honors semester hours required for completion across all rated programs is 30 credits.

For completion of the **University Honors Program**, students must earn at least 18 hours of Honors courses, including 6 hours of Honors Foundations and 12 credits in any combination of the following: honors electives (including additional Honors Foundation courses); departmental honors courses (up to 6 credits in honors contract courses); up to 6 credits of Independent Study; up to 6 credits in Randall Research Scholars courses; or graduate courses.

**Randall Research Scholars:** "During their freshman year, students complete an intensive series of courses on technology fundamentals, problem solving, project management and research fundamentals. These essential skills enable students to quickly learn and adapt to new knowledge domains and technical environments required for faculty-directed research projects. Throughout their sophomore to senior years the RRSP students will interview with faculty and select a project to work on as a research assistant with a faculty member who will act as project director. *Students will typically work on projects in areas related to their academic discipline; however, they may elect to work in an unrelated field to challenge themselves and broaden their exposure to academic research.*

**University Fellows:** The Fellows program emphasizes service, leadership, research/mentoring by faculty, professional internships, special Fellows seminars, and cutting-edge projects. Fellows receive excellent support in applying for jobs, prestige scholarships, and graduate/professional schools. Other special programming includes "annual domestic excursions and an optional international excursion."

Fellows also complete the **Black Belt Experience**. It is "the signature Fellows project, [and] creates an opportunity for students to explore the various issues affecting poverty in the Black Belt and to partner with individuals in Marion, Perry County, Alabama to create systemic change. Students are servant leaders and change agents who create projects that both respond to the needs of the community and capitalize on the students' particular interests, gifts, and abilities in preparation for lifelong civic action."

**Continuation and Graduation Requirements:** 3.30 for both.

**AP/IB credits** are **not** counted as replacements for honors courses.

**Course Offerings:** In the term we reviewed, UA Honors College offered at least 364 honors courses, almost all of them in honors-only class sections. About 40 of these were in English composition or literature, mostly the former. An excellent range in other disciplines followed, including math (13 sections), economics, computer-based honors, western civilization/history, biology, chemistry, physics (with calculus), a commendable series of 1.5-credit courses in "STEM-Business Honors." There were at least 30 of the STEM-Business sections, ranging from STEM-Business I to VII.

Here is the description: "Running alongside the STEM Path to the MBA, you will take a STEM Business Honors course each semester worth 1.5 credit hours that meets for 75 minutes per week. The class size is limited to 35 students, and each semester covers a business topic like Marketing, Accounting, or Operations Management, among others. You will engage in several group projects, closing out each semester with a case study based on the semester's business topic."

Another 200 or so were in honors interdisciplinary seminars and sections. Among them were "A Republic if You Can Keep It," "The Dark Side of Technology," "The Law and Social Change," "Art for Life's Sake," and the extremely timely "Gossip, Rumor, and the Media."

**Class Size:** The average size of the departmental honors courses was 29.4 students and for honors seminars 18.2 students. The overall average class size was **23.3** students. For all rated programs the overall average was **24.9** students.

**Honors Grad Rate Adjusted to SAT:** We estimate the six-year graduation rate of UA Honors students who entered the program (but not necessarily completers of honors requirements) to be 89-90%. This is higher than the average grad rate of other programs with similar test score requirements (86%).

**Grad Rate Adjusted to Freshman Retention Rate:** The university-wide freshman retention rate at Alabama is 86%. The estimated honors graduation rate in relation to this freshman retention rate is higher than that for other programs with similar freshmen retention rates.

**Ratio of Staff to Honors Students:** We estimate that there is 1 staff member for every **174.7** students. (Mean ratio for all programs is 1 staff member for every **127.9** students.)

**Honors Residence Halls, Amenities:** "The Honors Community is located in Ridgecrest North, South, East, and West. Honors students may, but do not have to, live in Honors Housing. Housing priority is based on date of housing application, and the earlier a student submits the housing application, the more housing options will be available to select during online room selection in the spring. The online housing application typically becomes available about October 1 of each year for the following fall. Living-Learning Communities allow students to have access to educational programs and extra-curricular activities exclusive to the Honors College."

 In the recent past, almost 60% of honors students living on campus resided in Ridgecrest North and South, while another 28% lived in Ridgecrest East and West.

These coed living-learning facilities form the center of the University's tightly-knit Honors community. "These buildings feature 4-bedroom suites with private bedrooms, 2 bathrooms, a living/dining area, and a kitchenette. The kitchenette has a full-size refrigerator, microwave, and cabinet space. The bedrooms feature height-adjustable beds with extended twin mattresses.

"In addition to the benefits of living with other Honors College students, faculty residents in each dormitory further increase the value of such an opportunity." Faculty-in-residence programs offer social events and serve as informal advisors for students living in those dorms.

**Honors Residence Halls, Availability:** We do not have data for this category.

**Prestigious Awards:** The awards that we track and include are listed in the section titled "Prestigious Scholarships." The awards are sometimes won by students who are not in an honors college or program, but increasingly many are enrolled in honors programs. It is also a trend that honors colleges and programs help to prepare their students for the awards competitions.

"Over the last 10 years, the Capstone [University of Alabama] leads the nation with 31 Goldwater Scholars, surpassing Princeton, Cornell and Harvard. In addition, UA is one of only four institutions, alongside Stanford, Princeton and Iowa State, to have the maximum number of nominees selected in 2017.

"The federal scholarship program honoring U.S. Sen. Barry Goldwater was designed to foster and encourage outstanding students to pursue careers in the fields of mathematics, the natural sciences and engineering.

"With 51 Goldwater Scholars, 15 Rhodes Scholars, 11 NSEP Boren Scholars and 16 Harry S. Truman Scholars in UA's history, we take pride in preparing our students through academic rigor and excellence to make significant contributions to research with national impact."

**UNRATED FEATURES**

**Continuation Requirements: 3.30 GPA.**

**Academic Strengths, National Rankings:** This is based on national rankings of *graduate* programs in all but engineering and business, where undergraduate rankings are used. One of the weakness of the *U.S. News* rankings is that they focus on too many wealth-related metrics while ignoring their own assessments of academic departments.

The average departmental ranking at Alabama is within the top 125 nationwide. Leading departments include business (45, a big rise), followed by physics (83), chemistry (88), economics (90), political science (96), history (98), and engineering (99).

**Internships, Professional Development, Community Engagement:** Honors Fellows, in particular, are engaged in community activities and leadership.

**Undergraduate Research:** "The McWane Undergraduate Research Fellowship awards up to $1,500 for students engaged in a research or creative project with a mentoring faculty member. These awards provide support for students who plan to be involved in a research or creative effort that is individual or collaborative. Scholarship recipients will verify their eventual participation in the proposed research endeavor and submit a one-page description of the research project to the Honors College."

Please see "curriculum" in this review for a description of the **Randall Research Scholars Program.**

**Honors Study Abroad:** The UA in Oxford study-abroad program "is thriving like never before. Housed in beautiful Worcester College, one of the university's primary constituent colleges, students can take full advantage of the Oxford experience. Oxford University itself is one of the oldest and most prestigious academic institutions in existence and Oxford has been a flourishing college town since the 13th century. In all its facets, Oxford offers an unparalleled opportunity for intellectual, architectural, and fun-filled explorations, both of the past and of the present. Our program encompasses all of Oxford's jewels, from the exclusive Bodleian Library to the heart of the town, to cutting-edge faculty, to our close proximity to London, Dover, Stratford-upon-Avon (Shakespeare's birthplace), and Canterbury (famous for its 11th century Cathedral and Chaucer's Canterbury Tales), all of which UA students visit on group excursions each summer."

Honors abroad in Germany, Czech Republic, Austria, and Italy "takes you to Munich (Germany), Prague (Czech Republic), and Innsbruck (Austria) with daytrips to several of King Ludwig II's castles in Bavaria, Stubaier Glacier and Bolzano (Italy)."

**Financial Aid:** The honors college and university are well-known for their recruitment of National scholars, especially **National Merit Finalists**, who receive:

- Value of tuition for up to five years or 10 semesters for degree-seeking undergraduate and graduate (or law) studies
- Four years of on-campus housing at regular room rate (based on assignment by Housing and Residential Communities)
- $3,500 per year Merit Scholarship stipend for four years.
- One-time allowance of $2,000 for use in summer research or international study (after completing one year of study at UA)
- $2,000 book scholarship ($500 per year for four years)

**National Merit Semifinalists** are eligible for the Presidential Scholarship, with a value of $104,000 over four years ($26,000 per year). "Students graduating with remaining scholarship semester(s) may use these monies toward graduate school and/or law school study at UA."

**Honors Fees:** None.

**Degree of Difference**: This is a rating based on the differences between (1) the average (2015, two-part) SAT scores for enrolled honors students (1400-1410) and (2) the average test scores for all students in the university (1190) as a whole. This rating is an indication of how "elite" honors students may be perceived as compared to students in the university as a whole. The score also provides an indication of how well-prepared the non-honors students in the university may be **Please keep in mind that neither the high nor low selectivity of an honors program determines how effective the program may be.**

**NAME**: THE HONORS COLLEGE AT FLORIDA INTERNATIONAL UNIVERSITY

**Date Established**: Faculty Scholars Program (1972-1990), Honors Program (1990-1997), Honors College (1997-present).

**Location**: Miami, Florida

**University Full-time Undergraduate Enrollment**: 45,813

**Honors Members in Good Standing**: 2,077 (mean size of all programs is 2,030).

**Honors Average Admission Statistics**: ACT, 27.2; new SAT score, 1272.

**Average High School GPA/Class Rank:** While class rank is not considered, the average high school GPA of incoming FTIC freshmen is 4.34.

**Basic Admission Requirements:** ACT, 25; new SAT score, 1170; 3.50 high school GPA, weighted.

**Application Deadline(s):** *Please verify with each program, as some deadlines could change.* Applications are open October 1—May 1 every year. The priority consideration deadline is January 15. Transfer students who wish to compete for limited scholarships should apply by the priority deadline date.

**Administrative Staff:** 15.

**Priority Registration: Yes,** honors students **register for all courses**, honors and otherwise, **with the first group of student**s during each year they are in the program.

**Curriculum Requirements:** The curriculum completion requirement (classes required to complete honors) defines not only what honors students should learn but also the extent to which honors students and faculty are connected in the classroom. If there is a thesis or capstone requirement, it reinforces the individual contact and research skills so important to learning.

The average number of honors semester hours required for completion across all rated programs is 30.0.

For first-year entrants, the honors completion requirement is 20 credits, including up to 6 credits for experiential courses and/or up to 6 credits for an honors thesis.

For transfer students and others entering after the first year, the requirement is 18 credits.

For students to complete the engineering and computer honors requirements, they must have 14 credits (6 for transfers) along with a non-credit design project that counts for upper-division honors college credit.

**AP/IB credits** are not traditionally counted as replacements for honors courses, but may be considered on a case-by-case basis.

**Course Offerings:** *FIU Honors College emphasizes interdisciplinary learning. All but a handful of honors enrollment is in honors-only class sections, most of them interdisciplinary rather than focused on a single academic discipline.* Several of these introduce honors students to the requirements and challenges of pre-business, pre-engineering, and pre-med majors.

A 26-section, first-year seminar of 3 credits, "The Origin of Ideas, and the Ideas of Origins," is described as follows: "What do we know? And how do we know it? As one of your introductory courses in the Honors College at FIU, this class will begin your journey in higher education by posing a series of epistemological questions and concerns for studying the nature of our intellectual pursuits. Our belief is that it is not just necessary to study something or learn something: one must be able to take a step back and understand the assumptions that are being made, the implications that our study has for the world, and where we stand in relation to all of these pursuits."

Beyond the seminars above, another 45 interdisciplinary courses were listed, such as "Entrepreneurship, Design, and Thinking," "Environment and Society," and "God and Man in the 'Great Conversation.'"

**Class Size:** The average honors class size at FIU Honors College is **21.1** students. For rated programs, the overall class size average is **24.9** students.

**Honors Grad Rate Adjusted to SAT:** Data unavailable.

**Grad Rate Adjusted to Freshman Retention Rate:** Data unavailable.

**Ratio of Staff to Honors Students:** Our estimate is that there is 1 staff member for every **138.5** students. (The ratio for all rated programs is 1 staff member for every 127.9 students.)

**Honors Residence Halls, Amenities:** The honors residence is Parkview Hall, which houses 214 freshmen and upperclassmen. Parkview is air-conditioned with suite-style rooms. There is all-you-can-eat dining at the Fresh Food Company, but it appears to be some distance away.

**Honors Residence Halls, Availability:** This rating compares the number of places in honors residence halls to the number of honors freshman and sophomore members in good standing. The ratio for the honors program is **.10** places. The average for all programs is .49 places.

**Prestigious Awards:** The awards that we track and include are listed in the section titled "Prestigious Scholarships." The awards are sometimes won by students who are not in an honors college or program, but increasingly many are enrolled in honors programs. It is also a trend that honors colleges and programs help to prepare their students for the awards competitions. Below are recent awards for FIU students:

Jose Sirven II
National Finalist, Truman Scholarship, 2017

Brian Garcia
Honorable Mention, Goldwater Scholarship, 2017
Jonathan Urra
National Finalist, Truman Scholarship, 2015

**UNRATED FEATURES**

**Continuation Requirements:** 3.30 for continuation for both.

**Academic Strengths, National Rankings:** This is based on national rankings of *graduate* programs in 15 disciplines, except engineering and business, where undergraduate rankings are used. The rankings listed below are for all universities, public or private. **"FIU recently placed in the Top 100 Public Universities by U.S. News."**

FIU has seven nationally ranked departments: earth sciences (118), history (134), psychology (148), business (151), education (158), engineering (162), and biology (218). In addition, according to U.S. News, FIU has the number one program in Florida for international business and global policy studies. In addition, *FIU reports that its law school graduates "consistently earn the highest bar passage rate of any of Florida's 11 law schools."*

**Internships, Professional Development, Community Engagement:** "Over the last academic year, Honors College students have been placed in a wide variety of internships, including: Univision, several law groups, the Make A Wish Foundation, St. Jude Children's Research Hospital, the Consulate General of Spain, several nonprofits, Amazon, Telemundo, US Southcom, Fiat Chrysler Group, VISA, local city and county government offices, UBS Private Wealth Management, several political campaigns, Bed Bath & Beyond, Nicklaus Children's Hospital, Allianz Global Investors, and several engineering firms.

"Also over the last academic year, Honors College students have completed over 36,000 cumulative hours of community service. Some of the most popular outlets for our students to volunteer are hospitals/medical centers, non-profits, government offices/facilities, Miami Dade County Public Schools, and places of worship."

**Undergraduate Research:** "The Advanced Research and Creativity in Honors (ARCH) program provides opportunities for Honors College students to engage in supervised research and creative projects under the supervision of FIU faculty experts from all academic areas. This is only open to Honors College students who benefit from a program which facilitates the completion of groundbreaking research, innovative products, and/or unique creative works."

**Study Abroad and Off-Campus Study:** FIU Honors College offers study-abroad programs in Costa Rica, France, Italy, Spain, China, Vietnam/Cambodia, Japan, United Kingdom, and South Africa. Below is the description of the Costa Rica program:

"Costa Rica is determined to become the first carbon-neutral country in the world by 2021. Students on this winter break trip will focus on the country's initiatives in social responsibility, 'green' development, biodiversity, ecotourism, indigenous community, and the fight against global warming. They will explore everything from ant farms to rainforest medicines, from volcanoes to snorkeling, from exotic birds to gulch-spanning ziplines, from crocodiles to frog ponds."

**Financial Aid:** "The Honors College offers 11 scholarships to qualified first time in college Honors students and an additional 6 scholarships to transfer Honors students." Florida Bright Futures Scholarship establishes lottery-funded scholarships to reward Florida high school graduates for high academic achievement and community service with per-credit scholarship award amounts.

FIU Presidential Scholarship requires a 1390 SAT or 30 ACT, 4.0 GPA; pays 100% tuition and fees plus books.

FIU Ambassador Scholarship requires a 1280 SAT or 27 ACT, 4.0 GPA; pays 75% tuition and fees plus books.

Transfer Academic Achievement requires 50 transferrable credit hours or an AA degree completed before term of entry and 4.0 GPA; pays 50% tuition and fees plus books.

Raise.me is a micro-scholarship program for high school students. Students must have at least a 3.2 GPA.

**National Merit Scholars** receive full tuition, fees, room and board, up to the cost of attendance as published by the Office of Student Financials.

**National Achievement Scholars** receive full tuition, fees, room and board, up to the cost of attendance as published by the Office of Student Financials.

**National Hispanic Recognition Scholars** receive full tuition, fees, room and board, up to the cost of attendance as published by the Office of Student Financials.

**Honors Fees:** None, except for honors residence hall.

**Placement Experiences:** "We do not officially track placement; however we can share with you the following exit survey results from the 2016-2017 academic year."

FT paid employment: 26%
Graduate or Professional School FT: 31%
Graduate or Professional School PT: 13%
PT paid employment: 12%
Starting or raising a family: 6%
Volunteer activity (e.g. Peace Corps): 8%
Other: 3%
Additional undergraduate coursework: 1%

**Degree of Difference**: Degree of Difference: This is difference between (1) the average SAT scores for recently enrolled honors students (1272) and (2) the average test scores for all students in the university (1200) as a whole. The difference may be an indication of how "elite" honors students may be perceived as compared to students in the university as a whole. Please keep in mind that neither the high nor low selectivity of an honors program determines how effective the program may be.

*Editor's Note: The Lewis Honors College at the University of Kentucky began operations in 2017. It is generously funded and has all the signs of becoming a major presence in public honors education.*

**NAME**: LEWIS HONORS COLLEGE

**Date Established**: 1961 as UK Honors Program. **2017** as Lewis Honors College.

**Location**: Lexington, Kentucky

**University Full-time Undergraduate Enrollment:** 22,621

**Honors Members in Good Standing**: 1989 (mean size of all programs is 2,030).

**Honors Average Admission Statistics**: ACT, 31.4; est. new SAT score equivalent, 1420.

**Average High School GPA/Class Rank:** 3.86, unweighted.

**Basic Admission Requirements:** ACT, 28; est. new SAT score equivalent, 1330; 3.50 HSGPA.

**Application Deadline(s):** *Please verify with each program, as some deadlines could change.* December 1, 2018, but prefers earlier.

**Honors Programs with new SAT scores 1403—1461:** Auburn, Central Florida, Delaware, Iowa, Kansas, Mississippi, Missouri, New Jersey Inst of Technology, Penn State, South Florida, Vermont, Virginia Commonwealth.

**Administrative Staff:** 14.

**Priority Registration: Yes,** honors students register for all courses, honors and otherwise, with the first group of students during each year they are in the program.

**Curriculum Requirements:** The curriculum completion requirement (classes required to complete honors) defines not only what honors students should learn but also the extent to which honors students and faculty are connected in the classroom. If there is a thesis or capstone requirement, it reinforces the individual contact and research skills so important to learning.

The average number of honors semester hours required for completion across all rated 50 programs is 30 credits.

Beginning in Fall 2018, these are the revised honors completion requirements for four honors options:

**University Honors** requires 30 honors credits, including 18 credits in honors courses, course conversions (honors contracts, 12-credit limit) or graduate courses; 6 credits in honors experiences; 3 credits in composition/communication; and a 3-credit thesis.

The **Global Scholars Pathway** option requires 35 credits, including 6 credits in honors interdisciplinary courses, 23 credits in business and economics, an average of 3 credits in study abroad, and a 3-credit management capstone.

The **Social Enterprise** option requires even more credits for completion—50. The curriculum is very similar to the Global Scholars Pathway, above, but 9 additional credits in business-related disciplines such as management, marketing, and accounting and credit for honors experiences is 6 credits.

Finally, the **Scholars in Engineering and Management (SEAM)** option requires 25 credits. At least three courses in engineering and one each in marketing and management are included. Six credits in honors experiences and a 3-credit engineering capstone are also required.

**AP/IB credits** are not counted as replacements for honors courses.

**Course Offerings:** Although we lack a comprehensive list of honors courses at this time, what we do have indicates that the LHC through Fall 2017 featured a series of courses structured around these broad subject areas: Honors in the Humanities; Honors in Natural, Physical and Mathematical Sciences; Honors in Social Sciences; and Honors in Arts & Creativity. *The courses within these categories do not, in general, focus narrowly on a single academic discipline even though they do have content mostly related to a given subject.*

For example, the Honors in the Humanities series has a section called "Early Modern Revolutions." The course description: "Much of the way we look at the world today in the 21st century can be traced to revolutions that occurred in Europe and America in the period from about 1600 to 1850. Some of these, of course, were political and military, such as the American and French Revolutions, but there were also revolutions in science, philosophy, economics, society, art, architecture, and music."

Another example from the Honors in Natural, Physical and Mathematical Sciences series is "What is Possible: Development of Biotechnology." The course not only recognizes that "biotechnology is playing an emerging role in many aspects of our daily lives (including in agriculture, medicine, biofuels, and industry)," but also "explores the multi-collaborative nature, thought processes, creativity and risk taking that led to both discoveries in basic sciences (i.e. the tool kit) and advances in biotechnology."

**Class Size:** Based on the class data that we have, which does not include enrollment in mixed or contract option classes, the average overall class size at LHC is **22** students. The average overall class size for all rated programs is **24.9** students.

**Honors Grad Rate Adjusted to SAT:** LHC has not been in operation long enough to establish a six-year honors graduation rate for freshman entrants.

**Grad Rate Adjusted to Freshman Retention Rate:** LHC has not been in operation long enough to establish a six-year honors graduation rate for freshman entrants.

**Ratio of Staff to Honors Students: Ratio of Staff to Honors Students:** There is 1 staff member for every **142.1** students. (Mean ratio for all programs is 1 staff member for every 127.9 students.)

**Honors Residence Halls, Amenities:** LHC excels at providing honors residential space. The four honors residence halls are Lewis Hall, Donovan Hall, Johnson Hall, and Haggin Hall. Together these residences house 1,343 honors first-year students and upperclassmen, a very high number. Each hall has air-conditioned, suite-style rooms, onsite laundry, a kitchen for the facility, and the same dining hall. Lewis is the newest addition (2017) to what is called, collectively, The Honors Residential College. Lewis Hall is also the home of LHC administration.

"All of these beautiful buildings are located on central campus, right across from the W.T. Young Library and in easy walking distance to dining in K-Lair, The 90, and Starbucks."

**Honors Residence Halls, Availability:** This rating compares the number of places in honors residence halls to the number of honors freshman and sophomore members in good standing. The ratio for the honors program is **.93** places for each first- and second-year student. The average for all programs is .49 places.

**Prestigious Awards:** The awards that we track and include are listed in the section titled "Prestigious Scholarships." The awards are sometimes won by students who are not in an honors college or program, but increasingly many are enrolled in honors programs. It is also a trend that honors colleges and programs help to prepare their students for the awards competitions.

UK students have won nine Rhodes Scholarships, two Gates Cambridge Scholars, four Marshall Scholars, 14 Truman Scholarships, and at least 20 Goldwater Scholarships award to outstanding undergraduates in the STEM disciplines.

**UNRATED FEATURES**

**Continuation and Graduation Requirements:** 3.00 for both.

**Academic Strengths, National Rankings:** This is based on national rankings of *graduate* programs in 15 disciplines, except engineering and business, where undergraduate rankings are used.

The average departmental rank at UKY is 84.9. The university has a nationally ranked department for each of the 15 disciplines that we track.

Nationally ranked departments at UKY include education (46), economics (68), history (69), psychology (75), business (78), political science (81), math (86), sociology (87), biology (90, (computer science (91), English (91), and engineering (99).

**Internships, Professional Development, Community Engagement:** "Credit-bearing Honors Experience options in Honors are:

"HON 395: Honors Research and Creativity. Independent research or creative projects supervised by a faculty member in the field. Work must result in a report or publication evaluated by the supervising faculty member.

"HON 352: Study and Travel Abroad. An experiential, travel-abroad course that requires pre-travel class preparation followed by travel abroad that will provide students with multi-cultural exposure, leadership, and a new frame of reference for understanding the world and their role in it.

"HON 399: Honors Service Learning and Community Engagement. A service- or community-based learning experience in the field under the supervision of a faculty member."

**Undergraduate Research:** "Honors requires six hours of experiential credit. This can include research but doesn't have to; it can also include education abroad, internship/co-op or community service courses. Undergrad research is usually handled through the student's major, but we do offer HON 395: Independent Work, for students who either want to do research unrelated to their majors or whose majors do not offer such classes."

**Study Abroad and Off-Campus Study:** "The LHC believes that international educational experiences are crucial for students to become well-rounded citizens of the world, and we strongly encourage students to investigate opportunities through the Education Abroad office that can suit any major, area of interest, duration, or language immersion.

"Additionally, the LHC is excited to be able to offer travel courses in which students may enroll to complete program requirements through the course designation HON 352. Coursework completed while on an Education Abroad program will count for toward fulfilling Honors Experience credit (with the exception of ISP 599).

"There are a variety of scholarships available to support student travel, including the Kate Johnson scholarship, Student Skills Development Award, or, if the travel is associated with a student's independent project, the Independent Project Grant."

**Financial Aid:** "The *Otis A. Singletary Scholarship provides full four-year In-State Tuition + $10,000 Housing Stipend (first & second years only and living on-campus in a University residence hall).* Students are required to be a member of the Lewis Honors College. Requires a minimum 33 ACT or 1490 SAT and 3.80 unweighted high school GPA.

**National Merit Finalists or National Hispanic Recognition** Scholars are eligible for the Patterson Scholarship, with the same value the Singletary Award, above.

"The Kate Johnson Scholarship helps to enable Lewis Honors College students to participate in activities to develop skills or to participate in some type of field-based academic effort. It is intended to offset the costs of research opportunities, education abroad experiences, conference travel, or summer programs."

**Honors Fees:** $250 per semester.

**Placement Experiences:** "Not enough data currently to report."

**Degree of Difference**: Degree of Difference: This is difference between (1) the average SAT scores for recently enrolled honors students (1420) and (2) the average test scores for all students in the university (1210) as a whole. The difference may be an indication of how "elite" honors students may be perceived as compared to students in the university as a whole. Please keep in mind that neither the high nor low selectivity of an honors program determines how effective the program may be.

**NAME**: JUDY AND BOBBY SHACKOULS HONORS COLLEGE

**Date Established**: 2006, formerly honors program begun in 1968.

**Location**: Starkville, Mississippi

**University Full-time Undergraduate Enrollment:** 18,312

**Honors Members in Good Standing**: ~1,650 (mean size of all programs is 2,074).

**Honors Average Admission Statistics**: Not listed; *estimated* ACT, 31.5; SAT, 1420.

**Average High School GPA/Class Rank:** Not listed.

**Basic Admission Requirements:** ACT, 30; SAT, 1400; 3.75 unweighted HSGPA.

**Application Deadline(s):** *Please verify with each program, as some deadlines could change.* December 1, 2018, preferably earlier; after that date, space available basis.

**Administrative Staff:** 14.

**Priority Registration: Yes.**

**Curriculum Requirements:** The curriculum completion requirement (classes required to complete honors) defines not only what honors students should learn but also the extent to which honors students and faculty are connected in the classroom. If there is a thesis or capstone requirement, it reinforces the individual contact and research skills so important to learning.

The average number of honors semester hours required for completion across all programs is 30 credits.

"To be recognized as an Honors College Scholar at graduation, and to receive the Honors designation (Collegium Honorum) on the diploma and transcripts, a student must complete at least 27 Honors credits with a 3.4 average in Honors courses and

1. complete the English composition requirement during the first year of full-time Honors coursework;
2. complete the transdisciplinary Honors sequence (6 credits);
3. complete two interdisciplinary Honors courses (6 credits);
4. complete three discipline-specific Honors courses or tutorials (9 credits);
5. complete a for-credit Study Abroad2; and
6. successfully write and defend an Honors thesis (3-6 credits).

**Course Offerings:** "Students pursuing the Cursus Honorum (Path to Honors) typically begin by taking our 'Quest' courses. These are small seminars (about 15 students in each section) focusing on core texts from the Western tradition as well as important works from Asia, Africa, and Latin America. These 'texts'—which include art, music, and film as well as literature—promote discussion of the Big Questions, such as: Why are we here? Is there a God? What is love? Should one exercise power over others? What is the purpose of art? and How do we know what we know? Such questions are at the heart of a liberal education.

"Beginning their second year Honors students may take interdisciplinary and problem-based courses in Fine Arts, Humanities, Mathematics, Natural Science, and Social Science. Examples of these ever-changing special topics courses include 'The World of J.R.R. Tolkien,' 'Culture, Society and Power,' and 'Ethics and Western Films.'

"Honors students can also take special sections of departmental courses and graduate courses for Honors credit. **The Honors Oxbridge Tutorial allows a student to define an individual topic of study with a professor in the tradition of Oxford and Cambridge.** All Honors students must have a senior capstone experience, and for some this means writing, presenting, and defending a formal Honors Thesis.

In Fall 2017, there were five sections of the "Quest" series and at least 44 sections in academic disciplines, including an impressive 11 sections in computer science, followed by multiple sections in biology/biochemistry, math, English (comp and lit), communications (public speaking), engineering, chemistry, philosophy, anthropology, political science, and philosophy.

SHC combines the "Quest" series with a strong range of departmental honors classes and appears to be a **blended** program with more emphasis on academic subjects than interdisciplinary courses. The tutorial courses appear to be true tutorials rather than honors contract courses; i.e., students meet only with the instructor who assigns readings and engages in extended dialogue with the student rather than having the student do extra coursework in a non-honors class section in order to earn honors credit.

**Class Size:** We estimate that the average honors-only class has about **16** students, not counting tutorials. For all rated programs the average was **17.5** students.

**Honors Grad Rate Adjusted to SAT:** We do not have data for this category.

**Grad Rate Adjusted to Freshman Retention Rate:** The university-wide freshman retention rate at MSU is 80%. The honors graduation rate in relation to this freshman retention rate is almost certainly higher, probably in the 84%-86% range.

**Ratio of Staff to Honors Students:** We estimate that there is one staff member for every **118** students. (Mean ratio for all programs is 1 staff member for every 127.9 students.)

**Honors Residence Halls, Amenities:** "The Shackouls Honors College is a residential College where students live together in the living-learning communities of Griffis Hall and Nunnelee Hall. Honors freshmen will be assigned to a room in either Griffis or Nunnelee hall with another Honors student. Roommate requests are encouraged; however, such requests may only be made for other Honors College students. Non-program roommates are not permitted." All freshmen are required to live in honors housing.

"Located in Zacharias Village, a true living-learning community has developed in Griffis Hall and Nunnelee Hall over the past six years. Classrooms, conference rooms, library, and computer lab complement student residences and food and social spaces." Griffis is also the administrative home of the college.

Both residence halls, in the north (east) zone of the MSU campus, are "new construction" dorms, with each double room having a private bath, microwave, refrigerator, wireless Internet, cable TV outlet, and individual room temperature control. Dining options include Moe's Southwest Grill and the Marketplace at Perry.

**Honors Residence Halls, Availability:** We do not have data for this category, but availability of honors dorm space for freshman, especially, is likely to be excellent.

**Prestigious Awards:** The awards that we track and include are listed in the section titled "Prestigious Scholarships." The awards are sometimes won by students who are not in an honors college or program, but increasingly many are enrolled in honors programs. It is also a trend that honors colleges and programs help to prepare their students for the awards competitions.

"Over the last five years, Mississippi State has had a Rhodes Scholar, a Gates Cambridge Scholar, two Truman Scholars, two Fulbright Fellows, and three Goldwater Scholars. The University has been recognized by the Washington, D.C.-based Truman Scholarship Foundation for "sustained success" in helping students both to win the $30,000 competitive awards and to prepare for public service careers. And most recently, the Goldwater Foundation, which recognizes the most promising undergraduate researchers across the nation in science, math, or engineering, awarded the Goldwater Scholarship to a Shackouls Honors student in the Bagley College of Engineering."

The university has a total of 18 Truman Scholars and 17 Goldwater Scholars.

**UNRATED FEATURES**

**Continuation and Graduation Requirements:** 3.40 for both.

**Academic Strengths, National Rankings:** This is based on national rankings of *graduate* programs in 15 disciplines, except engineering and business, where undergraduate rankings are used. The rankings listed below are nationwide and include both public and private universities.

The nationally ranked departments at MSU include education (95), engineering (110), history (125), math (144), physics (146), business (151), chemistry (154), biology (175), and psychology (181).

**Internships, Professional Development, Community Engagement:** "Through the generosity of NSPARC* [National Strategic Planning Analysis and Research Center, located in Starkville], we are able to provide supplemental funding for internships for students in the liberal arts and sciences. This is an important step because the pay associated with such internships often does not cover the full cost of travel to and living in a major city. The internships we have been developing will give our students in the liberal arts and sciences a broad range of venues in which to use the full panoply of their academic skills and education in a highly applied area. Furthermore, they will be expected to be able to work under pressure to produce high quality work quickly in high stakes situations.

"After these internships, our students would have real world experience bringing their academic skills and education to bear on a variety of real world problems. The internship itself along with expected letter of recommendation from their supervisors would stand as an informal credential testifying to their abilities and experience."

*"Mississippi State University's National Strategic Planning and Analysis Research Center (NSPARC) is expanding the boundaries of data science to create knowledge and innovations that drive human progress. Our expertise includes data analytics, predictive analytics, machine learning, artificial intelligence, system of systems, data governance, cybersecurity, cloud technology and high-performance computing. Known primarily for our work with smart government and more than 50 data innovations created in the last 10 years, **NSPARC has achieved national prominence in the data science field."**

**Undergraduate Research:** "The Undergraduate Research Symposium is held twice a year in the spring and summer semesters and is open to all undergraduate students engaged in research. The Symposium provides the opportunity for students to showcase faculty-guided, cutting edge research and creative activity by students from diverse departments, colleges, and research centers across campus through poster and oral presentation sessions.

"Students may submit group projects; however, there should be a designated principal presenter on the day of the symposium. The designated presenter should complete the registration form with his or her name and information. Co-authors and collaborators will be listed in the abstract booklet if included in the form. Prizes are awarded to the principal presenter only. Groups are allowed to submit individual abstracts and present different posters or give separate oral presentations for the same research. A large part of the project evaluation is being able to answer questions showing a deep understanding of the work that has been done."

**Study Abroad and Off-Campus Study:** "The Shackouls Summer Study at the University of Oxford is a highly selective program that affords the most academically qualified students with a true Oxford experience and scholarship support. The program runs each year for six weeks, from mid-May to late June, and is limited to fifteen MSU honors students. The Shackouls Oxford Program includes the following features not found in most other study abroad programs:

- An Oxford-themed seminar (e.g. J.R.R. Tolkien, C.S. Lewis, the Oxford Movement, British Art and Architecture, Contemporary British Politics)
- Tutorials with Oxford University faculty
- Associate Student status in the most prestigious Oxford colleges—e.g. Christ Church College, Trinity College, and New College—including dining hall, library, and pub privileges
- Oxford student ID card with Bodleian Library privileges
- Lectures given by Oxford academics and leading figures in British politics
- Performances at the Royal Shakespeare Theatre (Stratford) and the Globe Theatre (London)
- Tours of museums in Oxford, London, and Cambridge
- While a short summer program will offer flexibility to most majors, some students will elect to spend an entire term in Oxford taking four or more tutorials with Oxford faculty in one of the aforementioned colleges."

**Financial Aid:** "The Presidential Scholarships and the Provost Scholarships are Mississippi State University's most prestigious freshman awards. Each scholarship is awarded to 10-12 of the most outstanding entering freshman on a competitive basis."

**Presidential Scholarships**

"This scholarship covers tuition, fees, *room and board, research fellowships, and books for four years of undergraduate study. Non-resident students may also receive a scholarship to cover up to 100% of the out-of-state portion of tuition. Criteria: *Minimum* 30 ACT or 1330 SAT; outstanding high school academic record with a scholarship GPA of 3.75 or higher; exceptional high school and community leadership."

*Fully covers double-occupancy on-campus housing for up to four years, with an option to partially cover off-campus housing for the third and fourth year.

**Provost Scholarships:**

- Academic scholarship of $8,500 per year *($19,000 per year for non-resident)*
- $4,000 scholarship for study abroad
- A research grant of $1,500 for academic research and/or creative discovery
- A one-summer optional tuition credit of $1,000 ($2,400 for non-resident) and one summer of free housing in Griffis Hall
- An optional $750 travel grant to a conference (to be provided by Honors)

Criteria: Minimum high school GPA of 3.75 or higher; *minimum* 30 ACT.

**Honors Fees:** None.

**Placement Experiences:** We have no data for this category.

**Degree of Difference**: Degree of Difference: This is difference between (1) the average SAT scores for recently enrolled honors students (1400-1420) and (2) the average test scores for all students in the university (1180) as a whole. The difference may be an indication of how "elite" honors students may be perceived as compared to students in the university as a whole. Please keep in mind that neither the high nor low selectivity of an honors program determines how effective the program may be.

*Editor's Note: Although we do not have submitted data for Honors Carolina, we receive many requests for individual profiles of the program and hope that the summary review below will be helpful. We estimate that Honors Carolina would receive a 4.5 or 5.0 overall rating.*

**NAME**: HONORS CAROLINA

**Date Established**: 1954

**Location**: Chapel Hill, North Carolina

**University Full-time Undergraduate Enrollment**: 18,862.

**Honors Members in Good Standing**: Est. 1,900 (mean size of all programs is 2,030).

**Honors Average Admission Statistics**: Median ACT, 33; Median SAT score, 1440. "We require either an SAT or ACT score for all first-year applicants and sophomore transfer applicants. Please note that the writing portion of either the SAT or ACT is no longer required nor recommended. Additionally, we don't have a preference for one test over the other, so you may submit either score (or both). If you send us scores from multiple test dates, we'll take your highest score for each section of the test and consider those scores as we evaluate your application."

**Average High School GPA/Class Rank:** Top 3% of class.

**Basic Admission Requirements:** "We don't use formulas or cutoffs or thresholds; no one is automatically admitted or denied because of a single number. We read every application, thoroughly."

**Application Deadline(s):** *Please verify with each program, as some deadlines could change.* Must be accepted by university first, followed by honors invitation. University early action deadline is October 15, 2018, with decision by late January 2019. Regular deadline is January 15, 2019, with notification in late March.

**Other Honors Programs with new SAT scores from 1403—1461:** Auburn, Central Florida, Delaware, Iowa, Kansas, Mississippi, Missouri, New Jersey Inst of Technology, Penn State, South Florida, Vermont, Virginia Commonwealth.

**Administrative Staff:** 16.

**Priority Registration:** "…members of Honors Carolina register for honors courses before other eligible students each semester. They also receive priority status for wait listing of honors courses."

**Curriculum Requirements:** The curriculum completion requirement (classes required to complete honors) defines not only what honors students should learn but also the extent to which honors students and faculty are connected in the classroom. If there is a thesis or capstone requirement, it reinforces the individual contact and research skills so important to learning.

The average number of honors semester hours required for completion across all rated 50 programs is 30.0.

Graduation with Honors or Highest Honors at Honors Carolina requires a minimum of **30 credits** for first-year entrants: 24 course credit hours and a **6-credit thesis.**

To be an Honors Carolina Laureate, students admitted as first-semester freshmen must complete 24 credits; second-semester first-year students must earn 18 honors credits; and students admitted as first-semester second-year students must earn 15 credits.

**AP/IB credits** are not counted as replacements for honors courses.

**Course Offerings:** Honors Carolina offers a high number of honors course sections for the number of students enrolled. Almost all of the program enrollment is in sections that have 75%-100% honors students. Carolina allows non-honors students with high GPAs to take honors classes, a positive factor. A very small percentage of earned honors credit comes by way of honors contract classes. With the exception of some outstanding first-year seminars, honors courses are discipline-focused and extremely well-balanced, combining math and science offerings with sections in the humanities and social sciences. Overall, the program is a **discipline-based** program supplemented by interesting seminars.

In Spring 2018, about a dozen sections were in business, seven in history, six in biology, five each in economics, English, and political science, three each in philosophy and classics, and the remainder in American studies, computer science, psychology, public affairs, religious studies, and Spanish.

Seminars include "Gerrymandering," which explores "the problems introduced by gerrymandering and the technologies proposed to identify and prevent it," and "Combinatorics," where students "learn about the history of Combinatorics, its connections with the theory of numbers, its fundamental role in the natural sciences and various applications," including "what statistical physics is about, what is cryptography, and how the stock market works, and for everyone who likes mathematics."

One economics course is about game theory; a public affairs course looks at the philosopher John Rawls and his concept of justice. One math course is discrete math; another is calculus with functions of several variables.

There were no sections in engineering or physics. UNC does not have an engineering school.

**Class Size:** While the business and chemistry sections range from 30 to 45 students, the average size for other sections is **20-22** students. The average overall class size for all rated programs is **24.9** students.

**Honors Grad Rate Adjusted to SAT:** We estimate the six-year graduation rate of Honors Carolina students who entered the program (but not necessarily completers of honors requirements) to be 94%. This is far higher than the average grad rate of other programs with similar test score requirements (86%).

**Grad Rate Adjusted to Freshman Retention Rate:** The university-wide freshman retention rate at Carolina is extremely high at 97%. The honors graduation rate in relation to this freshman retention rate is somewhat higher than that for other programs with similar freshmen retention rates. UNC-Chapel Hill is tied with Michigan and UVA for the highest freshman retention rate among public universities. Only the most elite private universities (Yale, Harvard, Stanford, Brown, and a few more) have higher rates.

**Ratio of Staff to Honors Students:** Our estimate is that there is 1 staff member for every **118.8** students. (Mean ratio for all 50 rated programs is 1 staff member for every 127.9 students.)

**Honors Residence Halls, Amenities:** Honors Carolina residence halls have changed since our 2016 review. Now, the two residences are Horton Hall, in the Manning East Residential Community, and the adjacent Hinton James Hall, a 10-floor tower remodeled in 2013. Both are located in south campus, "only a few minutes' walk from the Dean Dome, Kenan Stadium, Rams Head Dining Hall, and beautiful study spaces in the Student and Academic Services buildings; Manning East places residents near the center of action."

Hinton James has eight-person suites and window air conditioners in each room. It also has cleaning services. "The walk to main campus where classes are is a solid 15 minutes. During the morning hours, you will see what seems like hundreds of people making their way up the hill to go to class. The walk is certainly doable and it's great exercise. If walking isn't your thing, the RU bus comes every 15 minutes and takes you right to the side of the Student Union. Going to Franklin Street? It is indeed an ambitious walk best saved for cool days in the fall, but you can hop on the U bus or ride the P2P if it's after 7:00 p.m."

Horton features four-person suites and central AC. The nearest dining appears to be at Chase Hall/Ram Market.

**Honors Residence Halls, Availability:** We do not have data for this category. *Note: Honors Carolina offers honors housing to all freshmen, and the Director reported in 2016 that 55% of freshmen choose honors housing while the rest to do not. Honors Carolina does not offer honors housing to sophomores.*

**Prestigious Awards (5.0):** The awards that we track and include are listed in the section titled "Prestigious Scholarships." The awards are sometimes won by students who are not in an honors college or program, but increasingly many are enrolled in honors programs. It is also a trend that honors colleges and programs help to prepare their students for the awards competitions.

UNC is one of the top three public universities in the achievement of prestigious awards at both the undergraduate and post-graduate level, and is likely the top public university when the following awards are combined: Rhodes (49), Gates Cambridge (5), Marshall (17), Churchill (16), and Truman (30).

UNC undergraduates have also won 46 Goldwater scholarships, and 15 Udall awards. Although we do not track Luce scholarships, for study in Asia, UNC students have won 37, "more than any other four-year institution, public or private."

**UNRATED FEATURES**

**Continuation and Graduation Requirements:** Cumulative GPA 3.00 for both.

**Academic Strengths, National Rankings:** This is based on national rankings of *graduate* programs in 15 disciplines, except engineering and business, where undergraduate rankings are used.

The average departmental rank at UNC is 25$^{th}$ or better nationwide among all universities. Outstanding departments are sociology (6), business (7), history (11), political science (11), psychology (13), chemistry (15), English (18), computer science (25), economics (29), education (30), biology (33), and physics (47). Again, please note that UNC does not have an engineering department.

**Undergraduate Research:** "Cutting-edge research is an integral part of the culture at Carolina. Honors Carolina students enjoy countless opportunities to work with faculty members conducting breakthrough research in almost any field. Honors Carolina students get involved in research projects, and many begin that work as early as their first year. Research may take the form of a senior honors thesis project, an advanced course in the major, a faculty-mentored research project, or participation in one of our competitive summer research fellowships."

**Note: The value of the awards listed below may have changed.**

"Burch Fellowships—Burch Fellows create their own unique educational experiences and travel the globe to pursue their passions. Designed for students with extraordinary ability, promise, and imagination, *Burch Fellowships provide up to $6,000 to support off-campus learning experiences like these: working with NASA astrobiologists to answer questions about the possibility of life on other planets; jamming with jazz musicians in Cuba; traveling to the Philippines to study how bamboo can mitigate the effects of climate change.*

"Carolina Blue Honors Fellowships in International Sports Entrepreneurship—The Carolina Blue Honors Fellowship enables students to embark on *a self-designed project focused on international sports entrepreneurship. Fellows receive up to $5,000* to support experiences like these: working for an Australian Baseball league franchise; leading a social media campaign for a pro cricket franchise in the India Premier League; helping a soccer start-up get off the ground in Tanzania.

"Froelich Honors Fellowships—The Will Froelich Honors Fellowship allows incoming first year students to study abroad, pursue a project of civic engagement, finance an internship, or work with a faculty mentor on independent research. Fellows receive $7,500 to fund experiences throughout their undergraduate career.

"Robinson Honors Fellowships—Robinson Honors Fellows delve deeply into the history and culture of Europe and the Mediterranean, from the golden age of Greece to the upheaval of World War I. Fellows receive up to $6,000 to pursue projects that explore art, literature, history, music, philosophy, political thought, and religion.

"Taylor and Gold Summer Research Fellowships—Taylor and Gold Fellowships support students engaged in faculty-mentored research projects during the summer. Fellows receive up to $4,000 to continue work they have begun with a faculty member, to get a head start on a Senior Honors Thesis, or to travel to distant libraries, labs, or archives that might otherwise be beyond reach.

"Thesis Research Grants—Research grants are available to help offset the cost of conducting a Senior Honors Thesis. The grants, up to $500, can cover the cost of equipment, supplies, software, publications, transportation, and other expenses."

**Study Abroad and Off-Campus Study:** Honors Carolina students have access to so many study-abroad and off-campus programs that not all of the information can be included here. Below are some of the opportunities:

"Honors Study Abroad programs are open to all UNC undergraduate students who are in good standing and have a 3.0 GPA. Financial aid can be applied to the program costs and Honors Carolina offers additional need- and merit-based scholarships.

"Honors Semester in London (Fall and Spring) *Students study at Honors Carolina's own Winston House on historic Bedford Square*, attend seminars within the shadow of the British Museum, conduct research at the British Library, and learn from professors who make London their home. Internships are available in fields ranging from global finance to healthcare and the arts.

"Weir Honors Fellowships in Asian Studies (Spring and Summer) Weir Honors Fellows become fluent in Mandarin and gain practical, independent work experience in China, home to one of the world's oldest civilizations and the 21st century's fastest growing economy. Fellows spend the Spring semester in Beijing for intensive language study, then complete an eight-week summer internship in either Beijing or Shanghai exploring careers in fields such as banking, law, journalism, public health, and historic preservation.

"Honors Semester in Cape Town (Fall) Students intern full-time and complete two academic courses on contemporary South Africa. Internships are available in public health, refugee resettlement, conflict resolution, medicine, urban planning, journalism, environmental conservation, the arts, and other areas.

"Honors Public Policy Seminar in Washington, D.C.: Domestic and Global Affairs Internship Program (Spring) Students enjoy first-hand engagement with the actors and organizations that influence domestic and international affairs in Washington, D.C. The seminar exposes students to a range of public policies which influence U.S. economic prosperity, national security, and America's role in the broader global community.

"Entrepreneurship in Silicon Valley (beginning in spring 2017) Students will work four days per week in internships and complete the requirements for an academic minor in entrepreneurship. Internships are available in young and maturing start-ups venture capital firms.

"Honors Carolina also offers a changing roster of field research seminars. These programs send faculty and students off campus to work on shared scholarly interests. Recent topics and locations include public health in Vietnam, energy and sustainable development in Germany and the Netherlands, Jewish life and the Holocaust in Poland, and security studies in Vienna, Bosnia, and Kosovo."

**Financial Aid:** "UNC's Office of Scholarships and Student Aid, along with the Morehead-Cain Foundation and the Robertson Scholars program, award merit- and need-based scholarships to members of Honors Carolina.

"While more than half of Honors Carolina students receive merit- or need-based academic scholarships, an invitation to join Honors Carolina does not automatically include a scholarship award.

"The Honors Carolina class includes a significant number of Morehead-Cain Scholars, Robertson Scholars, Carolina Scholars, Johnston Scholars, Pogue Scholars, and others."

According to the website Unigo, the Morehead-Cain Scholarship has a total value of "approximately $80,000 for in-state students and $140,000 for out-of-state students." The application deadline is October 15.

"The Robertson Scholars Leadership Program provides full tuition, room and board, and mandatory fees for each scholar for all four years of undergraduate study if the student maintains eligibility criteria. Scholars receive a laptop and have access to three summers of generous funding, as well as support for up to two semesters of study abroad.

"Approximately 36 awards offered annually. Generally, there are 18 awards offered at each eligible university [Duke and UNC-Chapel Hill].

"The Robertson Scholars Leadership Program is one of the most generous and visionary merit scholarship programs in American higher education. This program transforms students through their immersion in the intellectual and social life of two dynamic universities and their exposure to new and challenging environments."

**Honors Fees:** None.

**Placement Experiences:** None listed, but Carolina graduates attend the most prestigious institutions in America and abroad, and have excellent opportunities for employment as well.

**Degree of Difference**: This is a based on the differences between (1) the average (2015, two-part) SAT scores for enrolled honors students (1440) and (2) the average test scores for all students in the university (1305) as a whole. The test scores may be an indication of how "elite" honors students may be perceived as compared to students in the university as a whole. The scores can also provide an indication of how well prepared the non-honors students in the university may be. **Please keep in mind that neither high nor low test scores determine the overall quality of a program.**

**NAME**: UNIVERSITY HONORS COLLEGE

**Date Established**: Program founded 1969; *became the nation's only urban-focused honors college in 2014.*

**Location**: Portland, Oregon

**University Full-time Undergraduate Enrollment:** 21,633

**Honors Members in Good Standing**: 813 (mean size of all programs is 2,030).

**Honors Average Admission Statistics**: ACT, 28.6; SAT, 1283; 3.83 HSGPA.

**Basic Admission Requirements:** ACT, 26; SAT, 1250; 3.50 HSGPA.

**Application Deadline(s):** "December 1, 2018, is the priority deadline to be automatically considered for a scholarship." Admission is on a rolling basis.

"Students will be notified with a decision within about 10 weeks of their admission to PSU; see below for specific admission notification dates. Missing GPA, transcripts or test scores will delay the process. Due to the large volume of applications we receive, the Honors College cannot provide advance notice of admissions decisions.

"Honors College admissions decisions that are sent via email will go to the student's @pdx.edu email address if the student account is set up."

December 1, 2018 is the university scholarship deadline.

**Administrative Staff:** 3 staff and 8 core faculty.

**Priority Registration: Yes,** honors students register for all courses, honors and otherwise, with the first group of students during each year they are in the program.

**Curriculum Requirements:** The PSU Honors College is unique, combining "ways to think critically about the urban environment and the interdependence between the city and the global world." *It is "the only urban-focused honors college in the country."*

Completion of University Honors requires a minimum 45 quarter credits, the equivalent of 30 semester credits. The curriculum meets all university Gen Ed requirements.

The requirements are in four different areas:

The Global City (15 credits)—First-year sequence, foundations in reading and writing for research and scholarship focusing on sustainability, globalization and urbanization.

Urban Discourses (12 credits)—Research methodologies in urban history and sociology, urban arts and culture, and urban ecology.

Seminars, Research, and Internships (12 credits)—Explore methodological research in distinct disciplines, interdisciplinary questions, and research.

Thesis (6-12 credits)—Completion of a thesis project *in each student's disciplinary area.*

**AP/IB credits** are not counted as replacements for honors courses.

**Course Offerings:**

**First year: Foundations**

The Global City: Hon 101, Hon 102, Hon 103 (15 credits). "This year-long sequence serves as a foundations course in the four-year University Honors College curriculum and provides the basic intellectual framework for the social, cultural, political, and material study of the urban environment. 'The Global City' introduces the means to think critically about the urban environment and the interdependence between the city and the global world.

"This set of courses focuses on developing and refining student understanding and practice of the three writing tools dealt with throughout the Honors curriculum: summary of argument, explication, and placement in relation to a discourse community, as part of the preparation for writing the undergraduate thesis. While each section of the course will have different material, the writing tools studied throughout the year are the same from section to section. 'The Global City' sequence is taken in a cohort model, with students remaining with the same peers and faculty throughout the academic year. *Class size is limited to 24.*"

**Second year: Research Methods**

Urban Discourses: Hon 201, Hon 202, Hon 203 (12 credits). "The three connected courses of the sophomore year take the urban, and specifically the city of Portland, as an appropriately dynamic subject for research shaped by the three "domains" of academic knowledge: the social sciences, the humanities, and the natural sciences. Students progress through an integrated set of research projects that develop not only their understanding of the systems by which cities operate but also their own critical capacities as urban residents and knowledge producers. *Class size limited to 30.*"

Hon 201: Urban Social Sciences "examines urban structures and processes through the application of social science methodologies such as: spatial analysis, ethnography, interviews, surveys, and archival research, among others. We will explore and put into practice these skills by conducting original research in the Portland area."

Hon 202: Urban Humanities "examines the city as text, using humanities methodologies that produce close analysis of cultural artifacts and texts placed in cultural and historical contexts. Disciplinary approaches may include History, Languages and Literature, Film Studies, Gender Studies, Art History, Cultural Studies, and others."

Hon 203: Urban Ecology uses Portland "as a living laboratory [and] introduces methodologies in the natural sciences. We explore foundations of experimental design while also sharpening observational skills and awareness of physical and ecological patterns and processes in the city. Different focus areas depend on seasonal activity and include a range of topics such as stream ecology, plant science and ornithology.

**Third year: "Let Knowledge Serve the City" (12 credits)**

Honors Junior Seminars: Hon 407 (minimum 4 credits – maximum 12 credits). "At least one 4-credit Honors Junior Seminar is required; additional seminars are encouraged. Students choose from among a wide variety of interdisciplinary seminars, taught by Honors and departmental faculty, broadly focused around key methodological and interdisciplinary questions. Seminar classes challenge Honors students to think creatively and analytically as well as rehearse the essential research and writing skills necessary for the production of a senior thesis. *Class size limited to 20.*

"Honors Abroad: Hon 407 (4 credits – 8 credits). "The Honors College runs faculty-led global HON 407 seminars for Honors students every year. Past trips have investigated cultural and ecological sustainability in Borneo, studied sustainable development in the highlands of Nicaragua, explored global cities in Vietnam, and examined the history of plague and pestilence in London. These courses fulfill the HON 407 Junior Seminar requirement."

"Internships: Hon 404 (4 credits - 8 credits). "Students have the opportunity to gain experience, apply their academic learning, and make connections through approved cooperative education/internships. During their internship, students must enroll in and complete the online HON 404: Internship module on D2L. Honors students have in the past interned at OHSU, the U.S. Attorney's office, Portlandia, the National Institutes for Health, the Portland Art Museum, Mercy Corps, the Beaverton City Library, Willamette Week, and the Smithsonian, among many other organizations."

Research: Hon 401 (4 credits – 8 credits). "Students are encouraged to join ongoing research projects, conduct independent research, and develop creative projects under the supervision and mentorship of faculty."

Departmental H-seminars (4 credits – 8 credits). "Students may fulfill up to 8 credits of the junior requirements by completing approved H-seminars offered by departments across campus. A list of approved H-seminars is published on the Honors website each term."

**Fourth year: Community Engagement and Scholarship**

Senior Thesis (minimum 6 credits). "Honors students are required to complete a thesis in their major field during their final undergraduate year….Finally, the student presents the thesis at the Honors Thesis Symposium. Honors theses are published online through the PSU Library and are also available in the Undergraduate Research Commons, showcasing undergraduate research from universities nationwide."

**Class Size:** The class sizes are listed in italics above, in conjunction with courses taken in the first three years. The overall average is likely about **25** students. The overall average class size for all rated programs is **24.9** students.

**Honors Grad Rate Adjusted to SAT:** The six-year graduation rate of university honors program students who entered the program (but not necessarily completers of honors requirements) was 74.5%, lower than the average grad rate of other programs with similar test score requirements (85.5%).

**Grad Rate Adjusted to Freshman Retention Rate:** The university-wide freshman retention rate at PSU is 71%. Relatively few honors programs have an honors graduation rate that is higher than the university freshman retention rate—a plus for PSU Honors College. The freshman *retention* rate for the Honors College is 84%.

**Ratio of Staff to Honors Students: Ratio of Staff to Honors Students:** There is 1 staff member for every **79.4** students, but only if core faculty are counted. (Mean ratio for all programs is 1 staff member for every 127.9 students.)

**Honors Residence Halls, Amenities:** PSU Honors College students can choose to reside in Stephen Epler Hall, which features suite-style double rooms "with ensuite bathroom and kitchenette."

**Honors Residence Halls, Availability:** We do not have data for this category.

**Prestigious Awards:** The awards that we track and include are listed in the section titled "Prestigious Scholarships." The awards are sometimes won by students who are not in an honors college or program, but increasingly many are enrolled in honors programs. It is also a trend that honors colleges and programs help to prepare their students for the awards competitions.

We do not have data for this category.

**UNRATED FEATURES**

**Continuation and Graduation Requirements:** 3.25 for both.

**Academic Strengths, National Rankings:** This is based on national rankings of *graduate* programs in 15 disciplines, except engineering and business, where undergraduate rankings are used. The rankings listed below are nationwide and include both public and private universities.

Nationally ranked departments or specialties at PSU include urban policy (16), rehabilitation counseling (20), local government management (21), public management and leadership (37), social work (50), and public affairs (52).

**Internships, Professional Development, Community Engagement:** "Advising & Career Services maintains a list of internships available locally and around the world. Advising & Career Services also hosts multiple Career and Internship fairs throughout the year, such as the annual pre-health and volunteer fairs. Dozens of businesses, organizations, and other schools participate in these events.

"Most of the schools and colleges at PSU have internship advisers to help advise you regarding opportunities specific to your field of interest. *The School of Business, College of Urban and Public*

*Affairs, and College of Liberal Arts and Sciences have internship advisers located in their department.* Check with your school or college to find out what resources are available.

*"Portland's thriving nonprofit world can offer opportunities to students in all fields, even if you eventually plan on working in the private sector."*

**Undergraduate Research:** "In the final year of undergraduate study, all Honors College students complete a thesis. The thesis is a serious research project, representing a valuable opportunity for Honors students to work closely with a faculty advisor from their major department. Students generally take 8 credits of thesis coursework to complete the project in two terms; the minimum number of thesis credits required to graduate is six."

**Study Abroad and Off-Campus Study:** "PSU offers over 200 different programs in more than 80 countries around the world. Some of the programs are directly coordinated by Portland State, while others are offered through providers outside of PSU.

"The Honors College runs faculty-led global HON 407 seminars for Honors students every year. Past trips have investigated cultural and ecological sustainability in Borneo, studied sustainable development in the highlands of Nicaragua, explored global cities in Vietnam, and examined the history of plague and pestilence in London."

**Financial Aid:** "The University Honors College offers a limited number of Laurels Tuition Remissions awards to new and returning Honors students each year. Honors Scholarship awards are made for each academic year and are typically for $3,000 per academic year ($1,000 each term) and may be renewed for up to four years if the student maintains Honors eligibility. Awards are applied directly to tuition and cannot be used for any other purpose.

"Honors Laurels Scholarships are awarded to both newly admitted and returning Honors students. To maintain eligibility for the award recipients must be Honors students in good standing and meet Honors requirements for GPA and minimum enrollment.

*"The generous contributions of the **Institute for Sustainable Solutions** and Portland General Electric have made these competitive awards available to a small group of incoming freshman each year. These awards provide students with a **$2,500 grant per year** for two years as well as provide additional faculty mentoring and research partnerships."*

**Honors Fees:** There is a differential tuition of $7/credit hour. There is also a $10/class writing lab fee.

**Placement Experiences:** None listed.

**Degree of Difference**: Degree of Difference: This is difference between (1) the average SAT scores for recently enrolled honors students (1250) and (2) the average test scores for all students in the university (1120) as a whole. The difference may be an indication of how "elite" honors students may be perceived as compared to students in the university as a whole. Please keep in mind that neither the high nor low selectivity of an honors program determines how effective the program may be.

**Editor's Note:** *According to the university website, citing the* 2017-18 Almanac for The Chronicle of Higher Education, *Rowan University is the **seventh-fastest growing public doctoral institution** from 2005-2015, with 65.5 percent growth in enrollment.*

**NAME**: THOMAS N. BANTIVOGLIO HONORS CONCENTRATION IN THE HONORS COLLEGE AT ROWAN

**Date Established**: 1989 as an honors program at Glassboro State University; 2017 honors college.

**Location**: Glassboro, New Jersey

**University Full-time Undergraduate Enrollment:** 14,344

**Honors Members in Good Standing**: ~600 (mean size of all programs is 2,030).

**Honors Average Admission Statistics**: Not listed.

**Average High School GPA/Class Rank:** Not listed.

**Basic Admission Requirements:** ACT, 28; SAT, 1300. "Our application process takes into consideration high school academic records (i.e. grades, class rank) as well as extra-curricular activities and service projects. A teacher recommendation and essay response are required."

**Application Deadline(s):** *Please verify with each program, as some deadlines could change.* Applications will be reviewed on an ongoing basis after the following deadlines: Friday, December 14, 2018; Friday, January 11, 2019; Friday, February 15, 2019; Friday, March 1, 2019 (Final deadline).

**Administrative Staff:** 4 full-time and one part-time.

**Priority Registration: Yes,** priority registration at Rowan begins the day before regular registration.

**Curriculum Requirements:** The curriculum completion requirement (classes required to complete honors) defines not only what honors students should learn but also the extent to which honors students and faculty are connected in the classroom. If there is a thesis or capstone requirement, it reinforces the individual contact and research skills so important to learning.

The average number of honors semester hours required for completion across all programs is 30 credits.

Completing the Honors Concentration requires passing a minimum of 8 Honors courses (24-28 credits) with a grade of C or higher, ideally including 4 interdisciplinary courses and/or Honors courses outside one's major. Students must take at least one Honors course the first semester they enter the Concentration.

"Alternative course experiences (i.e., Internships, Study Abroad, Research, Senior Privilege) may be counted toward Honors course requirements with prior approval through an application process. A reflection paper is required at the conclusion of the experience.

"Rowan students in their senior year with a GPA of 3.0 or higher may apply to take graduate courses at undergraduate tuition rates (see the Undergraduate **Senior Privilege Policy** for more information). Honors students can apply to have graduate-level courses count toward their course requirements."

**Continuation and Graduation Requirements:** "Students must earn a cumulative GPA of at least 3.33 and a GPA of 3.45 in their Honors courses. Students must maintain a minimum cumulative GPA of 3.00 to remain in good standing with the Honors Concentration, keeping in mind graduate standards."

Honors students must also participate in at least two types of extracurricular activities *each semester*, from the following options:

**Service:** At least 14 hours of service projects of the student's choice. Service activities are those in which the student volunteers their time, talents, or resources to help another person, cause, or organization. Service activities may be performed on- or off-campus.

**Participation**: At least 14 hours of participation in Honors recommended activities. Honors recommended activities are those that enhance classroom education. These include field trips, speakers, events, groups, etc. Within these participation hours, each academic year Honors students must attend at least one educational speaker event, one art/theatre/ musical event, and one event focused on global or multicultural issues.

"Students must provide an account of taking part in these activities at the end of each semester. Students who have not completed their participation requirements will not be considered for funding for research assistantships, study abroad or conferences. One semester of incomplete, loss of, or late participation requirement will result in forfeiture of priority registration for classes. Two semesters without meeting participation requirements will result in removal from the Concentration."

**AP/IB credits** are not counted as replacements for honors courses.

**Course Offerings:** The Honors Concentration emphasizes courses in the academic disciplines rather than interdisciplinary courses, although there are some of the latter, including courses in the history of photography and the historical relation of protest music to social movements. One of the most interesting aspects of the Rowan Honors curriculum is **a series of 2-credit engineering clinics, more than 60 honors sections in Fall 2017.**

These clinics, **a collaboration by the four engineering programs [chemical, civil, electrical/computer, mechanical] at Rowan, "mix students of different engineering disciplines.** Students enroll in Clinics in each of their eight semesters at Rowan. The Freshman Clinic is focused on engineering measurements and reverse engineering. In the Spring semester, students work on a semester-long reverse engineering project. Reverse engineering is the systematic testing of existing products, for the purpose of improvement. For example, students have reverse engineered coffee makers, hair dryers, remote-control cars, electric toothbrushes, and portable water filters.

"The Sophomore Clinic is focused on engineering design. For perhaps the first time, students are exposed to realistic design problems best solved by multidisciplinary engineering teams. This course has significant communication components, both writing and speaking. Past projects include the design of landfills and baseball parks, and the design and construction of cranes, guitar effect pedals and small bridges. Students have also conducted energy audits of buildings on campus.

"In Junior and Senior Clinics, students work in small teams on open-ended projects under the supervision of one or more professor. Each team works on a unique project, which can be multiple semesters in length. A typical sequence includes: information search and review; development of semester goal and schedule; design/run/analyze (experiments) or design/build/test (prototypes); and presentation of results via written report and presentation. Most projects are funded by industry or governmental agencies."

The honors curriculum also included multiple sections of English, philosophy, business, history, math, computer science, and one section each in biology, chemistry, and physics.

**Class Size:** The freshman engineering clinics average 15-20 students, while the clinics in subsequent class years are much smaller. The average class size of other honors sections is about **15** students. For all rated programs the average for honors-only sections was **17.5** students.

**Honors Grad Rate Adjusted to SAT:** We do not have data for this category. Rated programs with similar entrance requirements have an average grad rate for honors first-year entrants of about 85%.

**Grad Rate Adjusted to Freshman Retention Rate:** The university-wide freshman retention rate at Rowan is 86%. We do not have the data to adjust the honors graduation rate in relation to this freshman retention rate.

**Ratio of Staff to Honors Students:** We estimate that there is one staff member for every **142** students. (Mean ratio for all programs is 1 staff member for every **127.9** students.)

**Honors Residence Halls, Amenities:** "We offer guaranteed cluster housing for Honors students interested in living among their peers. Our first year students reside in Holly Pointe Commons, while upperclassmen are housed in Rowan Boulevard or the Whitney Center. We allow non-Honors roommates (space available), as long as they meet the spirit of our learning community. Full time, unmarried undergraduates under age 21 with fewer than 58 credits are required to live in University Housing, unless they will be commuting from a parent or guardian's home within 40 miles of the Rowan campus."

New in 2016, the architecturally stylish Holly Pointe Commons has "7 floors on the 'tower' side and 4 floors in the 'curve.' Holly Pointe Commons located on the North side of campus. It has 1,415 beds and Glassworks Dining Hall, an all-you-care-to-eat dining hall."

Built in 2011, Whitney Center is a five-floor, air-conditioned apartment complex with 96 apartments for upperclassmen. Retail stores are located on the ground floor; nearby are the Rowan Boulevard Apartments, Parking Garage, Mullica Hall, Evergreen Hall, Enterprise Center, retail stores below Enterprise Center, Marriott Courtyard Hotel, and Rowan University's Barnes & Noble Bookstore.

Rowan Blvd. Apartments, with similar features, also house upperclassmen.

**Honors Residence Halls, Availability:** Although we do not have data for this category, the honors residence options listed above would seem to offer ample space for both first-year students and upperclassmen.

**Prestigious Awards:** The awards that we track and include are listed in the section titled "Prestigious Scholarships." The awards are sometimes won by students who are not in an honors college or program, but increasingly many are enrolled in honors programs. It is also a trend that honors colleges and programs help to prepare their students for the awards competitions.

Rowan undergraduates have won three Goldwater Scholarships, awarded to especially promising students in STEM disciplines, and at least one Boren Scholarship.

## UNRATED FEATURES

**Continuation and Graduation Requirements:** 3.00 for continuation. A cumulative 3.30 GPA and a 3.45 GPA in honors courses are required for honors graduation.

**Academic Strengths, National Rankings:** This is based on national rankings of *graduate* programs in 15 disciplines, except engineering and business, where undergraduate rankings are used. The rankings listed below are nationwide and include both public and private universities.

"The Henry M. Rowan College of Engineering was ranked #19 in the nation among the best undergraduate engineering schools [universities not offering a doctorate in engineering]. The ranking is a 14-place improvement since just four years ago, when the College placed 33rd in the annual report."

**"Our freshman to sophomore retention rate for the Henry M. Rowan College of Engineering is 92.2%, exceeding national and regional averages."**

**Internships, Professional Development, Community Engagement:** "The Engineering Outreach Office assists students in securing summer internships and professional careers after graduation. In the past, students have found positions with organizations such as Lockheed Martin, Amazon, DuPont, Exxon/Mobil, Inductotherm, General Motors, Glaxo SmithKline Pharmaceuticals, Johnson-Matthey, NASA, Campbell Soup Company, Boeing, PSE&G and Disney Imagineering, just to name a few."

**Undergraduate Research:** "Honors students are encouraged to conduct research and engage in creative work that supplements their learning in the classroom. Research/Creative Work Assistantships help students develop mentor-mentee relationship with a faculty member; familiarize students with research/performance processes and prepare them for possible graduate school work; encourage students to produce a finished piece of writing, performance, or other creative work that could be presented at a professional meeting or published in a student or professional publication or in an exhibition; and assist students in meeting Honors requirements through independent research/creative work. This is a competitive process. Students who receive awards will be funded with $800 for the semester or $1,600 for the year, which covers stipends and materials."

**Study Abroad and Off-Campus Study:** "There are many reasons why Honors students should take advantage of the opportunity to study abroad. Experiencing life in other countries and cultures; developing foreign language skills; broadening worldviews; and making lifelong friends while earning college credit are just some of them. Many students use study abroad experiences to prepare for graduate school and future employment. Most importantly, the experience will be one that you will remember and value for the rest of your life. Additionally, Honors Students may be able to receive up to $500 to reimburse travel expenses."

**Financial Aid:** "The Rowan University Scholars Program awards merit-based scholarships to eligible first time students who will be enrolled full time during the fall semester of their freshman year at Rowan. To qualify, students must have a minimum cumulative high school Grade Point Average (GPA) of 3.0 and a combined Evidence-Based Reading/Writing and Math SAT score of at least 1220 (ACT composite score 25). Applications for admission submitted before January 31 will be reviewed for scholarship eligibility. Individual award amounts are determined at the discretion of Rowan University's Division of Student Affairs based on the overall academic qualifications of the student, the competitiveness of the applicant pool and available funding."

**Honors Fees:** None.

**Placement Experiences (from engineering):** "Some of the companies that have hired our Alumni include the MD Department of Transportation; Navy (Nuclear Prop. Officer); NJ Dam Safety Office; NJ Department of Environmental Protection; NJ Department of Transportation; Port Authority of New York.

"Some of the graduate schools attended by our Alumni are Carnegie Mellon University; Cornell University; Drexel University; Lehigh University; Penn State University; Purdue University; Rowan University; University of New Hampshire; University of Texas at Austin; University of Virginia; University of Michigan; and Virginia Tech."

**Degree of Difference**: Degree of Difference: This is difference between (1) the average SAT scores for recently enrolled honors students (1300-1330) and (2) the average test scores for all students in the university (1190) as a whole. The difference may be an indication of how "elite" honors students may be perceived as compared to students in the university as a whole. Please keep in mind that neither the high nor low selectivity of an honors program determines how effective the program may be.

**NAME**: TEXAS A&M UNIVERSITY HONORS PROGRAM

**Date Established**: 1968

**Location**: College Station, Texas

**University Full-time Undergraduate Enrollment:** 50,735

**Honors Members in Good Standing**: 967 (mean size of all programs is 2,030).

**Honors Average Admission Statistics**: None listed.

**Average High School GPA/Class Rank:** None listed.

**Basic Admission Requirements:** "Incoming freshmen must complete a separate application to the University Honors Program and commit to living on-campus in the Honors Housing Community. The freshman application is competitive and considers high school class rank, standardized test score, and essay responses intended to evaluate vision, passion, commitment, willingness to take an intellectual risk, curiosity, and creativity. Because the applicant pool varies from year to year, there are no established cut-off scores for high school class rank or test scores. All interested students are encouraged to apply.

"Students not enrolled in an Honors Program may still register for Honors courses one week before the start of classes as an incoming freshman if they graduated in the top 10% of their high school class and have an SAT of at least 1360 (reading/writing + math, with minimums of 660 and 620, respectively) or a composite 28 on the ACT (minimum score of 27 each on verbal and math).

**Application Deadline(s):** *Please verify with each program, as some deadlines could change.* Application period begins July 1, 2018, and ends on December 15, 2018.

**Administrative Staff:** 4.

**Priority Registration: Yes,** honors students register for all courses, honors and otherwise, with the first group of students during each year they are in the program.

**Curriculum Requirements:** The curriculum completion requirement (classes required to complete honors) defines not only what honors students should learn but also the extent to which honors students and faculty are connected in the classroom. If there is a thesis or capstone requirement, it reinforces the individual contact and research skills so important to learning.

The average number of honors semester hours required for completion across all programs is 30 credits.

Graduation as an Honors Fellow requires 30 credits, including at least 21 honors credit hours, up to 3 credits in honors experiences, and 6 from a capstone/thesis.

Students can meet the honors requirement by taking any combination of departmental honors classes, graduate classes, honors contract classes, or independent-study classes.

**AP/IB credits** are not counted as replacements for honors courses."

**Course Offerings:** The only TAMU honors class data available is for honors enrollment in several different college-level and university-wide honors programs, not merely the University Honors Program. Adding to the difficulty is the fact that at TAMU students who are not formally enrolled in an honors program can still take honors classes if they have certain test scores and GPA credentials. The result is that we can only use percentages for all honors programs in reporting on courses, class sizes, etc.

*The class information we do have affirms the prominence of engineering on the TAMU campus.* Of 295 honors-only and mixed honors class sections, 38.7% were in engineering disciplines. Classes in business disciplines and communications each accounted for 8.33% (16.66% combined) of all honors sections, and math sections alone accounted for 10.8% of honors classes. Biology, chemistry, and physics enrollment was 11.8% of the total. Computer science enrollment was 4.4%. The remaining enrollment, about 18%, was in English, history, philosophy, political science, psychology, and sociology.

In order to offer honors courses in the disciplines listed above, a lot of mixed and contract sections were offered. A total of 102 unique contracts were completed in 77 different courses. Of 295 sections, 56% were large mixed sections, and the remaining 44% were honors-only. For all programs under review, enrollment by type of honors section was 75.8% honors-only, 15.4 % mixed, and 8.8% contract.

The TAMU Honors Program is, as we have noted before, a straight from the shoulder program, all about classes in the disciplines. It is almost purely a **department-based** honors program with only 4% of enrollment in honors core seminars.

**Class Size:** The average honors-only class size was 22.5 students; for all rated programs the average was 18.0 students. The average mixed section class size was 72.1 students, and for all rated programs the average was 68.6. The overall average honors class size was 50.3 students. For all rated programs, the average was **24.9** students.

**Honors Grad Rate Adjusted to SAT:** The six-year graduation rate of university honors program students who entered the program (but not necessarily completers of honors requirements) was 83.0%. This is somewhat lower than the average grad rate of other programs with similar test score requirements (85.5%).

**Grad Rate Adjusted to Freshman Retention Rate:** The university-wide freshman retention rate at TAMU is 90%. The honors graduation rate in relation to freshman retention is significantly lower than that for other programs with similar freshmen retention rates.

**Ratio of Staff to Honors Students: Ratio of Staff to Honors Students:** There is 1 staff member for every **324.1** students. (Mean ratio for all programs is 1 staff member for every **127.9** students.)

**Honors Residence Halls, Amenities:** "The Honors Housing Community (HHC) is the cornerstone of the University Honors Program first year experience and provides a true living-learning community for an interdisciplinary mix of high-achieving and highly-motivated students.

"Students in this program help each other to grow personally, professionally, and academically through a weekly seminar that has them identify their values and articulate those in relationship to their long-term goals. In addition to the seminar, first-year students benefit from living with other similarly-motivated students and sharing the experience in small 'family' groups."

The McFadden/Lechner honors residence halls can house about 400 freshmen students. The coed dorms have air-conditioned, suite-style rooms with shared baths. The nearest dining is at Sbisa. *First-year honors students are required to live in honors housing.*

**Honors Residence Halls, Availability:** This rating compares the number of places in honors residence halls to the number of honors freshman and sophomore members in good standing. The ratio for the honors program is **.83** places for each first- and second-year student. The average for all programs is .49 places.

**Prestigious Awards:** The awards that we track and include are listed in the section titled "Prestigious Scholarships." The awards are sometimes won by students who are not in an honors college or program, but increasingly many are enrolled in honors programs. It is also a trend that honors colleges and programs help to prepare their students for the awards competitions.

Aggies have won 7 Rhodes scholarships, 4 Marshall scholarships, and 4 Truman scholarships. Among the undergraduate awards won by Aggies, there have been at least 6 Udall scholars and 43 Goldwater scholars. TAMU students have also won an impressive number of National Science Foundation graduate fellowships.

## UNRATED FEATURES

**Continuation and Graduation Requirements:** Continuation requires a 3.50 GPA; graduation requires a cumulative 3.50 GPA and at least a 3.25 GPA in courses for honors credit.

**Academic Strengths, National Rankings:** This is based on national rankings of *graduate* programs in 15 disciplines, except engineering and business, where undergraduate rankings are used. The rankings listed below are nationwide and include both public and private universities.

The average departmental rank at TAMU is a very impressive 41.6. The university has a nationally ranked department for each of the 15 disciplines that we track, and all are in the top 70 nationwide.

Nationally ranked departments at TAMU include engineering (14), political science (24), chemistry (21), business (31), earth sciences (31), education (37), economics (39), math (39), computer science (43), physics (47), sociology (47), English (51), biology (62), psychology (66), and history (69).

**Internships, Professional Development, Community Engagement:** None listed.

**Undergraduate Research:** "The University Honors Program is housed in the same administrative unit as Undergraduate Research, which provides extensive opportunities and campus-wide support. The Honors Housing Community has a focus on helping students understand the value of attending a large research institution."

**Study Abroad and Off-Campus Study:** "More than 3,600 Texas A&M University students studied abroad last year, *ranking first in the nation among public universities and second among all universities* *in a study conducted by the Institute of International Education (IIE) and the U.S. Department of State's Bureau of Education and Cultural Affairs.*

"A robust study abroad program is essential to a university's ability to provide high-impact learning experiences to students, and it is heartening to know Texas A&M is among the best in the nation at providing these invaluable opportunities," Texas A&M University President Michael K. Young said.

"The 2017 Open Doors Report on International Exchange found that Texas A&M ranked second with 3,683 students abroad on credit-bearing programs during the 2015-2016 academic year behind New York University, a private university, which sent 4,481 students abroad.

"The total number of Aggies earning credit abroad last year increased by more than 450 students from the 2014-2015 academic year, with 3,219, and more than 650 students from the 2013-2014 academic year, with 3,021."

**Financial Aid:**

**National Merit Semifinalists** are eligible for the President's Scholarship with an award value of $12,000 total over four years. A single study-abroad stipend of $1,000 is also a part of the package.

**National Merit Finalists** are eligible for the National Merit Recognition Award, valued at $28,000 total across four years. In addition, Finalists receive National Merit Sponsorship and Supplemental Scholarships with a combined value across four years of $5,000.

These awards are "stackable" at TAMU, meaning students may also have other scholarships "stacked" on to the NMS awards:

*"National Merit scholars (semifinalists and finalists) will also compete for other freshman scholarship opportunities which are awarded in early January of the student's senior year.* **These scholarships are able to be added to the guaranteed scholarships listed above."**

**Honors Fees:** None.

**Placement Experiences:** None listed.

**Degree of Difference**: Degree of Difference: This is difference between (1) the average SAT scores for recently enrolled honors students (*estimated* at 1375-1400) and (2) the average test scores for all students in the university (1250) as a whole. The difference may be an indication of how "elite" honors students may be perceived as compared to students in the university as a whole. Please keep in mind that neither the high nor low selectivity of an honors program determines how effective the program may be.

*Editor's Note: Due to difficulties converting some UCI quarter unit data to match semester data from other programs, we are providing this unrated review instead of a rated review. Our **estimate** is that UCI CHP would likely be rated 4.0 overall.*

**NAME**: UNIVERSITY OF CALIFORNIA, IRVINE CAMPUSWIDE HONORS PROGRAM

**Date Established**: 1988

**Location**: Irvine, California

**University Full-time Undergraduate Enrollment:** 29,133

**Honors Members in Good Standing**: 950 (mean size of all programs is 2,030).

**Honors Average Admission Statistics**: ACT, 30.6; est. new SAT score equivalent, 1410.

**Average High School GPA/Class Rank:** 4.20, weighted.

**Basic Admission Requirements:** None listed.

**Application Deadline(s):** *Please verify with each program, as some deadlines could change.* Application period for all UC campuses is August 1-November 30, 2018. Honors invitation after applicants confirm UC Irvine as choice on or before May 1, 2019.

**Other Honors Programs with new SAT scores 1403—1461:** Auburn, Central Florida, Delaware, Iowa, Kansas, Mississippi, Missouri, New Jersey Inst of Technology, Penn State, South Florida, Vermont, Virginia Commonwealth.

**Administrative Staff:** 7.

**Priority Registration: Yes,** honors students register for all courses, honors and otherwise, with the first group of students during each year they are in the program.

**Curriculum Requirements:** The curriculum completion requirement (classes required to complete honors) defines not only what honors students should learn but also the extent to which honors students and faculty are connected in the classroom. If there is a thesis or capstone requirement, it reinforces the individual contact and research skills so important to learning.

The average number of honors semester hours required for completion across all rated 50 programs is 30 credits.

The CHP requires 54 quarter units (equivalent of 36 semester credits) for honors completion.

"The CHP curriculum consists of Honors Humanities Core and two core course track options: CHP Classic Track which includes Honors Social Science Core (Critical Issues in the Social Sciences) and Honors Science Core (The Idiom and Practice of Science, for non-science majors only), and Sustainable Societies which includes Critical Analysis of Health Science Literature, Environmental Issues Facing Sustainable Societies, Social Science Perspectives on the Sustainability of Societies, and Cities: Focal

Point for Sustainability Problems and Solutions. The CHP curriculum fulfills most of UCI's General Education requirements. The total number of courses and units is the same for both tracks.

**AP/IB credits** are not counted as replacements for honors courses."

*"Please note that we have added a new, second track in the sophomore and junior years called Sustainable Societies. Students in the sophomore and junior years customize their curriculum and select between "CHP Classic" and "Sustainable Societies," after having taken Honors Humanities Core in the freshman year.*

**Course Offerings:** "This year's cycle of **Humanities Core** is organized around the theme 'Empire and Its Ruins,' which will emphasize how humans have made sense of the rise and fall of societies and the effects of dominant structures on people who are marginalized. This quarter, we will address the formation and maintenance of the Roman Empire, the concept of "ruins" in Enlightenment-era philosophy and visual art, and the impact of the American ideology of Manifest Destiny on indigenous communities."

The **Social Science Core** "is team-taught by professors from the Schools of Social Science and Social Ecology and studies topics from the perspectives of political science, economics, logic and philosophy of science, and psychology, to name only a few. Sample topics have included authority, (dis)obedience and human society; decisions, compromises, and their rewards and penalties; learning and memory; and exotic societies (including our own).

Finally, the **Idiom and Practice of Science (Science Core-for non-science majors)** "will give you an understanding of the role science plays in addressing socially significant problems. You will learn how to understand scientific models and to judge the content, merit, and limitations of many issues of science in the modern world. Topics have included ozone depletion/global warming, earthquakes, biodiversity/conservation, genetic plant engineering, calculus and partial differential equations, evolution/aging, radiation/diseases, the mathematics of power, and the physics of music."

**Class Size:** While the humanities core seminars average about 18 students, CHP has a small number of humanities core *lecture* sections that are quite large, although they have breakout discussion sections that are significantly smaller. An estimate of the overall class not counting the core lecture sections is **17.6** students. The inclusion of the very large lecture sections would raise the average to more than 70 students—but CHP only has 3-4 of the large sections each quarter. The average overall class size for all rated programs is 25.4 students.

**Honors Grad Rate Adjusted to SAT:** The graduation rate of CHP students who entered the program (but not necessarily completers of honors requirements) is a very high 94.3%. *This is far higher than the average grad rate of other programs with similar test score requirements (86.1%).*

**Grad Rate Adjusted to Freshman Retention Rate:** The university-wide freshman retention rate at UCI is very high at 93%. The honors graduation rate exceeds the freshman retention rate. *Only three rated honors programs with freshman retention rates above 90% also had an honors grad rate that was even higher.*

**Ratio of Staff to Honors Students: Ratio of Staff to Honors Students:** There is 1 staff member for every **121.4** students. (Mean ratio for all programs is 1 staff member for every 127.9 students.)

**Honors Residence Halls, Amenities:** Freshmen living in honors housing are about evenly divided among three residences: The Shire, Loma, and Arroyo. While all of these have suite-style rooms and shared baths, they are not air-conditioned. However, the Irvine climate is generally mild, especially for the fall, winter, and spring quarters. The most convenient dining for Shire residents is Pippin; for the other freshman residences, it is the Anteatery.

Upperclassmen may choose to live in Arroyo Vista, with features similar to those in the freshmen dorms. Large, full-sized kitchens enable students to cook for themselves or they can purchase a voluntary meal plan for use in on-campus residence hall dining facilities.

**Honors Residence Halls, Availability:** This rating compares the number of places in honors residence halls to the number of honors freshman and sophomore members in good standing. The ratio for the honors program is **.59** places for each first- and second-year student. The average for all programs is .49 places.

**Prestigious Awards:** The awards that we track and include are listed in the section titled "Prestigious Scholarships." The awards are sometimes won by students who are not in an honors college or program, but increasingly many are enrolled in honors programs. It is also a trend that honors colleges and programs help to prepare their students for the awards competitions.

Numbers of scholarships won by UCI students: Rhodes (1), Marshall (2), Truman (8), Gates Cambridge (3), National Science Foundation fellowships (41 in the last three years), Fulbright Student Scholars (13 in last three years) and Goldwater Scholarships (33).

**UNRATED FEATURES**

**Continuation and Graduation Requirements:** GPA minimums are: Freshmen 2.80; Sophomores 3.00; Juniors 3.20; Seniors 3.20.

**Academic Strengths, National Rankings:** This is based on national rankings of *graduate* programs in 15 disciplines, except engineering and business, where undergraduate rankings are used. The rankings listed below are nationwide and include both public and private universities. **UC Irvine ranked 31st in the 2019 U.S. News rankings of national universities.**

The average departmental rank at UCI is a very impressive 32.5. The university has a nationally ranked department for each of the 15 disciplines that we track, and all are in the top 47 nationwide.

Nationally ranked departments at UCI include English (17), chemistry (20), sociology (23), education (24), physics (28), computer science (30), business (31), biology (33), history (34), psychology (36) math (39), engineering (40), earth sciences (41), political science (45), and economics (47).

**Internships, Professional Development, Community Engagement:** "CHP students are encouraged to participate in the many opportunities available to them, including those outside of the program. UCI offers myriad programs that contribute to future career development, including the Antrepreneur Center, the program and minor in Civic and Community Engagement, internships and career-readiness programs offered through UCI's Division of Career Pathways, experiential learning programs through Study Abroad, Academic Internship Programs (in Washington, D.C. and Sacramento), community engagement through the Blum Center for Poverty Alleviation, and various hands-on learning opportunities offered through UCI's schools and majors."

**Undergraduate Research:** "The Undergraduate Research Opportunities Program (UROP) encourages and facilitates research and creative activities by undergraduates from all schools and academic disciplines at UCI. The program offers assistance to students and faculty through all phases of the research process, whether it is with proposal writing, developing research plans through project management skills, awarding grants to fund research projects, scholarly journal writing through The UCI Undergraduate Research Journal, or presenting results of the research or creative project through the UCI Undergraduate Research Symposium."

**Study Abroad and Off-Campus Study:** "Students have access to the many study abroad opportunities offered through the University of California's Education Abroad Program (UCEAP), as well as the opportunity study through ANY international experience abroad that is not a part of that program (IOP). UCI Experiential Learning Programs abroad offer opportunities for students to engage in experiential or service learning abroad."

**Financial Aid:** "UCI merit-based scholarships are awarded to entering freshmen who demonstrate a high level of academic achievement as demonstrated by their high school GPA as reported on the admissions application, SAT (or ACT) scores, personal statements, and depth and breadth of the admissions application. These include the Regents' Scholarship and the UCI Alumni Association Endowed Scholarship."

**Honors Fees:** None.

**Placement Experiences:** "UCI Campuswide Honors Program alumni attend some of the most prestigious graduate and professional schools in the nation, pursue careers in many different fields, and are active, engaged members of their communities."

**Degree of Difference**: Degree of Difference: This is difference between (1) the average SAT scores for recently enrolled honors students (1410) and (2) the average test scores for all students in the university (1250) as a whole. The difference may be an indication of how "elite" honors students may be perceived as compared to students in the university as a whole. Please keep in mind that neither the high nor low selectivity of an honors program determines how effective the program may be.

News about new public university honors colleges often generates critical comments from readers who point to the "elitism" of such programs. These critics oppose the disproportionate allocation of resources to a relatively small number of students, arguing that the resources should benefit all students.

Comments along these lines appeared back in 2015 in response to Frank Bruni's New York Times column on honors programs, "A Prudent College Path." The opening of the new Honors Living/Learning Residence at Rutgers Honors College likewise brought forth the expression of similar views.

Some critics oppose honors programs as a matter of principle. A pubic university is for all of its students, not just an anointed few. Sooner or later, however, the argument focuses on the justifications or lack thereof for spending money on a select group of students instead of using more of it for disadvantaged students. Universities spend too much on honors residence halls, perks, and profs, the critics contend, or they spend too much on merit aid for talented students—or both.

First, as to the basic charge of elitism, the term clearly applies if it is used to characterize the official membership of highly qualified students in honors colleges and programs. In general, they are among the top 5-10 percent of the entire student body, based on high school gpa's and standardized test scores.

Second, it is true that specific components of honors programs, especially honors "benefits," do set honors students apart from the overall student body. Prominent among these benefits are special honors dorms and one form or another of priority registration for honors students.

Third, all honors programs offer smaller class sections to their students, especially during the first and second years of study. In order to provide these sections, academic departments must sacrifice "production" ratios in the interest of staffing these smaller classes.

If Professor A normally teaches three sections of microeconomics, each with an enrollment of 100, and then replaces one of these with an honors section of 20 students, the production ratios of both Professor A and the econ department are a little less impressive in the provost's eyes. The emphasis on "productivity" in public universities has become a sort of mantra in the eyes of many critics of state universities, many of them on the political right.

After conceding the above, the justification for this kind of spending actually depends on (1) whether public honors programs yield sufficient benefit to the whole university student body to warrant the emphasis they receive; (2) whether honors programs fill a legitimate need by providing slots for high-achieving students, in the absence of a sufficient number of such places at, well, elite colleges; and (3) whether the public universities need to offer honors programs and merit aid to remain competitive in order to keep top students in the state.

As former Penn State Schreyer Dean Christian Brady wrote in an article for the PublicUniversityHonors website, honors can be a "gateway" to transfer and non-honors students who find, after their first year or two in college, that they want to embrace greater challenges. (Dr. Brady is now Dean of the new Lewis Honors College at the University of Kentucky.)

Similarly, the University of Georgia's Center for Undergraduate Research Opportunities, though under the banner of the school's outstanding honors program, actually serves any undergraduate who wants to join in the excitement and promise of undergrad research. Another excellent program, Honors Carolina at UNC Chapel Hill, invites non-honors students with a strong academic record to participate in all honors classes.

Dr. Jeffrey Chamberlain, now Dean of the Hicks Honors College at the University of North Florida, agrees with Dean Brady that "Honors raises the game for the whole university. I am told repeatedly how good it is to have Honors students in non-Honors classes (and Honors students never take all of their classes in Honors). Furthermore, Honors students help non-Honors students in every imaginable way—Honors students are math and science tutors, writing consultants, even RAs, so they contribute to student success across the board." And, by the way, at a savings to the university.

Do elite colleges already provide enough classroom spaces for highly-talented students, without any need for honors programs? As I wrote on the PublicUniversityHonors site, the elite colleges and universities in this country, almost all of them private, simply do not have enough slots for the top 8-10% of students, based on test scores. Most of the highly talented students who are not accepted by elite private colleges will end up at public universities. Those public universities that allocate funds to support smaller classes and undergraduate research for talented students through honors programs, along with merit aid, are not only spending money to recruit students with higher test scores in order to enhance their prestige; they are also filling a real need by providing more slots for talented students. In addition, many universities are trying to keep talented students in state rather than seeing them leave, never to return. All too often, critics of public university spending ignore these needs.

Even if honors students are a boon to their campuses and fellow students and, arguably, need more options for a high-quality education, do these factors justify allocating dollars for their benefit instead of augmenting need-based aid?

MERIT SCHOLARSHIPS AND ELITISM

Critics claim that public universities not only spend too much on honors programming but in too many cases also fund and utilize merit aid inappropriately, especially at a time when the focus should be on providing more need-based assistance. But the uses of merit aid are many, as are the reasons that drive the aid decisions at individual institutions.

The main problem for leading institutions, especially, is how to balance quality, access, state interests (including revenue), and public perception. In general, the most vocal critics of merit aid believe that access is all-important, regardless of its impact on the other factors.

Two examples of that criticism have come from the New America Foundation: "Colleges' Pursuit of Prestige and Revenue Is Hurting Low-Income Students" and "The Out of State Student Arms Race," both by analyst Stephen Burd.

First of all, some of the arguments in these and other reports are valid. For one thing, there is no doubt that the *U.S. News* rankings drive many colleges to spend money on generating better metrics, especially those related to test scores, selectivity, and student/faculty ratios. Some schools have become proficient in gaming the system.

The *U.S. News* methodology formerly gave a combined weight of 9.25% to test scores and selection ratios. The use of the latter should be scrapped, given the increased use of the Common App and marketing geared to ramping up applications just for the sake of lowering acceptance ratios. (As for test scores, there are ways that colleges can game that metric as well.) The methodology also assigned a weight of 22.5% to multiple financial metrics that also pressure colleges to raise and spend more money.

State budget cuts and rising costs for instruction, research, and administration have also led to the need for more revenue. Just how much of the additional revenue is actually necessary for improved instruction is a matter of contention. (See for example Baumol's Cost Disease and The Bowen Effect.) The combined effects of state disinvestment and the obsession with prestige and rankings have undoubtedly led to the intense focus on increasing revenues.

But often merit aid is less related to rankings and prestige than it is to a more basic level of competition.

Some elite public universities (UC Berkeley, Michigan) offer higher percentages of merit aid than other public universities that are excellent but not so elite (although the average amounts of merit aid from Berkeley and Michigan are not especially large.) Why? The competition for UC Berkeley and Michigan includes many elite private schools, and sometimes even modest merit aid can be the deciding factor. Private universities such as Chicago, Northwestern, and Rice also offer significant merit aid, and do so to compete with the Ivies, Stanford, etc., who are so much in demand that they don't have to offer non-need-based aid. Rice just announced that students from families with incomes of $65,000 - $130,000 are eligible for free tuition; even students whose families earn as much as $200,000 will be eligible for half tuition discounts.

The University of Virginia and the University of North Carolina also compete effectively against private elites, but they have chosen to provide limited merit aid.

For public universities at the next level, Washington, Illinois, UT Austin, Wisconsin, the competition is often with other publics, and they more than hold their own. Partly as a result of being in high demand regardless of aid, UT Austin has one of the highest enrollments of Pell Grant recipients and offers little in the way of merit aid. The UC system seems to have found an enviable balance: UC campuses have no shortage of applicants, serve large numbers of Pell Grant recipients, and offer Regents merit scholarships to hundreds of students each year.

But when it comes to public universities with lesser reputations than those listed above, the balance between aid for competition or aid for access may tip too far toward competition, sometimes with an eye on improving rankings and revenue. New America singles out the University of Alabama and the University of South Carolina for criticism. How much of this criticism is valid?

The state of South Carolina now funds only 10 percent of the cost of education at the flagship university. Moreover, the number of college-age students in the state is declining. New America criticizes the University of South Carolina for awarding too much merit aid to out-of-state students, who still end up providing more revenue out of pocket than in-state students, and also help to sustain enrollment levels.

If the university allocated most or almost all of its aid to need-based students within the state, the revenue would drop dramatically and the expense per student would rise. The university would probably be unable to support its excellent honors college; for that matter, the university would eventually be unable to serve as many students period. So even though the state legislature undervalues higher education, the university and many citizens believe it is in the interest of the state to increase the number of college graduates (and their families) over the long haul, and not diminish the university in the process.

Is the percentage of non-resident freshmen (45%) too high, and the merit aid they receive too much? To answer those questions, one would need to know (1) whether many highly qualified (but low-income) in-state students are not receiving aid because the aid is going to out-of-state students with equal or lesser qualifications; and (2) how many of talented out of state students will remain in South Carolina after graduation. To the extent that highly qualified, low-income, in-state students are losing out, then the out-of-state aid is excessive.

Funding honors programs and offering merit aid to talented students can certainly increase the selectivity profile of a university and eventually enhance rankings and public perception. But there is a distinction between the aggressive gaming of the rankings and the more justifiable funding that is related to legitimate state interests. New America suggests that the extremely generous merit aid that the University of Alabama offers to talented out-of-state students is in part designed to improve rankings. But, contrary to that suggestion, the Alabama *U.S. News* ranking has crashed since 2012, when it was number 75, to number 129 in 2019.

The University of Mississippi is another flagship that offers generous merit aid. What is also true is that the state of Mississippi has the second lowest percentage of college grads in the nation, and Alabama the 7th lowest. Surely these states should find ways to sustain their flagship institutions, and merit aid, for now, is one of those ways. Who knows but that some day they might join UVA, UNC Chapel Hill, UT Austin, Wisconsin and others that can go forward without so much emphasis on merit aid.

Again, we agree with New America that many universities, including some major public institutions, do use merit aid, at least in part, for purposes of moving up in college rankings and sometimes excessively for revenue purposes. But the total picture is much more complicated, resulting in one of the most difficult issues to emerge from state disinvestment in higher education.

***And here's a proposed standard for balancing the factors:*** *If merit aid is denied to highly qualified, low-income students who are residents of the state, and goes instead to out-of-state students whose qualifications are about the same or less, then the merit aid is being used excessively for revenue purposes.*

**Curriculum**—the formal course of study required for honors program completion and, often, for graduation with honors.

**Honors Individuals**—the unduplicated count of individual honors students enrolled in a given term, as opposed to honors "seats" or honors "members in good standing."

**Honors Seats**—the number of classroom spaces occupied by honors students in a given term, this is a number larger than the number of honors individuals because each individual honors student frequently takes more than one honors class per term, thereby occupying two or more classroom spaces, or seats, in that term. If 25 honors individuals within a group of 200 total honors individuals take two honors courses instead of one, and the other honors students take only one course each, then the number of honors seats would be 225, not 200.

**Honors Members in Good Standing**—represents yet another way to enumerate the number of honors students; the number of members in good standing includes all honors individuals enrolled in a given term *and* honors students who are still planning to complete the honors requirements but who are not taking an honors course in the term.

**Discipline**—a term that is synonymous with an academic subject, such as math, chemistry, or philosophy.

**Academic Department**—the administrative unit that organizes courses, almost always in a single discipline, and assigns faculty to courses and sections in the discipline.

**Departmental Honors Program**—easily confused with a department-*based* honors program, departmental honors programs are offered by the academic department, often with little or no coordination with a university-wide honors college or program. For example, the history department selects a small number of excellent, highly motivated students to pursue departmental honors by taking a special research course and then completing an honors thesis for six credits, under the supervision of a history faculty member.

**Discipline or Department-Based Honors Program**—an honors program or college that offers few or no sections of its own but instead coordinates with academic departments to arrange honors course sections. A program of this type is not likely to feature seminars or interdisciplinary sections. An honors thesis is a frequent requirement.

**Core Honors Program**—an honors program or college that offers many of its own courses, often including seminars and interdisciplinary courses. Some core programs have set offerings in the academic disciplines as well, while others are entirely interdisciplinary in focus. Many core programs offer most of their courses in the first two years as honors versions of university General Education requirements, although this approach to meeting Gen Ed requirements is widely used by all types of honors programs. It is not unusual for most of the upper-division work for honors students in a core program to be centered on the honors thesis and associated research.

**Blended Honors Program**—an honors program or college using the most typical model of blending seminars, interdisciplinary courses, and discipline-specific courses. In many cases, these programs and those that are discipline-based (department-based) offer honors classes across all four years.

**Academic Department**—the administrative unit that organizes courses, almost always in a single discipline, and assigns faculty to courses and sections in the discipline.

**Blended Honors Program**—an honors program or college using the most typical model of blending seminars, interdisciplinary courses, and discipline-specific courses. In many cases, these programs and those that are discipline-based (department-based) offer honors classes across all four years.

**Capstone**—is sometimes offered as an alternative or replacement for an honors thesis. A capstone is usually a project undertaken by the student to demonstrate mastery of a subject area or procedure. Engineering students, for example, often complete involved and demanding projects pursuant to completing a capstone requirement. Other students in STEM fields can fulfill the requirement with experimental projects.

**Colloquium**—a seminar course that features different instructors and differing perspectives at each or several class meetings.

**Contract Section**—also referred to as an honors option, conversion, or enhancement, these are regular courses in which one or a few honors program students "contract" with the instructor to extra work in order to earn honors credit. Contract courses are often taken for upper-division credit in order to meet major or minor requirements. They are generally more than twice the size of honors-only sections and somewhat larger than mixed honors sections.

**Core Honors Program**—an honors program or college that offers many of its own courses, often including seminars and interdisciplinary courses. Some core program have set offerings in the academic disciplines as well, while others are entirely interdisciplinary in focus. Many core programs offer most of their courses in the first two years as honors versions of university General Education requirements, although this approach to meeting Gen Ed requirements is widely used by all types of honors programs. It is not unusual for most of the upper-division work for honors students in a core program to be centered on the honors thesis and associated research.

**Curriculum**—the formal course of study required for honors program completion and, often, for graduation with honors.

**Departmental Honors Course**—is a course for honors credit that concerns only the academic discipline offered by the department. Sometimes these are a formal part of completing a university-wide honors program and sometimes these are taken only to complete the departmental honors requirements for the discipline.

**Departmental Honors Program**—easily confused with a department-*based* honors program, departmental honors programs are offered by the academic department, often with little or no coordination with a university-wide honors college or program. For example, the history department selects a small number of excellent, highly motivated students to pursue departmental honors by taking a special research course and then completing an honors thesis for six credits, under the supervision of a history faculty member.

**Discipline**—a term that is synonymous with an academic subject, such as math, chemistry, or philosophy.

**Discipline or Department-Based Honors Program**—an honors program or college that offers few or no sections of its own but instead coordinates with academic departments to arrange honors course sections. A program of this type is not likely to feature seminars or interdisciplinary sections. An honors thesis is a frequent requirement.

**Experiences**—are activities outside the university's classroom for which honors credit may be awarded. These often include internships, public service, study abroad, research projects, teaching assistantships, and leadership education. Honors experiences are a trend in honors education.

**Honors-Only Section**—as the name suggests, this is almost always a class with honors students only or, in a few honors programs, a class in which 75%-90% of the students are in a university honors program and the other students have high GPAs and like the challenge and stimulation of an occasional honors class. For our purposes, both types are considered honors-only classes.

**Individuals**—the unduplicated count of individual honors students enrolled in a given term, as opposed to honors "seats" or honors "members in good standing."

**Members in Good Standing**—represents yet another way to enumerate the number of honors students; the number of members in good standing includes all honors individuals enrolled in a given term *and* honors students who are still planning to complete the honors requirements but who are not taking an honors course in the term.

**Mixed Honors Section**—or add-on section, is a course section that has honors and non-honors students enrolled in the same main section. Honors students in these main sections frequently meet in additional all-honors labs or discussion sections. Mixed sections are generally about twice the size of honors-only sections.

**Seats**—the number of classroom spaces occupied by honors students in a given term, this is a number larger than the number of honors individuals because each individual honors student frequently takes more than one honors class per term, thereby occupying two or more classroom spaces, or seats, in that term. If 25 honors individuals within a group of 200 total honors individuals take two honors courses instead of one, and the other honors students take only one course each, then the number of honors seats would be 225, not 200.

**Seminar**—a small class section, usually with fewer than 25 students and often with 10-15 students, where class discussion and participation are the norm. Seminars might be *interdisciplinary* or they might focus on only one academic subject, or discipline.

**Thesis**—is required by most honors programs for completion and graduation with some type of honors designation. The credit for an honors thesis can vary, with some having only 3 credits, many with 6 credits, and a few with 9-12 credits. Although some students with demanding majors, such as engineering, might avoid honors programs with a thesis requirement, the honors thesis is regarded as a very important component in the programs that require it. Often students are required to "defend" the thesis before faculty and other students or to make a thesis presentation. An honors thesis is excellent preparation for graduate or professional school and can be useful in gaining entrance to prestigious graduate programs.

Public University Press, in Portland, Oregon, has published two editions of *A Review of Fifty Public University Honors Programs* and a previous edition of *INSIDE HONORS.* Each effort is an improvement as a result of improved methodology and data.

The editor is John Willingham, also the founder of the website PublicUniversityHonors.com. John began researching and writing about public university honors colleges and programs in 2011, a time when many states had already made several annual cuts in funding for higher education. Some political leaders had become so focused on applying business models of "productivity" and "efficiency" to state universities that they lost sight of the critical need to offer the highest levels of quality in those institutions.

As a way of exemplifying the excellence that can and should be sustained in public universities, the editor compiled a rudimentary ranking of the honors programs in major state universities in 2012, hoping that readers would not only gain some comparative knowledge about the programs but also develop a greater awareness of the value that they all offer to highly talented students. Good intentions aside, the 2012 edition was a broad-brush attempt at describing the variety and complexity of honors programs. The next edition, in 2014, was an improvement but still lacked the extensive data necessary for a truly comprehensive study of honors colleges and programs. *INSIDE HONORS (2016)* marked a major turn toward an even more data-driven methodology.

*INSIDE HONORS 2018-2019* is the best attempt, thanks to the outstanding cooperation of honors Deans, Directors, and professionals in honors colleges and programs across the nation. Most of them have endured our repeated entreaties with patience, and, while thanking those who offered encouragement, we are also grateful to the several who voiced criticisms or concerns. Because of them, we have made many changes to the methodology and presentation of honors data.

The reason that the term "editor" applies to John more than "author" is that so much of the information in the book has come from the honors community. **Almost all of the quotes in the book are from honors professionals**. The assistant editor and marketing coordinator, Wendy Frizzell Willingham, is a graduate of the University of Wisconsin-Madison, where she was an honors student in foreign languages and education.

A Ph.D. scientist and statistician advises and assists John in the development of a master data sheet, based on about 500 documents and spreadsheets. The master data sheet is a compilation of data received from honors educators. John analyzes and categorizes all of the data from the programs and determines the impact of each category. The statistician standardizes and sums the raw data to produce both category and overall ratings. The two also worked together on an in-depth statistical study of honors completion rates.

John's background includes years of work in journalism and public administration, mostly in Texas. For three years, he was a regular contributor to the History News Network (HNN.us), writing several articles that covered the controversy in Texas over the adoption of social studies and science textbooks and curricula. His education includes a BA, *cum laude*, from the University of Texas at Austin, and an MA in history from UT Austin, including graduate minors in education and journalism. In 2013, he completed training in honors program evaluation offered by the National Collegiate Honors Council at the University of Nebraska. He also made a presentation on program evaluation at the NCHC Annual Meeting in Seattle in 2016. He is the author of an historical novel about the 1836 Texas Revolution, and his fiction and non-fiction have appeared in the *Southwest Review* literary quarterly, published by Southern Methodist University Press.

## EDITORIAL ADVISORS

**Vicki Been**
Elihu Root Professor of Law
New York University School of Law

**Erwin Chemerinsky**
Dean and Distinguished Professor of Law
University of California, Irvine, School of Law

**Richard A. Epstein**
Laurence A. Tisch Professor of Law
New York University School of Law
Peter and Kirsten Bedford Senior Fellow
The Hoover Institution
Senior Lecturer in Law
The University of Chicago

**Ronald J. Gilson**
Charles J. Meyers Professor of Law and Business
Stanford University
Marc and Eva Stern Professor of Law and Business
Columbia Law School

**James E. Krier**
Earl Warren DeLano Professor of Law
The University of Michigan Law School

**Richard K. Neumann, Jr.**
Professor of Law
Hofstra University School of Law

**Robert H. Sitkoff**
John L. Gray Professor of Law
Harvard Law School

**David Alan Sklansky**
Professor of Law
University of California at Berkeley School of Law

**Kent D. Syverud**
Dean and Ethan A. H. Shepley University Professor
Washington University School of Law

**Elizabeth Warren**
Leo Gottlieb Professor of Law
Harvard Law School